D0202953

NATIONAL UNIVERSITY
LIBRARY SAN DIEGO

Political economy and the Labour Party

The economics of democratic socialism, 1884–1995

Noel Thompson
University of Wales, Swansea

© Noel Thompson 1996

This book is copyright under the Berne Convention.
No reproduction without permission.
All rights reserved.

First published in 1996 by UCL Press

UCL Press Limited
University College London
Gower Street
London WC1E 6BT

and
1900 Frost Road, Suite 101
Bristol
Pennsylvania 19007-1598

The name of University College London (UCL) is a registered trade mark used by UCL Press with the consent of the owner.

British Library Cataloguing in Publication Data
A catalogue record for this book is available from the British Library.

ISBNs: 1-85728-160-8 HB
1-85728-161-6 PB

Typeset in Baskerville.
Printed and bound by
Biddles Ltd, Guildford and King's Lynn, England.

In Memoriam
Harold James Thompson
1916–94

Contents

Preface

With the widening of the electoral franchise in 1867 and again in 1884 the TUC had periodically sought to secure the election of trade union spokesmen and, through the efforts of organizations such as the Labour Representation League, 1869, and the Labour Electoral Association, 1886, a number of "labour" nominees had been elected with Liberal Party support. These so-called Lib-Lab MPs therefore owed allegiance to the Liberal Party but they also, as working-class trade unionists, provided an independent voice in parliament on labour questions and reserved the right to dissociate themselves from the Liberals on such issues. As the 1890s progressed, however, this Liberal/trade union alliance came under pressure and demands increased for independent representation of the interests of labour.

This pressure was, in part, a consequence of a revival of socialism in Britain in the 1880s with both Marxian and Fabian socialism having some impact within the Labour movement in this decade. The nature of that impact and the substance of these socialisms will be discussed below but at this point it can be said that the influence of socialist ideas was sufficiently strong to persuade many of the need for a separate party that would more effectively represent the interests of the working classes. To this end the Marxist Social Democratic Federation (SDF) was established in 1883 to secure the election of socialist MPs.

The old Liberal/trade union alliance also came under pressure as a result of the rapid growth of trade unionism that occurred in the last two decades of the nineteenth century, a growth that saw unionization embrace, almost for the first time, unskilled and semi-skilled sections of the workforce. Thus in 1900 trade union membership stood at over two million, having more than doubled in just over a decade. In such circumstances demands inevitably grew for the legislative protection of labour's material interests, as did the conviction that independent labour representatives would be better placed to pursue it. The growth of this "new unionism" together with the increasing impact of socialist ideas were important factors making for the creation of the Independent Labour Party (ILP) in 1893.

Further, as a result of the growth of employers' organizations in the 1890s and a number of court cases that threatened to erode trade union rights, the belief strengthened among trade unionists that labour representatives in parliament were necessary both to bolster the legal position of trade unions and to counter what was seen as the growing political influence of industrialists. In 1899, therefore, the TUC passed a resolution at its annual conference in favour of the establishment of a Labour Representation Committee (LRC) that would augment the representation and thereby increase the independence and strengthen the voice of labour in parliament. With the support of the TUC, socialist organizations (the SDF and ILP) and co-operative societies, the Committee was duly established in 1900 and it was after its electoral success in 1906, with the return of 29 candidates to parliament, that the Labour Party was founded.

Given the fundamental role played by the trade union movement in the formation of the LRC and then the Labour Party (the SDF disaffiliated in 1901 soon after the LRC's formation), it was almost inevitable that it was the unions' agenda that initially dominated the new organization and this should be borne in mind when the political economy of the nascent Labour Party is considered. Thus, for example, early in its parliamentary life the new Party successfully exerted pressure on the Liberal government to accept a bill drafted by the Party in conjunction with the parliamentary committee of the TUC. This, when passed as the Trade Disputes Act 1906, reversed the Taff Vale judgment of 1900, which had rendered trade unions liable to legal action for damages resulting from industrial action. Further, in the 1906–8 period it campaigned strongly on trade union issues related to factory conditions and workmen's compensation. Even so, to understand the kind of economic thinking that existed within the Party in the period up to 1929, it is also necessary to be aware of the many, varied and conflicting strains of socialist political economy that sought influence within its ranks. It is important to do so, first, because the Party from the outset comprised socialist organizations whose members were among the most active within it; secondly because the commitment of the Party to socialism became an increasingly important issue after 1906, and thirdly because, in however indirect or indeterminate a fashion, socialist political economy did impinge on the thinking of key figures within the Party and influence Party policy-making in this period.

Part I of the book is therefore primarily concerned with these disparate strains of political economy and the manner and extent to which they helped to shape economic thinking and policy formulation within the Labour Party immediately after its formation. It also discusses the nature of the ideological battle that took place for the economic mind of the Labour Party and the consequences that this had for the conduct of economic policy after the formation of the second minority Labour government in 1929. To that end the chapters in this section outline the distinguishing theoretical characteristics of Fabian socialism, guild socialism, syndicalism, Marxian socialism, anarcho-communism, liberal socialism and ethical socialism. In addition, to provide some indication of which ideas filtered into the Labour Party itself, Chapters 6 and 7 consider both the economic thinking of key figures within the Labour Party – Ramsay Macdonald and Philip Snowden – and some of the literature that the Party produced in the 1920s.

Part II of the book focuses, to begin with, on the experience of the Labour government of 1929–31 in relation to its conduct of the nation's economic affairs. Further, it looks at the theoretical basis upon which that conduct rested and the challenge to it by some within the Labour Party (Ch. 8). There follows a discussion of the fundamental economic rethinking that occurred in the aftermath of the 1931 debacle, with particular reference to what socialist political economists had to say on the stabilization of capitalism (Ch. 9) and the business of building a socialist economy (Ch. 10). Looked at from another angle, these chapters outline the short-run and long-run objectives of socialist political economy in the 1930s and the manner in which they dovetailed. This section concludes with a short review of some of the economic pamphlets produced by the Labour Party in that decade in order to consider the extent to which the socialist revisionism of the 1930s impinged on Party literature.

Part III is concerned with the translation of ideas into policy by the post-war Labour government (Ch. 11) and the subsequent rethinking of socialist political economy that was provoked by the relative dynamism of British capitalism in the 1950s and 1960s (Ch. 12). The final chapter of the section discusses some of the economic literature produced by the Labour Party in those two decades and the manner in which it reflected the revision of socialist economic thinking undertaken by Crosland, Jenkins, Strachey, Meade and others. It also considers the conduct of economic policy by the Wilson governments of 1964–70 in relation to the economic ideas and economic policy commitments that the Party articulated in the early 1960s.

Part IV begins with an account of the revision of socialist economic thinking that occurred within the Labour Party in the aftermath of the experience of the Wilson governments and in the light of the challenge to the hegemony of Keynesianism in the 1970s and 1980s. In this context, Chapter 14 considers the Alternative Economic Strategy that emanated from the left of the Party; while Chapter 15 discusses the attempt on the part of Keynesian social democrats such as Crosland, Jenkins and Meade to rethink their position in the context of changing material and ideological circumstances. Chapter 16 looks at the profound influence of Alternative Economic Strategy ideas within the Labour Party in the 1970s and early 1980s and considers the relation of economic thinking to policy-making in the Labour governments of 1974–79. The book concludes with two chapters on the state of economic thinking in the Labour Party in the 1980s and early 1990s. Chapter 17 considers the emergence of a rejuvenated liberal socialism articulated by writers such as Roy Hattersley, Giles Radice, Austin Mitchell and others, while the final chapter provides a critical account of the emergence of the supply side socialism that now dominates the economic mind and economic literature of the Labour Party.

The book is not intended to be a comprehensive survey of British socialist economics or the work of British socialist economists. Throughout, the emphasis is on political economy rather than economics and broad rather than narrowly theoretical questions: what socialist writers had to say as regards the failings of capitalism, whether its faults could be remedied, whether in a manner that permitted socialist advance and what form and direction subsequent socialist progress should take. Reference is made to more narrowly theoretical questions, e.g. price formation in a socialist economy, where that is deemed relevant, but for the most part it is the broad currents and themes of socialist economic thinking with which the work is concerned. As regards policy and policy formation, the focus is again upon the general rather than the specific. In particular, the work concentrates on the manner in which the overall policy thrust of the Party related to the currents of socialist economic thinking in a period, rather than the way in which particular pieces of economic advice and the precise input of individual economic advisers may or may not have impinged on the details of policy prescription.

The story told is a fascinating one, if sometimes horribly so. I have tried to tell it using, wherever possible, the words of those who have written the classic texts of British socialist political economy. The notes almost invariably refer to these and I have confined reference to those secondary texts that I have used, and that the reader may find useful, to a Bibliography at the end of the volume.

The work has benefited from the criticism of elements of its contents by those of my students who have read drafts of the earlier chapters as part of their final year *Economic opinion and unemployment* course, something that was often over and above the call of academic duty. Comments by anonymous referees on articles published in the *History of political economy* and *Researches in the history of economic thought and methodology* also proved useful. In addition, I would like to acknowledge the help of staff in the Library of the London School of Economics and Political Science and the Inter-Library Loans Department of the University of Wales, Swansea.

The book is dedicated to my father who would have greeted its appearance, as he did everything that I wrote, with the wry injunction to make the next book a western. Indeed, as I write this I can almost hear him say the words. The work does indeed provide an account of a few ideological shoot-outs and (in the final chapter) some indication of who, for the author, wear the white stetsons and who he would like to see bite the dust; but I fear, for all that, my father would still have reached for a Zane Grey rather than the present volume. He knew, of course, that I would never think the worse of him for that.

Noel Thompson
University of Wales, Swansea
1 December 1995

Part one

1884–1929

Chapter one
Marxism, state socialism and anarcho-communism

> I may fairly claim to have done more than any man living to spread knowledge of their [Marx's and Engels'] theories amongst English speaking peoples.
>
> H. M. Hyndman, 1907

> . . . this living death of Commercialism . . . no rest, no beauty, no leisure . . . all England become like the heart of Lancashire is now: a breeding sty for flesh and blood machines.
>
> William Morris, *Art and the people*, 1883

> I never was a Collectivist myself; I was always a Communist of the Morris School.
>
> Robert Blatchford, *The Clarion*, February, 1913

H. M. Hyndman

The first English edition of *Capital* was published in 1886, that of the *Communist manifesto* in 1887. Until the late 1880s, therefore, socialists in Britain were heavily dependent on the work of popularizers, fluent in the languages in which Marx's and Engels' work had been published, for access to Marxian ideas. Foremost among these was, undoubtedly, H. M. Hyndman (founder of the Social Democratic Federation) who, in works such as *England for all* (1881), *The historical basis of socialism in England* (1883), and *The economics of socialism* (1896), "really brought the great German's work to England".[1]

Certainly, the basics of Marxian political economy are to be found in these books. Thus Hyndman, like Marx, explained how "it is the socially necessary labour embodied in a commodity which measures its relative value"[2] and how exploitation must be understood in terms of the appropriation of the surplus value [unpaid labour time] that labour furnished over and above the cost of its subsistence. He made clear why Marx believed the lot of labour became increasingly impoverished, as a reserve army of labour, displaced by fixed capital, grew in numbers, and also how this would create an increasingly class conscious and revolutionary proletariat. Like Marx too, Hyndman argued that the social nature of production under capitalism must come increasingly into conflict with the individual ownership of the means of production and pointed to the "anarchy, absolute, unrestrained anarchy of individual exchange."[3] It was in consequence of this anarchy, he asserted, that economic crises occurred "at intervals constantly decreasing and their effects lasting longer";[4] although Hyndman's explanation of these lacked the sophistication of the "reproduction models" to be found in the second volume of *Capital.* That said, for Hyndman, like Marx, such crises clearly revealed the essential irrationality and waste of capitalism and were seen as advancing "the establishment of industrial monopoly. The smaller organisms in every department of trade . . . being relentlessly crushed out".[5] Like Marx, Hyndman also stressed that such a concentration of ownership acted as a constraint upon the expansion of production and exacerbated labour exploitation, while at the same time effecting a restructuring of industry that facilitated future state appropriation and control. This would occur, Hyndman believed, when, with the intensification of capitalist crises, a final irremediable and inevitable economic breakdown created the conditions for a revolutionary overthrow of capitalism and the transition to a socialism characterized by "the social production and social exchange of articles of use without profit".[6]

Hyndman was certainly the most important British popularizer of Marxian political economy in the period preceding the Great War. Yet E. J. Hobsbawm's view of this role is pertinent, "He was quite an orthodox follower of Marx in economic theory *as he understood it.*"[7] The problem was that Hyndman's interpretation of Marx was often limited, and dogmatic. With respect to its limitations there was, for example, the exposition of a crudely determinist theory of history that was not to be found in Marx's own work; a determinism that always carried with it the danger of political passivity and also the excision from socialism of an ethical dimension. In terms of his expositional limitations one could cite here too Hyndman's crude rendering of Marx's discussion of economic crises.

Hyndman's dogmatism was particularly apparent in his attitude to trade unions. Marx himself had argued that while in the short run trade unions might raise real wages and interrupt for a time the tendency for the labouring classes to become increasingly impoverished, in the longer term their efforts in this regard must prove ineffectual. However, such a view did not lead Marx to discount the importance of the struggle by trade unions for improved pay and conditions; on the contrary he saw it as a fundamentally important means by which the working class would acquire a sense of itself as a separate class with interests distinct from and antagonistic to those of the bourgeoisie. Thus the growth in political consciousness that was a necessary prerequisite for the revolutionary overthrow of capitalism was, in part, a by-product of industrial struggle. For Hyndman, though, because capitalism was characterized by the growth of a "reserve army" of the unemployed, by the growth of capitalist monopoly power and so, inevitably, by the increasing immiseration of labour, the efforts of trade unions were seen as necessarily futile. Thus *only* the struggle for a revolutionary transformation of existing economic arrangements, only "the collective ownership of the means of production, distribution and exchange, *managed by a democratic state* in the interests of the whole commonwealth" would effect "a complete emancipation of labour from the domination of capital and landlords".[8] One commentator has put the matter nicely. "Marx in the 1860s had done his best to take the trade union leaders as he found them . . . Hyndman did nothing but scold the Trade Unions . . . for not being what they were not."[9]

Hyndmanian Marxism was therefore unlikely to appeal to trade unionists and though it is true that members of Hyndman's SDF were among the most effective trade union leaders of the period prior to 1914, many such as John Burns and Tom Mann defected as a result of its stance on the inefficacy of trade union action. Given then the central role that trade unions played in its formation, Hyndman's Marxism was unlikely to exert a significant influence within the Labour Party.

Of course there are many reasons other than Hyndman's dogmatism for the limited nature of Marxian influence; not least the appeal of the competing *non-revolutionary* brands of socialism that existed at the time. These will be considered below. However, at this point one may hazard the view that they were, by virtue of their non-revolutionary nature, more likely to appeal to a British working class, steeped throughout the third quarter of the nineteenth century in the language and aspirations of reformism, than a political economy that anticipated and welcomed a violent, revolutionary overthrow of existing economic and social arrangements.

On the political front the SDF split from the Labour Representation Committee in 1901 and its retreat into a kind of ideological isolationism did nothing to further the permeation of Marxist ideas within the Labour Party. Further, whatever influence Marxism might have had was also diminished by the splits within Marxist ranks. In particular, in 1884, there was that between anarcho-communists such as William Morris, who sought a decentralized socialism that they believed could not, at that juncture, be achieved by parliamentary action and those, such as Hyndman, who favoured a parliamentary road to a socialism that would ultimately vest all ownership and economic power in the state.

In addition the fact that Hyndman's Marxism was infused with anti-religious sentiments, an anti-German jingoism and a racialist imperialism did not help in the business of popularization. The former would certainly have alienated the many British socialists whose political faith was rooted in biblically derived moral precepts. Further, the jingoistic and expansionist nationalism that Hyndman articulated would have been repugnant to those, and again they were many, whose socialism was of a pacifist kind that stressed, in however nebulous a manner, the international brotherhood of man.

As regards the alienation of those whose socialism was religiously rooted, another and more general point may also be made. Marxists such as Hyndman prided themselves on the scientific nature of their socialism. They had, courtesy of Marx, come to understand the *laws* of motion of capitalist development and the motive force of historical change. It was to those laws that they looked to effect that socialist transformation of society which they anticipated, rather than to any moral imperatives. To view the socialist transformation of society in this way had the advantage of instilling a self-confidence, not to say a positivistic arrogance, among those socialists who adhered to it: an intellectual and political self-confidence born of the belief that the doctrines to which they adhered could be validated in a rigorous, scientific fashion and that therefore, as adherents of a scientific socialism, they could speak about the future course of human history with absolute certainty. Yet all this ignored the ethical dimension of socialism and that belief in the need to transform men's souls, and not just their material circumstances, which inspired many to embrace socialism and lend their support to organizations such as the Independent Labour Party.

So while many reasons may be adduced to explain the negligible influence of Marxian political economy within the ranks of the Labour Party, Hyndman, in terms of the kind of Marxism that he purveyed, must bear some of the responsibility. In this context it is interesting to note that while Continental socialist political parties, adhering to doctrines of a Marxist hue, could count their support in hundreds of thousands and in the case of the German Social Democratic Party in millions, membership of the SDF, the only significant Marxist political organization, was a mere 9,000 in 1900. It is interesting to note too that in 1906 when *The review of reviews* asked the 29 recently elected Labour MPs which books had had the greatest influence on their thinking, Marx's *Capital* was mentioned only once. In that survey the book that was most frequently cited was, in fact, the Bible, with John Bunyan's *Pilgrim's progress* coming a close second.

It is true that Marxian socialism did emerge strengthened from the Great War. The revolution in Russia, currency instability and economic disintegration in central and eastern Europe, abortive revolutions in Germany, Hungary and Austria all seemed to substantiate the Marxian prediction that capitalism was doomed to imminent demise. Further, after 1917, communism could no longer be dismissed as a product of the perfervid, socialist imagination. It was,

Marxists could claim, a reality over one sixth of the globe. In the words of one commentator, it now had "the test of experience".[10]

Further, in Britain, in the immediate post-war period, the output of a new generation of writers – Noah Ablett, Maurice Dobb, Mark Starr, Eden and William Paul, J. T. Walton Newbold – turned the flow of Marxist literature into a torrent. There were also English translations of the works of Russian communists, such as Malinowski's *Short course of economic science* (1925) and Bukharin and Preobrahzhensky's *ABC of communism* (1922). However, while the influence of Marxism within the British Labour Movement in that period should not be discounted, particularly as regards the Marxian critique of capitalism, its constructive proposals had little impact. Leaving aside the antipathy of the greater part of the Labour Movement to ideas such as the dictatorship of the proletariat and the violent, revolutionary overthrow of the existing order of things, a centrally planned economy of the kind that Marxists sketchily proposed had little obvious relevance to the immediate problems that the British working-class were to confront in the 1920s.

William Morris

In some respects Morris too can be seen as a conduit for Marxian ideas in the period that saw the birth of the British Labour Party. That said, the Marxism that flowed from his pen bore a distinctive, Morrisian imprint; certainly it was very far from being the pure milk of *Capital* that Hyndman sought to supply. In any case, Morris's mind wrestled uneasily with the concepts and analysis of Marxian political economy. Thus on being asked after a lecture whether he accepted Marx's labour theory of value he replied with refreshing honesty that he did "not know what Marx's theory of value is. Truth to say my friends I have tried to understand Marx's theory but political economy is not my line and much of it appears to me to be dreary rubbish." Elsewhere he was to admit, "I don't think I shall make an economist even of the most elementary kind." "It is enough political economy to know that the idle class is rich because they rob the poor."[11] This in itself was a safeguard against any rigidly dogmatic Hyndmanian rendition of, or adherence to, Marxian economics.

That said Morris did take on board some of the central components of Marx's critique of capitalism – the exploitation and increasing impoverishment of labour, the reserve army of the unemployed, the tendency to periodic crises of increasing severity and the growing intensity of class conflict. Yet his explanation of these phenomena often deviated significantly from that of Marx. To give just one example, Morris explained general economic depression partly in terms of the volatility, born of caprice, of the money demands of the rich; partly in terms of a tendency to overproduction as capitalist producers sought to maximize output and partly in terms of simple underconsumption.

However if, deviations apart, Morris's critique of capitalism had on occasion a strongly Marxian flavour, it also had an aesthetic and a moral dimension that derived, in large measure, from the work of John Ruskin. For Morris, like Ruskin, capitalism not only exploited labour, it also corrupted it, or, more accurately, it corrupted its nature. The creative capacities of humanity were subordinated under capitalism to the desire for pecuniary gain. Instead, therefore, of "the intelligent production of beautiful things" labour was condemned to produce "vulgarities and shabby gentilities" that "pandered to degraded follies" and to do so as quickly and cheaply as possible.[12] In consequence what should have been an expression of the creative impulse, what Morris termed "joyful labour", degenerated into "useless toil".[13] The excessive division of labour and the acceleration of production required for the cheapness that a competitive capitalism demanded had destroyed the possibility of fusing labour and art. Instead the worker for the "whole of his life [came to be] hopelessly engaged in performing one repulsive and never-ending task". This, wrote Morris, was "an arrangement fit enough for the hell imagined by theologians but scarcely fit enough for any other form of society".[14] As a system, therefore, capitalism was not only materially but also morally and aesthetically bankrupt. Thus whereas, for Morris, "everything made should be a joy to the maker and a joy to the user",[15] capitalism crushed both the capacity to create and to appreciate the beautiful. It was devoid of both an aesthetic and a moral sense.

In addition, for Morris, capitalism, and the obsession with private gain that permeated it, not only destroyed the capacity to create what was beautiful and what was of real worth, it also destroyed the beauty of the natural world. On this Morris waxed more eloquent than almost any socialist writer of the period. Here he pointed in particular to the environmental consequences of the rapid and uncontrolled industrialization that the self-interested pursuit of profit had brought about. It was the capitalist pursuit of profit,

> which draws men into enormous, unmanageable aggregations called towns . . . ; profit which crowds them up when they are there into quarters without gardens or open spaces; profit which won't take the most elementary precautions against wrapping a whole district in a cloud of sulphurous smoke; which turns beautiful rivers into filthy sewers, which condemns all but the rich to live in houses idiotically confined at best and at the worst in houses for whose wretchedness there is no name . . . Why should one third of England be stifled and poisoned with smoke . . . why must Yorkshire and Lancashire rivers run with filth and dye?

For Morris the answer was plain – "profit and competition".[16]

If a competitive, profit-seeking capitalism corrupted the nature of labour and nature itself, it did the same to the character of social relationships. For competition "or war . . . whichever you please to call it, means at the best pursuing your own advantage at the cost of someone else's loss and in the process of it . . . not . . . sparing destruction even of your own possessions."[17] Such conflict was endemic to capitalism. There was the conflict between individuals pursuing a diminishing number of employment opportunities; between the organizers of labour, great firms, joint stock companies, capitalists in short;[18] and, most fundamentally, between the owners of the means of production and those with only their labour power to sell. However, it was not simply class conflict that Morris highlighted here but social antagonism in all its manifestations. In effect, capitalism destroyed the possibility of human fellowship.

While, therefore, Morris undoubtedly drew inspiration from Marx, his Marxism bore the stamp of his own concerns. Most obviously, like John Ruskin before him, Morris's critique of existing economic and social arrangements was rooted in a concern for the degeneration of art and the corruption of aesthetic values. It was this that evoked his concern for the nature of labour and the manner in which it had been debased under capitalism; for it was the degradation of labour that had effectively destroyed or perverted the artistic impulse.

So, for Morris, capitalism stood condemned not just for the economic but also for the moral and aesthetic impoverishment that it inflicted on society and, indeed, it was these latter aspects of his critique of capitalism that in large measure explain his popularity within the ranks of the Labour Party in the period prior to the Great War. It is the ethical and cultural dimension of his thought rather than his flawed exposition of Marxian political economy which, as we shall see, was to prove influential.

With respect to the prescriptive dimension of his political economy, it is useful to distinguish, as Morris himself did, between his short-run and long-run positions. As regards the short-run, there is, in fact, little to distinguish Morris from Hyndman and others who believed that the state should, under socialism, both own the means of production and assume responsibility for directing economic activity in the interests of society as a whole. However, while accepting that this might be necessary in a transition period, Morris recognized and emphasized the authoritarian dangers implicit in the centralization of ownership and power in the hands of the state. Thus in a review of a work by an American writer, Edward Bellamy, who advocated a centralized state socialism, Morris condemned the "impression which he produces . . . of a huge standing army tightly drilled". Elsewhere he was to write that: "men should not shuffle off the business of life on to the shoulders of an abstraction called the State."[19] "State Communism" should be seen, therefore, as a necessary phase of bastard socialism en route to the New Jerusalem: "a transition period during which people would be getting rid of the habits of mind bred by the long ages of tyranny and commercial competition and be learning that it is to the interest of each that all should thrive."[20]

Ultimately, though, Morris looked forward to state communism evolving in such a way that "communes", not the state, would become the source of economic decision-making, with society becoming "a great federation of such communes".[21] He looked forward, in other words, to the emergence of a decentralization of economic power with a gradual withering away of the authority and directive economic authority of the state. Morris's vision of socialism was, therefore, essentially an anarcho-communist one; a vision that was to receive its fullest expression in the utopian romance, *News from nowhere*, 1890. In that work the picture he painted was one of an economy characterized by small-scale, relatively unmechanized, units of production where the values of craftsmanship prevailed, where "useless toil" had been transformed into "joyful labour" and where the creative impulse was no longer constrained and corrupted by the pressures of commercialism. In this context the autonomy and the freedom of the worker would transmute labour into artistry. It would be a marketless, moneyless economy with a mutual exchange of services and goods proceeding on the principle of from each according to ability and to each according to need. But, above all, it was to be an economy that laid the basis for a society "bound together by honesty and mutual self-respect"; a society, in short, characterized by social equality and fellowship.[22]

It is also clear from a reading of *News from nowhere* that Morris believed that the economy that was to underpin his anarcho-communism would be primarily agrarian. He anticipated in that work the gradual withering away of the factory system and a parallel diminution in the use of machinery. In part this would be made possible by a more effective organization of economic life and, in part, by a more equitable distribution of wealth, which would facilitate the satisfaction of needs without recourse to mechanized mass production methods. In some measure also, Morris anticipated a voluntary scaling down of the desire to consume as the population increasingly sought satisfaction through the creative use of more leisure time, rather than increased consumption; in other words he anticipated the emergence of a kind of voluntary asceticism. Morris himself put it this way in an article written in 1894: "we should have so much leisure from the production of what are called 'utilities' that any group of people would have leisure to satisfy its craving for what are looked on as superfluities, *such as enjoying works of art, research . . . literature*."[23]

Morris's idealized socialist economy emerges, therefore, as an essentially pastoral, non-mechanized one characterized by small-scale or artisan production, with goods distributed not by market exchange or with the use of money but freely on the basis of need. In an increasingly complex, urban, industrial economy distinguished by large-scale, highly mechanized productive units and increasingly afflicted by the problems of urban squalor and industrial pollution that Morris himself so eloquently describes, it is understandable why, by way of reaction, this vision of socialism should have exerted such a powerful influence within the labour movement. One should also highlight here the appeal of the simplicity, autonomy and fellowship that were to characterize the communes whose emergence he anticipated; something that would have proved powerfully attractive to those beset by the complexities and social atomization of a rapidly changing industrial society.

That Morrisian political economy was indeed popular and influential within the early Labour Party there can be no doubt. In contrast to Hyndman, Morris's work was widely read by Party members. The survey conducted by the *Review of reviews*, to which reference has already been made, indicated that after the Bible and *Pilgrim's progress*, the two works that Labour Party MPs cited as most influential were Morris's *News from nowhere* (1890) and Robert Blatchford's *Merrie England* (1894). Further, as we shall see when we consider the writing of two key figures within the early Labour Party, Ramsay Macdonald and Philip Snowden, it is clear that Morris's work in general and *News from nowhere* in particular had a significant impact.

His vision of socialism, which highlighted the moral, the social and the aesthetic nature of the transformation that it would effect, was also given expression in the work of ethical socialists such as R. H. Tawney; his emphasis on the creativity of labour can be found in the writing of guild socialists such as A. J. Penty and A. R. Orage, while his concern with the decentralization of power had a significant impact on the thinking of other guild socialist writers such as S. G. Hobson and G. D. H. Cole. More generally, we can say that Morris's whole discussion of the decentralization of economic power, the organization of production to make it both pleasurable and creative, the motivation of labour by other than pecuniary incentives, the need to ensure that human rather than technical or profit-making considerations determined the scale of output and the need to establish social relations on a basis of fellowship and mutual respect, were to be reflected in the work of many socialist writers throughout the twentieth century. E. F. Schumacher's *Small is beautiful* is one of many works whose intellectual pedigree can be traced back to Morris and further to John Ruskin.

Robert Blatchford

One writer who, while exerting an important ideological influence within the early Labour Party in his own right, was also profoundly indebted to Morris was Robert Blatchford. The impact of Blatchford's *Merrie England* (1894) in the

1890s and 1900s was certainly as considerable as that of *News from nowhere*, even if it was neither as lasting nor as profound; in the 1890s alone it sold over a million copies. In addition the popularization of Blatchford's ideas was also effected by his paper *The Clarion* and by various social and propagandist activities connected with that newspaper. A contemporary of Blatchford's, writing in 1910, stated that *Merrie England* alone "has attracted more followers to the standard of English socialism than all or any other books contained in the library of the London School of Economics";[24] while Blatchford himself believed that his paper should be advertised under the slogan: "Mr Blatchford and the *Clarion* make more socialists than any rival establishment." However, if a consideration of Blatchford's thinking throws light on ideas that were undoubtedly influential, it is also important because its very popularity gives some indication of the state of economic thinking within the Labour Party itself. Thus works such as *Merrie England*, and for that matter *News from nowhere*, may, in this respect, be seen as reflecting as well as shaping that thought.

Robert Blatchford himself stressed his intellectual debt to William Morris. Thus he wrote in the *Clarion*, in 1899 that he was "not a rigid state socialist and never was, *I am, and always have been, a communist of the William Morris type*"; while again, in 1913, he stated in the *Clarion* that "Communist Anarchy of the Morris kind is what I call Socialism; the other thing, the State Socialism, or Collectivism, never appealed to me at all."[25] However this self-categorization is too simplistic. Blatchford certainly saw anarcho-communism of a Morrisian kind as the ultimate goal. Further, the moneyless, marketless and pastoral features of his conception of that goal also mirror the vision evoked by Morris in *News from nowhere*. Thus with the advent of socialism Blatchford wrote that he would

> set men to work *to grow wheat and fruit and rear cattle and poultry for our own use*. Then I would develop *the fisheries and construct great fish-breeding lakes and harbours*. Then I would *restrict* the mines, furnaces, chemical works and factories to the number actually needed for the supply of our own people . . . by degrees I would make all things free. So that clothing, lodging, fuel, food, amusement, intercourse, education, and all the requirements for a perfect human life would be produced and distributed and enjoyed by the people without the use of money.[26]

This is pure Morris. There also ran through much of what Blatchford wrote the ideal of fellowship. Thus he looked forward to the creation of a society in which "the makers of goods and the users of goods [would] carry on their work and their sales together *in a friendly way*".[27]

In addition, as regards his critique of capitalism, we can sense Morris again at his shoulder. Specifically there is a strong moral and aesthetic dimension. Thus competition is not only economically wasteful, it is "cruel and wrong".

"Through competition" too "millions of men are employed in *useless and undignified work*." Further, the "unfettered right of individual enterprise" not only made for "economic anarchy" it was also "*bad*". "It is bad because in a state of social warfare to termination point, the basest and the vilest have the advantage, for the vile man and the base will fight with less truth and fewer principles."[28] Elsewhere he wrote in Morrisian fashion of the pollution, adulteration and shoddiness that competition produced.

Similarly, Blatchford regarded what labour should be paid and what prices should be charged as essentially moral questions. An adequate and just level of wage payments was something that should be determined before production commenced and it should be in the light of this that what Blatchford termed "natural prices" were established. Taking the example of coal he wrote that if the nation fixed a "living wage" for colliers "then the nation ought to fix all wages and if the nation fixes wages, it must also fix prices".[29] Blatchford's work resonates with the language of moral economy and it should be noted that what he proposed, with respect to wages and prices, had been prefigured in the *Manifesto of the Socialist League* (1884), written by William Morris. In the *Manifesto* Morris had argued that one of the first acts of a socialist state should be to establish maximum prices and minimum wage levels.[30]

However, despite the strong parallels that can be drawn between Blatchford's critique of capitalism, his vision of what he termed "ideal socialism" and the anarcho-communism of Morris, it is clear that as regards what he termed "practical socialism" the state had a decisive role to play.[31] Thus in a work entitled *Britain for the British* (1902), he wrote: "Socialism is *only a method of extending State management* as in the Post Office and Municipal management, until State and Municipal management become universal throughout the kingdom."[32] Earlier, in *Merrie England*, he defined "practical socialism" as "a kind of national scheme of co-operation, *managed by the State*. Its programme consists essentially of one demand that the land and other instruments of production shall be the common property of the people."[33] So while, like Morris, Blatchford might emphasize that state socialism represented simply a staging post en route to an anarcho-communist ideal, a substantial part of his writing was nonetheless concerned with the minutiae of the transition period. In addition, as a number of commentators have pointed out, Blatchford's socialism did embody an admiration for order and discipline of an almost military kind that, he believed, could only be infused into civil society by the state. In this respect the authoritarian state socialism of a writer like Edward Bellamy was, unquestionably, influential and it is interesting to note that Blatchford strongly advised *Clarion* readers to read Bellamy's *Looking backward* and the work of another state socialist, Lawrence Gronlund, whose *Co-operative Commonwealth*, was published in 1884. There was, in short, much more of the state socialist in Blatchford than he was prepared to admit.

Blatchford's socialism therefore represents an uneasy mix of disparate elements, some derived from Morris, some from Bellamy and Gronlund and others, which can be traced back to a moral economy tradition. In that respect it was unique. That said, the circulation figures of the *Clarion* and the million copies of *Merrie England* that were sold suggest that his socialism, with its state socialist *and* anarcho-communist dimensions and its peculiar fusion of the ethical, the economic and the aesthetic, was also representative of the aspirations and the thoughts of many within the Labour Movement.

Chapter 2
Fabian political economy

> Now gentlemen, I am really a political economist. I have studied the thing. I understand Ricardo's law of rent and Jevons' law of value.
>
> G. B. Shaw, 1913

1883 saw the founding of the Fellowship of the New Life by Thomas Davison, a wandering philosopher, and Percival Chubb, a civil service clerk; its object being, through study and discussion, to cultivate "a perfect character in each and all". However, the Fellowship was soon to split between those who favoured the path of moral self-improvement and those who saw institutional and social change as vital to the business of perfecting character. It was the latter group that in 1884 founded the Fabian Society.

The first publications of the Society, while socialist in character, lacked both analytical and prescriptive precision. However, the situation was transformed by the advent of two men – the Irish wit and playwright G. B. Shaw and a civil servant at the Colonial Office, Sidney Webb. The literary flair of the former and the appetite for facts of the latter made them a formidable combination and together with figures such as Sidney Olivier, William Clarke, Beatrice Webb, Annie Besant and, for a time, H. G. Wells, they equipped the Society with a political economy that exerted a profound influence within the Labour Party at least until the early 1930s.

The Fabians indicted capitalism on two grounds. First it was characterized, and increasingly so, by the exercise of monopoly power and secondly its anarchic nature meant that it was productive of enormous waste. As regards the growth of monopoly power, the predatory competition that characterized capitalism had led to a marked concentration of ownership in important sectors of industry and while this did not usually result in monopoly strictly defined, it led to the emergence of syndicates, trusts, cartels and the collusive agreements that they spawned. This, in turn, resulted both in an underutilization of productive capacity, as capitalist entrepreneurs curtailed supply in order to maximize profit, and the consequent exploitation of the consumer who could no longer rely on market forces "to secure the utmost possible cheapness" of commodities.[1]

It should be said, of course, that such a view of things did not set the Fabian socialists apart from many other strains of socialism or, for that matter, from some radical liberal thinkers. Marx had pointed to the growth of monopoly as a characteristic feature of the later stages of capitalism when, as a mode of production, it assumed forms that increasingly obstructed the further development of productive forces. As regards the radical or "new" liberals, J. A. Hobson saw in the rapid growth of monopoly the essential cause of the maldistribution of the nation's economic surplus: a maldistribution that he believed lay at the root of over-saving, underconsumption, mass unemployment and the growth of economic pressures making for imperial expansion.[2]

There was, however, a dimension to the Fabian understanding of monopoly that did distinguish them from other socialists. For the Fabians argued not only that capitalism tended to monopoly in its later stages, as a diminishing number of large enterprises emerged, but also that even in circumstances that might conventionally be regarded as competitive, with industries characterized by numerous rival firms, monopoly power existed and was exploited. Here the Fabians made use of an essentially Ricardian theory of rent.

David Ricardo in his *Essay on profits* (1815) had argued that as a population expanded and as recourse was had to land of diminishing fertility to feed it, so owners of more fertile land, where costs of production were lower, would be able to exact rent from their capitalist tenant farmers up to the point where the rate of profit earned was no more than that prevailing on marginal land, that is that land last taken into cultivation. The more fertile the intramarginal land, the greater would be the rent the landowner would be able to exact. Rental income derived, therefore, not from any productive effort on the part of the landowner but from his fortuitous monopoly of a finite resource, that is intramarginal or better quality land.

What the Fabian socialists did was to generalize this analysis by applying it to other factors of production. Thus "interest" (as they termed supranormal profits) was explained in terms of variations in the productivity of capital investment in the same way as rent was explained in terms of the varying fertility of the land. Interest, as they saw it, represented the difference between the returns on the least productive or marginal capital investment and capital investment that, perhaps because of the quality of the industrial plant that it furnished or because of the advantageous site of the factory whose construction it financed, was more productive. It was, in short, a payment to those who owned (monopolized) non-marginal capital inputs.

Further, the Fabians stressed that the productivity of capital investment was often determined by factors unrelated to any sacrifice, forethought or organizational ability on the part of the owner/entrepreneur. Specifically the productivity of investment might be crucially influenced by the fortuitous location of other enterprises and the siting and construction of roads, docks, railways, housing, gas and waterworks by municipalities, the state or private entrepreneurs. As the Fabians saw it, therefore, owners of capital, like owners of land, were often the undeserving beneficiaries of "rental" payments that accrued to them as a result of their monopoly of a finite resource, e.g. a particularly advantageous location. Thus, no more than land rent could "interest" be considered a necessary cost of production.

Similarly those possessed of particular skills in short supply would be able to exact what the Fabians termed a "rent of ability". To take just one example the rewards of those in tasks involving "superintendence and direction" were high because, as Sidney Olivier put it, such occupations were "a virtual class monopoly" and would remain so until the superior educational provision enjoyed by that middle class was removed or extended to embrace the entire population. Only then would "the remuneration of such activity reach *the normal level or competitive value*".[3]

In summary, therefore, as Sidney Webb phrased it in 1892, "an additional product determined by the relative differences in the productive efficiency of the different sites, soil, capitals and forms of skill above the margin has gone to those exercising control over those valuable but scarce productive factors."[4] In short, the exploitation of monopoly power and its deleterious distributive consequences were endemic to capitalism.

Their use of the concept of the margin led the Fabians to link themselves with developments in mainstream economics in the last quarter of the nineteenth century. In Britain these developments were associated with the name of W. S. Jevons, and certainly the marginal utility theory of exchange value that he formulated in *The theory of political economy* (1871) did help set in motion theoretical developments in the field of microeconomics that were to dominate the next four decades. The Fabians were quick to insist upon such an association. It allowed them to reject Marxian political economy as based on a defunct (labour) theory of value and to claim that their own socialist political economy was soundly rooted in modern economic thinking and consistent with the theoretical advances that were being made in the *science* of economics.

However, while it is the case that Philip Wicksteed, one of those building on Jevons's theoretical achievements, played a vital part in converting G. B. Shaw from a labour to a marginal utility theory of value, Fabian political economy embodied little of what is to be found in the work of Jevons, Wicksteed or the other mainstream, neoclassical political economists of the period. The theoretical roots of their political economy were essentially Ricardian, though the economic thinking of the American Henry George may also, for a time, have proved influential. Certainly the latter's ideas, which had at their core an attack on the iniquities of rental income derived from landownership, circulated widely in Britain in the 1880s, both as a result of George's lecturing tours and the considerable sales of his *Progress and poverty*, first published in 1881.

Yet, whatever their sources of theoretical inspiration, the crucial point is that the Fabian view of things led them to condemn "competitive capitalism" as irremediably monopolistic and as producing, in consequence, a distribution of wealth that could be defended neither on grounds of equity nor on the basis that it was necessary to call forth the existing level of output.

If, however, the Fabians saw contemporary capitalism as corrupted by the increasing growth of monopoly power, they also saw it as economically anarchic. Capitalist production was "anarchic and unsound", "anarchical and reckless" and characterized by "competitive confusion".[5] Lack of knowledge and uncoordinated decision-making meant that supply rarely matched demand, productive resources were wasted through misallocation, underutilization or duplication, and labour often found itself redundant. "Who can estimate", the Webbs wrote, "among how many different boards and committees, partnerships and combinations, in how many entirely uncoordinated centres of management, unaware of each other's proceedings and constantly in conflict or confusion the direction of . . . British . . . industry is dispersed."[6] In effect the fragmented, competitive, self-interested pursuit of gain precluded the exercise of any informed and organizing intelligence and colossal economic waste was the inevitable consequence. Producers were ignorant of the intentions of their rivals, the extent of the market and the needs of society. Further, as regards those needs, they were also ignorant for reasons other than the absence of information resulting from market anarchy. Thus as a consequence of the maldistribution of wealth that followed from the pervasive nature of monopoly power, the market failed to indicate accurately the nature of social requirements. So the market transmitted information only about the needs of those with the requisite purchasing power.

Economic waste resulted, therefore, from the ignorance contingent upon anarchy and also from the misinformation as to society's real needs which, in such circumstances, the market supplied. Further, waste was also a consequence of what the Fabians considered to be the needlessly complex and roundabout system of distributing and exchanging commodities which, among other things, produced a needless proliferation of retail outlets. In addition, as regards that system of exchange, there was the "elaborate deception of consumers by enormously expensive advertisements" which made for irrational and ill-informed choices on the part of consumers with a consequent wasteful misallocation of resources.[7] This latter was subjected to particularly scathing attack in H. G. Wells's *Tono-Bungay* which was, and remains, one of the finest satirical indictments of mass advertising ever penned. Advertising was one factor, though not the only one, producing what one Fabian writer categorized as the "anarchic irresponsibility" of the private consumer.[8]

To obviate or remedy the iniquities, inequities and structural deficiencies inherent in the capitalist market economy Fabian socialists suggested a range of expedients. First, having distinguished, as they believed, the source and nature of unearned income, they considered that taxation should be used to secure it for social purposes. As G. B. Shaw saw it, rent and interest could and should be transferred to the state "by instalments" and, in general, Fabian socialists favoured a radically redistributive fiscal policy.[9] However, it is clear that they saw it as doing only a part of what was required to eliminate the evils of an increasingly monopolistic capitalism. In particular such a policy would do little to mitigate the inherent economic anarchy of the system. They believed therefore that only by the extension of public ownership to a point where the greater part of the nation's productive capacity was under social control could all evils finally be exorcized.

To begin with, such an extension would mean that "rental income" would be directly acquired for social uses without the intermediation of the tax system. It would no longer be necessary, therefore, to rectify the adverse distributive consequences of the growth of monopoly power *after* they had occurred. For that reason alone Fabian socialists advocated social ownership on a substantial scale. But there was more to it than that. For socialism was not just about rectifying distributive injustices; not just about securing the economic surplus for social use, even if, for Fabian socialists, that was undoubtedly important. Socialism was also, fundamentally, about the elimination of waste and inefficiency through the social organization and control of the nation's productive capacity. Only in this way could socialism provide an effective antidote to the competitive anarchy of the market economy. So Fabians advocated the "taking over of the great centralised industries" by the state or municipalities in order to lay the basis for a "consciously regulated co-ordination" of economic activity.[10] The extension of public ownership was therefore to be the means of organizing and controlling economic activity in the interests of society as a whole. Only this would make possible the elimination of the "competitive confusion" that characterized contemporary economic life; only this, and the consequent attenuation of the influence of anarchic market forces, would permit the ordering of productive activity in a manner that eliminated waste, maximized efficiency and accelerated the growth of output. These things could not be effected through the medium of private firms whether operating in a competitive or a monopolistic economic market environment but only by means of publicly owned enterprises operating under state or municipal control.

On that basis rationality, not blind instinct, would be made to govern economic decision-making; intelligence would replace the haphazard interaction of market forces and the laws of chance would give way to the certainty that resulted from the scientific management of economic affairs. In short, the extension of public ownership and the attenuation of the influence of market forces would allow "organised co-operation" to be "substituted . . . for the anarchy of the competitive struggle".[11]

Once the nation's productive capacity, by one expedient or another, had passed into public control, the socialized enterprises that emerged would be administered by a new breed of manager pursuing objectives of a radically different kind and motivated by considerations very different from those of the people who ran privately owned undertakings. Specifically their primary concern would be the efficient satisfaction of society's needs. As regards motivation, the managers of public concerns would be fired not by the pursuit of profit but by the ideal of social service. Stress on this ideal as a motive to enterprise was not, of course, a monopoly of Fabianism, but Fabian socialists did see in it the essence of the new spirit that would govern the administration of socialist enterprises and the management of a socialist economy in general.

The Fabians believed that the replacement of the capitalist entrepreneur by the professional manager was a process that had already progressed to a considerable extent under capitalist auspices. The growth of large-scale units of production, often wielding monopolistic powers and participating in collusive agreements, had already rendered obsolete the entrepreneur's traditional function of taking the initiatives and risks necessary to hone his firm's competitive edge. The expert administrator was already taking the place of the capitalist swashbuckler. All that remained to be done was for such bureaucratic expertise to be utilized for social purposes rather than private profit.

Fabian socialists therefore advocated the extension of public ownership both on grounds of equity – it permitted the social use of an economic surplus that would otherwise accrue to the unproductive – and on grounds of efficiency, in that it allowed for the rational, scientific organization and control of economic life. This extension was, however, to be effected gradually. To this end a number of methods were suggested. G. B. Shaw, for example, believed that the "socialisation of rent" by way of taxation would convince existing property owners of the pointlessness of insisting upon their titles to the means of production.[12] An apposite fiscal policy could therefore be used to secure a peaceful transition from private to public ownership. Further, once municipal or state owned enterprises were established their superior efficiency would ensure the eventual bankruptcy of their rivals. As Annie Besant put it, "the economic forces which replaced the workshop by the factory will replace the private shop by the municipal store and the private factory by the municipal one."[13] Competitive pressures could therefore be used to secure a transference of productive capacity to social ownership. In this context it was also suggested that public authorities, through the administrative power that they wielded, could act to disadvantage private concerns or advantage their publicly owned rivals. As Shaw wrote, only partially tongue in cheek, "a skilfully timed series of experiments in paving, a new bridge, a tramway service, a barracks or a smallpox hospital" could "significantly alter the economic prospects of any enterprise". They could be used, in effect, to blunt the competitive edge of private enterprise and to sharpen that of public concerns and so accelerate the extension of social ownership. Finally, as regards the extension of public ownership, that could also be effected by means of compulsory purchase with a measure of compensation for existing owners.[14]

However, whatever the preferred form of transference, Fabian writers emphasized its gradual, piecemeal and inevitable nature. The whole was summed up in Sidney Webb's famous phrase, "the inevitability of gradualness", which highlighted the reformist nature of the socialist path that the Fabians proposed. In addition, the allusion to inevitability gave their proposals a pseudo-scientific authority linked, as it frequently was, to a social evolutionism derived from a bastardized Darwinism. Indeed, the word "evolution", with its scientific connotations, flowed frequently from their pens and, while it was often used as a synonym for reformism and to distinguish their *evolutionary* from Marxian *revolutionary* socialism, they also used it to convey the idea that what they proposed represented the next stage in the ineluctable, scientifically dictated progression of mankind to ever more organized and sophisticated forms of social existence. In the words of one writer, what they proposed represented "the lesson of evolution in social development . . . the substitution of consciously regulated co-ordination among the units of each organism for their intermittent competition".[15] Thus the Fabians, like the Marxists, were able to claim that they swam with the tide of history; though it was, of course, history according to Darwin, not Hegel.

As with their critical economics, so with their view of the shape of things to come, the Fabians stressed the scientific nature of what they had to offer. In so doing they could and did claim the authority and the kudos which, in this period, attached to those who practised "science"; a period when the natural sciences, in particular, were so obviously advancing humanity's understanding and mastery of the physical world. Thus the view prevailed, in Fabian ranks, that it was they and not the Marxists, shackled as they were to an obsolescent theory of value, who purveyed a truly scientific socialism, and, in general, they exuded all the intellectual self-confidence that one might expect to attach to such a faith. Certainly they prided themselves not only on drawing theoretical inspiration from modern, scientific economics but also on their adherence to a scientific, empirically grounded methodology. Their theories, as they believed, were supported by and inductively rooted in a painstaking accumulation and assimilation of *the facts*, while their policy prescriptions were derived from actual, piecemeal experimentation with public (largely municipal) ownership.[16]

Of course, this belief in the *inevitability* of gradualness, in the necessary evolution of society in a direction that could be scientifically predicted, carried with it the danger of political passivity and there are certainly passages in the writings of the Fabian socialists which suggest that, on a theoretical level, this was a danger to which, on occasion, they did succumb. Sidney Webb, for example, wrote in 1892 that it needed "nothing but a general recognition of development" of "English social evolution in the direction of collectivism and social ownership" and "a clear determination not to hamper it, for Socialism to secure universal assent. *All other changes will easily flow from this acquiescent state of mind*". He also wrote of "*blind social forces . . . inexorably working out our social salvation*". Similarly Annie Besant wrote that: "all we can do is to *consciously co-operate with the forces at work*, and thus render the transition more rapid than it would otherwise be."[17] However, while Fabians sometimes came close to suggesting that the best thing socialists could do was to get out of the way of the juggernaut of history, it must also be said that they were among the most active of socialists in attempting to realize their vision of socialism in partial and practical ways.

None the less, the prescriptive passivity implicit in certain aspects of their political economy was a potential weakness and one which, as we shall see, was to leave its mark on the Labour Party's economic literature in the 1920s and its conduct of economic policy in the 1929–31 period. In addition, there was one other and more fundamental deficiency that was to have profound consequences both as regards policy formulation and the conduct of the nation's economic affairs by the minority Labour government of 1929–31. This related to their critical view of the competitive market economy where uncoordinated endeavour, the burgeoning of monopoly power and the relative or total ignorance of producers and consumers were productive of waste, inefficiency and economic chaos. Given such a view, given that the market as a pricing, allocative and distributive mechanism was essentially and irredeemably flawed, its use as a means of implementing economic policy was effectively ruled out. Specifically, such a conception of the market ruled out the use of expansionary strategies that revolved around the increase of purchasing power as a means of expanding output and employment. These, in the Fabian view of things, would not solve the problem of the ignorance of decision-makers in a market economy; they would not eliminate the abuse of monopoly power or the wasteful nature of contemporary retailing; nor would they facilitate the reorganization and scientific management of industry that could only proceed once public ownership had been substantially extended. Indeed expansionary monetary and/or fiscal policies might be expected to exacerbate, not mitigate, the evils that characterized contemporary capitalism.

Now it is true that *The minority report of the Poor Law Commission* (1909), which bears the Fabian imprint of Beatrice Webb, did advocate public expenditure to reduce the amplitude of the economic cycle and thence the depth and economic waste of the slump, but the objective here was avowedly to "regularise" rather than increase demand. "We think", the signatories of the Report stated, "that the Government can do a great deal to *regularise* the demand for labour as between one year and another by a more deliberate arrangement of its orders for work of a capital nature." However, the Report argued that this would involve "*no artificial stimulus to demand*", that is there would be no addition to and expansion of aggregate demand over time but simply a change in the timing of part of the annual expenditure of £150 million by "national and local authorities" on "works and services".[18] Such an alteration in the timing of the expenditure would mitigate the worst economic excesses of the slump but it would not touch the roots of unemployment and poverty. On that the Minority Report is clear. These would remain "a constant feature of industry and commerce *as at present administered.*"[19]

Consistently with their critical analysis of the market the Fabians could not therefore advocate expansionary fiscal and monetary policies to tackle unemployment because the mechanism that would give these policies effect – the market – was seen by them as fundamentally defective. This ruled out, therefore, a whole range of economic measures which, given the economic circumstances that Labour confronted when in office in the interwar period, were singularly apposite. What Fabians were left with, having turned their back on the possibility of such macroeconomic management, was the experimental and incremental extension of public ownership, which, in an age of mass unemployment, was as inapplicable as it was uninspiring. Even the contra-cyclical strategy of the Minority Report was rendered redundant in such circumstances, for that had presupposed that extra spending in the slump would be funded out of the prior accumulation of budget surpluses and no such surpluses were available to Labour when it took office in 1929. Hamstrung in these ways, the temptation would then be to rely on the inexorable unfolding of the evolutionary forces making for the advent of socialism.

That it was Fabian political economy that came to dominate the minds of those who mattered in the Party and thence the positions which, in the 1920s, the Party took up on economic questions, gave these prescriptive deficiencies considerable historical significance. For what they did was to seriously circumscribe Labour's options and, in so doing, constrain its room for policy manoeuvre when it finally came to power. That Fabian political economy did exert such influence will be shown in Chapter 7, while a discussion of historical consequences of that hegemony will form the basis of Chapter 8.

Chapter 3
Guild socialism

> To medieval social arrangements we shall return, not only because we shall never be able to regain complete control over the economic forces in society except through the agency of restored Guilds, but because it is imperative to return to a simpler state of society.
>
> A. J. Penty, *Guilds and the social crisis, 1919*

Although the origin of Guild Socialism is normally dated to the publication in 1912 of a series of articles by S. G. Hobson in A. R. Orage's paper *The new age*, A. J. Penty's *Restoration of the gild system* in 1906 must certainly be seen as the seminal work. His book was, above all, a fundamental attack upon the equation of socialism with the extension of state ownership or what he termed "collectivism". As Penty saw it, the primary objective of "collectivism" was to eliminate competition but it was the destruction of commercialism that was the real prerequisite for the building of socialism. This was so because it was adherence to the principles of commercialism that had corrupted contemporary capitalist society through their impact on the nature and purpose of labour; those principles ensuring that the exigencies of the balance sheet would triumph over considerations of creativity, beauty and social utility.

Collectivism of the kind proposed by the Fabians amounted to "state commercialism" and was, at root, an attempt to remedy the evils resulting from the avarice of the few by appealing to the avarice of the many. It was rooted in the fallacy "that government should be conducted solely in the interests of man *in his capacity as consumer*", which meant subjecting the producer to what Penty termed the "demoralizing tyranny of an uninstructed majority" interested only in the cheapness of what they sought to purchase.[1] That, for Penty, would entail the progressive subdivision of the labour process and increasing recourse to mechanization – developments that had already reduced labour to the mechanical and repetitive. It was this denial of the opportunity for creative labour that represented the quintessence of capitalism's iniquity for it was this that robbed humanity of what was necessary to be fully human. All this, of course, has a strongly Morrisian flavour.

It was the liberation of humanity's creative potential that, for Penty, was central to a socialist transformation of society, and to this end he advocated the transference of economic power to guilds of producers or, as Penty phrases it, the transference of "the control of industry from the hands of the financier to those of the craftsman."[2] These were to be akin to the guilds of the Middle Ages in that they would be imbued with a concern for the ideals of good workmanship and service to the community. They would ensure that considerations of commercial advantage no longer drove productive activity, and instead of shoddy wares "the cheapness of which is paid for by the lives of their producers and the degradation of their users", producers, skilled in their craft, would create only what was beautiful and useful.[3] Thus Art would triumph over pecuniary gain, effecting what Penty termed "a regeneration of the spiritual life of the people".[4] The crucial agent in this transformation was to be the trade union movement which would provide the means of securing the kind of control over workshops and factories that was a necessary precondition for the formation of producer guilds. As Penty put it "the first force which will be instrumental in restoring the Guilds is the Trade Union movement", which, he believed, represented "the new centre of order" in society.[5]

The restoration of the gild system embodied many elements central to what was to be termed guild socialism: the setting of the producer centre stage, the emphasis on creative labour as the primary objective of social transformation, the rejection of state collectivism, the decentralization of economic power, the role given to trade unions in that process and, thence, the belief that the motive force of social transformation lay outside the sphere of politics.

Such ideas, it must be said, were blended with a medievalism that undoubtedly gave the work an anachronistic flavour. Thus the book's anti-commercialism spills over into a more general desire for a marked diminution in the volume of international trade and a gearing of industry to local markets. Further, Penty's aversion to the division of labour and mechanized mass production is often indistinguishable from a general antipathy to industrialism *per se* and along with this there went an emphasis upon the need for agriculture to play a more prominent part in the economic life of the nation. However although at other times such aspects of the work might have ensured that it sank without trace, it was published in a period when certain developments made many of its central themes seem particularly relevant to sections of the Labour Movement.

To begin with, while the period 1906–14 was one of political advance as far as the parliamentary representation of the Labour Party was concerned, and while it also saw Parliament, courtesy of the Liberal government, improve the legal position of trade unions through the Trades Disputes Act, 1906, it was also one that saw a decline in real wages, a growth in capitalist power through the concentration of ownership and growing threats to the economic position and status of sections of the workforce, e.g. through an acceleration in skill-destroying technical change. In these circumstances it is understandable that parliamentary socialism and traditional trade unionism were often seen as ineffectual and, in consequence, more sympathetic consideration was given to alternative ways of improving and protecting the lot of labour.

Further, in relation to these alternative ways, the growing strength and militancy of the trade union movement should be noted. Thus between 1888 and 1910 trade union membership tripled. Also in the period after 1900, there were amalgamations that resulted in the formation of new national unions such as the National Transport Workers Federation. There was also the growth of inter-union co-operation epitomized by the Triple Alliance of 1914, involving the transport workers, miners and railwaymen. In addition, the membership of those new national unions showed themselves to be particularly militant in the period immediately prior to the Great War. Thus it has been estimated that the number of days lost through strikes rose from around 6.5m in 1910 to 7.6m in 1911 and to 38.1m in 1912 and, as regards trade union militancy, the years 1912–14 saw national strikes by all three of the national unions that came together to form the Triple Alliance.

In this respect the publication of S. G. Hobson's *National guilds*, in 1914, with its guild socialist rejection of the political road to socialism and its emphasis on the crucial role to be played by trade unions, was well timed. The book was based on the 1912 articles in Orage's *The new age* and went through three editions by 1920. Its full title was *National guilds, an inquiry into the wage system and the way out* and it was upon the commoditization of labour and its consequences that Hobson, like Penty, directed the greater part of his critical fire. It was the wage system, involving the purchase of labour's powers at a subsistence or near-subsistence wage, that permitted the exploitation of the labouring classes who, in forfeiting all claim to their product, allowed the surplus that they created to be distributed as rent, profit and interest to the unproductive. Further, for Hobson, the selling of labour meant the selling of labour's creative powers and, in consequence, "social inertia and spiritual death"; social inertia, in that this made for a "passive or subdued citizenry"; spiritual death in that by forfeiting control over their creativity labourers sold both soul and body.[6] Social emancipation required, therefore, the abolition of the wage system.

Such a stance led Hobson to reject utterly the Fabian position; both its support for the Liberal social and economic reforms, which he saw as designed to repair what must be destroyed, and its advocacy of state socialism or collectivism that left the wage system intact. The latter was the cardinal sin. Private capitalism simply became state capitalism with no alteration in the status and powers, and only limited improvements in the economic position, of labour. For, with the compensation of private owners which the Fabians proposed, the labourer would simply be subjected to exactions that "would bear as heavily on labour as the present burden of rent, interest and profits".[7] In addition, Fabian collectivism, in bestowing on the bureaucrat the task of organizing the "industrial army", effectively ignored the application of democratic principles to industry. The Fabian attitude to democracy was, as Hobson saw it, "arrogant and supercilious", characterized by a reliance upon the state bureaucracy efficiently administering social reforms.[8] It stood opposed therefore to the notion of an active citizenry, which the guild socialist adherence to industrial democracy embodied.

Hobson was also clear that the transition to guild socialism, while in some measure partaking of gradualism, would none the less involve conflict. He wrote of "the complete organisation of labour upon a footing of industrial war" and of "the class struggle" as "the sternest of stern realities".[9] In this respect too, Hobson's guild socialism was markedly different from Fabianism.

Guild socialism alone provided the way out of the wage system and, as with Penty, it was the trade union that Hobson saw as furnishing the embryo of the guild. "The trade unions are undoubtedly the natural nuclei of future industrial organisation."[10] What Hobson looked to, therefore, was first the widest possible extension of trade unionism and then, through merger and integration, the emergence of one union for each industry. Once established such unions, wielding immense power, would "make tireless and unrelenting inroads upon rent and interest"; this absorption of surplus value being "the kernel of the future economic revolution".[11] In addition they would press for co-management of industries, so rendering increasingly untenable the powers of management and laying the basis for an eventual transference of the greater part of economic power to the guilds.

For Hobson, the guild, once established, would be responsible for all aspects of production in a particular industry. In that way it would take over the role of the existing capitalist class. Further, "it would assume, instead of the State, complete responsibility for the material welfare of its members."[12] In these respects it would enjoy considerable autonomy. However, ownership of the means of production should, he believed, be vested in the state. Also, the general policies pursued by the guilds, for example with respect to levels of output, should be pursued only after consultation with state representatives and, where there was a divergence of views, Hobson was clear that the state must have the final say. Its view should prevail even over that of a Congress of all the guilds. In addition, the state would have the right to tax the guilds on a per capita basis. To a greater extent than many guild socialists therefore, Hobson saw the state as having a considerable role in co-managing the economy. So while guild socialism, for Hobson, "rejects State bureaucracy . . . it [also] rejects Syndicalism because it accepts co-management with the State . . . subject to the principle of industrial democracy." Hobson therefore had "no sympathy with a certain narrow school of thought that argues for the restriction of politics to the Guild or its equivalent".[13]

Finally, the State would have a range of what Hobson saw as essentially political functions to perform, independently of the guilds. These would embrace the legal system, health, the armed forces, the conduct of foreign relations, education and central and local government administration. The performance of these functions would be untainted by economic considerations or pressures and, in consequence, Hobson believed that an exclusive concern with them would help bring about a purification of the political process.

Yet although he differed from many guild socialists in terms of the considerable role that he gave to the state and while he had no truck with Penty's medievalism, his primary objective was a quintessentially guild socialist one; it was to effect a revolution based upon the "aesthetic and ethical proposition" that "the value and significance of human labour are not in the same category as the inanimate elements that go into wealth production".[14] Labour should not be treated as a commodity. It was something that had an aesthetic, a moral, indeed, a spiritual significance. Social relations had to be established on a basis which reflected that; a basis that, above all, allowed individuals to express their creativity in their work. Only then would they and society be truly emancipated.

Hobson was one of the first writers to "modernize" Penty's guild socialism. It was, however, G. D. H. Cole, in the periods immediately prior to and after the Great War, who was to prove guild socialism's most formidable theoretician and popularizer. In works such as *Self-government in industry* (1917) and *Guild socialism restated* (1920) Cole, like Hobson, jettisoned Penty's medievalism and his abhorrence of large-scale production and developed guild socialist doctrine in ways that rendered it both applicable to an industrial society and consonant with the growing power and militancy of the trade union movement in Britain.

As we have seen, the Fabians believed that the most fundamental failing of capitalism was its wastefulness and the impoverishment that resulted from it. For Cole, its cardinal sin and most repugnant feature was its destruction of the freedom and individuality of the worker. Thus industrial capitalism treated "men as means to production instead of subordinating production to the wellbeing of the producer".[15] As the Fabians saw it, the primary object of socialism should be to eliminate waste by substituting an efficient public administration of economic activity for the individualistic pursuit of economic gain. This, they believed, would lay the basis for a general improvement in the material wellbeing of society. For Cole the primary objective of socialism should be freedom for the creative impulse and this required not so much the extension of state control over economic activity as the extension of self-government and, in particular, self-government in the workplace. Thus like Penty and other guild socialists Cole believed that the nationalization or municipalization of productive activity could not be seen as synonymous with socialism. It should be noted though that Cole, unlike some guild socialists, did accept that nationalization or municipalization could provide a useful first step to the democratization of decision-making and thence self-government in industry.

Like William Morris, however, Cole believed that the essence of socialism lay in making possible creative, or as Morris had it, "joyful" labour. Indeed *Self-government in industry* ends with a quotation from Morris whom Cole refers to as "the greatest of the democratic writers" and, with biting irony, as "a quite unpractical Socialist who was so little in the swim he refused to join the Fabian Society".[16] Thus while differing markedly in their conception of what guild socialism should be, both Penty and Cole drew inspiration from this common source. Both believed that "the guild system [would] bring Morris into his own".[17]

Crudely put we can say that for the Fabians human liberation was a function of increasing output more equitably distributed. It lay in the sphere of consumption. For guild socialists like Cole liberation was to be sought in the sphere of production and any society "which organise[d] its industry on the basis of consumption [would] be inevitably servile". Greater consumption of itself would "not make less dreary or automatic the life of the worker who is subjected to bureaucratic expert control and divorced from all freedom and responsibility".[18] Only in so far as the labourer secured control over production would the servility of capitalism be eliminated. Thus Cole and other guild socialists possessed a deep antipathy to the growth of an irresponsible (in the political sense) state bureaucracy; an antipathy that they shared with "distributivists", such as Hilaire Belloc, whose book *The servile state* certainly had an influence within guild socialist ranks. Belloc too, for similar reasons, believed that the abolition of destitution and poverty by Fabian methods could well occur without, in any meaningful sense, liberating the working classes from their servile state.

For Cole the Great War showed *par excellence* what would occur when the state took responsibility for substantial areas of economic activity. As he wrote in 1917, "every act of government during the war seems to leave labour with diminished power to control its own destiny." Thus the Munitions Act, 1915, which allowed state control to be exercised over the type of labour used in armaments manufacture and its mobility amounted, in Cole's eyes, to a "profit-sharing arrangement" between the state and capitalists with a view to the exploitation of labour. The gradual extension of public control recommended by the Fabians entailed the same dangers.[19]

Cole's vision of guild socialism is described in greatest, not to say excruciating, detail in *Guild socialism restated* (1920). These details, and in particular the institutional complexity of his vision, need not detain us, although it should be said that that complexity was an inevitable consequence of Cole's search for a decentralized socialism minus the market mechanism. What are fundamental are the themes that run through the work, namely Cole's emphasis on the decentralization of power and decision-making, the separation of economic and political power and his stress on "active citizenship" and "self expression" as vital to the building of a socialist society. Thus he argued strongly the need for worker-controlled units of production possessing a considerable measure of autonomy.

That said, it should be noted that in *Guild socialism restated*, *Self-government in industry* and other works by Cole in this period, national institutions, both those representing the producer (e.g. national guilds and the national guilds congress) and those representing the consumer, were to play a vital role. In addition, unlike some guild socialist contemporaries, Cole saw the state as having a crucial role in representing the interests of consumers. As regards major investment decisions, for example, "the State, as the representative of the consumers, must have in it a voice equal to that of all the producers".[20] Also, while the national guilds and the National Guilds' Congress would assume responsibility for "the organisation of supply and demand . . . [and] the control of prices" this function must be performed "in consultation with the consumer" represented either by the state or other institutions representative of consumer interests. In this respect, Cole describes the determination of prices as a "*social* function", not one to be performed by the guilds in isolation.[21]

Here the guild socialist position, as articulated by Cole, differs profoundly from that of the syndicalists who also emphasized the autonomy of workshops and factories and likewise looked to a decentralized socialism. Cole, unlike the syndicalists, believed that the interests of the consumer had to receive expression and thence institutional embodiment. He recognized, therefore, as the syndicalists did not, potential conflicts of interest between the producer and society that could not be evaded by assuming that because society as a whole was made up of producers, no such conflicts could arise. As he saw it what was required was not just workers' control but a partnership between the State and the Guilds.

Both Fabian socialism and guild socialism were given impetus by the Great War. Thus if the Fabians could claim that the experience of war showed clearly that through the extension of social control over economic activity great things could be achieved, for the guild socialists it demonstrated how far removed this state of affairs was from socialism. Further, the war confirmed that the concentration of economic power involved in state collectivism did indeed bring the dangers of authoritarianism in its wake. If the state had in fact brought order to economic life it had also used coercion to do so. If state collectivism had allowed a more effective prosecution of the war this had been at the expense of trade union rights and a general infringement of civil liberties. It is understandable, therefore, that guild socialism, with its stress on the need for the decentralization of power through the autonomy of worker-controlled productive units, should have expanded its influence and enjoyed considerable popularity after 1918.

The war also provided opportunities to advance the guild socialist cause. Specifically the pressing need for the co-operation of the workforce in the standardization and expansion of output allowed a measure of encroachment on the decision-making power of management – a development that guild socialists such as Cole were quick to advocate and encourage. Indeed encroaching control was seen at this time as the primary means of pursuing the guild socialist ideal. In addition, disenchantment with the trade union leadership's preparedness to co-operate with the state and capitalist entrepreneurs alienated many and led to the growth of rank and file activity, such as the Shop Stewards Movement, which saw the workplace as the crucial battleground.

It is not surprising, therefore, that guild socialism did exert a significant influence within the Labour Party in the immediate post-war period and, in particular, within the Independent Labour Party that actually endorsed the guild socialist programme in 1922. Also, in this period, guild socialism was briefly given successful practical expression through the National Guild of Builders. There was too an acceptance by several major unions of the idea, inimical to Fabianism, that publicly owned industries could and should be jointly managed by representatives of the state and the workers.

However, the influence of guild socialism within the Labour Party and the labour movement was to be relatively short-lived. Unemployment rose rapidly in the aftermath of the immediate post-war boom and, in consequence, trade unionism, the key agency for guild socialist change, was severely weakened. Further, with the economic downturn came the collapse of the National Guild of Builders in 1923 and, in such circumstances, it was inevitable that guild socialism would begin to lose both its plausibility and its attractiveness.

Moreover, as regards the rapidly diminishing influence of guild socialist ideas in the 1920s, there were the ideological rifts within guild socialism itself; in particular over the role of the state in the guild socialist scheme of things. On the tactical plane too there were divisions between those who favoured a more or less combative approach to the advance of guild socialism. Some believed guild socialism would come through the slow permeation of the values and attitudes of craftsmanship, while others favoured direct action, in particular "encroaching control", as the best means by which trade unions could lay the basis for the creation of guilds. There also existed a minority who eschewed a peaceful and gradual means of transferring economic power, favouring more revolutionary methods: many of these were to move into the British Communist Party when it was established in 1921. Finally, with respect to its declining influence, it should be noted that G. D. H. Cole, guild socialism's most prolific propagandist and most important theoretician, effectively abandoned the cause shortly after the publication of his *Guild socialism restated.*

However, guild socialism was not the only political economy of decentralized socialism advanced in Britain in the period immediately prior to the First World War. Syndicalists too denied the existence of a political road to socialism, categorized the extension of public ownership as the growth of state capitalism and saw in social welfare legislation a means of inducing dependency and securing control over the labouring classes. Like the guild socialists they also saw as dangerous any concentration of economic power in the hands of the state and, like them, they looked to the abolition of the wage system and the emergence of a decentralized socialism, built around the nuclei of trade unions, as the means by which labour might be emancipated. Where they differed was, first, in their belief that the construction of socialism required revolutionary conflict and the seizure of power by means of a general strike; secondly, in their view that the ownership of the means of production, not just its control, should be vested directly in the trade unions; and thirdly, in their belief that trade unions should, on that basis, have the absolute power to make crucial economic decisions about production, allocation, distribution, etc. after consultation with other unions. Thus there was no question, as there was with G. D. H. Cole, of a partnership between the state and the guilds. One could also add that while both sought the destruction of the wage system the syndicalists took their stand here much more obviously on the critical analysis of Marx.

It has sometimes been argued that syndicalism was a foreign import and not part of any indigenous tradition of socialist political economy, and certainly British syndicalism owed much to French and American influences in particular. Movements pressing for workers' control had come into being in France and the United States in the last decades of the nineteenth century prior to the growth of British syndicalism. For example, in France, the trade union movement had evolved in a decentralized manner on the basis of *syndicats*, or groups of workmen in the same industry. These in turn were federated in *bourses du travail*, which co-operated with each other and acted collectively through the *Confédération Générale du Travail.* Until 1914 too, the *Confédération* articulated a political philosophy that embraced the notion that capitalism was to be forcibly overthrown by trade union action, with socialism being built on the foundation of producers' organizations owned and controlled by their workers.

In the United States, syndicalism was advanced by the Socialist Labour Party under the leadership of Daniel de Leon. Again, as with the French syndicalists, de Leon advocated the overthrow by militant industrial action of a capitalist system that would be superseded by trade union based producer organizations. To that end the syndicalist International Workers of the World was founded in 1905.

French syndicalism and American industrial unionism proved influential in a number of countries including Britain. James Connolly, for example, was influenced by the work of de Leon during a period in the United States and became an important figure in the spread of syndicalist ideas in Britain through organizations such as the Socialist Labour Party. A key figure too was Tom Mann, who in part derived his syndicalism from Connolly and in part from his experience of industrial disputes during a period in Australia. In 1910 Mann established a paper, the *Industrial syndicalist* and, one year later, the Industrial Syndicalist Education League, both of which played an important role in the spread of syndicalist ideas in the British Labour Movement prior to 1914.

Yet, as one commentator has pointed out, British syndicalism was not simply an ideological import.[22] Again, as with so may strains of British socialism in this period, one can find the roots of an indigenous tradition in the work of William Morris. Morris too poured scorn on the political road to socialism. There is also in his work a strong anti-state bias and a stress on the need for a revolutionary overthrow of capitalism. Morris in his emphasis on craftsmanship, skill and the autonomy of labour also addressed many of the concerns that found expression in syndicalist, as they did in guild socialist, literature. Syndicalism in Britain was therefore, at least in part, home grown.

The infusion of foreign ideas occurred against the backdrop of, and indeed helped to provoke and shape, that unparalleled wave of industrial unrest which swept Britain in the years immediately prior to the Great War. These were also years characterized by the growth of rank and file movements challenging union hierarchies and, indeed, it was one of these, the Unofficial Reform Committee of the South Wales Miners' Federation, that produced one of the classic texts of British syndicalism – *The miners' next step*, published in 1912. However, the syndicalist movement was to undergo a process of disintegration in Britain in the 1913–14 period, largely as a consequence of internecine disputes; even if it was not until the mid-1920s that it can be said to have finally given up the ghost in Britain. That said, at no time did it prove influential within the Labour Party, though it may have played some part in preparing the ground within the trade union movement for the favourable reception (already noted) accorded to some guild socialist ideas in the immediate post-war period.

Chapter 4

Liberal socialism and the challenge to Fabianism

> No general theory of socialism dependent for its working on some large view of the feasibility of social service as an adequate economic motive is likely to be adopted in this country.
>
> J. A. Hobson, *Incentives in the new industrial order*, 1922

As we shall see in Chapter 7, it was Fabian socialism that in terms of its influence within the Labour Party emerged as the dominant strain of socialist economic thinking in the 1920s. Yet, for a time, in the immediate post-war period, that dominance was contested by what may be termed a liberal socialist political economy. As regards that challenge three figures are of particular significance – John Strachey, Oswald Mosley and, most importantly, J. A. Hobson, and it is with their contribution to socialist political economy that this chapter is concerned.

Hobson had begun political life as a Liberal but like many on the radical wing of the Party he was alienated by its abandonment of liberal values and principles during the war and increasingly saw the Labour Party as the best means for their future defence. By 1917, in a work entitled *Democracy after the war*, he had gravitated sufficiently leftwards to be able to write that he had come to accept the socialist analysis of the evils of capitalism and, shortly after, he joined the Labour Party. In the early 1920s Hobson's influence upon economic thinking within the ILP was unquestionably profound. His critique of capitalism and the policies he advocated were advanced in papers such as the *Socialist review* and the *New leader*, while one of his most important works, *The Economics of unemployment*, was published in 1922 and, among many others, strongly influenced G. D. H. Cole. Further, in the immediate post-war period, Hobson became Chairman of the Labour Party Advisory Committee on Finance and Trade Policy and, in the early 1920s, he also made a decisive contribution to the deliberations of the ILP Living Wage Commission whose report – *The living wage* – will be discussed in some detail below. That report was published in 1926 and co-authored with H. N. Brailsford, E. F. Wise and

Arthur Creech Jones. It represented by far the most formidable challenge that Fabian political economy had to confront, and Brailsford, having worked closely with Hobson on the Living Wage Commission, was quick to acknowledge Hobson's crucial input to the document.

John Strachey after an initial flirtation with Conservatism at Oxford joined the Labour Party in 1924 largely as a result of the influence of two men – E. D. Morel and Arthur Ponsonby – who, like Hobson, had moved into the ranks of the Labour Party as a consequence of the disillusionment they felt with the Liberal Party's conduct of policy during the course of the war. It was shortly after this, in 1925, that his first major work – *Revolution by reason* – was published. It was a book that in terms of its critique of capitalism, its hostility to Fabianism and its policy prescriptions shared considerable common ground with *The living wage* and there is, indeed, strong evidence to suggest Hobsonian influence. However, before considering this and the work itself in more detail, it is important to point out that Strachey's book owed much to Oswald Mosley. In fact its long title was *Revolution by reason, an outline of the financial proposals submitted to the Labour Movement by Mr Oswald Mosley* and the book was dedicated "to O. M. who may one day do the things of which we dream". Indeed it was, in large measure, an amplification, and an superbly lucid one, of ideas contained in a small pamphlet of Mosley's also entitled *Revolution by reason*, which had been published in March 1925 some months before Strachey's work. However, while some commentators have seen Mosley as the thinker and Strachey as the popularizer it is more accurate to see both pamphlet and book as the product of a joint intellectual effort.

In considering the political economy of liberal socialism it is, nevertheless, with Hobson that we should begin, both because his major works pre-date the publications of Mosley and Strachey and because there are good reasons for believing that Strachey's work in particular owes much to Hobson. From the publication of *The physiology of industry*, with A. J. Mummery in 1889, Hobson had advanced the view that capitalism was fundamentally flawed at a macroeconomic level. For capitalism, as Hobson saw it, was characterized by a tendency to over-saving and thence over-investment with a consequent over-expansion of productive capacity in relation to effective demand. The inevitable result of this was a tendency to periodic economic convulsions characterized by glutted markets, squeezed profitability and the under-utilization of productive resources, in particular labour.

In the *Physiology* this tendency to over-saving was explained by reference to the prevailing Victorian emphasis on thrift but by the 1890s, in works such as *The problem of the unemployed* (1896), Hobson's thought had taken a more radical turn with his linking of over-saving and over-investment to the maldistribution of wealth. Such a maldistribution was seen as following on from the growth of exploitative monopoly power and thence the accumulation of unearned income in the hands (or bank balances) of those, the idle rich, with a high propensity to save, as opposed to those, the working-classes, with a high propensity to consume. Thus Hobson saw general economic depressions in terms of a sectoral imbalance between producer and consumer goods industries, which in turn was rooted in a skewed and morally indefensible distribution of wealth.

The solution lay, therefore, in eliminating this maldistribution and to that end, in *The problem of the unemployed* and subsequent works, Hobson advocated a radically redistributive fiscal policy both to enhance working-class purchasing power and to provide the wherewithal for increased state expenditure. As he put it in *The economics of unemployment* (1922) "if the surplus income of the rich, which produces . . . congestion and . . . stoppages, were absorbed, either by increasing the share of the workers or by the needs and uses of an enlightened state, or both, this economic disease [depression and mass unemployment] would be remedied."[1]

In addition, Hobson saw a role for the extension of public ownership, for he saw it as a means of appropriating the unearned income or "unproductive surplus" that would otherwise accrue to those whose ownership of the means of production allowed them to wield monopoly power. That there was considerable scope for such an extension Hobson had no doubt. Indeed he believed that it would and should ultimately encompass all industries where mechanization and the routine nature of production permitted economies of scale sufficient to produce a pronounced concentration of ownership. As Hobson put it in *The evolution of modern capitalism* (1926) the "growing socialisation of industry must be regarded as the natural adjustment of society to machine production" for "large routine businesses where mechanical, methods are dominant . . . tend towards a condition where competition disappears".[2]

Of course, there is much here of a Fabian hue, but Hobson's position is, in fact, markedly different. For Hobson believed in the necessary existence "of even larger domains of industrial activity which, not conforming to this economy [of scale], would remain in a state of competition and private enterprise".[3] In other words there were significant sectors of industry whose production methods did not lend themselves to mechanization and standardization and that had, therefore, no inherent tendency to oligopoly or monopoly. This was particularly true of industries that catered for highly differentiated human needs and where, therefore, craftsmanship and skill were the vital inputs. Hobson recognized that such industries might not be of great importance at present but, as society became more prosperous and individuals spent a diminishing proportion of their income on mass produced essentials, such industries, producing non-standardizable, quality products would, he believed, assume increasing significance. Here, in the absence of economies of scale, competition would prevail and, in such circumstances, there would be no need for any extension of public ownership. Thus "the field of private enterprise in all departments of effort would", as he saw it, "grow faster than the field of Collectivism."[4]

In marked contrast to the Fabians, Hobson looked forward not to a fully collectivized but to a mixed economy; an economy too that would provide increasing scope for private enterprise and individual initiative to respond creatively to a growing demand for high quality, non-standardizable products. Public ownership would therefore encompass only those highly mechanized, mass-production industries that satisfied the routine, basic needs of the population. Given, then, his views on the scope for the beneficial extension of public ownership and his position on the central role to be played by the market in the course of economic progress, it would seem legitimate to apply to Hobson the label of liberal socialist. Certainly his opinions on these matters set him markedly apart from the Fabian socialists.

The nature of his critique of capitalism and the policies that he derived from it understandably drew a sympathetic response from many in the Labour Party and it was not long before his ideas fed through via the Living Wage Commission into the most important policy document produced by the ILP in the 1920s – *The living wage* (1926). The essential policy thrust of this was the Hobsonian one of expanding working-class purchasing power. To this end what it proposed was the institution of a "living [minimum] wage", enhanced social welfare provision in the form of family allowances and an increase in non-remunerative public investment. These policies were to be implemented in conjunction with the extension of public ownership and the creation of an institutional basis for national economic planning. However, planning and public ownership were to follow on from, not precede, the greater prosperity that increased working-class purchasing power would create. Thus, as the authors of *The living wage* saw it, a Fabian-style programme of "nationalising certain industries piecemeal" would best be carried forward only when "an upward movement in wages generally" had brought a trade revival in its wake.[5] Only when the imbalance between saving/investment and consumption had been rectified could the extension of public ownership be successfully set in train.

As regards the expansion of effective demand, the authors of *The living wage* also saw a role for monetary policy. The policy was, however, to be an essentially permissive one. As they saw it "the expansion of the market" would necessitate "the expansion of credit and currency to keep pace with the output of goods and services"; an expanding market required, in effect, a monetary policy sufficiently expansionary to ensure that the money supply rose in line with output.[6]

The economic strategy of *The living wage* was absolutely consistent with Hobson's liberal socialism. What the authors proposed was to use the market to secure certain immediate socialist objectives and lay the basis for subsequent socialist advance. In contrast to the Fabians who saw it as a mechanism that was fundamentally flawed, they proposed a strategy in which it played the crucial role of a transmission belt conveying the effects of increased working-class consumption in such a manner as to drive the macroeconomy forward. Further, the strategy relied on the market forces set in motion by the expansion of purchasing power to produce both a more efficient and a more socially beneficial allocation of resources, as well as their fuller utilization. Thus the authors wrote of "the living wage" that "its purpose is to serve as an imperious demand for efficiency and intelligence alike in the production and distribution of wealth".[7] In their view higher labour costs brought about by the institution of a living wage would, through the market forces they unleashed, necessitate a corresponding improvement in efficiency if profits were not to be squeezed or eliminated. It was for that reason that the pamphlet "urge[d] that the figure for it [the living wage], should be estimated somewhat higher than our present level of industrial efficiency would warrant" for then it would represent "a demand addressed to industry, with the avowed purpose of stimulating a better organisation of the total co-operative output."[8] In addition, if in this context higher wages provided the stick, then increased market demand would furnish the carrot necessary to encourage a more efficient utilization of resources. Thus the strategy involved increased purchasing power "playing on the industries which cater for mass consumption", which would precipitate not just "a higher volume of production" but also encourage "the technical re-organisation and re-equipment of industry".[9]

It was also believed that increased market demand from the working classes would promote a reallocation and utilization of resources more in harmony with society's real needs. Thus while Hobson and his co-authors accepted that it would be necessary, in some measure, consciously to guide the flow of investment into socially useful channels, that is to divert it deliberately from luxury-good production and some forms of foreign investment to industries oriented to the production of necessities, they none the less considered that such a reallocation of resources could also be expected to occur "spontaneously" under the pressure of market forces. This was so because "the additional and more stable demand from wage earners for the produce of these industries will make them an attractive and safe investment".[10] Thus given a more equitable distribution of wealth these writers, again in marked contrast to Fabian political economy, believed that the market could be relied upon to transmit an accurate idea of social need and, by so doing, effect a transference of resources to the production of necessities. As E. F. Wise put it in his defence of the ILP living wage proposals at the Labour Party Annual Conference in 1927, "less will be spent in Bond Street and at Monte Carlo but vastly more will be spent on food, textiles and other things".[11]

In addition to its role as a mechanism promoting efficiency and a socially beneficial allocation of resources, Hobson believed that the market could also often be relied upon to furnish the incentives necessary to encourage energetic and innovative productive activity. Here again Hobson clearly and consciously distanced himself from the Fabians and their emphasis on "the spirit of service" as the key motivator within their socialist commonwealth. As he saw it, "no general theory of socialism dependent for its working on some large view of the feasibility of social service as an adequate economic motive" was likely to work; a sense of social service "is not likely to have any considerable effect as a motive in the mind of men who continue to do the same work under the same technical conditions and even the same personal control as before".[12] The belief that the desire for material gain, the profit motive, the predatory individualistic instincts that the market fostered could be "eliminated from the whole industrial system" was, as Hobson saw it, "a facile conviction".[13] The problem with what he termed "Labour socialism" – and this covered Fabianism – was that it too often failed to "recognise that over a large area of industry, prize-money, in the shape of profit, must continue to be a serviceable method of getting the best results of inventive ability, risk and enterprise into the productivity of industry".[14] Again, this whole emphasis on individual initiative and market incentives would suggest a liberal socialist categorization of Hobson's position.

Of course it was recognized that market forces would often, of themselves, fail to produce that fundamental reorganization of industry and rapid reallocation of resources that Britain required. The authors of *The living wage* did, therefore, give an important role to public institutions such as an Industrial Reorganisation Commission, a National Investment Bank and a nationalized banking system in what they believed would be a fundamental, planned, reorganization of the economy. Thus the National Investment Bank and a nationalized banking system would use the funds accumulated by the Post Office Savings Bank, municipal banks and nationalized insurance companies to promote amalgamation and generally "foster efficiency for the general good".[15] Ultimately too it was envisaged the National Investment Bank would become "one of the most powerful means by which the [public] penetration and control of industry [could] be promoted" and "would . . . in association with an Industrial Commission and the councils of the nationalized services [act as] . . . the planning and directive centre of the nation's industrial life".[16]

Nevertheless, the new stream of purchasing power in the hands of the working classes, transmitted through the market, was to be *the* vital and indispensable prerequisite for the whole process of transformation. If it was not a sufficient condition for socialist economic change, it was certainly seen as the fundamental one. It would raise the level of economic activity, eradicate unemployment, create the economic climate necessary to facilitate the process of restructuring and rationalization and also encourage investment in that part of the economy which remained in private hands. Increased working-class consumption was, then, the prime mover in the economic strategy that Hobson and the other authors of *The living wage* proposed.

The fullest exposition of the Strachey–Mosley critique of capitalism can be found in the former's *Revolution by reason*. Like Hobson they believed that capitalism was characterized by an inherent tendency to general economic depression and like Hobson they explained it in terms of an imbalance between the producer and consumer goods sectors of the economy: an imbalance that derived from a distribution of wealth skewed in favour of those who wielded economic power through their ownership of the means of production and against those whose only resource was their labour. For Strachey and Mosley such a maldistribution of wealth led to over-investment in the expansion of productive capacity, which in turn resulted in an increase in the output of consumer goods beyond that for which there was an adequate demand at existing prices. What resulted was a price fall in the consumer goods sector of the economy with a consequent contraction in that area of productive activity. Further, price deflation produced an appreciation in the real value of savings or investible funds that would persuade potential investors to refrain from committing them. Rather, in such circumstances, they would have an incentive simply to reap the windfall gains to be derived from holding such funds in liquid form. In this way the depression would be rapidly transmitted to the producer goods sector. The general level of economic activity would therefore decline and mass unemployment eventuate. As Strachey phrased it in *Revolution by reason*,

> if it [a nation] saves more than a certain proportion of its income *it will not spend enough money to absorb the goods and services produced by its existing instruments of production without a general fall in prices*. But a general fall in prices acts . . . as the most effective check to further productive activity. Hence if its proportion of savings is too high it will year by year add to those instruments of production and therefore to its productive capacity, without increasing at all its power of consumption at a given price level. Thus it will soon be able to produce more than it allows itself to consume.[17]

This whole emphasis upon sectoral imbalance and the critique of capitalism derived from it are clearly Hobsonian; though it should be noted that there is no actual acknowledgement of intellectual indebtedness in either the book or the pamphlet version of *Revolution by reason*. Yet given the already noted influence of Hobson's ideas within ILP ranks and the closeness of the parallels with Hobsonian analysis it is difficult not to believe that, either directly or indirectly, Hobson was the key influence upon these writers' critical analysis. In this context it is also worth noting that in the early 1920s, before joining the Labour Party, Mosley worked closely with the Liberals and was a member of the 1917 Club which, in addition to Strachey's early mentors Ponsonby and Morel, included Hobson as an active member.

Further, their neo-Hobsonian critique laid the basis for a set of economic policies that followed closely those advanced in *The living wage*, though there were important differences of emphasis. As in *The living wage*, so in *Revolution by reason*, the way out of depression and the first steps along the socialist road were to be found in the expansion of working-class purchasing power. As Strachey put it, "what we need are not new secondary [i.e. capital] but primary [i.e. consumer] goods. Any policy that will lead to an increase of the ratio of spending to saving will produce a higher percentage of primary goods to secondary goods. And this is what is necessary for our economic well-being, for the essential condition for the working of modern industrial production is the creation and maintenance of a steady and widespread effective demand for goods and services."[18]

However, as regards the specific means by which this was to be achieved, what Mosley and Strachey proposed did differ from the strategy advanced in *The living wage*. There, working-class purchasing power was to be raised, essentially, by a redistributive fiscal policy; for Strachey and Mosley, a publicly owned banking system and an expansionary monetary policy were the key ingredients. Thus they advocated the nationalization of the banks in order to create "a public banking system, capable of giving such accommodation to industry as [would] enable it to increase the purchasing power of the workers". This policy would be reinforced by the creation of an Economic Council that would ensure the use of such monetary facilities "by forcing up . . . money wages and other receipts . . . of the working-classes" through the setting of progressively rising minimum wage rates that enterprises would be expected to meet. Thus monetary policy would have the threefold function of, first, giving the necessary accommodation to employers to raise working-class purchasing power; secondly, increasing public influence and control over the private sector in proportion to the credit that the public banking system bestowed; and thirdly, helping to overcome the tendency to price deflation as output expanded. In this last respect the authors of pamphlet and book were avowedly indebted to J. M. Keynes and the policy of price stabilization that he proposed in *The tract on monetary reform* (1923). Monetary policy was, therefore, central to the Strachey–Mosley strategy.[19]

Strachey and Mosley did also advocate the more general extension of public ownership and economic planning. Indeed they believed the latter would be facilitated by the financial leverage that could be exerted through the kind of publicly owned banking system that they proposed. Thus planning was necessary, in particular, to ensure that demand was expanded in line with the nation's capacity to produce. Here the Economic Council would play a crucial role, assuming responsibility for establishing the "total potential production of 'useful' goods and services with existing productive resources" and then calculating "what minimum wage, at present prices, this would make possible for the worker".[20] In line with this it would be responsible for ensuring the rapid expansion of output through the co-ordination, reorganization and, where necessary, control of industry, to allow it to cope with a managed expansion of working-class purchasing power. Thus it would, in Strachey's words, "tell the mine owners and the railway companies [for example] that they must create national corporations which would provide the community with the essential commodity, coal and the essential service, transport, with the utmost efficiency possible."[21] If they failed to do so then such industries would have to be taken into public ownership.

However, as with the authors of *The living wage*, so with those of *Revolution by reason*, planning would be conducted in response to the needs of the working classes as these were expressed through the market. Thus it would be the information furnished by the market, after the expansion of working-class demand, which would serve to guide that process of rationalizing and reorganizing industry which was seen as a precondition for any future, lasting prosperity. This was, of course, in marked contrast to the Fabian notion of the planned or "scientific" organization of industry, by which planning originated with the bureaucracies of the state and municipalities and proceeded only once the nation's means of production had been taken into public ownership. The Fabian approach to planning was directive, that of the liberal socialists reactive.

Strachey believed that to begin by nationalizing and then "planning the organisation of supply" was "to begin at the wrong end" and to do so would, as he saw it, run the risk of creating "*an economic dictatorship under which an all-wise Government provided only those things it thinks its citizens might want.* We prefer to let those citizens express their real wants by giving them purchasing power".[22] Planning would not, therefore, be "planning in the abstract", as was the case with Fabianism, "but to meet demand". "There is", wrote Strachey, "an essential difference between planning to meet a genuine, spontaneously manifested, new demand and planning to give the people what the Government thinks they ought to want".[23] The former was what writers like Hobson, Mosley, Strachey and other liberal socialists understood by planning; the latter was what the Fabians sought. The former put the consumer and freedom of choice at the centre of things; the latter put the planner there. Given this, the label of liberal socialist again seems the appropriate one.

What was offered by Hobson, Strachey, Mosley and other liberal socialists was, therefore, radically different from the Fabian economic strategy and represented a profound challenge to it. To begin with, while the Fabians looked to a diminishing role for the market through the extension of social ownership, the liberal socialists sought to utilize it to achieve socialist objectives. It was to provide the transmission belt that would convey to the economy as a whole the motive force of increased working-class demand; it could be relied upon as an allocative mechanism ensuring an efficient and socially beneficial allocation of resources; it could be counted upon to promote efficiency and the incentives it provided would act as a spur to productive activity.

Secondly, while it is important not to minimize the extent to which the liberal socialists believed in the need to extend public ownership, it should be stressed that this was only one element and certainly not the most important one in their strategy. They did not envisage, and they did not desire, a fully collectivized economy and in any case they had much more to offer in terms of economic policies. As such, they avoided a limiting obsession with nationalization and municipalization. Their strategy embraced radical fiscal and monetary policies and in so doing dovetailed short-term, electorally attractive measures of social amelioration with longer-term socialist objectives relating to the control and restructuring of the economy.

By way of contrast what the Fabians had to offer, primarily, was a long-term strategy that aimed at creating a fully collectivized economy. This had little relevance to the immediate material problems that the working class confronted in the 1920s and, in particular, that of unemployment. Thus industrial rationalization, as the Fabians themselves recognized, was a necessary concomitant of the extension of public ownership, if that was to bring the predicted productivity and output gains. The scientific reorganization of Britain's productive capacity was, after all, what the Fabians sought and that must, among other things, entail the elimination of that wasteful duplication of plant and equipment that characterized existing, anarchic economic arrangements. Thus, in the short run, the pursuit of Fabian policies would be likely to exacerbate not mitigate the most pressing problem of the period.

In contrast, the liberal socialists, beginning with that problem, furnished the kind of short-term strategy that would, in the words of E. F. Wise, "convince . . . people that Socialism . . . really meant something." As he saw it, such an approach made "Socialism . . . attractive to the ordinary working men and women who were not so much interested in . . . problems of administration, organisation and finance and so on . . . but . . . wanted to see results quickly."[24]

However, considerations of electoral advantage aside, the liberal socialists furnished a strategy embodying a raft of short-term policies that might be implemented within the expected lifetime of a Labour government and relevant to the most pressing problems that such a government would be likely to confront. This is what the Labour Party manifestly lacked in 1929–31 and this deficiency (one of the most serious consequences of the dominance of

Fabian thinking) explains much about Labour's subsequent performance when in office. They also offered a more decisive break with the past than the gradualism of the Fabians. The channelling of increased working-class demand into the marketplace would, it was argued, effect an immediate and profound change in the structure, organization and control of economic life. It would also represent an immediate and significant redistribution of economic power.

Further, while it was the Fabians who wrote of the need for a scientific reorganization of industry, it was the liberal socialists who actually advanced ideas as to how to set about the business of national economic planning. On the surface this may seem surprising. Yet when it is recognized that the Fabians believed the destruction of the market was a necessary precondition for effective planning, while the liberal socialists believed the market could be used by the planners, it is less so. For the Fabians planning had to await a prior, substantial extension of public ownership; for the liberal socialists it could begin once the requisite institutions and macroeconomic strategy had been put in place.

Finally, one should note that while the Fabians were concerned primarily with the maximization of output, the liberal socialists were more interested in the business of consumption. Indeed they stressed consumer sovereignty as against the authority of the planner or the bureaucrat. Further, their policies were designed to make consumer sovereignty a meaningful concept for all and not just for the rich few. In general theirs was a more hedonistic and certainly a more libertarian economic philosophy than that of the Fabians and, indeed, both Strachey and Hobson can be found voicing fears about the kind of authoritarianism that might emerge should the planners rather than the consumers come to rule the roost. Power in the hands of planners was centralized; power in the hands of consumers was dispersed. The latter was certainly to be preferred to the former.

However, at the 1928 Labour Party Annual Conference a motion to refer back to the Party's National Executive the adverse report of a Commission of Inquiry on the Living Wage Programme of the ILP was defeated by 2,780,000 votes to 143,000. As far as the Labour Party was concerned, therefore, the living wage strategy was dead in the water. At the same Conference the approval of *Labour and the nation* confirmed the dominance of Fabian political economy. So, for the second minority Labour government the way forward was to be an essentially Fabian one and they were to realize too late that it ended in a cul-de-sac ! As for liberal socialism, it was not a case of RIP 1928. It was, as we shall see, not dead, only sleeping.

Chapter 5
R. H. Tawney and the political economy of ethical socialism

> That is where the mere economics of social reform – Fabianism etc. – breaks down. They study the room but they open no windows in the soul.
>
> R. H. Tawney, *Commonplace book*, 1913

From its origins in the early nineteenth century, British socialist political economy embodied a powerful moral component. This was, perhaps, most apparent in its critique of capitalism but it was evident too in the nature of the prescriptions that many socialist writers put forward. As regards the critique, capitalism was to be condemned not just because it was productive of waste and inefficiency, not just because it failed to raise working-class living standards and make effective use of the productive capacity it created but also (for many primarily) because it was productive of injustice, iniquity and the degradation of human kind. Thus it failed to match reward with desert, it induced self-seeking immoral behaviour, it fostered predatory and acquisitive instincts, it atrophied humanity's creative abilities, it encouraged the abuse of power and its corollary servility. Not only did it materially impoverish and demean, it also irredeemably corrupted Man's soul. Such were the essentials of the moral condemnation of capitalism that ran through much of the work of socialist political economists in nineteenth-century Britain.

With respect to policy prescription, the ethical dimension of socialism imprinted itself in a number of ways. Thus, in the early nineteenth century the attempts by Robert Owen, William Thompson and others, to institute a system by which goods exchanged according to the labour they embodied was, in many respects, an attempt to reconstitute a moral economy founded on "just" prices. Further their communitarian experiments were avowedly an attempt to create "new *moral* worlds" whose influence would gradually permeate and transform the old. Similarly the emphasis placed on the creation of producer co-operatives by mid-century Christian socialists such as J. M. Ludlow was born of a determination to establish a basis, if only in microcosm, for the moralization of productive activity. Later in the century, with Morris and *News from nowhere*, we have again, as with the Owenites, the idea of communities functioning on a moral basis of reciprocity rather than the self-seeking basis of exchange.

It is not surprising, therefore, that it was an essentially ethical socialism that initially prevailed within the ranks of the Independent Labour Party after its foundation in 1893; its first leader, Kier Hardie, deploying the language of moral economy in particularly eloquent fashion to denounce the evils of capitalism. In addition the survey of the reading habits of Labour Party MPs in 1906 to which reference has already been made clearly evidences the force of the ethical, indeed the religious, basis of political conviction within the Labour Party. What was true of Hardie and the early Labour Party MPs was true of many within the Party as a whole; on economic questions what they adhered to was a moral rather than a political economy, still less a socialist economics.

For that reason alone and in order to understand the nature of some of the thinking within the Labour Party on matters of economics, it is of particular importance to consider one uniquely powerful articulation of the political economy of ethical socialism; namely that to be found in the work of R. H. Tawney. Indeed in books such as *The acquisitive society* (1921) and *Equality* (1931) it was Tawney who gave that political economy its classic early-twentieth-century expression. However, it is important to focus on Tawney too because it was he who drafted important Labour Party policy pamphlets – such as *Labour and the nation* (1928) and *For socialism and peace* (1934), which will be considered in later chapters – and, as that might suggest, his was an influential voice as regards policy formulation. Thus he may be said to have both reflected a powerful current of thinking within the Labour Party and made a substantial contribution to the potency of its influence.

The essence of Tawney's critique of capitalism was that it had destroyed the moral basis that had previously underpinned social and economic relationships. In contrast to previous socio-economic systems, such as feudalism, ethics had been detached from economics and the idea accepted that productive activity was "a mechanism moving by quasi-mechanical laws and adjusted by the play of non-moral forces in which methods of organisation and social relationships [were] to be determined solely by considerations of economic convenience and productive efficiency".[1] While, under capitalism, ethics might have a place in the *private* life of the individual, they had no part in determining the nature of social and economic relations. The onset of capitalism had, therefore, effected a demoralization of economic life, a view that was to be historically grounded by Tawney in his *Religion and the rise of capitalism* (1926).

This demoralization manifested itself in a number of ways, most obviously in the treatment of human beings as means to the end of private profit and wealth creation rather than as ends in themselves. As Tawney wrote in his *Commonplace book*, a private journal kept for the years 1912–14, "under present arrangements men are used not as ends but as means", and again, "industry creates poverty by refusing to treat men as ends or respect their personalities".[2] In such a squalid ethical atmosphere the working class was not simply exploited, it was debased. Workers became "hands", a mere extension of mechanism, rather than human beings with creative capacities and above all, for Tawney, souls.

It was the dominance of this instrumental conception of human beings that lay too at the root of the class division and social tensions that characterized capitalism. For, in such circumstances, as Tawney saw it, society was inevitably "divided, in its economic and social relations, into classes which are ends and classes which are instruments".[3] Where such a division prevailed labour would be paid not a just or a fair reward for the services it rendered but as little as was necessary to guarantee its supply. Similarly, those who saw an increase in their material well-being as the object or end of economic activity would act to secure a reward proportionate not to the service that they rendered but the economic power that they deployed. This, for Tawney, was the essence of the "privilege" that he saw as scaring and corrupting contemporary society – "by privilege I mean payment whether in money or social position without corresponding services".[4]

Such "privilege" was particularly apparent under existing economic arrangements, as there had emerged, with the evolution of capitalism, a class of "functionless property owners" who did not even assume the entrepreneurial responsibilities of superintendence and direction but simply appropriated "the surplus arising from the more valuable sites, the better machinery [and] the more elaborate organisation" of industry.[5] It was they, in short, who secured the rental income that the Fabians had highlighted as deriving from the monopoly of finite resources whether of situation, capital equipment, land or talent. It was they who saw their interests as ends and the labouring classes as the means to further them.

These social divisions, rooted in the moral wasteland at the heart of capitalism, corrupted both the nature of productive activity, by debasing labour into a mere instrument of production, and also its purpose. Thus, for Tawney, "the purpose of industry [should be] service, to supply men with the material means of a good life".[6] Its true rationale was to provide what was useful and beautiful and in so doing lay the material basis for what Tawney saw as the primary end of humanity's spiritual fulfilment. However, under capitalism, where functionless property owners wielded economic power not with an eye to the service of society but to the individualistic end of personal gratification, resources were allocated and productive activity directed to satisfy their capricious desires. Thus they "exercise[d] a demand which diverts to the supply of luxuries productive power which would be directed to the multiplication of the necessities of common humanity".[7]

Further, the overriding emphasis upon wealth acquisition and the expansion of output, which a means-oriented attitude to human beings produced, had obscured the fact that "the merits or demerits of an industrial system [were] not to be measured solely, or even principally, by the success with which wealth [was] distributed amongst the parties involved, but by the extent to which the relationship existing between [them] was such as to develope [*sic*] self-respect, self-reliance and enterprise".[8] Again and again Tawney was to make this point. The primary purpose of economic activity was not material, it was ethical and spiritual; it was about providing the opportunity for creative self-expression, moral behaviour and the possibility of human fellowship. Only when individuals were viewed as ends in themselves, rather than wealth-creating instruments, would economic activity be organized in such a manner. Only then would it be recognized too that an improvement in society's material circumstances would not of itself bring content and a sense of human fulfilment. That would come only when human relationships rested on manifestly moral foundations; what Tawney termed "'rules of life' which are approved as just by the conscience of mankind".[9]

For Tawney, therefore, the essential rottenness of capitalism was moral. The "heart of the problem", Tawney wrote, "is not economic. It is a question of moral relationships. This is the citadel which must be attacked . . . the immoral philosophy which underlies much of modern society". In this context, therefore, capitalist power and "economic privilege" "must be abolished not, primarily [as the Fabians believed] because they hinder the production of wealth but because *they reproduce wickedness*". Similarly in writing of unemployment and low wages Tawney stated, that "we ought to feel about [them] . . . what decent people feel now when there has been *a gross miscarriage of justice*".[10] This is the language of an ethical socialist political economy.

Such language was even more evident when Tawney came to set out the fundamental objectives that socialists should pursue. For, as he saw it, what was needed, what must underpin any lasting socialist transformation of society, was the remoralization of economic life. Service, co-operation and social justice must displace the egotistical avarice of possessive individualism as the basis upon which productive activity proceeded. In effect a social ethics, and for Tawney that meant a Christian social ethics, must come to infuse every aspect of economic life and thence the social relationships that life dictated. Only then would society cease to be riven by class division and be capable of pursuing common purposes for the common good; only then would it be characterized by social harmony and, most importantly, only then would it be possible to unleash "the spiritual energy of human beings in all the wealth of their infinite diversities", with "external arrangements, whether political or economic" being strictly subordinated to that end.[11]

Yet, if this was the vision, Tawney accepted that the construction or, more accurately, the reconstitution of a moral economy required practical, even prosaic policies to translate it into a material reality. Here, as regards policy prescription, Tawney focused in particular on the evil of functionless property drawing inspiration, though not, it must be said, in equal measure, from both Fabianism and guild socialism. Thus in his work Tawney deployed on a number of occasions the Fabian socialist explication of the sources from which functionless property derived its income. For example, in *The acquisitive society* he wrote of "the normal effect of private property" as being that of "transfer[ing] to functionless owners the surplus arising from *the more valuable sites, the better machinery, the more elaborate organisation*".[12] Here Tawney was clearly thinking in Fabian economic categories, even if they were invested with a moral resonance; like the Fabians too he argued that unjust rewards were those that derived from the adventitious monopoly of non-marginal factors of production and like them he made a clear distinction between the manager (with his professional expertise) and the capitalist rentier who made no contribution to the production process and whose existence and reward were therefore, in an economic and a moral sense, unnecessary. Like the Fabians also he believed that, for the future, a political alliance might be struck between managerial and other kinds of labour.

Tawney's remedies for this evil of rentier income were also of a Fabian hue. To begin with he believed that much could be achieved by a progressive fiscal policy. This would allow "the pooling" of these "surplus resources by means of taxation and the use of the funds thus obtained to make accessible to all, irrespective of their income, occupation or social position, the conditions of civilisation which, in the absence of such measures, can be enjoyed only by the rich".[13] Thus Tawney looked to progressive taxation to appropriate from those who provided no service, that to which they had no right, in order to furnish what he termed a "social income" "available on equal terms" to all. This "income" would assume a variety of forms. It would encompass the provision of health care, education and housing; it would also involve social welfare payments in relation to sickness, old age and unemployment. In essence, for Tawney, it represented communal provision financed by the progressive taxation of individuals; a practical implementation of the socialist dictum from each according to ability to each according to need. Such a policy also involved a social determination of the allocation of resources on the basis of need rather than the capacity to pay and thence the capacity to profit.

Like the Fabians too, Tawney saw the extension of public ownership and control as a crucial antidote to functionless property and unmerited rewards. However, he was also convinced that that extension must assume a variety of institutional forms. There were, to begin with, "certain great services which cannot solely be resigned to exploitation for private profit because the public welfare is so intimately dependent upon them, that those who own them become, in effect, masters of the nation."[14] Given their strategic significance these services, such as transport and the coal industry, should, as Tawney saw it, be nationalized. This would secure the economic surplus they created for social use but, more importantly, it would also allow these industries to be carried on more efficiently and with an eye to the general, long-term economic interests of the nation. In this context it should be noted that Tawney was a member of the Royal Commission on the coal mining industry, chaired by the Liberal peer Lord Sankey, which, in 1919, recommended nationalization as providing the best institutional framework for that industry's rejuvenation.

Yet if nationalization had its place, Tawney was clear that it was not the only form in which public ownership might be extended to achieve socialist objectives. Thus he suggested not only municipalization (e.g. of urban land) but also state partnerships with private enterprise and the acquisition of controlling interests in private companies. Further, in order to extend state control without a concomitant extension of ownership he suggested the appointment of state directors to the management boards of key private firms. Thus "the achievement of the ends for which public ownership is desired need not always involve a change of owners", while public ownership was also "clearly compatible with the widest diversities of constitution and government".[15]

However, one aspect of these diverse means of extending public ownership which would be common to them all was worker participation in the business of management. For Tawney, industrial democracy had to be extended to give workforces real decision-making powers. A considerable measure of self-government was vital. First, only that could prevent the workers, either in private or public enterprises, from being treated as means to the ends of managers rather than ends in themselves. Secondly, self-government also entailed responsibility for the provision of good service. Here Tawney believed that every occupation should assume the form of a profession, "being governed by standards other than the immediate advantage of the particular individuals or companies which compose it." This would, as he saw it, "substitute a relationship of co-ordinate service to the community, for the present subordination of the hired wage earner to a master who employs him for profit."[16] Thus with self-government and with the adherence to professional standards all occupations and all companies would become part of that interlocking system of rights and (service) obligations that Tawney saw as providing the social cohesion and unity of social purpose that possessive individualism signally failed to furnish. Thirdly, the exercise of decision-making power by workers was seen by Tawney as integral to unleashing creative ability and thence that "growth towards perfection of individual human beings" which in his view was the primary end of economic activity. For all these reasons Tawney was sympathetic to the general aims of the guild socialists and a strong advocate of the guild socialist idea of encroaching control as a means of extending industrial democracy and furthering self-government by the workforce. Thus he wrote in support of "the principle of trade unionism being applied not merely . . . to questions of wages and hours but *to all questions of industrial policy*".[17] He was also, for a time, an active member of the National Guilds League.

Yet Tawney was also adamant that self-government could not be absolute. The purpose of industry was service to the community and, ultimately, it was society that must determine whether that service was being effectively provided. The state, therefore, had "a right to satisfy itself that the service [furnished by an industry or company] is faithfully discharged".[18] To that end Tawney envisaged state and consumer representatives on the management boards of public and private enterprises, along with representatives of the workforce and management itself. "Industry must be subordinated to the community in such a way as to offer the best service technically possible." It must be subordinated too in such a way as to ensure that: "those who offer faithful service should be honourably paid and those who offer no service should not be paid at all."[19] It would therefore be the state's responsibility to ensure the fair remuneration of labour, whether by way of minimum wage legislation or other expedients, and to sequester payments that were considered unwarranted. It was, in effect, the ultimate guarantor of the remoralization of economic life.

Thus both Fabian and guild socialist currents ran through the prescriptive dimension of Tawney's moral economy. Of the two the Fabian influence was the more powerful but, that said, as regards public ownership, what he offered was a pluralism of a distinctly non-Webbian kind. Though the state might have ultimate authority, economic power was to be dispersed. It was to be dispersed by way of industrial democracy and self-government; it was to be distributed among differently constituted public and public/private enterprises and it was to be split as well between the private and the public sector. So although Tawney emphasized the need for a substantial extension of public ownership, stating in 1938 that "it would be fatal" for a Labour government "once more to evade the task of effecting a real transference of economic power, on a substantial scale, from private to public hands",[20] he none the less believed that where private enterprise furnished a service commensurate with its rewards and where the evil of functionless property was absent then the conduct of business could usefully and legitimately be left in private hands. Profits were acceptable where they constituted a necessary cost of production. Thus even in *The acquisitive society*, a savage indictment of the moral basis of contemporary capitalism, Tawney stressed that "a clear discrimination should be made between the payment needed to secure the necessary supplies of capital, the reserves required to meet risks, the salary of the employers as managers" and those payments that derived solely from the monopoly of a scarce resource.[21] He accepted, therefore, that a mixed economy could provide the requisite material basis for the moral regeneration of economic life and thence the construction of a socialist society.

It was the case too, both as regards his critique of capitalism and his vision of socialism, that what Tawney offered was qualitatively different from the political economy of the Webbs. Thus while he accepted that much could be done along Fabian lines and while he drafted the quintessentially Fabian *Labour and the nation* (1928), the fact remained that "modern society [was] sick" not as a consequence of the wasteful and ineffective utilization of resources and the impoverishment that resulted but from "the absence of a moral ideal".[22] That, in the final analysis, was where Fabianism fell short. It studied the room, it suggested a more rational arrangement of the furniture, but it opened no windows in the soul.

For Tawney capitalism was damned not just, or even primarily, because it was inefficient and impoverished a large part of the population. Though guilty in that respect, its real and all-encompassing sin was that it was based on principles that engendered injustice. It lacked a moral foundation for behaviour in the economic and social spheres of human existence. By the same token the New Jerusalem could only be built if that failing were rectified and for Tawney that meant it could only be built on the foundation of Christian moral principles. This did not mean socialists should neglect the economic or fail to advance policies that would alleviate the material impoverishment of the masses. But such policies, if necessary, were certainly of themselves insufficient for the construction of a socialist society. Socialist aspirations must transcend the material and with that in mind he wrote in his *Commonplace book*, that: "when three or four hundred years hence mankind looks back on the absurd preoccupation of our age with economic issues . . . the names they will reverence will be those of men who stood out against the prevalent fallacy that the most important problems were economic problems."[23] Under existing arrangements it was economic concerns that dominated; under socialism it would be a concern with moral and spiritual enrichment that would prevail.

In this context it is interesting to note that in the "age of affluence" that followed the Second World War there was, on the part of some socialist writers, a comparable call for the de-prioritization of the economic and an elevation of moral concerns and objectives. Thus in the 1950s, when it looked as if the policy instruments required for sustained economic growth and an unending increase in material prosperity were, in fact, available and could be applied within an essentially capitalist framework, there were those who declared that it was socialism's ethics not its economics that must henceforward be seen as the distinguishing characteristic of its political philosophy. At the present juncture too, in the mid-1990s, it is a moral discourse of rights and duties that often infuses the speeches of the current Labour Party leader. The ethical socialist tradition therefore remained a powerful one within the Labour Party and was to continue not only to mould its rhetoric but also to shape its thinking on economic and other questions.

Chapter 6

Political economy in the early Labour Party: Ramsay MacDonald and Philip Snowden

Socialist change must be gradual and must proceed in stages, just as the evolution of an organism does.

Ramsay MacDonald, *Socialism*, 1907

The line of advance to which socialists attach greatest importance is by way of public ownership. All other ways are merely palliative.

Philip Snowden, *Socialism and syndicalism*, 1913

MacDonald joined the Fabian Society in 1886 and the ILP shortly after its foundation in 1894. He became secretary to the Labour Representation Committee when it was established in 1900, was elected to Parliament in 1906 and shortly after, in 1911, became leader of the Labour Party, a post that he held until the outbreak of war in 1914 and then again from 1922 until the break-up of the Labour Government in 1931. He wrote a number of works in the pre-war and immediate post-war period; works that evince a fascinating, if sometimes incoherent, blend of the disparate intellectual currents that characterized British socialism in these decades. Four in particular are worthy of note and will be used here to illustrate the salient characteristics of his thought in the pre- and post-Great War periods – *Socialism and society* (1905), *Socialism* (1907), *Socialism after the war* (1918) and *Socialism, critical and constructive* (1921).

Underpinning much of what MacDonald wrote was the idea of social evolution; the view that just as life evolved from simple to more complex organisms better adapted to their environment, so society progressed "slowly and by organic adaptation".[1] However, as he saw it, what distinguished the evolution of human society was the gradual emergence of a social and institutional framework that was "more and more capable of expressing the *moral* consciousness of man". Thus, for MacDonald, society evolved in such a way that, ultimately, social interaction came to rest upon a truly moral basis.[2]

A number of points can be made about this view of things. First it implied an evolutionary view of social progress with the emphasis on gradual adaptation to changing material circumstances. Secondly, as it was expounded by

MacDonald the notion of social evolution took on a determinist character. Thus one finds him writing in 1905 of "the iron law of social evolution" and, as regards the transition to socialism, he was clear that it could be made only when capitalism had been "allowed to complete itself".[3] Thirdly, MacDonald used the idea of social evolution to affirm a scientific authority for his socialism, claiming to apply to the progress of society the insights that biology, and specifically Darwinism, had recently contributed to an understanding of the evolution of species. As MacDonald put it, "Biology alone was competent to give the clue to the proper understanding of the process of evolution because it was the science which dealt with the modes of change followed by organisms."[4] Thus MacDonald believed his socialism was every bit as scientific as that of Marx, though embodying an evolutionary rather than a revolutionary conception of historical progress. Fourthly MacDonald's writing is riddled with biological analogies where society is represented as a single living organism. Such a view of course militated against any idea of conflict, in particular class conflict, as the route to socialism, for that implied an organism at war with itself. Here again MacDonald was at pains to emphasize the gulf which separated his position from that of Marx. For him, "Socialism mark[ed] the *growth* of Society, not the uprising of a class."[5]

With respect to the influences that were important in shaping the evolutionary and organic aspects of MacDonald's socialism, that of Herbert Spencer was of particular importance, as it was for a number of Fabians, among them the Webbs and Shaw. Thus in *Socialism and society*, he wrote that "Spencer's general philosophy . . . has . . . contributed to the stability of socialist thought, *mainly by his clear exposition of the fact of social evolution*".[6] It is not surprising therefore that in sharing this influence MacDonald should also have shared much else with the Fabians and in particular their general conception of socialist advance. Thus, as one might expect of social evolutionists, there was the common emphasis on gradualism. In fact MacDonald was often to make the link explicit. As he wrote in *Socialism*, "socialist change must be gradual and must proceed in stages, *just as the evolution of an organism does*". Elsewhere he linked this gradualism to a conception of the piecemeal nature of the transition to socialism. Thus "when the tendencies begun by scores of experiments – factory laws, public health laws, municipalisation – are followed out, joined together, systematised, Socialism is the result."[7] In this, and many other passages in MacDonald's writing, his conception of the gradual, piecemeal, reformist, growth/evolution of socialism is clearly conveyed.

As regards the common intellectual influences upon MacDonald and the Fabians that of Auguste Comte is also important: the positivism of Comte fed through into a common emphasis on the scientific nature of the socialism that they propounded. This can be seen clearly in MacDonald's social evolutionist interpretation of history, which he overtly linked to insights he considered he had derived from advances in the biological sciences. However, MacDonald stressed too the positive basis of his "constructive" socialism, seeking like the Fabians to convey the scientifically organized nature of economic life under socialism as against "the *unregulated clash* of individual interests . . . and the *haphazard* expenditure of individual effort with all their accompanying *waste* of economic power", that characterized capitalism.[8] The socialist solution would also be implemented by means of "*scientific experimenting*" gradually "bring[ing] order where there is now chaos, organisation where there is now confusion, law where there is now anarchy". Elsewhere MacDonald wrote of creating "order out of chaos and reason out of chance".[9] The language is clearly that of positivism and Fabianism.

A Fabian flavour is also apparent in his treatment of economic depressions, which, for MacDonald, epitomized the waste created by an anarchic capitalism. Here after a cursory nod in the direction of Hobsonian underconsumptionism MacDonald proceeded in a quintessentially Fabian manner both in terms of analysis and remedies. Thus he wrote in *Socialism and society* that

> however desirable it may be to increase the powers of consumption enjoyed by the wage-earning classes, that of itself will not obviate industrial crises, because it will only be a further incentive to the individual producer to produce a greater proportion of the market's demands. A rising demand is a spur upon supply . . . There can be no steadiness of industry as long as there is anarchy in production. The flow of production must be regulated at the source. The instruments of production must be socialised before unemployment is obviated.[10]

For MacDonald, as for the Fabians, the problem of unemployment would only be solved when the public ownership of the means of production permitted the systematic estimation of needs and the deliberate matching of supply with demand; simply raising the level of working-class consumption, however desirable on other grounds, was not a solution.

MacDonald's social evolutionism gave a Fabian flavour of another kind to the constructive aspect of his socialism. For he stressed, as did the Fabians, that what he proposed was in harmony with contemporary developments; that his constructive socialism moved with the historical tide. Thus MacDonald argued that in proposing to replace the unregulated and wasteful competitive pursuit of individual self-interest by the national and municipal organization of economic activity, socialists simply sought to confirm what was already occurring. The economic forces unleashed by competition had produced the emergence of trusts and monopolies that by regulating output, price, the purchase of raw materials and the marketing of products had, through the national and regional organization of industries, gone a long way to eliminate the waste that the anarchy of competitive capitalism created. The trust had this to its credit, it "reduces waste and is also always striving to estimate demand so that it may thereby regulate production." So the socialist "whilst he warns against combination controlled by capitalist interests, or by capitalist machinery . . . accepts and values the gains of combination itself and proposes to harness them to communal well-being."[11] Thus nationalization and municipalization would involve the community confirming and reaping the organizational gains that the growth of trusts and monopolies had secured, while, at the same time, effecting a switch in objectives from private gain to social service. This transition would also be made all the easier by virtue of the contemporary emergence of a new class of professional managers whose interests no longer lay in the maximization of profits and whose services could as easily be used in a socialist as a capitalist economy. Socialism here, as elsewhere, involved simply the confirmation of contemporary developments; as MacDonald put it, though in words, it must be said, as redolent of Marxism as Fabianism, "the life of the coming epoch, germinates in the bosom of the order which is maturing."[12] While, therefore, MacDonald might condemn what he saw as the economic determinism of Marxism, his work, like that of the Fabians, also had a strong determinist element.

As regards the rationale for extending public ownership, the manner in which it was to be extended, the way in which public enterprises were to be managed and with what objectives, MacDonald's thought again bears the imprint of positivism and Fabianism, though other influences are also apparent. In *Socialism and society* MacDonald proposed a fairly all-encompassing criterion for determining when extension was warranted. Thus public ownership should be extended to "all those forms of property in the use or abuse of which the whole community is more interested than private individuals".[13] However this extension was seen by MacDonald as gradual and piecemeal. It should be determined not by reference to "theoretical considerations of the rights of the state" but "by practical experiences of the working of Socialistic *experiments from time to time*".[14] Again, this is very Fabian. However, as regards the management of public enterprises, while, like the Fabians, he clearly saw the new breed of professional managers that capitalism had created playing a fundamental role, MacDonald's thinking during the war and in the immediate post-war period also (as we shall see below) reflected the influence of guild socialism.

Like many Fabians MacDonald emphasized the point that the need for greater state intervention in the economy had "received a wonderful proof" during the war. "Competitive and disorganised individual initiative in an open market [had] had to be superseded by national control" in order that the nation could conduct the war effectively.[15] At the same time, MacDonald recognized that the coercive use to which the enhanced powers of the state were put had generated considerable concern among sections of the Labour Movement. In consequence he believed that socialists had to consider with some care the question of what authority the state should wield in economic and other matters and how its power should be circumscribed or counterbalanced to guard against the emergence of "a servile political and military state".[16] And, in works such as *Socialism and the war* and *Socialism, critical and constructive*, he emphasized at a number of points the positive aspects of guild socialist thinking in this respect. Indeed, in the latter work, he clearly envisaged something resembling the kind of "encroaching control" favoured by guild socialists such as G. D. H. Cole. Thus he put forward the idea of democratically elected workshop committees taking responsibility for the hiring and firing of labour, for labour discipline and for the appointment of officials such as foremen. Further, he argued that these workshop committees should be consulted on questions related to production and should be treated as "a recognised part of the management organisation".[17] They should also deal with wage rates and wage differentials and, ultimately, they might enjoy sufficient autonomy to "act as a sort of contracting body delivering the required product and receiving for distribution, on scales and ratios which [they themselves] settle, an agreed return." Such a view of things, however speculative, was undoubtedly infused with the spirit of guild socialism.[18]

In addition, MacDonald believed that such representative bodies would make an important input to decision-making in nationalized and municipalized enterprises. This would occur through boards of management "which were representative of both the community *and the workmen*".[19] The "administration of industry would not be taken outside the ultimate responsibility of the State" – and here MacDonald distinguished his position from the more decentralist forms of guild socialism – but was, none the less, "to be a task conducted by a specialized organisation [board] built up from officials and functionaries *from the working organisation itself and belonging to it*".[20] Such worker representation and control MacDonald saw as vital for the emergence of a spirit of social service and as fundamental, therefore, to the successful working of socialism. However, this was to be a conception of the management of the public corporation that was to be jettisoned by the Labour Party in the years to come.

David Marquand in his splendid biography of Ramsay MacDonald has pointed to two fundamental and sometimes conflicting dimensions of his personality.[21] On the one hand there was the practical politician with a nose for power; on the other there was the impassioned utopian who could inspire with vibrant images of the promised land. Both aspects of the persona are there in the prescriptive component of MacDonald's political economy. The former is reflected in his Fabianism and aspects of his guild socialism; the latter in his discussion of the ultimate objectives that socialists should keep before them. As regards these, Ruskin, both directly and indirectly, left a definite imprint on MacDonald's thought. There was too more than a little of William Morris in what he wrote. In addition, as with the other Labour MPs of 1906, one should not discount the influence of the Bible, with which MacDonald, through his early upbringing, was well acquainted. Finally, there was also the influence of those with whom he mixed in the South Place Ethical Society and East London Ethical Society, both of which he joined in the late 1890s. Specifically there was his acquaintance with J. A. Hobson, whose study of John Ruskin was published in 1898.

Such influences reflected themselves in a number of ways but in particular in MacDonald's continual emphasis on the ultimately ethical nature of the objectives that socialists pursued. Thus he frequently made the point that while organizational efficiency, the elimination of waste and the expansion of output were important intermediate objectives, they must not be seen as the ultimate goal. Indeed he warned that their pursuit could sometimes obscure the goals, which, for socialists, should be paramount. As he wrote in 1921,

> To-day there is an active and pernicious propaganda asking labour to consider nothing but its economic interests . . . This, for the moment, may be made the basis of what are called advanced and revolutionary movements but the general effect on the mind of the working- class masses is to set before them self-regarding goals. Its psychological result is to induce them to think first and foremost of their own immediate advantage and it obscures the spirit of social service and the end of communal well-being.[22]

This stress on the ethical and, in particular, the moral imperative of social service, is a key component of his vision of the good or socialist society, and indeed his critique of capitalism too was often clearly driven by a sense of moral revulsion. Thus the distribution of wealth under capitalism was condemned on the grounds that it was "without any reference to the *moral requirement* that service must be the reason why men possess and production the only title to enjoyment". As it was, under capitalism "ownership" had "nothing to do with *moral justice*".[23] Further, the periodic unemployment that characterized capitalism should be condemned not just for the waste it involved but also because it forced the labourer to take as long as possible on each task and so "to work *dishonestly*". In addition, as the prime motive to labour under capitalism was pecuniary gain it precluded labour that was a "response to *moral and spiritual motives*".[24] MacDonald looked ultimately, therefore, to the "establishment of [a] State where . . . the economic machine will no longer hold spiritual things in subjection; a society that would be organised in such a way as to reflect 'the moral consciousness of man' ". As he put it, in terms of his evolutionism, "Today we are in the economic stage . . . Tomorrow we shall be in the moral stage."[25]

A socialist society should also be one that gave scope for the exercise of the population's creative faculties. Like Ruskin and Morris, MacDonald attacked capitalism for the corruption of craftsmanship and the destruction of human creativity. "The purpose which must dominate the morality and the thought of the businessman is a favourable balance sheet . . . The result is inevitable, the arts languish, the vulgar Empire of plutocracy extends its gilded barriers." Under existing arrangements it was "cheapness" that capitalism demanded; "the cheapness of sweating which destroys craftsmanship", negating at every point "the desire to acquire and deploy artistic skill".[26] Under socialism, in contrast, "art is . . . restored to life . . . under conditions of joy and freedom";[27] there would, in effect, be the material freedom for the creative impulse to flourish. Here the language, the sentiments, the vision are those of Ruskin and Morris.

MacDonald's writing therefore represents a fascinating tapestry of the many and diverse strands of socialist and anti-capitalist political economy that flourished in the period that saw the birth and progress to power of the Labour Party. Positivism, social evolutionism, Fabianism, guild socialism, the work of Ruskin, the socialism of Morris are all reflected. What resulted often lacked coherence and it certainly did not amount to a systematic exposition of socialism or socialist political economy, but then one suspects that this uneasy combination of disparate ideological elements was more common than not within the Labour Party of the period. In that respect MacDonald's eclecticism was representative.

This eclecticism also gave his socialism a kind of ideological richness, but that said, the lack of theoretical sharpness or coherence meant that it provided an unstable basis for either the advocacy or the defence of policy prescriptions and this was to be of fundamental importance as regards his leadership of the first two Labour Governments. In the heat of battle the utopian vision had little to offer and the tendency would be to fall back on moral rhetoric, the incrementalism of Fabian political economy or the determinism of a social evolutionary view of the emergence of socialism. The problem was that in the economic storms of the inter-war period these provided a better basis for prescriptive inertia than the effective conduct of policy.

As Chancellor of the Exchequer in both the inter-war Labour governments Philip Snowden was a key figure within the Party. He was *the* acknowledged expert on matters financial and economic and many commentators have seen his stance on economic questions as explaining, in large measure, the failure of these governments to tackle effectively the problems that confronted them and, in particular, that of unemployment. However, leaving aside the degree of blame that attaches to Snowden in these matters, an appreciation of his political economy is none the less crucial to any understanding of the state of economic opinion within the Labour Party and the policies to which it adhered in the 1918–31 period.

Although it should be said at the outset that Snowden's grasp of economics was considerably more assured, there are similarities between his political economy and that of MacDonald. In particular they shared an evolutionary and, at times, essentially determinist conception of the advance to socialism. Thus in Snowden's view of things socialism was "the next social system in the order of evolution" and it would come about as the "culmination of a series of evolutionary changes or slow developments which would gradually establish the new economic and social order in which the instruments of production and distribution would be socially owned and controlled".[28] Socialists should not seek to anticipate history. Each social order must fulfil its "destined purpose". Only when that purpose had been fulfilled would it give place to "a new order in which social organization more fittingly adapts itself to economic evolution".[29] As with MacDonald the language and instincts are those of gradualism; yet there is too something of a Marxian flavour in Snowden's conception of the emergence of a new social order that would more easily accommodate economic progress. It was also the case that the periodization of history in his works paralleled that to be found in the *Communist manifesto*, though Snowden made clear that the progress of history was not a consequence of class conflict but must be seen in terms of organic growth.

Consistent with this view of historical progress was Snowden's belief that the socialization of economic life should be experimental and piecemeal. There would be a "gradual transformation of the capitalist system into a co-operative commonwealth".[30] This would be achieved in four ways. First by further extending the legislative limitation of private property rights through measures governing the hours and conditions in factories, mines, shops, etc.; secondly by extending the kind of social welfare legislation already passed by the Liberals in the period prior to the Great War; thirdly by the taxation of unearned income and finally by the extension of the municipal and national ownership of economic activity. However, "the line of advance to which socialists attach greatest importance is by way of public ownership. All other ways are merely palliative."[31]

As regards that line of advance, capitalism itself was already preparing the way. Like MacDonald, Snowden identified in contemporary capitalism an ineluctable tendency to monopoly. This development enhanced the exploitative power of capitalism but it also laid the basis for the extension of public ownership. As Snowden saw it,

> the Trust is a great step forward in economic advance. Like every advance it brings disadvantages . . . But the Trust . . . is doing a necessary work. Competition has served the purpose of weeding out the incompetent and ill-equipped capitalists. The Trust is concentrating industry and is evolving Capitalism to that stage where the public ownership and control of the great industries will be possible. Competition, the Trust and then socialism.[32]

Trusts had eliminated the waste resulting from competition; they had rationalized industries; they had concentrated ownership (for the most part) in the hands of the competent few and in doing all this had, in effect, prepared the ground for the extension of social ownership. All that was required to turn profit-oriented concerns into public corporations driven by the ideal of social service was the requisite Act of Parliament. Snowden also believed that the degree of monopoly power exercised within an industry was the criterion that should determine its "ripeness for public ownership and control".[33] In that respect land, "the railways, the mines, shipping and other forms of transport, the production of electrical power . . . and banking and insurance are ripe for the application of nationalization".[34]

All this bears the imprint of Fabianism, as does Snowden's critique of the distributive failings of capitalism. For here, even more overtly and certainly more clearly than MacDonald, he used that generalization of Ricardian rent theory which is one of the distinguishing features of Fabian political economy. Landowners were seen as securing rent from their monopoly of good quality land or land that was fortuitously situated in relation to urban or industrial developments. Similarly, the capitalists through their monopoly of innovations or more productive capital equipment were able to exact rent in the same way as the owners of fertile land. "Capital too exacts its economic rent", wrote Snowden. "Just as the landlord gets an unearned income from the increase in the value of land, so the capitalist gets an unearned increment from improvements in productive methods and in other ways not the result of his own efforts or abilities."[35]

If this analysis of the distributive evils of capitalism echoes that of the late-nineteenth-century Fabians so too does Snowden's solution: that unearned income that did not result from any contribution to production should be taken by the state by fiscal means. "Both local and national taxation should aim primarily at securing for communal benefit all [these] unearned . . . increments of wealth."[36] To this end Snowden suggested the use of income tax, death duties and the taxation of any increase in land values. However, he was clear that while taxation might mitigate it could not solve the problem of the maldistribution of wealth; that could be achieved only by the social ownership of the means of production. For then all rental income would accrue to the state and local authorities and could be used for social purposes.

At a macroeconomic level Snowden like the Fabians saw the waste resulting from economic anarchy as the primary failing of competitive capitalism. In this respect the war had shown what could be achieved under state direction. It had "led to the exposure of the wasteful and inefficient methods of capitalist production and proved how far short of the maximum output pre-war production had fallen".[37] The most obvious form of waste was that of unemployment, and Snowden linked this, as did the Fabians, to "the lack of organisation and to the chaos of unregulated production".[38] Thus capitalists produced with no knowledge of the intentions of their rivals or the extent of profitable demand. "Production [was] largely speculative" and subject to all the excesses and errors of speculation.[39] Inevitably, in such circumstances, there were periods when, either partially or generally, demand did not match output and labour was rendered redundant. Under socialism the problem would not exist because the social control of productive activity could be used to ensure that supply was always commensurate with demand. Also the organization of production by the state and local authorities "would provide for the easy transfer of labour from where a reduced amount was needed to an industry or locality where more was required".[40]

However, short of full-blown socialism, Snowden believed such solutions were not available. Like Beatrice Webb in the *Minority report of the Poor Law Commission*, he therefore considered the possibility of using "schemes of national development" to provide employment for those who were the victims of existing economic disorder. It is, however, important to be clear about what Snowden believed a Labour government might do, not least because of the dismissive attitude of the 1929–31 government to the possibility of using public investment expenditure as a means of reducing the level of unemployment and, specifically, its condemnation of the proposals emanating from Keynes and the Liberals.

Here it can be said that, in general, Snowden's position was consistent with the negative Fabian view already documented. Yet, in works such as *Socialism and syndicalism* (1913) and *Labour and the new world* (1921), there are elements of ambivalence that one might not expect given the vehemence with which he was to attack Keynesian remedies in the late 1920s and 1930s. It is true that in the 1921 work he lays down quite exacting criteria for state financed schemes of national development. The two points to keep in mind when considering such schemes, he argued, were first that the work had to represent "new industry" and second "*it should be remunerative*, that is it should add at least as much to the total of national wealth as the support of the scheme has taken from the store".[41] Thus we have here a rehearsal of some of the arguments against the utility of public works schemes that Snowden and others were to deploy to justify the negativism of Labour's conduct of macroeconomic policy during the 1929–31 period. Yet at other points in the same work we find

Snowden arguing that even if public work brought "no financial return, if it has made the men anew, restored their self-respect and brought back their strength, it is a scheme that can be justified as social economy".[42] Further, in similarly positive vein, he stated that as the problem of unemployment was "the pressing question of our time . . . it must be faced with a determination to spend *whatever sums, however large*, may be necessary to remove the scandal from our society of a class of human beings industrially and socially superfluous."[43]

Given his subsequent attitude to spending and the imperatives of a balanced budget there is a profound irony in such statements, but they do show that, in the early 1920s at any rate, Snowden was not the unabashed advocate of the negative Treasury view of public works expenditure that he subsequently became. However, the fact that he did ultimately succumb so completely to fiscal orthodoxy provides further evidence that those who formulated their economic thinking within the confines of Fabianism lacked a theoretical basis for those expansionary policies that sometimes appealed to both their economic commonsense and moral sensibilities. Thus Fabian political economy provided little that could be used to justify a "determination to spend . . . large sums" on a programme of national economic development and to provide men such as Snowden with the intellectual conviction and the political nerve necessary to resist the rhetoric of sound finance. Without that the temptation would always be to succumb to the traditional Treasury view of fiscal management and balance the books – a temptation to which Snowden with his instinctual attachment to parsimony and sound money was, in any case, particularly prone.

As regards other influences on Snowden, that of Marx was largely negative. Thus Snowden dismissed *Capital* as a work whose "style was neither interesting nor clear", offering the further pertinent comment that "very few have either the time or inclination to make a careful study of these ponderous volumes".[44] More specifically, while he might share Marx's periodization of history, he emphatically rejected what he interpreted as Marx's economic determinism. Further, he attacked the idea that class conflict was either history's motive force or an inevitable precondition for the emergence of socialism. Like MacDonald, he emphasized throughout his work that "though Socialism is primarily the cause of the working-class it is not in its aim and object a class movement." "Industrial slavery [would] be abolished by the enlightened self-interest and ethical impulses of *all* classes."[45] Nor, for Snowden, would class conflict engender the "social spirit" that was the essential basis of a socialist community. In any case it simply did not reflect the realities of the complex variegated nature of the class structure of British society, or the fact that the Labour Party was increasingly attracting middle-class support.

In this context Marxian notions of revolution as the means of socialist transformation were also given short shrift. Leaving aside the deleterious social and economic repercussions that would follow from such a transition to socialism, the fact was that the British working class, because it had achieved so much by "peaceful agitation", would certainly not "abandon that means for methods of a different character".[46] A constitutional, piecemeal approach to socialism was one that was in harmony with the traditions and expectations of working class agitation in Britain and could therefore be expected to command the greatest support.

Finally if there was a Fabian aridity about much of what Snowden wrote, there was too an inner ethical fire. This is most apparent in his condemnation of capitalism. Leaving aside the immorality of the waste it generated, there was the kind of men it made and the kind of social practices it encouraged. Its competitive aspect in particular provoked Snowden's moral ire. For, it developed "not the human but the animal instincts of men", making them "hard, selfish, cruel and acquisitive".[47] Further, the separation of workers from the means of production was to be condemned not just because it laid the basis for the appropriation of unearned income, but also because it encouraged parasitism on the one hand and servility on the other. Snowden also damned on moral grounds "the slavery and mechanical character of modern industrialism", which "[had] destroyed the individuality and originality of the workers"; such sentiments being liberally interspersed with quotations from Ruskin on the "joy of creative work".[48] Yet, when it came to the crunch, when it came to the articulation and implementation of practical policies, Snowden's Fabian head and parsimonious instincts invariably triumphed over his Ruskinian soul. At the end of the day, as he himself put it, socialism had to be paid for. There could be no such thing as a free socialist lunch.

Chapter 7
The economic literature of the Labour Party, 1918–29

> Mr Lloyd George . . . is ready to mortgage the future as gaily as ever; but to the electorate the style of his proposals is too suggestive of a moneylender's advertisement. Wise men throw such things into the waste paper bin without more ado.
>
> Labour Party, *How to conquer unemployment* (1929) on the Liberal proposals for increased public investment expenditure

Both Marxian and guild socialism were given fresh impetus by the war, yet, for reasons that have already been touched upon, they had little lasting impact on the political economy of the Labour Party in the post-war period. Liberal socialism for a time threatened to dominate the policy debate but by the late 1920s it too had been decisively rejected. The influence of ethical socialism lingered on but in terms neither of analysis nor of economic policy prescription did it have a distinctive impact, though R. H. Tawney did play an important part in drafting *Labour and the nation*, on the basis of which the Labour Party fought the 1929 general election.

The genre of socialist political economy that did emerge fortified by the war and that did come to dominate not only the minds of the men who mattered – MacDonald and Snowden – but also the economic literature that the Party produced, was that articulated by the Fabians. The war seemed to have provided proof positive of the Fabian view that it was by the extension of purposive public control over the economic and social life of the nation that great things could be achieved. It was, after all, not the anarchic pursuit of self-interest but the efficient, scientific, public administration of economic activity that had won the war; surely then it could best deliver the benefits of the peace.

The war also seemed to have confirmed the Fabian prediction of the ineluctable progress of society in the direction of collectivism. Thus by the war's end the munitions industry, investment, the railways, food distribution and the allocation and use of labour were, to a greater or lesser extent, under the control of the state. It is true that in the immediate post-war period controls were dismantled and state intervention in the economy was considerably reduced but there was no obvious reason why such retrograde steps could not be reversed, and there now existed a literature, e.g. E. M. H. Lloyd's *Experiments in state control* (1920) and *Stabilisation, an economic policy* (1923), which showed how the public regulation and control of economic activity could be effectively implemented. Works such as Sidney and Beatrice Webb's *Constitution for the socialist commonwealth of Great Britain* (1920), the second edition of their *Industrial democracy* (1920) and their *Decay of capitalist civilisation* (1923) are all testimony to the intellectual self-confidence of Fabianism in this period, and the economic literature of the Labour Party in the 1918–29 period provides substantial evidence of the profound and growing influence that it had.

One need look no further than *Labour and the new social order* (1918) to substantiate this. The very language in which it is written distinguishes it as an essentially Fabian document. Thus as regards the distribution of the national product the problem was that:

> We have allowed the riches of our mines, the *rental value* of the lands superior to the margin of cultivation, the *extra profits* of the fortunate capitalists, even the material outcome of scientific discoveries . . . to be absorbed by individual proprietors and then devoted very largely to the senseless luxury of an idle class.[1]

Further, this maldistribution was accentuated by an increasing tendency to "trustification", which laid the basis for a more intense exploitation of the consumer.

It is all there. The notion of the margin and of an economic surplus accruing in the form of rents and supranormal profits to the unproductive, who then effect a wasteful allocation of the nation's resources in favour of the production of luxury goods. In similar Fabian vein, the pamphlet argued that this economic surplus should be appropriated and used for the common good. This was "to be secured on the one hand by the nationalisation and municipalisation of productive resources and on the other by the steeply graduated taxation of private income and riches".[2]

The surplus once acquired in these ways would be used for national purposes. It would provide a source of cheap investment funds that could be used to increase productive capacity and improve the efficiency of enterprises. It would also be utilized in such a way as to provide increased public funding for "scientific investigation and original research" relevant to industrial production, investment in the nation's infrastructure and the wherewithal to enhance social welfare provision.[3] It would, in short, furnish the social investment necessary for the construction of an efficient and truly civilized society.

Along with the maldistribution of wealth, argued the authors of *Labour and the new social order*, went general economic waste and inefficiency or, as they phrased it, "the disorganisation, waste and inefficiency involved in the abandonment of British industry to a jostling crowd of separate private employers with their minds bent not on the service of the community but . . . only on the utmost possible profiteering".[4] Again the language is manifestly Fabian, though with a flavouring of ethical socialism.

As regards the remedy, this was couched in Fabian terms of scientific organization, rational economic decision-making and the spirit of social service. What was wanted was a "genuinely scientific reorganization of the nation's industry no longer deflected by individual profiteering".[5] Thus the industry and resources of the country should be organized not with the maximization of profit but with public service in mind. It was science and intelligence, not the self-interested pursuit of gain, that were required to ensure rapidly rising living standards and the full and effective use of the nation's resources. What was needed was "a deliberately thought out systematic and comprehensive plan" with economic needs and objectives met not in line with the capacity to pay but in the order of their "real national importance".[6] Conscious, rational, scientific, economic decision-making was to replace instinctual responses to market stimuli. Such sentiments were to appear again and again in the Labour Party's economic literature of the 1920s, most obviously in *Labour and the nation* (1928).

Labour and the new social order also embodied the ideas on contracyclical government expenditure that had previously found expression in the *Minority report of the Poor Law Commission*. In fact, as early as January 1917 the Labour Party Annual Conference had passed a resolution expressing the view that it was the "duty of Government" deliberately and systematically to prevent unemployment by arranging public works and the orders of National Departments and local authorities in such a way as to maintain the aggregate demand for labour in the whole kingdom approximately at a uniform level from year to year".[7] To this end it recommended that governments should have prepared and have to hand public works schemes that they could "set in motion when the demand for labour fell".[8] Again, in August 1917, in a submission on War Aims to the Inter-Allied Conference, the Labour Party emphasized the need, on the cessation of hostilities, for public works that "together with the various capitalist enterprises that may be in progress" would "maintain at a fairly uniform level, year by year, and throughout each year, the aggregate demand for labour".[9] So the call in *Labour and the new social order* for plans "to prevent any considerable or widespread fluctuations in the total numbers employed in times of good or bad trade" by such means simply represented a reiteration of the need for a contracyclical strategy.[10] It should be emphasized once again, however, that this strategy was conceived of in terms of preventing oscillations around a "normal" (for capitalism) level of unemployment. As in the *Minority report* the view was that unemployment would remain an affliction as long as the economic system was characterized by uncoordinated and self-interested economic decision-making.

Ideas and policies similar to those in *Labour and the new social order* were to find expression in the economic literature produced by the Labour Party throughout the 1920s; all of which, in greater or lesser measure, bears a Fabian imprint. Thus while economic and political developments may have affected the content and thrust of particular documents, the general themes, as we shall see, were to remain those of 1918.

Understandably, with the collapse of the post-war boom, the focus and policy emphasis was on unemployment, soaring as it did in 1920–21 towards 20 per cent of the insured working population and never, subsequently, falling below the one million mark. Here, initially, Party literature stressed the impact of the war and, as importantly, the consequences of a pernicious Versailles Settlement. Given the economic dislocation caused by war, particularly in Central and Eastern Europe and Russia, "hundreds of millions of civilized human beings have ceased to exist for us, in the sense that they neither buy from us nor sell to us"[11] and this decline of trade with Germany, Russia and what had previously been the Austro-Hungarian Empire would, it was argued, "alone account for most of our present employment". Further, problems created by the war had, undoubtedly, been exacerbated by the peace. Thus the fact that the reparations burden imposed on Germany had "lamed the biggest productive machine in Europe in time of world shortage [was] a general disaster".[12] This, superimposed on the inherent periodic tendency to slump under capitalism, almost entirely explained the unparalleled magnitude of the unemployment that beset Britain in the early 1920s.

This analysis of the problem was advanced in a number of pamphlets published by the Labour Party in the early 1920s but most notably in *Unemployment, the peace and the indemnity* (1921) and *Unemployment, a Labour policy* (1921). However, the latter pamphlet is also significant as it emphasized the need to maintain working-class, domestic demand in the light of the loss of markets in Continental Europe. Thus it argued strongly against a proposed introduction of short-time working as a solution to the problem of unemployment on the grounds, first, that it reduced the earnings of those affected to a level that did not permit a "reasonable" standard of living and, secondly, that deflationary macroeconomic repercussions would ensue. Specifically, "the reduced purchasing power of the workers *directly* affected, lessen[ed] the demand for all other kinds of commodities and services and so caus[ed] an ever-widening circle of workers to become unemployed or under-employed."[13] Short-time working might benefit the individual employer but to the extent that it dampened aggregate demand it did damage to the economy as a whole drawing more and more workers into "the vicious circle of under-employment and *under-consumption*".[14] In effect, therefore, the pamphlet deployed a crude notion of a negative multiplier.

So the government had by its foreign policy made impossible the early restoration of the foreign market and, in its support for short-time working, now proposed "to add to its achievements the destruction of the home market by reducing the purchasing power of this country".[15] While, therefore, *Unemployment, a Labour policy* (1921) was the product of a joint Labour Party/TUC committee chaired by the Fabian Sidney Webb, both the language and the analysis have a Hobsonian resonance. Certainly the whole emphasis upon underconsumption as central to the problem of unemployment and on the need to maintain the purchasing power of the workers is very much in line with Hobson's position, as is the pamphlet's suggestion that working-class demand might be maintained by "a diversion of purchasing power from the richer classes".[16] It is also interesting to note here that the view that this *diversion* of purchasing power would have no *net* effect on unemployment because it was simply a redistribution from one section of society to another was strongly rebutted in a manner that was essentially Hobsonian:

> a wide distribution of purchasing power among the community in the form of wages . . . produces quite a different effect from the possession of an equal amount of purchasing power by the richer classes. *Money available for investment has no necessary immediate effect in maintaining economic demand in the home market but purchasing power distributed in the form of wages or maintenance to the workers immediately results in a stimulation of economic demand.*[17]

Thus the pamphlet embodied a Hobsonian awareness of the economic consequences of the differing relative propensities to consume and to save/invest of the rich and of the working-classes.

In this context a pamphlet published some time later in 1926 and entitled *On the dole or off?* is significant. In it, an interesting distinction is made between measures designed to "regularise" production and the "stabilisation of purchasing power". The first implied the contracyclical regulation of government orders "in such a way as will keep the wheels of industry revolving steadily"; the second denoted "the scientific manipulation of credit and currency to maintain the amount of purchasing power in the hands of the people and so maintain production".[18] The first was of course Fabian in provenance, the second very much the strategy being articulated by Strachey, Mosley and others within the ranks of the ILP. The pamphlet, however, proceeds in a way that is more critical of the latter than the former strategy. There are problems with both because neither "the perfect regularisation of production" nor "the perfect stabilisation of prices is possible".[19] However, the particular problem with a monetary policy aimed at the stabilization of purchasing power was that while it might "maintain a steady confidence and the output of goods by capitalist enterprise, it would not of itself promote the comprehensive and *scientific development of resources and economic possibilities which are essential for the absorption into employment of a growing population and for a progressive improvement of the standard of life of the workers*".[20]

This is quite clearly a critique of the liberal socialist position from a Fabian standpoint. Further, the pamphlet argues that there were major problems involved in maintaining purchasing power and stabilizing prices by means of a redistributive fiscal policy even though such a policy might be applauded for other reasons. The argument here is interesting both because it represents a critique of the "living wage" strategy and because it runs contrary to what had been argued in *Unemployment, a Labour policy*. Taxation "would *not* create a net addition to the purchasing power of the country", it would "only transfer purchasing power from one body of people to another". This represented an important shift in position from 1921 and, taken together with the critical comments on a contracyclical monetary policy, it represented a ruling out of options and a narrowing of focus as regards the conduct of economic policy. One year later, of course, the Hobsonian "living wage" policies of the ILP were to be overwhelmingly rejected by the Labour Party Annual Conference of 1927.

Further, although in *On the dole or off?* definite reservations were expressed as to what might be achieved by the contracyclical placement of government orders, such a policy was nevertheless presented in a positive and more detailed form. Thus it was suggested that when the Labour Party was again returned to power it should, in times of relative prosperity, set aside £10 million per annum to be spent in periods when the level of economic activity was falling. "The effect of the policy would be to reduce purchasing power during the good years and increase it in the bad times."[21] It was also argued that if this did not prove sufficient then public works schemes should be "financed during a depression by bank borrowings"; though the pamphlet expressed concern about the liabilities that would be incurred and the need, therefore, for selectivity as regards such schemes.[22] More generally though, the impression conveyed in this and other pamphlets such as *Work for the workless* (1924) is that public works schemes might mitigate but did not unearth the root causes of unemployment. Thus the 1924 pamphlet, drafted by Sidney Webb, stated that "Labour recognised . . . that schemes of work . . . can never solve the problem of unemployment, even though they may be *some use as stop gap ends*", for the root of the problem lay "in the present system of industry".[23]

Nevertheless, to implement a contracyclical policy effectively, *On the dole or off?* proposed the establishment of an Employment and Development Board. This was to have three functions. First, to establish the different directions in which economic development, by way of public works expenditure, was possible. Secondly, to assess the relative importance of specific schemes with a particular eye to their impact on employment and living standards, and thirdly, to consider the magnitude of capital expenditure involved. However, it was also argued that such schemes of development must be pursued in conjunction with the economic reorganization that the extension of public ownership would allow and here the pamphlet made particular mention of the power industry, mining, transport and the land. Thus in *On the dole or off?* the substance of the economic programme, the emphasis within it and the means of implementation were essentially Fabian.

It was, however, on the basis of *Labour and the nation* (1928), a statement of the Party's aims and principles that secured the overwhelming approval of the 1928 Labour Party Conferenc that Labour fought the 1929 election. This was a wordy fusion of ethical and Fabian socialism with the latter clearly predominating as regards its economic policy prescriptions. Science, service and efficient administration are the key themes that run through it. Thus it was by "the fullest utilisation of *scientific* knowledge and administrative skill" that a social order would be created that would maximize "economic welfare and personal freedom". It was "by *science*, co-operation and the spirit of service" that "the world [could] be made a more tolerable abode for future generations". Output could be increased through "the progress of *scientific* knowledge and the art of administration. Further, the Labour Party would set about the whole business of economic management in a "practical and *scientific* spirit" for as a Party it stood for "the deliberate establishment, *by experimental methods*, without violence or disturbance", of a just society.[24]

This Fabian veneration of science and efficient administration is a marked characteristic of the pamphlet. In terms too of its specific policy prescriptions it was also very much in the mould of Fabian gradualism with the occasional nod in the direction of ethical socialism. The object was "to convert industry *step by step*, and with due regard to the special needs and varying circumstances of different occupations from a sordid struggle for gain to a co-operative undertaking carried on for the service of the community"; something to be achieved in part by the piecemeal extension of public ownership to mining, power, land, transport and the Bank of England, "*without haste* . . . with careful preparation, with the use of the best technical knowledge and managerial skill, and with due compensation."[25] In addition there was a reiteration of the commitment to establishing an Employment and Development Board that would initiate and, with the help of a Treasury grants, finance a series of public works schemes. The document also suggested the creation of a National Economic Committee that would ensure that "economic policy was accurately adjusted to the needs of the moment" by the provision of accurate economic information.[26]

As regards the general conduct of fiscal policy, the emphasis in *Labour and the nation* and in other literature produced in the late 1920s was now very much on a “prudent and economical administration of the nation’s income”. A Labour government would act in such a way as to curtail expenditure that added “little or nothing to national well-being” and raise tax revenue “from those elements in the income of society which contribute little to social efficiency”.[27] In this way it would conduct the nation’s economic affairs according to the principles of “good housekeeping”. “Good Housekeeping” was, indeed, the subheading of this section of the pamphlet and the intention of the Party was clearly to make sure that the costs of any programme of social reform were met out of current revenue. Socialism must be paid for.

This attitude is also reflected in *How to conquer unemployment* (1929), the Party’s response to the radical economic strategy of employment-creating public investment advanced by the Liberals in *Britain’s industrial future* (1928) and *We can conquer unemployment* (1929). The whole of *How to conquer* was characterized by adherence to a set of mutually conflicting responses to what the Liberals were proposing. On the one hand, the Party argued, with some justification, that what Lloyd George and the Liberal Party were advocating had been “stolen without acknowledgement” from the plans that the Labour Party had been proposing since 1917.[28] At the same time, the Party argued that such policies involved “clapping a plaster of relief works on the patient’s back”, mortgaging the nation’s financial future and having recourse to “madcap finance” to cover the costs.[29] In short the Labour Party contrived to argue that the Liberals were proposing policies appropriated from Labour, which were both ineffectual and financially unsound!

However, when it came to the business of explaining why the financial underpinning was “madcap” the pamphlet was far from clear. What the Liberals proposed was to borrow £250 million to finance investment on infrastructural development. *How to conquer unemployment* did not rule out such borrowing *per se* but only provided the funds were expended in ways that were “directly productive of future revenue or which will be socially or industrially productive” and only on condition that provision was made for the repayment of the loan when increased revenue was not immediately forthcoming.[30] Thus the pamphlet insisted that the increase in investment expenditure entailed by a public works programme, “except when it is directly reproductive”, should be met out of taxation.

By 1929, therefore, the Party’s stance on public investment expenditure was characterized by half-heartedness, qualification and confusion. It is unsurprising then, that when the Party assumed responsibility for the conduct of economic policy in the 1929–31 period, economic depression and rapidly rising unemployment precipitated a speedy abandonment of any attempt to reconcile the practices of good housekeeping – meeting increased expenditure out of taxation and balancing the budget – with its erstwhile commitment to employment-generating public investment. Ambivalence with regard to the latter ensured that any conflict would be resolved in favour of adherence to the former. Here we see clearly the negative consequences of that Fabian suspicion of an expansionary fiscal policy that has already been remarked upon.

On the conduct of monetary policy the pamphlet had nothing to say other than that it should be pursued with the objectives of stabilizing the exchanges and the purchasing power of money. There is no indication that these twin objectives might be in conflict and nothing is said on which should prevail and why. Nor is there any discussion of the constraints imposed on the conduct of monetary policy by the Gold Standard. The major concern was that the Bank of England should be under public control; to what end was a question that received little consideration. Presumably, once instilled with the necessary spirit of social service and already possessing the requisite expertise the Bank could be relied upon to pursue whatever monetary policy was in the public interest.

That said, Philip Snowden, at least was clear what that policy should be and it was one that did not entail any monetary expansion that might jeopardize the value of the currency. Thus in a debate at the Labour Party Annual Conference of 1928 on the "Banking and currency supplement" of *Labour and the nation*, Snowden stated that it did not "matter whether prices are high or low *provided they are stable* because if prices are stable wages and other conditions will adapt themselves to that fixed condition of things".[31] For Snowden, then, it was for labour to make the adjustments necessary to ensure sound money, even if such adjustments entailed the reduction of money wages. This was fundamentally at odds with the liberal socialist view of things and much more in line with the views of those whose determination to effect wage reductions had precipitated a general strike two years previously. For Snowden the priority was price stability; for the liberal socialists it was raising real wages and maintaining the level of working-class demand necessary to ensure full or near-full employment.

As regards redistributive policies, *Labour and the nation* is also redolent of both Fabian and ethical socialism. The aim was to appropriate collectively those "surpluses" that were the product of "social effort" so that they "shall be applied by society for the good of all". This was to be effected by taxing income of the unproductive and those who added little to "social efficiency". Specifically, the pamphlet suggested a "complete revolution in the national attitude to the inheritance of wealth",[32] proposing a substantial increase in death duties and a graduated surtax on incomes over £500. In addition, there would be taxation of income derived from the rent of urban land; though Party policy insisted that, ultimately, all land should be publicly owned. Further, revenue raised from these sources would permit the elimination of taxes on necessities and the development of "indispensable social services" to improve working-class living standards. However, the document was at (Fabian) pains to point out that such policies were not class based. In advocating such measures the Party was speaking not just for the "wage-earners", "but, *with the exception of an insignificant fraction*, for the whole community."[33] Thus throughout, it was argued that what the Party offered were policies that transcended class.

However, while Fabianism dominated the literature, the language used to justify and elucidate such policies was often that of ethical socialism. Thus, for example, *Labour and the nation* condemned contemporary economic life as a "sordid struggle for gain". In addition, it stressed the ideal of fellowship, arguing that the economic policies advanced by Labour were the practical embodiment of the notion that "men are all, in very truth, members one of another". It even quoted John Ruskin to the effect that "there is no wealth but life"; a clear indication of the pen of Tawney.[34] Moreover, the conception of economic activity as "service" to the community was emphasized throughout but, of course, "service" was a notion with a Fabian as well as an ethical socialist pedigree. In general terms, though, the analytical thrust and the objectives of the political economy embodied in *Labour and the nation* were essentially Fabian.

Some have also seen a guild socialist influence in some of the immediate post-war literature and in *Labour and the new social order* allusion was certainly made to "economic democracy". However, the kind of democracy proposed was an insipid affair. Thus the consumer co-operative movement was held out as the great example of the workers' capacity for economic self-government, and there was certainly no suggestion of significant worker participation in the decision-making of socially owned enterprises. Economic democracy was understood rather in terms of the ultimate responsibility of the managers of such enterprises to the parliamentary representatives of the community. In short, the notion of economic democracy was severely circumscribed.

Given then the political economy of the Labour Party in the 1920s how did it fare when it took office in 1929? That and the longer-term consequences of its conduct of economic policy in the 1929–31 period are the questions that will be considered in the next three chapters.

Part two

1929–45

Chapter 8
Labour in office, 1929–31

> Without any adequate theory of the transition, the Labour Party was bound to be defeatist in the circumstances of 1929. Socialism was impossible and capitalism was doomed: there was nothing to do but govern without conviction a system it did not believe in but saw no real prospect of changing.
>
> R. Skidelsky, *Politicians and the slump*, 1967

When it came to power in June 1929 economic fortune looked as if it might smile on the incoming minority Labour Government. That year proved the best for exports since 1918; in the spring unemployment was on a downward trend; 1928–9 saw industrial production and GDP growing at a rate of 5.1 and 2.4 per cent per annum. If such trends had continued the government might have acquitted itself satisfactorily. It might have set about the gradual, piecemeal extension of public ownership and rationalization of industry that it proposed; it might have financed public works on a sufficient scale to accelerate the prevailing tendency for unemployment to fall; and it might, in a climate of growing prosperity, have acquired the increasing revenue necessary to effect a significant increase in social welfare expenditure. All this could also have proceeded in a general climate of growing domestic and international confidence, which would have diminished business anxiety about any adverse impact of such policies on the level of profitability and mitigated any City concern over the maintenance of the exchange rate. In short, even within the policy constraints it had established for itself, there would have been some freedom of manoeuvre and the likelihood of a measure of success.

With the collapse of the United States economy and the global economic shockwaves that resulted these possibilities evaporated. In a situation of rapidly rising unemployment (over 2 million by July 1930), falling industrial production, squeezed profitability and mounting bankruptcies, social and economic reform of the kind articulated by Labour was increasingly seen by the government, in particular Snowden, Chancellor of the Exchequer, as a luxury that could not be afforded. Further, the existing scale of public works was now manifestly inadequate in relation to the magnitude of the unemployment problem, while any notions of fundamental industrial restructuring on the basis of extended public ownership had necessarily to be abandoned in the light of the precarious political position of the minority Labour Government. What Labour desperately needed in view of the rapidly deteriorating economic circumstances was a set of macroeconomic policies that would tackle the problem of unemployment, impart sufficient forward momentum to the economy to restore business confidence and make possible some tentative steps, at least, in the direction of ameliorating the material lot of Labour's constituency. But, as we have seen in the previous chapter, the essential components of such a strategy were exactly what had been ruled out by the triumph of Fabianism.

Of course the absence of a theoretical structure in terms of which such a strategy could be articulated and defended was not the only obstacle in the way of its pursuit. Even a Labour Party enthusiastically embracing the economic doctrines of liberal socialism would still have had to confront a depression of unparalleled severity and a Treasury implacably wedded to the notion that "whatever might be the political and social advantages very little additional employment can, in fact, and as a general rule be created by state borrowing and state expenditure";[1] confronted too by a Treasury possessed of an unparalleled intellectual and imaginative capacity when it came to outlining the administrative, practical and theoretical impediments to an expansionary programme of public investment. It was also the case that business and international confidence was fragile and might not have taken kindly to a radical departure from accepted principles of fiscal and economic management. Even so, the absence of the theoretical constructs and conceptual framework in terms of which a radical economic strategy could be formulated and defended was one important factor condemning the minority Labour government to policies of negation, restriction and inactivity.

Where new ideas are absent the old almost inevitably hold sway and what that meant was balanced budgets (which as revenue diminished implied expenditure cuts) and the deflationary defence of an overvalued exchange rate. It also meant acceptance of the Treasury view that increased public investment expenditure must necessarily prove ineffective as a means of reducing the level of unemployment and adherence to a Micawberite faith that something, to be specific the economic cycle and world trade, must eventually turn up.

It is true that with the formation of the Economic Advisory Committee in February 1930 MacDonald did enlist the services and trawl the opinions of professional economists and others – Keynes among them. However the Committee was divided on the most effectual remedies for unemployment. In particular there was a division of opinion between economists such as Keynes and the practical men, industrialists such as Sir John Cadman, and also a divergence of views within the ranks of the economists themselves, most notably between Keynes and Lionel Robbins. The Economic Advisory Committee was never likely, therefore, to help the Labour Government circumvent the policy impasse in which it found itself.

All this said, some commentators have suggested that public adherence to the principles of economic orthodoxy, together with a covert, practical deviation from them (by way of increased expenditure on support for the unemployed and, more tentatively, on roads), helped produce an economic outcome as favourable as could have been expected in the circumstances and better than was achieved by most governments in the 1929–31 period.[2] However, this does not rule out the likelihood that the Labour Government could have done still better had it not been so hamstrung, and therefore conservative, in terms of the macroeconomic policies it pursued. Nor does it deal with the fact that the government simply did not grasp the range of policy options on offer. Adherence to a political economy that ruled out the possibility of expansionary fiscal and/or monetary policies meant, when incremental socialism was no longer feasible, adherence to the economic orthodoxy emanating from the Treasury. In effect, Labour put itself in a position where there was no alternative. It must also be said that, whatever the general economic performance under the second minority Labour Government, its conduct of economic policy undoubtedly paved the way for political disaster in 1931.

If, however, Fabianism provided no way forward except into the arms of the Treasury, it was also the case that Philip Snowden, in particular, found the resultant embrace anything but uncongenial. Fiscal rectitude, sound money and free trade were the fundamental tenets of his economic philosophy. If socialism had to be paid for that meant budgets had to be balanced. If this could not be achieved then socialist advance must be halted. Socialism could not be built on the foundation of a nation living beyond its means. Further, socialist progress must proceed on the basis of a currency the domestic and international value of which was stable, and that meant ensuring that monetary policy remained in the hands of financial experts immune from pernicious, political pressures. As regards free trade, that was a practical expression of the international brotherhood of man and, for Snowden, and many others, a central article of socialist faith. If then, to quote Churchill, "the Treasury mind and the Snowden mind embraced each other with the fervour of two long-separated kindred lizards" it was with a passion rooted in a shared economic *Weltanschauung*.

It did not help, of course, that on matters financial and economic Snowden's was *the* authoritative voice within the Party. But the fact that that voice retained its authority almost until the end suggests that for most of the Party it was not perceived as dictatorial. It is true there was dissent and that, as unemployment rose, dissent and frustration grew, but within the Party only one small group, that surrounding Oswald Mosley, actually put forward a feasible, radical, economic alternative. An ILP rump, including James Maxton, Archie Kirkwood, John Wheatley, Campbell Stephen and others, fulminated against the ineptitude and the drift of economic policy and the material impoverishment it inflicted upon the working class but, for all this, the Party retained a remarkable unity. In part this may have been dictated by the exigencies of its minority position but also, surely, by the absence of a non-Fabian theoretical framework in terms of which economic questions and alternative strategies might have been considered. It was, indeed, only when MacDonald and Snowden moved to implement the recommendations of the May Committee on National Expenditure, 1931, for cuts in unemployment benefit amounting to £66 million, and even then only over the "means test" component of those cuts, that the majority of the cabinet and the Party parted company with the prime minister and his chancellor. Even at the death the fundamentals of Fabianism went largely unchallenged and indeed it would live to fight again in various guises and mutated forms after 1931.

During the course of the minority Labour Government there was, in fact, only one significant challenge to Fabianism and thence to Treasury orthodoxy and this originated with Oswald Mosley and John Strachey, who had already confronted its ideological hegemony in the 1920s. As early as March 1930 we find Strachey complaining of the Labour Party showing "perceptible Conservative tendencies" and by October 1930 his frustration had increased to a point where he wrote of Snowden as: "determined . . . to prove that a socialist Chancellor of the Exchequer can be the champion of laissez-faire. He stands immovable upon economic principles which Mr. Mill and Mr. Jeavons [*sic*] would have thought amateurishly inflexible and doctrinaire."[3]

Such frustration was shared by Mosley. Indeed matters were made worse for him by the fact that at the outset of the government he had been drafted onto a committee under the chairmanship of the Lord Privy Seal, J. H. (Jimmy) Thomas, which had responsibility for the co-ordination of Labour's employment policies. However with its lack of executive powers, the absence of a clear remit and under an inept, ineffectual and sometimes inebriate chairman, the Thomas Committee came, for Mosley, to epitomize the impotence, incompetence and inertia of the government's response to rapidly deteriorating economic circumstances.

It was, in particular, the impetus of this acute frustration that led Mosley, with Strachey's help and support, to set out his ideas for a radical alternative to existing economic policies. This was done first, in a Memorandum in January 1930, (rejected by the cabinet in May 1930 and subsequently by the Party at its annual conference in October 1930) and then, in a Manifesto (signed by 17 Labour MPs and the miners' leader A. J. Cook), which was published in

December of that year. Further, as a result of the Party's rejection of his ideas, Mosley resigned from the cabinet in May and, shortly after the conference, abandoned Labour altogether, establishing the New Party (February, 1931) and then the British Union of Fascists.

What the Memorandum and the Manifesto sought was an employment-creating programme of home development based upon a substantial restructuring and modernization of the British economy. The proposals had both a short-term and a long-run dimension. In the long run, the objective should be a fundamental rationalization and reorganization of the nation's industrial base both to satisfy more fully the needs of the domestic market and to enable British industry to compete more effectively in those markets where competition was still a possibility. For the most part though, Mosley assumed that international markets would, for the future, be less important and that British industry was destined to become less export oriented. This was due first, to the growth of protectionism, secondly, in the aftermath of 1929, to the generally depressed state of world trade, and thirdly, to the rise of low-cost (labour) producers, particularly in East Asia, with whom British industrialists could not hope to compete while maintaining the living standards of their labour force. Thus Mosley mounted a fundamental challenge to the notion, underpinning the government's stance on economic policy, that Britain's economic fortunes would be restored and unemployment alleviated by an eventual revival of the export trades. For that reason his strategy of industrial regeneration was focused on the home market and was geared to greater national self-sufficiency, and to that end it sought to raise and maintain the level of purchasing power in the domestic economy.

To implement this programme of rationalization, restructuring and redirection, Mosley proposed a number of measures. First there should be a fundamental reorganization of the machinery of government to provide the strong central planning and control that his strategy required. Specifically, in the Memorandum, Mosley proposed the creation of a small executive committee under the chairmanship of the prime minister. This would include ministers with substantial economic responsibilities, advised by a "body of experts employed on a full-time basis by the state" and serviced by an independent secretariat of 12 senior civil servants.[4] Also, to be able to act swiftly and decisively, there would need to be a reform of parliamentary procedures to remove the traditional checks and balances that could so easily be used to obstruct the effective implementation of a radical strategy.[5]

In terms of institutional changes, Mosley also proposed the establishment of a development bank to fund the reorganization, re-equipment and modernization of British industry, rejecting the idea that the existing banking system could be relied upon to provide the necessary finance. As he saw it, the current tentative and ineffectual approach to rationalization on the part of the

Bank of England and the clearing banks was proof positive of the need for this. What Mosley had in mind, therefore, was something along the lines of a state finance corporation that would use substantial capital assets to fund and facilitate the process of restructuring.

Crucial to the whole strategy of modernization and expansion was the regulation of trade and the insulation of the domestic market from, among other things, the exogenous shocks of world price fluctuations, organized "dumping" and competition from "slave labour . . . in oriental countries."[6] Such regulation could also be used to provide a captive or near captive domestic market that a rationalized and re-structured manufacturing sector would service. For Mosley, in the Memorandum, trade should be regulated and planned by means of an import board, which would use its bulk purchasing powers to conclude favourable trading deals with Britain's trading partners. In addition, while he saw tariffs as largely ineffective in insulating the domestic market against currency fluctuations, they nevertheless had a place in the economic proposals put forward in the Manifesto. Thus commodity boards, representing producers and consumers, would grant the protection of tariffs on certain conditions related to pricing, efficiency improvements and the remuneration of workers in the industry concerned. In general terms what he sought, therefore, was "an organisation planning, allocating and regulating . . . trade rather than leaving these great things to the blind forces of world capitalistic competition."[7]

Internationally, free trade no longer existed. Adherence to it would be likely to promote a precipitate, forcible and unplanned restructuring of Britain's industrial base, exacerbating the problem of unemployment and causing long-term economic weakness. Conversely, protection would allow the country "consciously to choose the forms of production best suited to it and to see those industries were permanently established here, protected from the interference of quite arbitrary external factors".[8]

Imperial preference would also form an important part of this commercial policy and of national economic planning in general. As the authors of a pamphlet written in support of the Mosley Manifesto put it, "the Dominions have, for the most part, foodstuffs and raw materials to sell and we have manufactured goods to sell. This natural balance of trade should be developed under a commonwealth plan of mutual advantage."[9] Thus a restructured, rejuvenated and essentially industrial British economy would be complemented and serviced by a colonial periphery providing, for the most part, primary products.

Such were the essentials of the long-term strategy. In the short run, though, it would be necessary to tackle the problem of unemployment more directly. Indeed, as Mosley recognized, the rationalization and restructuring that he proposed would, in the short term, merely exacerbate the problem of unemployment. What he therefore put forward, after consulting with Keynes, was a £100 million road development programme and an additional £100 million programme of capital expenditure financed by government borrowing in the form of a development loan. This, together with a retirement pensions scheme and the raising of the school leaving age, would reduce unemployment by 700,000 within a year. Further, these measures would dovetail with the long-term dimension of the strategy by upgrading the nation's social and infrastructure, so helping to lay the basis of a more modern, advanced, competitive industrial economy, albeit one now geared to the servicing of domestic and empire markets more than previously. In addition the rise, or at least maintenance, of working-class purchasing power that these measures would secure would create a general economic climate more conducive to restructuring and ensure that it occurred with particular reference to the domestic market.

Economic planning, increased government investment expenditure, protection, imperial preference and greater national self-sufficiency in manufactured goods: these were the essentials of a strategy that would raise working-class living standards and, ultimately, guarantee a level of aggregate demand sufficient to eliminate and prevent the re-emergence of mass unemployment. It was essentially a defensive strategy based on the pessimistic premise that there could be no return to the level of exports that Britain had enjoyed in the nineteenth century. Yet it was too a strategy that sought to provide a radical alternative to the policy inertia induced by the melding of the Treasury and the Fabian mind. It is true that it was not manifestly socialist but, as Strachey and Mosley made clear, it did not in any sense involve the abandonment of socialist objectives. It was simply a temporary suspension of their pursuit or, more accurately, *un reculer pour mieux sauter*. Thus, as regards the extension of public ownership, Strachey wrote that "the immediate question is not a question of the ownership but of the survival of British industry. Let us put through an emergency programme to meet the national danger; afterwards political debate on fundamental principles can be resumed."[10] In effect, a rejuvenated capitalism was seen as a necessary prerequisite for future socialist advance, not least because it was a prerequisite for Labour's retention of political power.

In some superficial respects these proposals echoed those of mid-1920s liberal socialism, but the echoes are faint and distorted. For example, it is clear that the market was to play a less central role than that which Strachey and Mosley had previously ascribed to it in 1925. Certainly a prime objective was to raise working-class purchasing power and secure the salutary macroeconomic consequences that would result, but that rise was to be a consequence of what was proposed, not the agent of change. Thus central to the strategy was the idea of a preconceived national economic plan and a small, powerful, central economic committee that would play a highly interventionist and directive role in implementing it. In the mid-1920s, market-mediated working-class demand would determine planning priorities; by 1930, these priorities were to be predetermined by the "economic overlords". In short, in the mid-1920s planning was conceived of as reactive; in the Mosley proposals it was to be directive.

What was proposed also contrasts with the emphasis on the dispersal of economic power implied by the role given to the working-class consumer in *Revolution by reason*. Thus, in the 1930 proposals economic policy-making was to be concentrated in a few competent and powerful hands, while, in addition, existing parliamentary constraints on the exercise of that power were to be considerably loosened. The Mosley Manifesto and *Revolution by reason* did, however, have this in common. Both were rejected by the Labour Party and with that rejection in October 1930 went the last effective challenge to the dominance of economic orthodoxy. Thereafter the road was straight and untrammelled to the fiscal retrenchment proposed by the May Committee Report and the demise of the Labour Government that was to follow the attempt by MacDonald and Snowden to implement its recommendations.

Chapter 9

Socialist economic management and the stabilization of capitalism, 1931–40

> Socialist thinkers and economists have been too ready to ignore the overriding necessity of maintaining production and life in the transition period – a period likely to be long – during which the transfer of economic power to the state is being effected.
>
> E. F. M. Durbin, *The politics of democratic socialism*, 1940

The collapse of the Labour Government in 1931 and the political and economic circumstances surrounding that collapse raised certain fundamental questions about the nature and fate of capitalism, the general economic strategy to which Labour had been committed and the theoretical basis upon which it had rested. These were questions which, in the 1930s, socialist thinkers had therefore to address as a matter of urgency and the answers that they furnished had a profound impact on the evolution of socialist political economy in Britain in that decade.

A number of writers were to tackle these issues and indeed the early 1930s witnessed the formation of a number of groups that fostered a rethinking of many aspects of socialist political economy and Labour Party economic thinking, both critical and prescriptive. Thus even before the demise of the Labour Government, the New Fabian Research Bureau (NFRB) was established in March 1931 in order to remedy the paucity of ideas as to how to tackle the growing economic crisis. The Bureau initiated research on international, political and economic issues and it enlisted the services of an impressive array of economic expertise that included, among others, Hugh Gaitskell, E. F. M. Durbin, James Meade and Colin Clark – Durbin and Gaitskell in particular playing an important role in organizing the work of many of the economic committees that were set up under the Bureau's auspices.

The XYZ Club was founded in January 1932 by a few individuals who worked in the City and were sympathetic to the aims of the Labour Party. Here the key figures were Nicholas Davenport, Vaughan Berry and Cecil Spriggs, city editor of the *Manchester Guardian*. The aim was to educate the Party in the machinery of finance, a subject on which its leaders and members had hitherto shown a woeful ignorance. The Club therefore became a valuable source of advice on the financial aspects of Labour Party policy and one increasingly tapped by its policymakers. In addition, the financial experts were joined in 1934 by three socialist economists – E. F. M. Durbin, Hugh Gaitskell and Douglas Jay. In terms of its influence, as one writer has put it: "it has, indeed . . . some claim to have exercised, in a quiet sort of way, more influence on future government policy than any other group of the time and to have done so in the most private manner."[1]

Finally, there was the Society for Socialist Inquiry and Propaganda (SSIP) which was established in early 1931 with the dual aim of remedying the absence of socialist thinking within the Labour Party and popularizing socialist ideas. It involved, among others, Ernest Bevin, G. D. H. Cole, Colin Clark, E. F. Wise and H. N. Brailsford. Under its auspices lecture courses were initiated and study guides and reports produced. It existed for only a short time (1931–2) but, in the words of one its members, Margaret Cole, it "did a good deal to galvanise up-to-date thinking within the labour movement."[2]

These organizations provided part of the institutional apparatus within which and by means of which a process of ideological revision was set in train. The ideas and the policies that they generated went a long way to tackle the questions mentioned above and often fed through into Party policy-making and the economic literature that Labour produced in this period, particularly via the Finance and Trade Committee of the National Executive, chaired by the formidable Hugh Dalton. This Committee was a prime initiator of discussion, research and new thinking within the Labour Party and made considerable use of the output of the NFRB and the XYZ Club. In addition, the fact that the Committee had as members trained economists such as Gaitskell and Durbin was something that not only fostered economic thinking within the Party but also, undoubtedly, enhanced the quality of the thinking that was done.

It is also worth noting here more specifically that in the 1930s there was, for the first time, a generation of university-educated economists with socialist or at least Labour Party sympathies upon whose ideas the Party could draw and who could be incorporated into its policy-making structures. In the 1920s it could avail itself of the services of few such individuals; by the 1930s an embarrassment of intellectual riches was available to it. Evan Durbin, Hugh Gaitskell, Colin Clark and James Meade all read politics, philosophy and economics at Oxford. Durbin moved on to take up a fellowship at University College and then a lectureship in economics at the London School of Economics. Gaitskell after working for a year as a Workers' Educational Association tutor, became a lecturer in economics at University College London. Colin Clark became a research assistant at the LSE and Meade began his long and illustrious career as an economist with an Oxford fellowship, a career that in the

1930s involved participation in the Keynesian revolution and its aftermath. Douglas Jay read Greats not PPE at Oxford, but an All Souls fellowship was secured by a paper on neoclassical economics and he took up a post on *The Economist* in 1933. In short, in the 1930s all those mentioned had careers as professional economists, while, at the same time, their services were available to the Labour Party.

Any discussion of political economy and the Labour Party in this decade must therefore begin with their work. For, directly and indirectly, they had a definite influence upon the formulation of economic policy. That said, the economic writing of the "non-professionals" must not be neglected and in this chapter consideration will also be given to the work of G. D. H. Cole and John Strachey. In terms of central themes this chapter will discuss the opinions of these writers on the likelihood and means of stabilizing British capitalism prior to further socialist advance, while the next will consider their views on the construction and operation of a socialist economy once that task had been accomplished.

E. F. M. Durbin

E. F. M. Durbin's first major book *Purchasing power and trade depression* was published in 1933. With respect to the work of the writers mentioned above, it is unique. For while accepting capitalism's capacity to rebound, eventually, from the depths of the slump, it denied that policies were available to a social democratic government that would in any significant sense accelerate the process. Strachey too, of course, consistently with the brand of Marxism-Leninism that he espoused in the early 1930s, denied the efficacy of any of the mooted social democratic remedies for depression. However, unlike Durbin, he also asserted that capitalism's demise was imminent and inevitable. For Durbin this was not so. Market forces would ultimately ensure that capitalism emerged phoenix-like from the economic ashes, even if at some considerable economic cost.

In fact Durbin was soon to shift from the position that he took up in *Purchasing power* and throw off the policy inertia that it implied, but it is none the less important to consider this work at the outset because it established a large part of the theoretical basis that underpinned his subsequent analysis and policy proposals. An understanding of it is therefore central to our appreciation of Durbin's contribution to economic debate within the Labour Party and among socialist economic thinkers in the 1930s.

The work provided an analysis of the causes of economic depression in terms of the economic fluctuations that Durbin saw as endemic to capitalism. It drew theoretical inspiration from a number of sources but most obviously from

Friedrich Hayek's *Prices and production* (1930), Keynes's *Treatise on money* (1930) and D. H. Robertson's *Banking policy and the price level* (1926). The influence of Hayek was, however, manifestly the strongest and in this context it is pertinent to note that he and Durbin where colleagues at the LSE in the early 1930s and that Hayek read and made suggestions for the improvement of Durbin's *Purchasing power* prior to its publication.

Durbin accepted Hayek's fundamental proposition that the trade cycle was caused by an expansion of credit to capital goods producers, which permitted an increase in the level of their investment beyond what was warranted by the voluntary savings of the community. This predisposition on the part of the banking system to overexpand credit he saw as resulting, in large part, from a desire to stabilize prices when the improvements in efficiency that followed capital investment should have dictated a fall in prices in line with costs. Price stabilization in this context, with costs falling, produced windfall profits and this in turn touched off a wave of further investment, which the banking system sought to accommodate. In addition, Durbin believed that as a result of previous waves of overinvestment there existed a state of near-permanent excess capacity in the capital goods sector, a situation that encouraged owners to borrow to set that capacity in motion at the least sign of recovery.

Eventually, though, there would come a point when the banking system would be forced to contract credit for prudential reasons to protect its cash reserve ratio. Thus "the banks to protect themselves refuse to extend credit any further and to offset the new outflow of cash, they may even seek to reduce the outstanding volume of credit."[3] However, investment by capital goods producers had been proceeding on the expectation of continuing windfall profits; but now, with this contraction of credit and its resultant deflationary impact, such expectations were destined to be frustrated. As Durbin described it, "At once it becomes unprofitable and even impossible to complete the existing plans of investment . . . As soon as the Rate of Investment falls to a lower level, the whole existing structure of production is rendered unstable because the contraction in the stream of active money will exert *a depressing effect on the price level of consumption goods and render still further degrees of investment unprofitable.* A cumulative process of losses, contraction and bankruptcy must begin" and "a contraction in real investment".[4] Moreover, this depression in the capital goods sector would be relatively rapidly transmitted to the consumer goods sector with general economic depression and mass unemployment eventuating. "This", wrote Durbin, "is the period of maximum depression."[5]

Now such a theoretical stance might lead one to expect that Durbin would argue for an increase in public investment or an expansionary monetary policy as a means of setting things to rights in the capital goods sector and thereby reversing the cumulative contraction in economic activity. It was, after all, the contraction in credit by the banking system that precipitated the downward spiral. However, in 1933, Durbin's response to such policies was that of a good Hayekian. It was negative. As he saw it, the cautious pursuit of such expansionary policies would do "nothing or very little to improve things";[6] while if they were more vigorously pursued they would "merely repeat the Trade Cycle and lead to a new crisis".[7] In the latter case, what Durbin feared was that expansionary measures would set in motion the kind of inflationary boom that would ultimately add further to the problem of excess capacity in the capital goods sector. Thus "the economic system is between the devil of unemployment in the capital goods industries and the very deep waters of unbridled inflation."[8]

For Durbin there were, in fact, only two ways out of the depression that afflicted capitalism in the early 1930s. "Either the rate of voluntary saving must be increased" to allow a non-windfall-profits-based expansion of investment, an expansion that did not sow the seeds of a subsequent slump, or there must be a "slow and painful" elimination of excess capacity in the capital goods sector.[9] To increase voluntary saving Durbin believed it would be necessary to redistribute wealth in favour of those with a relatively high propensity to save. This was unacceptable on grounds of equity alone, for it involved a redistribution from those with lower to those with higher incomes. "It therefore seems to me that there is no real alternative to the slow and painful readjustment of the structure of production to a lower rate of capital accumulation . . . *a boom has to be expiated by economic pain and ills sufficient to satisfy the most neurotic and sadistic inflationists.*"[10] The problem here, of course, was that this might be politically disastrous for "it is unlikely that the opinion of democracy has yet reached a significantly advanced state to permit the execution of a policy which involves the continuance of immediate distress".[11]

As to the longer-term objective of taming the trade cycle, Durbin was more optimistic. A contracyclical monetary policy aimed at stabilizing prices he ruled out as certain to set in motion inflationary pressures and thence to cause a future boom and subsequent slump. But he did suggest that a monetary policy aimed at keeping consumer *money income* stable might do the trick. This would necessitate an active policy of monetary management and it would also involve a measure of price deflation. However this deflation would follow from a real fall in production costs; it would be slow and steady and would be the way of transmitting the benefits of increased production to a consumer whose *money income* remained stable. The important point, though, is that in *Purchasing power*, the policy prescriptions that Durbin did furnish were focused on the long run. They were not relevant to the immediate problems that confronted British capitalism – mass unemployment and general economic depression.

However, as regards those problems, Durbin, under the influence of James Meade, was soon to jettison his negative policy stance. This can be seen in *The problem of credit policy* published in 1935, though the shift is prefigured in his *Socialist credit policy*, which appeared shortly after *Purchasing power* in 1933. He wrote in 1935, "it no longer seems to me to be true that the only method of bringing equilibrium out of Trade Cycle fluctuations lies in further deflating during the period of depression", and went on to suggest a combination of monetary and fiscal policy that would "banish unemployment forever" and "double the standard of living in thirty years".[12]

In the 1935 work Durbin retained his two-sector – consumer goods and producer goods – model of the economy. Again, as in 1933, he believed that problems might arise as a result of an over-expansion (in relation to available voluntary savings) of the capital goods sector, financed by bank credit. Again the emergence of excess capacity in this sector was what was seen as precipitating a general contraction in the level of economic activity. However, whereas in 1933 Durbin had rejected a contracyclical policy of price stabilization as inflationary and therefore destabilizing, by 1935 he discussed, in positive terms, the use of producer and consumer credits as a means to that end, the aim being to ensure that real income increased in line with the output of final goods. Yet, while it might be possible in theory to secure price stabilization by such expedients, he accepted that the practice of such a contracyclical policy would prove difficult in the context of an individualistic capitalism. Specifically the adverse impact on business confidence of such policies could neutralize their impact. It might also be difficult, once such a policy had been embarked upon, to prevent the simultaneous expansion of consumer credits and credit to producers.

There was though another possible way forward. "It would not be utterly impossible," wrote Durbin in 1935, "even within the present institutions of our economy to unbalance the budget continuously and make up the deficit by the issue of varying amounts of unbonded credit to an amount determined by the course of physical productivity." That is, unfunded budget deficits could be used to create the necessary increase in purchasing power to prevent price deflation occurring with rising output.[13] But again, because of the adverse impact of such a radical departure from fiscal orthodoxy on business confidence, Durbin had doubts about the efficacy of such a policy.

However, whatever expedients were adopted, Durbin believed that what was crucially necessary was closer public control over the conduct of monetary policy: "the initiation", as he put it, "of the fundamental institutions of a Planned Money". For Durbin that need not necessarily mean the nationalization of the banking system, though in the early 1930s he was prepared to advocate that; however, it did entail what he termed "a monetary system planned under a unified control".[14] Thus the central bank should have the authority to control the policy of "every organ which directly affects the flow of money income and expenditure" and would do so "in the light of its knowledge of the existing financial and industrial position and future trends". Such control was necessary if the problem of depression was to be tackled and absolutely vital to the kind of long period credit policy necessary to "remove the inherent instability of industrial circulation, cure the Trade Cycle or achieve the stabilisation of prices in the long run".[15] Financial planning and the institutional structure that permitted it were fundamental prerequisites for policies designed to solve the immediate problem of unemployment and, for the future, prevent the incidence of booms and their attendant slumps.

As to the specifics of a strategy to counter depression, Durbin recommended a cheap money policy pursued in conjunction with open market operations (to increase the liquidity of the banking system), government guarantees upon private investment, public works schemes and direct government investment. Taken together such a package could raise purchasing power to the point where unemployment in the consumer goods sector was reduced to zero. As regards the non-inflationary elimination of unemployment in the capital goods sector, Durbin looked to the rise in the level of voluntary saving which would attend an increase in national income as the economy moved out of depression. In addition, as the recovery got under way, the government could take an increasing fraction of the rising money incomes which would result "either in the form of voluntary loans or by taxation for the purposes of capital expenditure".[16] In this way Durbin believed it might simultaneously control the level of consumer expenditure and the level of capital investment in a way that both secured employment objectives and prevented the emergence of inflation. To the extent that the government was successful, the trade cycle would be tamed and a *permanently* high level of employment could be secured in the economy as a whole. Dynamism and stability could be realized prior to the demise of capitalism and the emergence of a full-blown socialist economy.

In contrast to *Purchasing power and the trade depression*, therefore, and despite continuing reservations about some elements of an expansionary strategy, Durbin's 1935 view as to what could be done is decidedly positive and optimistic:

> Theoretical reasoning seems to establish an extremely strong a priori case for believing that a centralised Banking Authority will remedy precisely those deficiencies from which our existing monetary system suffers . . . Disastrous fluctuations in economic activity could be cured forever and the more elastic free moving policy of stable prices be safely pursued. A new financial machine and a redistribution of power within it might release for another century the productive powers of mankind.[17]

The period between *The problem of credit policy* and Durbin's next major work, *The politics of democratic socialism* (1940), saw the publication of Keynes's *The general theory of employment, interest and money* (1936). The *Politics* has therefore sometimes been seen as part of the revisionism set in motion by the permeation of Keynesian ideas within the Labour Party, a permeation manifest certainly in works such as Douglas Jay's *The socialist case* (1937) and James Meade's *Introduction to economic analysis and policy* (1936). Yet the contracyclical or, as he termed them, "prosperity" measures advocated by Durbin in 1940 were really no different from those that he had advanced before the appearance of *The general theory*. Thus he was as clear in 1940 as he had been in 1935 that depression could be dissipated by an expansionary monetary and fiscal policy and that if a contracyclical policy "were pursued with sufficient vigour it would prove possible to control the volume of business activity and to use that control to prevent all large scale fluctuations in it".[18] Indeed in 1940 he was sufficiently optimistic to believe that it would be possible to "reduce general unemployment to zero and maintain it there indefinitely".[19] While, therefore, *The general theory* may have helped confirm Durbin in his thinking as to what needed to be done, it did not significantly alter the salient characteristics of the macroeconomic strategy he proposed. Further, Durbin was critical of the fact that the work did not deal with the dynamic problem of fluctuations. As such it did not address the problem of how to avoid sowing the seeds of an inflationary boom when tackling the problem of slump and unemployment. To a very large extent, therefore, Durbin arrived at the position he occupied in 1940 independently of Keynes, though not, it must be said, of Hayek. In 1940 he was critical too, as he had been throughout the 1930s, of any reliance upon a purely Keynesian strategy.

Durbin was convinced that if depression was to be finally eliminated from the economic system it would be necessary for the government to assume a wide range of economic responsibilities. Social control of the economy would have to be extended and monetary and budgetary policy conducted with an eye to a very different range of objectives than previously, e.g. the level of capacity utilization, the volume of output, the price level, the level of consumer income and the state of employment. To fulfil these responsibilities it would also be necessary to extend public ownership and to provide the state with whatever additional powers it required to replace individual economic decision-making by planning in significant areas of economic life. Only then would the economic basis of a socialist society be laid. As Durbin put it in 1935, "before a superior form of social life which is free from personal indignity, free from arbitrary authority and free from class distinctions can be brought into existence the fundamental institutions of property and profits must be replaced by the institutions of social authority in economic affairs."[20] However, a consideration of Durbin's discussion of how exactly this might be done must be reserved for the next chapter.

James Meade

In contrast to Durbin the influence on Meade of Keynes and the young generation of Keynesian economists, sometimes referred to as the Cambridge Circus, was profound. Meade was an early convert to the belief that the stabilization of capitalism at a full employment level of output was possible and took an important part in the discussions of Keynes's work that preceded and followed the publication of *The general theory*. His *Introduction to economic analysis* clearly rests on Keynesian foundations. Certainly the work is imbued with a Keynesian optimism that the faults in capitalism that had caused mass unemployment were remediable. At the outset Meade asserts: "we can start by dismissing the theory that there is some fundamental flaw in the existing monetary and pricing system . . . the problem of unemployment is capable of solution *without any revolutionary changes in our economic system*."[21] Monetary and fiscal policy could be conducted in a market economy in such a way as to ensure that the problem of unemployment was solved. Pump-priming public expenditure together with a reduction of interest rates by the banking system would be sufficient to stimulate private investment and move the economy in the direction of full employment. As regards the balance between monetary and fiscal policy the "reduction of interest rates by monetary policy" was to be "the main permanent instrument of control" while "increased public expenditure on public works above the normal should be regarded as only a temporary measure".[22]

With respect to maintaining the investment component of aggregate demand, Meade acknowledged the problem of time lags: lags between the initial decision to increase public investment and the time when that decision bore fruit in terms of actual employment-creating investment expenditure. There was, however, no such problem with the consumption component. There is, Meade wrote, "a form of expenditure which should be capable of almost simultaneous expansion and that is the purchase of consumption goods by individuals".[23] Here he suggested the possibility of a contracyclical use of the existing unemployment insurance scheme. The idea was that contributions from workers and employers should be levied at a rate that would just make the scheme self-financing at a "standard volume of unemployment". When the volume of unemployment was above this level, receipts would be less than payments and the difference would be covered by "new notes issued by the Bank of England"; when unemployment was below the standard rate, then the excess of receipts over payments would be used to pay off the Unemployment Assistance Board's debt to the Bank. Along the same lines, Meade also suggested that the taxation of income could be varied in a comparable way and with similar objectives. Thus "consumer credits" built up in times of prosperity when tax revenue exceeded expenditure would be repaid in less prosperous times to boost consumer demand. Meade acknowledged that for such a system to work governments would have to have "the power, intelligence and courage to raise and lower rates of taxation at the appropriate time" but, potentially, this was an instrument that could be quickly used, and to powerful effect, on the level of aggregate demand.[24]

Presciently, Meade also discussed the problem of inflation were such a policy to be pursued. Here he quite clearly envisaged some kind of trade-off between unemployment and inflation and some non-inflationary level of unemployment. Thus he wrote of a "standard" volume of unemployment where money wage rates rose in non-inflationary fashion at the same rate as the marginal productivity of labour. However, this "standard" rate could also be considerably reduced "if those who are responsible for fixing money wage rates [would] refrain from demanding a rise in wage rates as long as there is any considerable volume of unemployment".[25] Some kind of restraint as regards wage claims was therefore necessary if employment policies of the kind that Meade was proposing were to be successful. As we shall see there was much in this that anticipated the kind of policy positions that adherents of Keynesianism within the Labour Party would take up in the post-war period.

Douglas Jay

Douglas Jay's treatment of depression in *The socialist case* was also indebted to Keynes both directly through his reading of the *The general theory* and indirectly through Meade's *Introduction*. However, Jay was also clearly influenced by the work of J. A. Hobson and E. F. M. Durbin. As this might suggest, the work is characterized more by its eclecticism than by its theoretical coherence. However, the essential thrust of his argument is the same as that of Meade; the failure of capitalism to work in such a way as to fully utilize labour and other resources *can* be remedied prior to the advent of full-blown socialism.

Jay began by considering, sympathetically, the view that over-saving was at the root of capitalism's macroeconomic difficulties. This argument, as he saw it, did not depend for its force on the idea that saving represented a leak from aggregate demand. Rather, its substance lay in the notion of sectoral disequilibrium, with over-saving producing excessive investment in the expansion of productive capacity and, simultaneously, a fall in the demand for consumer goods sufficient to cause their prices to fall below costs of production. J. A. Hobson is referred to as "the most distinguished representative of this school of thought"; but, while recognizing Durbin's very different explanation of the causes of over-saving, Jay also saw his *Purchasing power and trade depression* (1933), as proceeding along similar lines. These deflationary pressures in the consumer goods sector would ultimately have an adverse effect on the demand for producer goods and so a cumulative contraction in the level of economic activity would be triggered. "Neither on theoretical or empirical grounds. . . does it seem possible to doubt", wrote Jay, "that a rapid increase in savings will cause general losses in the consumer goods trades and consequently a fall in the demand for capital goods. It is almost bound, therefore, to start a cumulative deflation."[26]

Jay then proceeded to discuss Keynes, both his position in the *Treatise on money*, where fluctuations in the general level of economic activity were seen as resulting from a deviation of aggregate savings from aggregate investments and in *The general theory*, when actual saving and actual investment were assumed to be equal but not necessarily at a full employment level of output. As Jay saw it, both works emphasized increased investment as the primary means of eliminating depression and unemployment. In the *Treatise* this was to be brought about by reducing the rate of interest in long-term capital markets; in *The general theory* it was to be achieved by an increase in public investment expenditure.

Jay himself believed that an increase in consumption and/or investment expenditure would do the trick. However, like Meade, he considered that the best and most "direct and beneficial way" to move the economy out of a slump was "to stimulate consumption".[27] He also believed, like Durbin, that a recovery produced by increased investment could sow the seeds of a subsequent slump. Thus Hobson, Durbin and Keynes, in different ways, underpinned Jay's policy prescriptions.

Like Meade, Jay also argued that consumption should be stimulated not by way of an increase in wages but by other means. Here, among other things, Jay suggested a reduction in indirect taxation and a remission of working-class rates, both of which were to be financed by a budget deficit. His reason for suggesting these expedients was that in altering the ratio between costs and profits a straightforward rise in wages would adversely affect profitability, dampen the demand for capital goods and so trigger off a cumulative contraction in the level of economic activity.[28]

A concern with sectoral imbalance, which in large measure derives from the influence of Durbin, also manifests itself in Jay's discussion of a situation where the consumer goods industries were operating at full capacity and earning "normal" profits, while excess capacity existed in the producer goods trades. In such circumstances increased government expenditure would simply precipitate a rise in the price of consumer goods and inflict "forced saving" on the population as a whole. Given this, it would be necessary for the government to act to maintain effective demand while prohibiting and/or taxing new investment. Such a policy Jay believed would "effect a transfer of resources into the consumers' trades". "Alternatively, the surplus labour and capital in the producers' trades might be taken on directly by the Government and used for the production of consumers' necessities".[29] Such policies, Jay recognized, would involve substantial interference by a socialist government with the interests of consumer, worker and capitalist. Jay also argued at this time that the nationalization of the Bank of England would be necessary to implement an effective demand management policy.

In the case of Durbin, Meade and Jay we have professional or university educated economists, embarking on the task of revising socialism in the light of a prolonged period of mass unemployment and within the framework of what may be loosely termed mainstream economics. Yet in the 1930s this undertaking was not the exclusive preserve of the professionals. Others too played a part, in the case of John Strachey a unique one.

John Strachey

Durbin, Meade and Jay can be seen as insiders with the opportunity to influence Labour Party thinking through the policy-making structures that it had established. Strachey in contrast was an outsider. During the greater part of the 1930s he was associated with the Communist Party and in works such as *The coming struggle for power* (1932), *The nature of capitalist crisis* (1935) and *The theory and practice of socialism* (1936), he showed himself to the be most effective popularizer of Marxism-Leninism in the English language. Prior to the Seventh Congress of the Communist International, 1935, this had led him to damn western capitalism as doomed to imminent demise; fascism was interpreted as a last desperate throw of the political dice to salvage it, and the reformist policies of social democratic parties were branded "social fascist". The political economy that he and other communists advanced to underpin this position was correspondingly long on the critical analysis of capitalism's irremediable flaws and correspondingly short on policy proposals that stopped short of a revolutionary transition to an economy run on Soviet lines. However, after the Seventh Congress the Communist International altered its position and adopted a policy of seeking to secure the support and co-operation of social democratic parties in a "popular front" aimed at arresting the rise of fascism; there arose the urgent need to formulate economic policies that would provide a basis for such co-operation, polices that, at the same time, would lay the basis for the transition to a socialist economy.

Strachey was quick to grasp that a popular front politics entailed a fundamental revision of the political economy to which the Communist Party had previously adhered. It required in short the formulation of a popular front economics, an economics that would involve both a reassessment of the longevity of capitalism and an economic strategy consistent with its short-run survival. Only on this basis could co-operation with a social democratic party such as that of Labour proceed. *A programme for progress* (1940) sought to provide just that. While, therefore, Durbin, Jay and Meade aimed to revise the Fabian gradualism that had contributed to the disaster of 1931, Strachey's task was that of revising a Marxism that had failed to engage constructively with the fundamental problems that the British economy confronted. In fact, the positions to which their respective revisionisms led them were remarkably similar and Strachey may, in fact, be seen as playing a important role in popularizing the revisionist political economy that emerged in the 1930s and, also, in popularizing it among those who would not have read, or have wanted to read, the works of Durbin, Meade and Jay. His role was the vital one of both expounding and broadening support for a new socialist political economy.

Strachey's Marxism had led him to believe that capitalism's basic defect was that it was on the one hand characterized by an inherent tendency for the rate of profit to fall; on the other, it was afflicted by economic depressions caused by a deficient demand stemming from the impoverishment of labour. To the extent that the latter problem was resolved by a rise in working-class incomes the former problem would become more acute. To the extent that the problem of profitability was successfully addressed, wage costs must fall and the problem of deficient demand would be exacerbated. In short, twentieth-century capitalism was between a rock and a hard place.

However, by the late 1930s, Strachey had come to believe that the dilemma might be temporarily resolved if a way could be found of increasing demand that did not at the same time increase costs, squeeze profitability and imperil the dynamism of capitalism. Two ways were open: a redistributive fiscal policy and an expansionary monetary policy. To pursue the latter Strachey believed it would be necessary to nationalize the Bank of England and "the seven considerable joint stock banks". That done, the banking system could be made to furnish the funds necessary for the state to embark upon a capital investment programme. It could also lend to private entrepreneurs who were "willing to produce either independently or in conjunction with the government, the roads, schools, hospitals and houses, which the nation required".[30] Such a monetary policy would not adversely affect the rate of profit of capitalist enterprises; on the contrary by reducing the cost of finance and increasing capacity utilization it would be likely to raise it. The tendency for the rate of profit to fall could therefore be reversed at the same time as the problem of deficient demand was tackled.

The second manner in which aggregate demand could be increased was by way of a redistributive fiscal policy in favour of those, the working-classes, with a relatively high propensity to consume. Now given the dilemma that Strachey believed capitalism confronted, his chief concern here was to effect this redistribution by means that would not impinge upon the rate of profit and thus adversely affect the employment of labour. What he suggested, therefore, was that increased taxation should fall on the "rentier and financier interest". This would mean an increase in tax revenue derived from rent and interest payments, which could be used to finance increased family allowances, old age pensions and unemployment benefits. Thus the "mass of the population" would benefit, their purchasing power would be increased, while capitalist profits and thence the dynamism of the system would remain relatively unaffected.[31] Like Meade, therefore, Strachey believed that increasing purchasing power in the hands of the working-class consumer was crucial to the solution of the immediate and pressing problem of unemployment and that that, in turn, was a necessary prerequisite for the construction of a socialist economy.

G. D. H. Cole

Finally, as regards the stabilization policies put forward by socialist writers in the 1930s, it is necessary to consider the work of G. D. H. Cole, who, after the comparative silence of the 1920s, published extensively on economic questions in the following decade.

Even in *The next ten years* (1929), a work that appeared immediately prior to the onset of the great depression, Cole had sought to alert his readers to the weakness of British capitalism and the problems this posed for a smooth transition to socialism. In the past, he stated, "socialists [had] argued about the form of the future society and the best means of attaining it" while taking "the stability of the capitalist order for granted" and "treating capitalism with the respect due to a going concern".[32] However, although, by 1929, unemployment had fallen significantly from its 1921 peak, exports had risen to 81 per cent of their 1913 level and the economy was showing other signs of strength, it was still, for Cole, no longer permissible to view capitalism in that way; it could no longer be taken as a "going concern". For socialists it was imperative, therefore, to tackle capitalism's immediate failings and their adverse economic consequences; it was necessary to stabilize capitalism in a manner that would lay the basis for its subsequent socialist transcendence. How exactly that could be done was, in substance, the intellectual challenge that Cole took up in much of what he wrote in the 1930s.

Yet despite Cole's forebodings as to the stability and dynamism of capitalism, it must be said that the spectre of *imminent* breakdown did not haunt the pages of *The next ten years*. British capitalism may not have been displaying the kind of economic buoyancy that characterized the pre-war period but there was no need to anticipate its immediate demise. By 1931, however, Cole's view of things had changed radically. In an article, appositely entitled "The crisis", written with Ernest Bevin and published by the *New Statesman and Nation* in October of that year, Cole made clear that even the "drastic proposals" he was advancing might prove "less than the situation requires; for it is hardly possible to exaggerate its gravity". What he had to offer, therefore, was very much in the nature of "*an attempt . . . to avert collapse.*"[33] Indeed, at this date, he was profoundly pessimistic about the prospect of capitalist stabilization. For Cole, capitalism was teetering on the edge of the economic abyss and, in consequence, he himself teetered on the brink of accepting the necessity of its revolutionary transformation.

But even in 1931, and more so subsequently, the spirit of Keynes and Bevin prevailed over that of Marx and Lenin. Both Cole and capitalism clawed their way back from the brink. For if, in "The crisis", Cole's policy prescriptions were based only on the "*assumption*" that the temporary stabilization of capitalism was "still possible if we use our wits" and the *assumption* that "a transition to a better system" could therefore be made "without an intervening period of sheer chaos and disaster", that assumption was increasingly taken as fact, as the 1930s progressed and western capitalism regained a measure of stability.[34]

In the early 1930s Cole tackled the problem of stabilizing capitalism and preparing the ground for socialism with considerable urgency and on a number of fronts. To begin with, there was what could be achieved by way of monetary and exchange rate policy, something that involved consideration of both the domestic and the international dimension of the problems that British capitalism confronted. As his starting point Cole took Keynes's *Treatise on money*, in which the latter had argued that the central banks of the major creditor nations should co-operate in the pursuit of an expansionary monetary policy designed to raise and then stabilize the level of world wholesale prices, the aim being to restore levels of profitability internationally by widening the gap between costs and prices and also to reduce the real indebtedness of debtor nations. Cole considered such a policy in an article published in 1931 and agreed that currency and credit could "be issued in accordance with the expansion of world productive power . . . so as to keep world prices stable."[35] He also argued, though, that if such a policy was to have the benefits envisaged, there was need for a thoroughgoing revision of international debts and, in particular, the termination of reparations payments. However, Cole was soon to express grave doubts about the overall feasibility of such a strategy. Thus he noted that it was difficult to compile a general price index for a single country and he went on to state that it would be "impossible to compile such an index for all countries taken together".[36] In the absence of such an index, as he recognized, the practicability of international price stabilization must be called into question. Also, the degree of international economic co-operation necessary for the "world system of currency management" required to attempt the stabilization of the general level of world prices would, he argued, be unlikely to be forthcoming.

What then of internal price stabilization as a means of putting capitalism on firmer foundations? In his 1931 article Cole saw it as an objective worth pursuing. His fear, however, was that, the pursuit of internal price stability would prove inimical to exchange rate stability and that would hinder the recovery of world trade. Also, following on from this, if the emphasis was placed on managing a national currency with the objective of stabilizing internal prices, that, for Cole, removed the possibility of recreating "a single world currency valued equally in every country" to replace the Gold Standard that had been abandoned by Britain and 26 other countries in September 1931.[37] This absence of an international medium of exchange he saw as a serious matter, a major obstacle to international recovery. His hope, therefore, was that somehow it would be possible to reconstitute some kind of "modified gold standard which would be compatible with price stability".[38] This, though, remained an aspiration rather than a well articulated policy.

This aside, Cole argued in his 1931 article that despite the adverse international consequences it might involve, monetary policy should be pursued by a nationalized Bank of England in such a manner as to halt the downward trend of domestic prices. By 1932, however, the emphasis was shifted from price stabilization to a monetary policy managed "not to stabilise prices but to interfere with their free movement as little as possible and to adjust the supply of money to the needs of a community at a price level *whose changes are determined by the efficiency of production*".[39] He was to make the point again in 1933, when he wrote of the "considerable dangers" of pursuing the objective of price stabilization and of the need to allow prices to fall in line with productivity.[40] The words might have come from the pen of Evan Durbin.

However, in the 1933 piece, Cole added another element to his position, which rendered it distinct from that of Durbin, arguing that once, by way of an expansionary monetary policy, prices had been raised to a point where a measure of economic buoyancy had been restored the best policy was to let them fall "as productivity increases but not to the full extent of the increase of productivity, the balance being preserved *by a deliberate policy of raising wages* and also, where necessary, by using the instrument of taxation".[41] Cole's fear was that as productivity rose and prices fell, money wages might simply fall at the same rate or, with labour-displacing productivity gains, more rapidly. Either way the chronic tendency to deficient aggregate demand that characterized capitalism would re-emerge. For Cole, like Hobson, saw economic depression as a consequence of a maldistribution of income in favour of "capitalist recipients" who then saved and invested "in times of prosperity an unduly large part of the total available purchasing power".[42] The deficient demand for *final products* which resulted was what precipitated price deflation and unemployment. What was needed, therefore, were policies designed to raise the share of wages and/or the state's share of national income as productivity rose. Only that, together with the requisite monetary policy, would ensure the kind of increase in the demand for final goods necessary to put capitalism back on an even keel. To this end Cole discussed the possibility of issuing consumer credits or, in his words, "the creation of additional purchasing power in the form of non-repayable gifts".[43]

However, he undoubtedly had some reservations about such a policy; in part because it might be interpreted as an acceptance of the views of those such as Major C. H. Douglas, whom Cole and others saw and castigated as a currency crank, but also because he saw consumer credits as having a dangerous inflationary potential. Consumer credits could, therefore, be usefully employed only "*at exceptional times of deflation*".[44] In any case, he asked, "why should not the State create the required additional money and use it to pay wages to the unemployed in return for useful work of a non-competitive and not directly remunerative kind?"; that is work that would not exacerbate the inherent tendency over-investment. In this context, therefore, he advocated an extensive programme of state-financed public works along the lines that the Roosevelt administration was pursuing in the United States.

Like many others on the left Cole viewed what was happening in America with a mixture of hope, admiration and not a little scepticism, scepticism at least with respect to the New Deal's ultimate success. Indeed the New Deal must be seen as an important influence persuading many in the Labour Party to consider favourably expansionary policies of a kind that are normally associated with the name of Keynes. Cole wrote of Roosevelt's "courageous opportunism"[45] and that neatly captures his response and the reaction of many others. He admired the determination of Roosevelt to embark on a radical economic strategy; he applauded too his willingness to take on the opposition to his policies that he confronted in the business and political communities. At the same time Cole believed, with some justification, that the strategy was devoid of substantial theoretical underpinning and was largely driven by short-term considerations. Yet he admitted that while, in the past, he had believed that "no such planned and balanced development of economic forces could be achieved within the limits of a system based on private ownership and relying for its incentive to produce on the expectation of profit", his "scepticism [was] now rather of the long-run than of the short-run. I do not doubt the possibility, or even the probability, of American reflation being able to bring about "*a temporary revival*".[46] Something of the same should therefore be implemented in Britain: a strategy that would increase wages, raise demand and upgrade the social and industrial infrastructure of the nation, pursued in conjunction with an appropriate monetary policy.

So, in the 1930s, a number of socialist political economists put forward policies the object of which was to drag capitalism out of the economic abyss. They might differ over the urgency and the magnitude of the task; they might approach it with more or less enthusiasm and with degrees of optimism that varied between thinkers and over time. Yet all were agreed that the immediate objective of saving capitalism could be embarked upon with a reasonable expectation of success. Revolution was not necessary to break the log-jam that had blocked socialist progress. Contemporary economic theory and American practice both pointed a way forward. Reformist socialism was not redundant and if socialist advance had been interrupted an apposite combination of fiscal and monetary policies would both restore the momentum and lay the basis for an eventual transition to a fully socialist economy. But with what building blocks should such an economy be constructed, how should they be put together and on the basis of what principles would economic activity then proceed? It is with the answers that socialist political economists furnished to these questions in the 1930s that the next chapter is concerned.

Chapter 10
Building a socialist economy: the market, planning and public ownership, 1931–40

> The market mechanism will be neither retained as the tyrannical arbiter of the economy nor yet done away with and replaced by a predetermined plan, but . . . transformed until it itself becomes an instrument of the plan.
>
> John Strachey, *Left News*, 1941

Given then that the health of capitalism could, in large measure, be restored by the apposite combination of monetary, fiscal, exchange rate and wage policies, given that the evil of mass unemployment could be largely eliminated, living standards raised and economic progress resumed, what need was there for the building of a socialist economy and what form should the construction take?

As regards the first question, many emphasized the temporary nature of the respite that expansionary policies would provide, arguing that unless fundamental changes of a socialist nature were made to existing economic arrangements the forces making for depression would reassert themselves. What socialism offered to them was not only a way of ending the depression but also the establishment of a stable and balanced economic order as a safeguard against future slumps. Thus many socialist writers believed that while macroeconomic stabilization policies of the kind that they proposed would introduce a measure of order into capitalism, economic life would remain essentially anarchic and chaotic as long as economic decision-making was primarily rooted in a self-interested individualism. Only socialism would permit the conscious, rational, planned conduct of economic activity necessary to ensure long-term economic stability and thence sustained, non-cyclical economic growth.

Many also made the point that the *effective* implementation of the expansionary policies they advanced required further intervention in the economy along socialist lines. Thus the management of the level of aggregate investment would require publicly controlled institutions, such as a national investment board, whose activities would have a significant impact on the functioning of the capital market. Many also believed that it would necessitate a substantial extension of social ownership in order to furnish the means of controlling the investment plans of key sectors of industry. The apposite conduct of monetary policy would also require at least the nationalization of the Bank of England and, many believed, that of the joint stock banks as well.

Further, it was argued by some that intervention of the kind mooted to stabilize capitalism would probably damage what dynamism and vitality it still possessed because it would go some considerable way, in the words of Cole, to "undermine the incentives and initiative of private investors and private captains of industry without setting up in their place the new driving force of Socialism".[1] Again, to circumvent this difficulty, it would be necessary to extend social ownership in order to establish motives for efficient productive activity other than those of profit and pecuniary gain.

Finally, many writers accepted that while economic stabilization policies laid the basis for a substantial improvement in the material position of the working classes and a more equitable distribution of wealth, further measures of a socialist kind would be required to realize more fully the ideals of liberty, equality and fraternity. Specifically, they emphasized the fundamental role that an extension of public ownership would play in the business of redistribution alongside redistributive taxation.

Socialism was therefore seen by writers in the 1930s as essential for *sustained* economic and social progress and this chapter is concerned with what, in economic terms, the transition to a socialist economy would actually entail. Specifically it will focus on socialist discussion of the nature, instruments and objectives of planning, the role of public ownership and the problem of rational economic calculation in a planned economy. While, therefore, the previous chapter was concerned with how socialist political economists believed capitalism might be saved, this is concerned with their views as to how it might be transformed.

As we have seen, Fabians, such as the Webbs, stressed the importance of the scientific management of economic affairs on the basis of public ownership. Under the socialist commonwealth they envisaged collective decision-making rather than egotistic impulses would determine the quantity and quality of what was produced, the distribution of the national product and the allocation of scarce resources. The Webbs looked, therefore, to a planned economy, though, with the possible exception of their *Constitution for the socialist commonwealth of Great Britain*, they contributed little to a political economy of planning or to the discussion of the problem of economic calculation under socialism. That said, they were clear that the market could not be accommodated within their vision of a socialist economy and, as the 1930s progressed, they were to view with increasing enthusiasm the marketless planning that was pursued in the Soviet Union. In contrast, liberal socialists such as Hobson viewed things differently. The market, given a more equitable distribution of wealth, could be used to transmit to producers and planners a relatively accurate conception of what society wanted and how best, therefore, the nation's resources might be allocated.

For the most part the writers with whom we will be concerned in this chapter also believed that planning and the market could be reconciled; with important exceptions, most notably G. D. H. Cole, they believed that, given certain preconditions, the market could be used as a means of determining prices and gathering the information necessary for the economic calculations and decision-making of socialist planners. In short, what the 1930s witnessed, and what this chapter discusses, is the resurgence of a liberal or market socialism.

Barbara Wootton: Fabian echoes

In the 1930s Barbara Wootton was one important participant in the debate among socialist political economists that revolved around planning and the market in the context of a socialist economy. Here her major contribution was *Plan or no plan* (1934) a work that influenced, in addition to others, the young Douglas Jay. In some respects this book, like that of many of the writers whose work will be discussed in this chapter, reflected a positive attitude to the market mechanism. However, at the same time, it expressed definite Fabian reservations and concerns about how it might be accommodated within a planned socialist economy. The positive aspect comes across clearly at the outset of the book with Wootton stressing that before any consideration of the failings of the price mechanism or any search for possible substitutes could be usefully undertaken it was imperative to understand the functions it had performed and what the market economy had actually achieved. "It is only if we clearly understand the job that a piece of machinery has to do . . . that we can judge the efficiency of its working" and "before we make any criticism of this form of organisation, we must give due weight to the commonplace that in the last century and a half this system has provided the mass of people with an abundance and a variety of forms of consumption never before equalled in the history of mankind".[2] Such a view of things and such a positive attitude to the market, expressed as it was in 1934, certainly marked a significant break with most of what had gone before.

As Wootton saw it there was "nothing in the nature of the price mechanism which would prevent it from functioning in an egalitarian society".[3] The reason why an egalitarian society functioning on such a basis had not yet emerged had nothing to do with the incompatibility of socialism and the market mechanism but rather was due to the fact that "the left-wing liberal school of thought, whose dreams are pervaded with images of such a society, does not count very numerous or influential adherents".[4] *Plan or no plan* may be seen therefore as an attempt to set about the necessary task of persuasion and to provide that school with more substantial theoretical underpinning.

That said, Wootton made clear that the market mechanism was characterized by important deficiencies. With respect to income distribution, for example, it failed to match effort and reward. So, while Wootton accepted that interest and "normal" profits were economically necessary payments, which would be made even in the context of a totally planned economy, that did not mean they were morally defensible. There was, as she saw it, "all the difference in the world between being paid for the sweat of your brow, and being paid for giving permission to someone else to use the plant and materials of which you are the owner".[5] Powerful moral arguments could therefore be levelled against the inequitable manner in which the existing economic system functioned. Thus Wootton shifted the critique of rent and interest from the economic to moral ground. For the "old" Fabians such payments had no economic justification; for Wootton and, as we shall see, for Douglas Jay they were ethically indefensible. Yet Wootton believed that these failings might be rectified while still retaining the price mechanism, in particular, by means of redistributive taxation. Thus one could conceive of a society where there were "no marked inequalities in the conditions of living" but where "economic questions were settled by reference to the price mechanism".[6]

Wootton also considered that the existing price system was characterized by certain institutional rigidities that had been built into it, especially over the previous two decades. These prevented the market functioning in the manner suggested by conventional economic theory and, in particular, impaired its allocative efficiency. Specifically, the public regulation of price movements, which "under a price economy are the recognized signals that a new orientation of production is due", had this effect, thereby inhibiting economic growth and ultimately damaging the interests of those whom price regulation was supposed to benefit. "Thus we are getting the worst of both worlds . . . neither the crude vigorous growth of Victorian capitalism nor the ordered progress of a planned economy."[7]

The market also had deficiencies of a macroeconomic nature. Most obviously there was the periodic incidence of slumps that Wootton saw as resulting from the false expectations, limited knowledge and "clusters" of mistakes that characterized the behaviour of participants in a market economy. Here, while acknowledging his influence, Wootton believed that Hobson's thinking had led many into error. The system was not flawed in the manner he had suggested. "It is not the rules of the game", as she put it, "that bring us to stagnation" but the fact that "we have not learnt to follow the rules accurately".[8] That is, the essential problem was that economic actors failed to acquire and act on accurate information. To some degree the fault lay with the economic actors themselves but in large part too it lay with the monetary system, which, as writers such as Hayek (*Prices and production*) and Keynes (*Treatise on money*) had shown, created the informational problems and consequent errors in decision-making that were the major precipitant of economic booms and the slumps that followed.

There was, however, no need for drastic remedies. It should be possible by way of a monetary reform to "change the oil without redesigning the whole engine."[9] The elimination of the ignorance and errors, the "clusters of mistakes" that caused macroeconomic disturbances did not necessitate the abandonment of the pricing mechanism. To begin with it was wrong to suppose "that those who live under that [price] system will always behave as foolishly in the future as they have done in the past".[10] More importantly, the appropriate contra-cyclical conduct of monetary policy would allow capitalism to circumvent "the periodical choke-ups which arise from the fact that everybody's plans are made in complete independence of everyone else's".[11] Wootton stressed, therefore, that despite the depth and the prolonged nature of the slump that it was experiencing "the chances of a revival of capitalism . . . are very much greater than they are reckoned by many socialists". In addition, and in contrast to some socialist writers, she went on to make the point that "the recurring depressions of capitalism [had] been setbacks on an upward course *not stages of a progressive decline*".[12]

Yet, a policy that aimed finally to eliminate mass unemployment would require more than this. There would also have to be the conscious matching of aggregate supply and aggregate demand and this would involve planning of a kind that could be implemented effectively only under a more "socialised system of output". As Wootton saw it, this was because a "capitalist community" did not dare permit "public authorities" to set in motion plans to provide employment, for the resultant increase in output would inevitably bring down prices and diminish profitability. Within a "socialised" economy, however, such considerations would not apply.

Further, while planning could in some measure be beneficially applied to a capitalist economy, it was the case that "unless planners have full control of the main instruments of production" there would be a major obstacle in the way of effective planning, "*and control practically implies ownership*".[13] Thus Wootton, like other socialist political economists of the period, supported the extension of public ownership on the grounds that it gave the planners the necessary power to plan effectively.[14] Specifically, it allowed them to make saving and capital accumulation a social function. This was important because, as Wootton and others believed, taxation had reduced the capacity of private savers to fulfil this function adequately. Thus the public ownership of productive capacity was necessary to allow the appropriation at source of a sufficient part of the economic surplus to ensure both a high level of capital investment *and* increased social service provision.

There is in all this much that anticipated the broad outlines of the kind of socialist economic thinking that was to be articulated more fully in the late 1930s by Jay, Meade and Durbin. The manner in which Wootton discussed the market and the functions it performs while critical was not dismissive. Her recognition of what the market did and the difficulties of setting economic calculation on a different basis also marked a departure from much (in terms of socialist political economy) of what had gone before and anticipates some of what is to be found in the works of Meade and Jay. So too does her discussion of the resilience of capitalism, its longevity and the remediability of some of its central, macroeconomic defects. Thus Wootton, in *Plan or no plan,* made clear that capitalism had achieved much and, rightly managed, could be made to achieve more.

For all that she carried with her more than a little Fabian baggage. This is apparent at a number of points but most obviously where she discussed ultimate objectives. For, after a peaceful transition to socialism by way of a gradual extension of public ownership to embrace "the instruments of production", Wootton envisaged the creation of a new planning authority that would have control over the greater part of the nation's productive capacity. Wootton also considered that this authority might come to make certain decisions on the basis of information different from that provided by the price mechanism. However she also considered that, as regards the price of consumer goods and the distribution of labour, the planning authority might seek to use the information that the market provided.

For this planning authority to function effectively, Wootton believed also that it would have to secure the support and the services of what she saw as a rapidly expanding middle class. "The appealing and simple motif of the class war [had therefore] to be dropped."[15] Successful economic planning required "an extremely high standard of administrative competence" and that competence must come, primarily, from the ranks of the middle classes. Like the Webbs, Wootton had a technocratic rather than a democratic conception of planning. Thus it was necessary to "recognise once and for all that economic administration is a job for experts and hand it over to them. Detailed democratic control of economic affairs is at best a hopeless morass and at worst . . . a hypothetical pretence."[16]

All this also went hand in hand with a generally favourable view of the Soviet Union that again mirrored the attitude of the Webbs and, as we shall see, G. D. H. Cole. Thus Wootton saw Soviet planners as having the "power of trying out new and bold ventures . . . which is one of the most conspicuous points of contrast with the Western world, suffering as the latter does from widespread and disabling paralysis of the collective will". Further, the Soviet Union was characterized by a considerable measure of equality and no unemployment.[17] For Wootton, therefore, an extension of economic democracy to encompass the planning process would simply replicate the paralysis afflicting contemporary capitalism.

In addition, Wootton, like the Webbs, saw planning as something that would involve the transcendence of class or sectional interests. Successful planning after all would "require that an entire nation, ignoring its sectional and class conflicts of interest, should unite in doing something which is to the evident advantage of practically all the members of that nation." For Wootton, like the Fabians, "the motif of class warfare" was redundant.[18]

E. F. M. Durbin: economic planning and economic power

As we have seen in the previous chapter Durbin, after some initial scepticism, came to believe that the State could move the economy back towards a full employment position by means of the appropriate combination of monetary and fiscal policy. Under the influence of James Meade, and to a lesser extent Keynes, that belief strengthened as the 1930s progressed, to the point where he considered that it was possible, through state action, to maintain full employment indefinitely. Yet growing optimism as to what might be achieved by way of expansionary macroeconomic policies never led Durbin to question the need for planning and the extension of public ownership over a considerable part of the economic system. Both were seen as fundamental to the construction *and maintenance* of a more buoyant, crisis-free economy and a more just and equitable society.

There were a number of reasons why Durbin believed this to be the case. First, he saw contemporary capitalism as characterized by certain irreversible developments which, in the longer term, would destroy its dynamism. Specifically Durbin cited the growth of trade union power, the redistributive taxation that had financed expanded expenditure on social welfare provision and increasing "central control of industry, trade and finance". Trade union power had "jammed" the labour market and in so doing had destroyed "the free-moving, self-adjusting, perfectly sensitive competitive capitalism of the theoretical textbooks". Redistributive taxation had struck "heavily at the funds available for capital accumulation and economic progress", while the 1930s had witnessed moves in the direction of a cartelization of British industry that had necessarily resulted in the growth of restrictive monopoly power. What had emerged as a consequence of the latter development was, in Durbin's words, a kind of "state-organized, private property, monopoly capitalism".[19]

As Durbin saw it, all these developments could be traced to a popular reaction to the insecurity and inequality generated by an unrestrained capitalism or, as he phrased it, "a short-sighted adaptation of the institutions of laissez-faire capitalism to the needs of ordinary men and women."[20] However, short-sighted or not, democracy and democratic pressures made such developments inevitable and, short of the overthrow of democracy itself, irreversible. While capitalism might be stabilized, therefore, its long-term dynamism and flexibility would become increasingly precarious unless apposite socialist policies were pursued.

For that reason alone social ownership had to be extended and the state had to set about the task of economic planning. Thus the state or state-controlled institutions had to take over the function of saving and accumulation to maintain an adequate rate of capital investment. Further, nationalization *and* planning were necessary to circumvent the adverse consequences of the growth of monopoly power. Thus even after the extension of social ownership, decisions as to pricing and output could not be left in the hands of nationalized corporations because the managers of even socialized concerns would have an interest in restricting output and maximizing the surplus that they generated. As Durbin put it in 1934, in an unpublished Memorandum, "nationalized industries" too "might build up their own vested interests".[21] He argued, therefore, that "the only way of becoming . . . reasonably sure that [monopoly] power is not exerted is to take *all final responsibility for output policy out of the hands of those who could benefit in any way from restriction*".[22] Such power should be vested in a Supreme Economic Authority.

Here he departed substantially from a conception of nationalization that was taking root in certain sections of the Labour Party and that looked to the creation of autonomous public corporations managed by those with business expertise; a conception that was clearly articulated in Herbert Morrison's *Socialisation and transport* (1933). Durbin's views were also at odds with those of others, such as Cole, who stressed the need for the democratization of decision-making within nationalized enterprises. Thus Durbin's whole emphasis was on the need for a strong, central control that could override, when and where necessary, considerations of industrial democracy and corporate autonomy. As he wrote in *The politics of democratic socialism*: "Responsibility in the socialized sector must from the beginning be upwards . . . upwards to bodies concerned primarily with the interests of the consumer, with society as a whole, with the rational and common good of wealth production."[23] What he wished to avoid was the kind of uncoordinated syndicalism that could result from the creation of autonomous, self-serving, national corporations.

Such an attitude is apparent too in his discussion of the threat that trade unions posed to economic flexibility and economic growth. Thus Durbin accepted that under capitalism one might expect trade unions to act to advance and protect the interests of their members with little consideration for the wider economic consequences of their behaviour. It was, indeed, just such action that was at the root of the loss of flexibility in the labour market that threatened the self-adjusting capacity of the capitalist system. However, under socialism, and in the context of socialist planning, he looked forward to the "supersession in the trade union and Labour Movement, in practice as well as in theory, of the last element of Syndicalism".[24] Thus the Supreme Economic Authority would ensure that trade unions took a wider view of their responsibilities and did not advance wage and other claims that threatened the dynamism or stability of the economic system. As he put it in an unpublished Memorandum written in 1935, "The organized workers who claim with justice that the interests of the community should not be over-ridden for the profits of the few, should go on to add that those same interests must not be over-ridden for the wages of the few."[25]

To plan effectively was to ensure the long-term dynamism of the economic system and for Durbin effective planning required a fundamental transference of economic power out of the hands of private capitalists. While, therefore, there were other reasons for the extension of social ownership, the transference of power was viewed by Durbin and others in the 1930s as one of the most fundamental. Even as regards the implementation of an effective anti-depression and contracyclical policy of the kind outlined in the previous chapter, it was necessary that the state secured complete control over certain economic levers: specifically, for Durbin, control over the banking system to implement the requisite "planned" monetary policy. Thus he looked to a nationalized Bank of England to provide a "unification of policy control", in order to "control the policy of every organ which directly affects the flow of money income and expenditure".[26]

But, as Durbin recognized, socialists sought to attain many economic and social objectives in addition to that of full or near-full employment. He wrote in 1940 that he wished "to use the power of the State" not only to pursue "expansionist policies within the growing socialised sector of the economy" but also "to restore and maintain a high level of active accumulation; to moderate insecurity still further; to curb the cyclical oscillations of economic activity by a control of the income and investment position of the community; and to secure much greater equality in the distribution of the product of industry". As Durbin emphasized, the attainment of such a wide range of economic objectives was "only [made] possible . . . by the supersession of private property as the seat of industrial control".[27] For him, nationalization represented "a programme for the acquisition of economic power by the state" and that was the basic prerequisite for the construction of a socialist economy. That said, it should be emphasized that for Durbin it was *control* that was vital and if that could be secured without the extension of public ownership, all well and good.

As regards the general rationale for planning and the concentration of economic authority in a central planning body, Durbin, in terms reminiscent of the "old" Fabians, contrasted the existing uncoordinated system of individual economic decision-making with the situation that would prevail where a central planning institution, such as the Supreme Economic Authority, made decisions on the basis of a comprehensive view of their social and economic consequences. Here Durbin wrote of "the enlargement of the field surveyed when any economic decision is taken" in contrast to the narrow, self-interested focus of individual enterprises.[28]

Durbin's discussion of the economic principles by reference to which the Supreme Economic Authority would exercise its powers of decision-making, once acquired, will be discussed below. However, it should be noted that like all the writers considered in this section he believed that there should be a free market for consumption goods and that the price information transmitted by the market should be used by the planners in their economic calculations. This would not only make for rational economic calculation but also for greater sensitivity to the changing needs of society (as consumers) and thence to greater flexibility in the business of planning.

With respect to the extension of social ownership two other considerations where important for Durbin. First, like the Fabian socialists, Durbin argued that the increasing divorce of ownership from control that characterized contemporary capitalism rendered the institution of private property literally "useless". Private property owners no longer served a useful economic function in terms of managing their assets with a view to their efficient exploitation; in large-scale enterprises professional managers now usually fulfilled the functions that private capitalists had previously performed. As Durbin put it, "the propertied classes are now parasitic in the final sense that their income is purely a distributive share and contributes nothing to the increase of production."[29] Social ownership should be extended, therefore, because private property had lost its moral as well as its economic rationale.

Secondly, a number of studies in the 1930s had suggested that the extent to which fiscal policy could be used to effect a substantial redistribution of wealth was becoming increasingly limited. Given this, Durbin, like a number of other writers, saw the extension of social ownership as an increasingly important means of implementing what he termed "a clear and unambiguous equalization programme".[30] Here again he had something in common with the "old" Fabians.

James Meade: the political economy of liberal socialism

Like Durbin, Meade also believed that the market mechanism must play a fundamental role in the efficient functioning of a socialist economy, and, in his *Introduction,* the Industrial Planning Commission that he proposed would utilize "a pricing system similar to the pricing system of a competitive economy".[31] For Meade, planning without the price mechanism was impossible and, for the most part, he was hostile to interference with it. Such interferences produced a misallocation of resources, they infringed consumer sovereignty and diminished consumer utility, and the distributive objectives that they sought to achieve (e.g. by way of food subsidies) could be more easily and more efficiently achieved by fiscal means.

Yet Meade also argued the need for the extension of public ownership, seeing it as a necessary adjunct to the business of macroeconomic management and as a means of attaining the objectives of greater efficiency and equity. In his *Introduction* he envisaged a situation where the state would own sufficient property to be able to ensure not only "that the optimum amount of national income is saved", but also "to achieve a considerable degree of equality in incomes and to finance its ordinary expenditure *without resort to commodity or income taxes*".[32] To that end Meade argued that public ownership should embrace those industries characterized by monopolistic practices. This would allow the elimination of payments that could not be justified in terms of a factor's marginal product and, by thus abolishing monopoly profits and rents, go a long way towards achieving the kind of material equality that socialists sought without interference, direct or indirect, with the price mechanism. As regards macroeconomic management, public ownership would also permit a higher level of capital investment than if "monopolistic concerns", with their interest in constraining output, were left in private hands. In addition the "socialisation" of those industries in which capital investment was already high and in which the state could not secure control over their level of investment expenditure by other means would also permit closer control over the level of aggregate investment. However, throughout his economic writing, Meade made clear that to attain particular objectives it was "control" or "management" rather than "ownership" that was important; this was a theme that, as we shall see, was also to loom large in the political economy of post-war socialist revisionism.

To facilitate control over the level and direction of investment in the economy Meade also advocated the creation of a National Investment Board; an idea whose pedigree could be traced at least as far back as the Liberals' *Britain's industrial future* (1928), where it had played a key role in the public investment programme that lay at the heart of their economic strategy. Under the auspices of the National Fabian Research Bureau, the idea of such an institution had been taken up and developed by a number of writers. Of particular importance here was the work of Colin Clark, who envisaged a Board that would have the power to acquire funds through the issue of bonds and that would exert control over a range of financial institutions, in particular the joint stock banks; though, unlike many socialist writers, Clark did not advocate their nationalization. In addition in his *Control of investment* (1933) he argued for an element of tax revenue to be earmarked for the Board's use.

Among socialist writers opinion varied considerably as to the powers, composition and responsibilities of the National Investment Board, a diversity of opinion that can be seen, in particular, in *Studies in capital investment* (1935), a New Fabian Research Bureau publication edited by E. A. Radice. Specifically there was disagreement on the extent and form that control over the banks, insurance companies and building societies would take, disagreement over whether the National Investment Board should have independent powers to acquire funds, and disagreement too over the degree and nature of political control that should be exerted over it. Only on the general need for some kind of control over the aggregate level and direction of investment were all agreed.

Meade saw the National Investment Board as a key instrument of what he envisaged as socialist planning. However, it should be emphasized here that when Meade wrote of planning it was planning of a largely macroeconomic, one could legitimately say Keynesian, kind. It was a question of managing aggregates (aggregate demand, aggregate savings, aggregate investment, general consumption and public expenditure) rather than planning of a discriminatory kind that sought to fundamentally reshape and restructure the economy at a microeconomic level and/or set it dancing to a radically different tune. This was a very different and certainly more circumscribed conception of planning than that adhered to by some socialist political economists. Thus, as we shall see, G. D. H. Cole saw planning as a means of achieving a much wider range of objectives by means of a more diverse range of planning instruments and institutions than those envisaged by Meade.

As regards socialist planning or, more accurately, management of the economy, Meade also considered the likely impact of what he proposed on Britain's international position. Thus, like Durbin, Gaitskell, Strachey and a number of others, he believed that the pursuit of expansionary policies would require the adjunct of exchange rate flexibility. Likewise he confronted the problem of capital flight that might arise with the advent of a Labour administration pursuing a radical economic strategy, a problem that was seen as having a particular relevance in the aftermath of 1931, when, it was believed, City interests had effectively torpedoed the Labour government. Here again, the taking of certain economic powers and their planned use was what Meade and others such as Gaitskell and Durbin proposed. Specifically they advocated the use of bank rate, exchange control and an Exchange Equalization Account to prevent both an outflow of funds and any dramatic fall in the international value of sterling. Meade was confident that such measures or a combination of such measures would do the trick. "Financial panics may take a number of forms," he wrote in 1935, "but all of these can be effectively dealt with."[33]

Finally as regards his discussion of the pursuit of redistributive objectives a particular conception of the role to be played by a competitive market lies at the heart of what Meade had to say. While concerned to reduce inequality,

Meade believed that the owners of productive factors should be rewarded, as in a perfectly competitive market, according to their marginal products, whether in the form of wages, interest or profit. He therefore rejected the view that redistribution could best be effected by increasing wages, if that entailed increasing them above the marginal product of labour, or lowering interest and profit, if that meant reducing the reward of capital below its marginal product. Similarly commodity taxes were rejected as a means of redistributing income, on the grounds that they resulted in an allocation of resources different from that desired by consumers.

Meade's preferred instrument for the reduction of income and wealth inequality was direct taxation. Of course an increase in direct taxation had its drawbacks. It might adversely affect the growth of output by increasing leisure preference and, by eroding the motive to save, it could diminish the rate of capital accumulation. Nevertheless, for Meade, it was, in economic terms, a relatively unobjectionable means of achieving greater material equality.

Like Durbin, therefore, Meade in the 1930s furnished powerful arguments in favour of accommodating the market within a socialist economy.

Douglas Jay: the market, public ownership and redistribution

In considering the distribution of income and wealth Jay too, in *The socialist case*, started from the neoclassical argument that, on the assumption of perfect competition, it is the case that when goods exchange at marginal cost, no supranormal profits are earned and factors of production are rewarded according to their marginal product. Given this it had to be accepted that interest and profit were necessary payments to maintain the existing level of factor inputs, interest being the reward for waiting and profits for risk-taking. However, what is necessary, Jay argued, is not necessarily what is just. Hence if the competitive market distributed the national income in a manner consistent with the contribution of factors to production, that did nothing to ensure that income matched needs or that reward was commensurate with effort. As Jay pointed out, it was often possible to produce the service of "waiting" with little exertion or sacrifice, while many of the most poorly paid jobs involved considerable physical effort. There was, therefore, no ethical basis for the distribution of wealth that even a competitive market effected. As has been noted such arguments can also be found in Barbara Wootton's *Plan or no plan* – an influence that Jay acknowledged in his preface to *The socialist case*.

Further, the market also failed on grounds of equity because in many instances it was not truly competitive. The existence of monopoly power and monopolistic practices, inheritance laws that ensured that all did not start from the same point in the competitive race, the monopoly of educational privileges by a small fraction of society, all ensured that this was the case.

Yet, despite these failings, the market was something with which socialists must learn to live. As Jay wrote, "it may be that in an imperfect world it is the only, or perhaps least undesirable system which is in fact available."[34] The prices generated by the market might be neither economically (where monopoly power was wielded) nor morally defensible but, none the less, they often provided the only basis available for rational economic calculation. The objective of socialists should therefore be not to abolish the market but to render its operation consistent with a socialist concern for justice and equity. It was indeed the pursuit of such an objective, by way of redistribution, that Jay believed lay at the heart of a distinctively socialist political economy: that, rather than the objective of macroeconomic stabilization.

As he saw it there were three main ways of redistributing wealth: trade union pressure for higher wages, legal confiscation of property and taxation. The first method was for the most part acceptable, but was outside the control of government; the second was "extremely inequitable, perhaps even more so than violence"; the third was acceptable and lay within the power of government to effect. Redistributive taxation must, however, be directed against "unearned income", both because inequalities resulting from earned income were not large and because they were "usually paid in virtue of highly important services".[35] It is not surprising, therefore, that the key component of the redistributive fiscal policy proposed by Jay should have been an inheritance tax.

What Jay looked to then was an economic system in which prices were freely determined by market forces, where "free consumers' choice and free competition [were] retained unimpaired but unearned income [was] being gradually distributed in social services". This he saw as "a perfectly conceivable system . . . we may regard it as a halfway house towards socialism. *Indeed it is more than halfway. For the utilisation of unearned incomes to raise the standard of living of the poorer wage-earners must always remain the real heart of socialism.*"[36] As socialism progressed, market forces could be increasingly relied on both as regards the distribution of income and the pricing of commodities. With respect to the latter, "as inequality is diminished the money, or price calculus will lose much of its falsity" and provide a more accurate indication of the relative intensity of different social needs, rather than simply those of the rich.[37] As regards the former, with "the gradual suppression of unearned and grossly unequal incomes, the structure of *competitive* earned incomes worked out by the price system" would approximate "much more closely to a real reflection of abilities". Thus for "the foreseeable stages of socialism, the general plan is to allow wages and salaries to be settled by competitive principles and supplemented by State services" with redistributive taxation used to bring about a closer approximation of effort and reward.[38]

What role was there then for the traditional (Fabian) policy of extending public ownership? The short answer here is that, regardless of what might be achieved by way of macroeconomic stabilization and redistribution, it was, for Jay, fundamental. To begin with public ownership was an important antidote to the growth of monopoly and monopolistic practices, though Jay accepted that alternative policies might be appropriate here. Public ownership could also be justified because of the economic leverage that it gave to the state in periods of trade depression. Thus if output were curtailed or production suspended as a consequence of depressed profitability, the power "to suspend the working of the profit motive" would enormously enhance the power of government to act and allow the level of output to be maintained even in periods of loss. In this context Jay, like many other liberal socialists of the period, believed the banking system should also be nationalized because of the vital role that it could be made to play in this respect.

However, Jay recognized that this would still leave "a very large class of industries to which nationalisation would only be appropriate at a very late stage if ever"[39] and here he had particularly in mind new, small and speculative ventures. There were also what he termed "established, but not unified industries", whose development might best be influenced indirectly through the tax system and by way of commercial policy.[40]

G. D. H. Cole, socialism without the market

The writers whose work has been discussed so far took a positive (if critical) view of the role that the market could play in the context of a socialist economy. However, one writer who took a fundamentally different stance, and whose position certainly reflected an important current of thinking within the Labour Party in the 1930s, was G. D. H. Cole. Of course, as we have seen, Cole believed that by way of the requisite expansionary monetary and fiscal policies a measure of economic vitality could be restored to the capitalist system without any significant alteration in existing economic arrangements or the market mechanism. Yet he was equally adamant that that vitality would be transient.

First, Cole doubted the ability of governments to control whatever revival their policies brought about. There was no question, therefore, of returning to an "*equilibrium* on a basis of maximum production" and every reason to expect the recurrence of crises of increasing intensity.[41] Secondly, expansionary policies did not destroy the power of private monopolists that would still be used to restrict output even in a situation of more buoyant demand. Thirdly, the continued existence of monopoly power would also serve to maintain that maldistribution of wealth that was the root cause of over-saving, over-investment, underconsumption and slump. Fourthly, while an expansionary monetary policy might go some way to ensure a higher level of investment and thence of economic activity, it did not solve the problem of distributing credit in a socially optimal fashion. Fifthly, Cole believed that state involvement in the economy by way of a substantial public investment programme might well "undermine the incentives and initiative of private investors and private captains of industry", adversely affecting the capitalist system's economic dynamism;[42] thus capitalism might be robbed of its virtues along with some of its vices. For Cole, this was an argument that could also be used against building socialism by way of an adherence to a gradualist reformism. For, if public investment had this adverse effect, so too would a strategy involving a redistributive fiscal policy and a growth in social welfare expenditure, as it would be likely to erode "dangerously . . . the funds which must be left for investment in the hands of the rich if Capitalism as a system is to continue to work".[43] For that reason alone Cole saw a "gradualist policy" as necessarily "suspect". Sixthly, there were limits to the pursuit of a public works policy within existing economic structures. The effective implementation of such a policy would involve a level of public expenditure that governments would find difficult to sustain and capitalists would find increasingly intolerable in terms of servicing the increased public indebtedness that would result. Further, under capitalism, the state was limited as to the kind of public works it could undertake. Thus they had to be works that did not compete with private enterprise, "for otherwise it will be in danger of causing capitalist recession instead of capitalist revival."[44] Finally, it was necessary to move on rapidly from a purely expansionary programme if the waste involved in competition was to be eliminated. For these reasons, therefore, Cole emphasized the need for the speedy and substantial extension of public ownership as the basis for comprehensive socialist economic planning.

As regards that extension, Cole was clear that effective economic planning could not be implemented "while at any rate the major industries, including the key industry of finance, remain in private hands".[45] Public ownership of these industries was, at the very least, necessary to give the state the powers it required to plan. Once acquired, such powers would be deployed through a number of institutions whose functions Cole was to discuss at length in two major works in the 1930s, *The principles of economic planning* (1935) and *The machinery of economic planning* (1938).

At the base of the planning pyramid would be industrial planning commissions; commissions responsible for planning a particular group of related industries. The plans formulated by these bodies would then be fed through to a National Planning Commission that would thus be "thoroughly equipped with the fullest statistics that the various industries and services, trading agencies and government departments could supply". Armed with its own staff of technical experts, this commission would be responsible for the formulation of a National Plan using both the information with which it was furnished by the industrial commissions and its own estimation of future "trends in productive organisation and the structure of demand". However it would be an *advisory* rather than an *executive* body. The crucial decisions as to the shape of the National Plan and the manner in which it was to be executed would lie with a National Planning Authority, "so constituted as to represent the interests of the general community".[46] In addition there would be a Department of Economic Inspection, which would assess the "efficiency of each branch of production from a technical point of view", a National Income Planning Authority that would determine levels of remuneration in the light of working conditions, hours and the supply of and demand for particular labour services, and a National Investment Board that would be "entrusted with the function of allocating the available supply of capital among different uses in accordance with the National Plan". This latter institution would therefore have distinctly greater powers than the National Investment Boards that figure in the political economy of some of the other writers discussed in this chapter and the previous one.[47]

Such a burgeoning of bureaucracy clearly indicates that Cole had a more all-encompassing conception of socialist economic planning than any of the other writers considered in this chapter – a view confirmed whenever Cole outlined what he saw it as entailing. He wrote in 1932, for example, that what was needed was:

> (a) a collectively planned economy designed to secure the right relative application of resources to the various kinds of production, (b) a mechanism of income distribution that will base the amount of income which it distributes on the magnitude of the available productive resources, (c) a system of controlled prices to preserve the proportion between the planned production and the amount of income to be distributed, (d) a controlled financial mechanism designed to correct disequilibria due to the time factor or any tendency to leave available income unspent.[48]

Thus the planning authorities were to perform the pricing, distributing, allocative and equilibrating (macroeconomic and microeconomic) functions of the market.

In this context Cole's view of the market's role under planning also clearly differentiated him from the other writers discussed, though his criticisms of the manner in which it functioned under capitalism were, in many respects, very similar. Like Jay and others, he argued that market price failed to provide an accurate idea as to the social utility of commodities because of the unequal value of money to the rich and the poor. As he wrote in 1935, "price offers in the market represent not proportionate lumps of expected satisfaction or of desire but only lumps of desire weighted in accordance with the size of the offerer's income and capacity for being satisfied."[49] Of course other writers believed that with a more equitable distribution of wealth such problems could be rectified without abandoning the market. For Cole, however, under socialism, "new standards of valuation" would "come into play".[50] Thus planners would take account of needs, not just money demand. When determining the socially optimal allocation of resources they would formulate and work with some standard of social utility "which cannot be identified with the price standard accepted by most economists as sufficient for the measurement of purely economic goods".[51] In addition they would have to work with some measure of "real cost", which would involve "attributing values" to factors of production before taking into account the "amounts of the 'scarce' factors of production used in the production of goods".[52] Cole was not clear as to how this process of attribution would proceed but his intention was obvious; to have and work with some notion of the "social opportunity costs" involved in employing particular factors of production in particular tasks.

More generally what he sought was to establish estimates of demand price and supply cost calculated on a very different basis from that which operated in a market economy. As Cole saw it there would "need to be, not a single system linking together all value-prices in terms of a universal equivalent but *two* distinct commensurabilities, one of products offered for sale one with another, and the other of the scarce factors of production one with another"[53]; the first presumably based on estimates of social utility, the second on estimates of social opportunity cost. How these were to be married was, however, another problem to which Cole failed to provide any convincing solution.

Similarly, to secure the socially optimal distribution of the National Product, the planning authorities should again seek to take account of need. Thus they would act to ensure that part of the National Product – and Cole hoped and expected it would be a growing part – took the form of a "social dividend", the magnitude of which would vary with the needs of the recipients. As Cole put it, at the outset of the process of distribution "a certain part of social production will . . . be removed from the price market and transferred definitely to the realm of collective decision about what is to be produced."[54] Part would also be distributed as wages and here considerations of supply and demand *would* enter into the calculations of the planners. However, Cole believed that wages would have a diminishing significance and ultimately would come to be viewed as little more than pocket money; for social service rather than the desire for pecuniary gain would come to be the prime motive for productive effort. As Cole envisaged it in the *Principles*, "the less we offer men differential monetary advantages, the more we shall have to make them willing to give good service because they feel the giving of good service is part of their own duty."[55]

Cole did accept a continuing and important role for the market as a mechanism transmitting to planners some idea of what society desired *once its basic needs had been satisfied.* As he wrote in the *Principles of economic planning*, "both the planned and the planless economy have the same necessity to adjust their output to what consumers are prepared to buy at prices at which producers are prepared to sell."[56] That said, commodities would be priced by publicly owned industries with regard to a wider, social view of the costs of production than that employed by private entrepreneurs under capitalism, and throughout his discussion of the political economy of planning Cole looked to establish forms of economic calculation under socialism in which money and the price mechanism would play little or no part. As he wrote in 1935, "Decisions involved in the national plan ought to be made as far as possible *in terms of real things and only translated subsequently for convenience into money terms.*"[57] In this and other respects his political economy was radically different from that of Durbin, Meade, Jay and, for the most part, the Wootton of *Plan or no plan.*

This whole debate over economic calculation may seem an esoteric one and in some respects it undoubtedly was. But it also encapsulated vitally important questions about the nature of socialism. Among other issues it raised that of economic freedom and in particular the extent to which the freedom of the consumer could be accommodated under socialism. "Market socialists" stressed the need for planners to take on board the information that consumer choices, freely made, transmitted through the market. Such an approach, they argued, expanded the realm of economic freedom, while the information thus acquired, if acted upon, made for a more efficient utilization of resources in relation to individual consumer needs. In contrast, for Cole, with his conception of an expanding social dividend, consumer choice would be constrained as remuneration increasingly took that form. Further, as he saw it, prices were to be not so much the result of consumer choice, not so much the consequence of decisions taken independently of the planners, but rather, as he put it in 1932, "under socialism" prices would "come to be regarded much less as data than as controlled expressions of the results of the concrete decisions about the organisation of production and real incomes."[58] That is, under socialism, planners would determine, not react to, a configuration of prices and do so in the light of *their* view as to how available resources might best be utilized and the national product best distributed.

One final aspect of Cole's discussion of planning needs to be considered, namely that relating to the conduct of international trade. Here Cole attacked what he saw as the Labour Party's traditional adherence to free trade principles. Such an adherence had made for a peculiar "ideological hybrid" with demands for public ownership and regulation of industry sitting uneasily beside a "desire to leave trade free".[59] However, Cole believed that the socialization of industry would inevitably involve the state in the planning of trade, if only because it would then have to provide for the marketing of its products. What Cole proposed, therefore, was the establishment of Import Boards that would regulate imports with reference both to that portion of home demand that they believed domestic producers would be unable to satisfy at a given price and to the overall value of imports that the nation's exports would permit. The value of the country's exports would in turn be determined by decisions of the planning authorities that would establish where productive capacity might best be geared to the satisfaction of domestic demand and where to the satisfaction of foreign demand. As regards the business of international trade itself, this would be conducted on the basis of bulk purchase and sale.

As Cole saw it, such planning of international trade, in contrast to other means of control, such as tariffs and quotas, need not be restrictive. It would not be necessary to pursue a commercial policy designed to protect or create jobs by excluding imports because planning would ensure that all labour resources were fully utilized whether in export industries or in catering for home demand. In these circumstances, Cole considered that "a planned economy [would be] free from the bias against imports which has dominated for centuries the commercial policy of most industrial nations".[60] There was, therefore, no reason to expect that Import Boards would act in a restrictive way. That said, Cole was of the opinion that in the internationally planned economy of the future it was "unlikely that any great industrial country will ever again come to export so large a proportion of its total output as Great Britain was in the habit of exporting in the course of the Nineteenth Century".[61] The expectation was therefore that economic planning in general would lead to an economy more geared to the demands of the domestic market, a view that in the 1930s transcended political divisions being as clearly articulated, for example, in Harold Macmillan's *The middle way* (1938) as in the Mosley Manifesto.

At the root of Cole's view of the manner in which a socialist economy would function was a visceral distrust of the market mechanism. As regards the conduct of international trade it is clear that he looked ultimately to a situation where socialist nations would exchange goods on a barter basis. Moreover, his emphasis on the growing importance of the social dividend and the declining significance of wages suggests a situation where the market would be circumvented and goods distributed on the basis of need. He was also quick to point out the extent to which the market mechanism and the prices it generated failed both to embody the social costs of production and to convey an accurate estimate of social requirements. What Cole looked to, therefore, was an informational basis for economic calculation different from that which the market provided.

However, Cole was swimming decidedly against the stream in the 1930s.

For in that decade, as we have seen, most British socialist political economists made their peace with the market and sought to accommodate it within their vision of how a socialist economy would function. What emerged in this decade was a more liberal and also, it must be said, a more theoretically rigorous socialist political economy; one that consciously sought to deploy the insights, analytical tools and theoretical constructs with which a training in neoclassical economics had provided many of its proponents. The fruits of this training manifested themselves in a number of ways, but in particular in a more precise understanding of the functions that the competitive market could, and did, perform and that would have to be replicated in any socialist economy from which the market mechanism had been banished or where its operation was constrained.

Economic calculation in a socialist economy

This understanding was particularly apparent in the discussion of the possibility of rational economic calculation in a socialist economy that took place in the interwar period. Thus many socialist political economists, whatever their particular views on the details of how such calculation should proceed, were agreed that socialist planners should aim, as far as possible, to reproduce that configuration of prices that prevailed when a perfectly competitive system was in equilibrium; for such prices, neoclassical economics argued, would ensure a full and efficient use of available factors of production and, for a given distribution of wealth, the maximization of social utility. Such a view of things had come out of a debate over whether rational economic calculation was possible under socialism, the origins of which can be traced back to the publication by Ludwig von Mises in 1920 of an article entitled "Economic calculation in the socialist commonwealth". In it he insisted that the magnitude and complexities of the information-gathering and computational problems involved in socialist planning, in the absence of market information on the relative scarcity of productive factors, meant that those factors could not be efficiently utilized. In short, he argued that under socialism rational economic calculation was an impossibility.

The subsequent response came from a number of writers but in particular Oskar Lange and Abba Lerner and in Britain from, among others, H. D. Dickinson, Durbin, Meade and F. M. Taylor. A full discussion of the complexities of the ensuing debate both with von Mises and other writers such as Hayek and Robbins and within the socialist camp have been furnished by a number of authors and need not be repeated here.[62] But, in broad outline, what socialist writers believed they provided during its course was a refutation of this Misesian charge; a refutation that rested on essentially neoclassical foundations.

One of the classic rebuttals was Lange's *On the economic theory of socialism* published in 1936. Lange's focus, like that of the other writers mentioned, was on the equilibrium that neoclassical writers saw as being established under perfect competition. This equilibrium was characterized by the full and efficient utilization of resources as producers equated the ratios of the marginal productivities of the factors they employed to their relative costs and increased output to the point where the marginal cost of a product equalled its price. Simultaneously, consumers maximized the satisfaction they derived from their consumption by allocating expenditure in such a way as to equate the ratios of the marginal utilities of the commodities they purchased with their relative prices. The price mechanism operated to equate the demand for and supply of each commodity and thence the demand for and supply of commodities as a whole. Under perfect competition, therefore, all factors of production were fully and efficiently utilized and consumer satisfaction maximized. Further, all market participants would be rewarded according to the marginal product of the factors that they provided and the scale of their factor inputs, that is according to their contribution, in this respect, to the production process.

For Lange, under perfect competition, the price mechanism brought about this desirable state of affairs by a process of trial and error: "if the quantities demanded and the quantities supplied diverge the competition of buyers and sellers will alter the prices . . . And so the process goes on until . . . equilibrium is finally reached."[63] It was this process, he believed, that could be replicated by socialist planners. To do so, as in a capitalist economy, consumers would be left free to maximize their utility in the marketplace. However, with the social ownership of the means of production, producers were no longer guided by the imperative of profit maximization to an efficient utilization of resources available to them. Instead, as Lange saw it, they could be directed to the same end by means of two rules established by a central planning board. First, it would instruct producers to choose that combination of factors that minimized their average cost price of production, and secondly it would instruct them to produce up to a point where, as under perfect competition, the marginal cost of production was equal to the price at which their products sold. Thus producers would, in effect, be given instructions that would cause them to act in the same manner as producers in a perfectly competitive market.

As, under socialism, the means of production were now publicly owned, producers would, of course, be confronted by factor costs established by the central planning authority. So while the prices of consumer goods would be freely determined in the market by the demand of utility-maximizing consumers, the planning authorities would establish the factor prices that producers used as the basis for the calculation of costs and thence optimum output levels. If these factor prices truly reflected relative factor scarcities they would produce a full and efficient utilization of resources in relation to consumer demand. If they did not then surpluses and shortages of productive factors would emerge. However, the planning authorities would then, by a process of trial and error comparable to that which occurred under competitive capitalism, alter factor prices in such a way as to eliminate shortfalls and surfeits and so, eventually, move the economy to an optimum utilization of resources. Thus under socialism the same position could be established as that which would emerge under a perfectly competitive capitalism and by a comparable process; the difference being that under socialist planning, where the process of trial and error was consciously managed, Lange believed it would be more rapidly completed.

One other point of note here is the element of decentralization involved in a "market socialist" conception of planning. Thus while the central planners determined and altered factor prices, decisions as to how best to produce up to the point where marginal cost equalled price were left in the hands of technically knowledgeable plant managers. Further, consumers were left free to deploy their income as they chose.

Writers in Britain such as Durbin, Dickinson and Taylor all sought in comparable, if different, ways to use neoclassicism to furnish the analytical tools, concepts and criteria that would permit rational economic calculation on the part of socialist planners. As early as 1933, Dickinson, like Lange, had put forward a "trial and error" solution to arriving at a configuration of prices which would achieve efficiency objectives, categorizing it as a "process of successive approximation", though Fred Taylor had been first in the field as regards this notion with an article published in 1928.[64] What Dickinson argued was that, given the "openness" of socialist production, all the information necessary to establish the supply and demand schedules of individual enterprises could be easily obtained and, on the basis of this, an equilibrium set of prices could be established that met neoclassical efficiency criteria. Trial and error might be necessary to arrive at this configuration but he believed that that would entail a much shorter series of successive trials than was involved in a competitive market.[65]

Like Lange, Durbin too believed that plant managers could be guided by rules that supplanted the imperatives of profit maximization and led them to meet neoclassical efficiency criteria. Thus planners should instruct them to "calculate the marginal productivity to them of all mobile resources" and then to move them "to positions of highest calculated product".[66] However, he argued further that, given the practical difficulties in calculating marginal cost, managers should be instructed to produce up to the point where average cost equalled price. This was in contrast to the view of Lange, Lerner and others who insisted on the marginal-cost-pricing rule for public corporations. Lerner in particular was highly critical of Durbin's position here, insisting that the ease or otherwise of managers adhering to the marginal-cost-pricing rule was not something with which economists should be concerned. Rather, their job was that of specifying those pricing rules that made for the full, utility-maximizing and efficient use of resources.

Lerner also introduced the concept of marginal opportunity cost as a means of ordering "the economic activity of society [so] that no commodity is produced unless its importance is greater than that of the alternative that is sacrificed". If that objective could be attained then he believed that "we shall have completely achieved the ideal that the economic calculus of a socialist state sets itself".[67] However, an ideal it was to remain, as Lerner did not furnish a solution to the enormous theoretical and computational problems that would have been involved in rendering such a calculus operational. In this context Durbin's emphasis on practicality rather than theoretical purity carries more than a little weight.

Meade too believed that neoclassical efficiency criteria were appropriate to the running of socialized industries and should be applied by socialist planners. In fact, socialist planning was the only means of ensuring that such criteria prevailed. Thus as capitalism had become increasingly monopolistic, it had generated a set of prices markedly different from those that would be generated by perfect competition. That this was the case had been shown quite clearly in the work of contemporary economists such as Joan Robinson – *The economics of imperfect competition* (1933) – and Edward Chamberlin – *The theory of monopolistic competition* (1933). Meade suggested nationalization and planning as a remedy for this and also argued that the extent of the departure of existing from perfectly competitive prices could be used as a measure of how pressing the need was for the extension of public ownership over particular sectors of the economy. Thus in 1935, in an "Outline of economic policy for a Labour government", Meade wrote that "in those industries in which there is least perfect competition . . . there is greatest need for state control of industry".[68] Consistent with this, Meade proposed that firms or industries once nationalized should adopt marginal cost pricing as regards their products and marginal revenue pricing of the factors that they utilized. Such a pricing policy would both make for efficiency and ensure that socially owned concerns satisfied consumer needs better than existing privately owned enterprises wielding monopoly power and concerned simply to maximize profits.

It is beyond the scope of this book to discuss the theoretical and other difficulties inherent in the solutions to the problem of socialist economic calculation that these writers furnished. Critiques are numerous and readers may take their pick. However, what is important to note is that these theorists not only considered they had rebutted the fundamental flaws that von Mises and others (for example, Hayek and Lionel Robbins) believed they had detected in the economic case for socialism but they were also convinced and convinced others that they had established a more or less practical set of criteria and guidelines by reference to which socialist planners and socialist managers could conduct the business of economic life efficiently. Specifically, with regard to enterprises owned by the state or municipalities, they believed they had provided important insights and rules on pricing policy. So, while much of what they wrote would have been unintelligible to those outside the ranks of professional economists, and while much of it had little immediate relevance to the practical task of building a socialist economy, their achievement was none the less of fundamental importance, not least because it instilled and bolstered the belief that in economic terms socialism could be made to work and work more efficiently than the existing capitalist economy. In addition, their work also underlined the positive role that the market and market economy concepts could play in the construction and running of a socialist economy.

Labour Party economic literature in the 1930s

Finally, it is necessary to consider briefly the imprint left by the socialist economic thinking, discussed in this and the previous chapter, upon some of the economic literature produced by the Labour Party in the 1930s. Here there is no question but that it did reflect, in some measure, the intellectual ferment that followed the traumatic events of 1929–31. That said, a residual Fabianism remains as much in the language as in the policies advanced. Thus arguments to the effect that the primary objective of Labour Party economic policy was "to convert industry . . . from a *haphazard struggle for private gain* to a *planned national economy* owned and carried on for the *service* of the community", certainly had a strong Fabian resonance.[69] Further, this idea of a scientifically planned, publicly owned, economic order supplanting the market anarchy of competitive private enterprise and the motive of service replacing that of profit, were to surface again and again in policy documents in the thirties as they had in the 1920s. Similarly, the view that the crucial choice before policymakers was that between public ownership and private monopoly also found frequent expression. As it was phrased in *For socialism and peace* (1934), the "choice [was] between the conduct of industry as a public service, democratically owned and responsibly administered and the private economic sovereignty of the trust and combine."[70] What still lay at the heart of the Labour Party's economic literature in the 1930s, therefore, was the assumption that socialism could only be built on the foundation of a substantial extension of public ownership, particularly into those industries where private monopoly power prevailed. Such an extension was seen as the "only basis on which ordered planning of industry and trade [could] be carried out". "Banking and credit, transport and electricity, water, iron and steel, coal, gas, agriculture, textiles and shipping, shipbuilding, engineering . . . in all these the time has come for drastic reorganisation and for the most part *nothing short of immediate public ownership* and control will be effective." A General Enabling Act was also proposed, "giving the State power to acquire any land, rural or urban" and it was envisaged that such power would be extensively used.[71] Nor do the policy statements embody much notion of a mixed economy: The Labour Party "contends that the only way of establishing social justice is by *getting rid of production for private profit* and substituting production for the use of the community". In so far as the role of the private sector was discussed, it was in terms of its statutory reorganization and rationalization, the criteria that would be applied to this process and the objectives with which it would be pursued.

That said, it was the case that the literature of the 1930s did reflect the historical experience of 1929–31 and some of the new economic thinking discussed above and in many respects therefore it *was* qualitatively different from that of the 1920s. In particular there was emphasis on a swift and decisive transference of economic power to the state, something which was absent from the Fabianism of the 1920s, with its stress upon piecemeal gradualism. The transition to an economy built on public ownership must be rapid and substantial. As the authors of *For socialism and peace* put it, what was wanted was "a rapid advance to a Socialist reconstruction of national life".[72] In the early 1930s this was to include too the nationalization of the banking system and the setting up of a "National Banking Corporation", though debate continued within the Party as to whether the clearing banks should indeed be nationalized. In fact, the Party's position on that changed over time. In documents such as *For socialism and peace*, *Socialism and the condition of the people* (1934), *Labour's financial policy* (1935) and *Why the banks should be nationalised* (1936) they were to be nationalized; in *Labour's immediate programme* (1937) they were not. But the important point to note is the stress that was now placed on the need to secure public control over money and credit. No less than eight out of the 20 pages of *Socialism and the condition of the people* were devoted to "banking, finance and investment". Further, in detailing its "four vital measures of reconstruction", *Labour's immediate programme* listed finance first: "The control of the financial machine, of currency, banking and investment policy [was] now in the forefront of the Labour Party's Programme."[73]

Another fundamental point of contrast with the literature of the 1920s was the emphasis placed on the pursuit by Labour of apposite policies of macroeconomic management. Here it is interesting to note that, by way of theoretical underpinning, *Socialism and the condition of the people* effectively reproduced, in simplified form, the explanation of economic fluctuations that Keynes furnished in his *Treatise on money*.[74] Thus it reasoned that where aggregate saving was greater than aggregate investment, "the money forthcoming for the purchase of goods falls short of the money spent on their production, and there is a fall in prices and decline in employment", the excess of savings being used to cover these windfall losses. Further, "the more savings are diverted into the mere financing of losses the less are available for fresh investment . . . the less expenditure there is on capital goods, and the greater is the decline in prices and employment". As the authors of the pamphlet saw it, this was the British experience of the early 1930s, which had seen a cumulative contraction in the level of economic activity. Where, on the contrary, aggregate investment was greater than aggregate saving then windfall profits and an unstable boom would occur. Such had been the case in the run up to 1929. A primary "object of the national control of investment" should therefore be "*to make investment equal to savings*" as well as "to divert it into socially useful channels".[75] In that way "financial policy" could be used to "bridge more adequately the gulf between production and consumption . . . avoid[ing] the booms and slumps which have for so long been so regular a feature of our financial system".[76] Thus under the influence of Keynes and others the Party was, by the 1930s, clearly discussing the problem of general economic depression using theoretical constructs markedly different from those of the 1920s and this had important implications for the kind of economic policies that it advanced.

It was in the context of this view of slumps that the Party's proposals for "national economic development" were put forward. This programme of development was to be carried through under the auspices of a National Investment Board that would, in conjunction with a nationalized banking system, "co-ordinate the mobilisation and allocation of that part of the national wealth which is available for investment". It would formulate a "scheme of national investment" and so "act as an instrument of Government engaged in operating national planning". However, the literature also envisaged its powers being used as a means of macroeconomic management: it would be responsible for "a bold programme of national development which would not only diminish unemployment substantially, but, by increasing public revenue and reducing expenditure on unemployment benefit, will relieve Budgetary stringency". So the literature took on board the Keynesian point that such a policy of investment expenditure would not only create employment but would also, through its impact on the general level of economic activity, solve the problem of balancing the Budget.[77]

Moreover there was in the literature a clear expression of the multiplier and a recognition of the implications it had for the cost of employment creation. *For socialism and peace* stated that:

> it should not be forgotten that new expenditure in development not only creates employment directly and indirectly, in respect of the particular schemes of work put in hand, but *creates further employment in*

> *an ever-widening circle*, through the payment of wages to those who are now unemployed and who, through their increased purchasing power, are enabled to buy additional goods and services.

Further, as regards the cost of such employment creation, it should not be forgotten that "many items in the programme . . . are directly revenue producing and would pay for their own cost".[78] The parallel with Keynes's defence of public works expenditure could not have been closer and, indeed, in *Socialism and the condition of the people*, specific reference was made to his *Means to prosperity* (1933).[79]

As regards the task of controlling the level of aggregate investment the nationalized Bank of England, through its conduct of monetary policy, would also play an important role. This it would do "by buying or selling government securities and by raising or lowering the Bank Rate", thereby affecting the level of private investment.[80] It should be said too that this policy of demand management was also seen as one that aimed at price stabilization.

But if the influence of Keynes can be detected, there are also definite liberal socialist inflections. Thus *For socialism and peace* saw "the prevailing economic depression [as] in large measure the result of the operation of an economic system which fails to distribute purchasing power in effective relation to its capacity to produce". In consequence "more spending power must be provided for the great body of consumers whose income is represented by wages and salaries". To this end the pamphlet recommended the extension of the Trade Boards Act, the improvement of the existing agricultural wages machinery and the creation of adequate wages machinery on a national scale. As with Hobson and others, therefore, the objective was to move the economy out of depression by increasing working-class purchasing power. In addition "taxation" could also "be used to secure a better distribution of wealth *and purchasing power*".[81] This is all strongly Hobsonian, though it should be said that the articulation of such a position also reflected the general climate of opinion within the Party, created by Durbin, Meade, Gaitskell, Jay and others. This was important too as regards the reception and articulation of Keynesian ideas, whether those of the *Treatise*, *The means to prosperity* or *The general theory*. That said, it should be noted as regards the last that while a memorandum on it and its policy implications was produced for the Labour Party by Gaitskell, Durbin, Jay and Clark, "*specific* commitment" to the use of Keynesian techniques to effect economic expansion" was removed "at the drafting stage" of *Labour's immediate programme*.[82]

Even so, while the extension of public ownership and the rhetoric of science, efficiency and rationality might still dominate the Labour Party's economic literature in the 1930s, that literature now also emphasized the need for macroeconomic management using both monetary and fiscal policy.

In that respect it expressed and reflected some of those powerful theoretical currents within socialist political economy that this chapter has identified and which were to flow even more strongly in the post-war period. Yet, as Elizabeth Durbin has made clear, *Labour's immediate programme* emphasized the need to achieve the stability of trade and employment, not its expansion by means of the levers of demand management. The triumph of such Keynesian ideas within the Labour Party was to lie in the future.[83]

As regards the external dimension of the conduct of economic policy, though the idea of fluctuating exchange rates and other expedients had been mooted by writers such as Meade and Durbin, while protectionist ideas were also current and while G. D. H. Cole advanced the idea of planned trade, the Party continued to adhere to the idea of a stable exchange rate and never wholeheartedly accommodated the idea of protection, though the idea of boards to regulate the flow of imports was put forward in Party literature. Free trade aspirations were still articulated, in particular by the leadership. Yet, given the generally protectionist climate of the 1930s, there was a recognition that a compromise had to be struck between economic principle and economic expediency and to that extent, positive proposals aside, the Party did not commit itself to any fundamental dismantling of the protectionist structures that had been erected since 1932.

Part three

1945–70

Chapter 11

Theory into practice, 1945–51

> . . . whether one tries to look forward from 1945 or backwards from forty years later, those years [1945–51] appear in retrospect, and rightly so, as years when the government knew where it wanted to go and led the country with an understanding of what was at stake.
>
> Alec Cairncross, *Years of recovery*, 1985

The Labour Party took with it from the inter-war period a determination to effect a substantial and swift extension of public ownership, a commitment to a fundamental redistribution of wealth, a pledge to enhance social welfare provision, a preparedness to use monetary and fiscal policy as the basis of macroeconomic management and a general insistence on the need for planning, along with an ambiguous notion of what economic planning entailed. It is the purpose of this chapter to consider the extent to which these commitments, in the Labour Party economic literature of the 1930s and elsewhere, were actually fulfilled in terms of the conduct of policy.

Taking the last commitment first, to evaluate the success or otherwise with which socialist economic planning was implemented by the post-war Labour governments, it is vital at the outset to consider the nature of the ambiguity alluded to. For, as regards one conception of planning, the record may be deemed that of failure, while, as regards the other, it was one of considerable achievement. In essence the ambiguity in the use of the term "planning" lay in this. For some, such as Meade and Jay, planning meant, in effect, macroeconomic management, with fiscal and monetary policy being used to manipulate aggregate demand to secure, primarily, non-inflationary full employment, such demand management being supplemented where necessary by exchange and import controls to cope with any balance of payments difficulties either on current or capital account. The objectives of economic management having been achieved, in particular that of full employment, the price mechanism could, with certain provisos, be left to effect an efficient allocation of resources.

For others, such as G. D. H. Cole, economic planning involved the state determining social and economic priorities and then ensuring the appropriate allocation of resources in relation to the needs it had identified and the goals it set. This view of planning downplayed the role of the price mechanism and emphasized the importance of direct, often physical, controls to secure the desired outcome. It also emphasized the supply-side aspect of planning and thence the need for a microeconomic and discriminatory dimension.

Of course the division between the two conceptions of planning was not always clear cut. Those who conceived of planning in terms of macroeconomic management did admit the need for some direct controls, in particular over overseas investment, imports, building and even the prices of particular products. Without them, it was believed, the government might not be able to use fiscal and monetary policy to achieve its full employment objectives. Further, the proponents of planning of the directive, microeconomic kind accepted the need for Keynesian-style demand management as a supplement. Thus the complaint of someone like Cole was not that such macroeconomic management was unnecessary in the context of a planned economy but that it neither encompassed nor was sufficient for socialist planning. Nevertheless, though they shared some common ground, when it came to efficiently allocating scarce resources and distributing the national product in an equitable fashion, there was this crucial difference between the two conceptions: while the former sought to supplement, the latter, in large measure, aimed to supplant the price mechanism.

Along with an emphatic general commitment to planning – "the Labour Party offers a national plan", "Labour will plan from the ground up" – the 1945 Labour Party Manifesto, *Let us face the future*, embodied both conceptions, as did much of the economic literature produced by the Labour Party in the immediate post-war period. Thus while recognizing what might be achieved by way of maintaining "a high and constant purchasing power", it also made the point that "if the slumps in uncontrolled private industry are too severe to be balanced by [such] public action – as they will certainly prove to be", then "control of private industry" and "an extension of the public sector" would be necessary to achieve the objective of full employment.[1] Further, the Manifesto suggested the use "of suitable economic and price controls to secure that first things shall come first . . . *There must be priorities in the use of raw materials . . . It is either sound economic controls – or smash*".[2] This commitment to both conceptions of planning is also particularly apparent in the 1945 Manifesto's discussion of the role to be played by a National Investment Board. Thus, as regards national investment, it was to have the directive planning function of "determin[ing] social priorities" but also the contracyclical, macroeconomic management role of "promot[ing] better timing in public investment".[3]

The influence of a directive, discriminatory, supply-side view of planning was apparent in the immediate post-war period and, indeed, underpinned what one commentator has termed "Mr. Attlee's supply-side socialism"[4] – measures that aimed, however tentatively and unsuccessfully, to restructure and modernize the British economy with a view to effecting a substantial increase in labour productivity. However, for a number of reasons, its influence waned considerably as the period progressed.

To begin with, and crucially, there was the problem of the instruments by means of which such planning was to be rendered effective. Stafford Cripps, who initially articulated support for this kind of planning, pursued the idea and the practice of a manpower budget, which had been used during the war and which, he believed, could continue to provide the basis for economic calculation in manpower terms. This would enable planners to establish how this particular scarce (in the post-war period) and vital resource might best be allocated to satisfy those national needs that they identified. Planning on this basis had, after all, proved successful during the war and directive powers were available in the immediate post-war period to ensure that, once determined, the desired allocation of labour resources could be effectively secured. However, it was soon recognized that directive measures permissible in war were increasingly unpalatable in time of peace.

Of course, that still left open the possibility of manpower allocation by means of wages planning and this proposal did indeed come from a number of quarters. Figures such as Durbin, Crossman and others within the Party were strong advocates of such planning as a means of attaining a distribution of labour consistent with planning objectives, without recourse to overt coercion. Such views were pressed with particular force at a time when there was a labour shortage in strategic industries, such as coal, but opposition from within the Party and, in particular, the trade union movement prevented "wage planning" being taken on board by the government. In so far as the government did introduce a wages policy it was one involving the co-operation of the trade union movement; a policy of voluntary restraint (in the 1948–50 period), the aim of which was the macroeconomic one of damping down inflationary pressures, rather than effecting a planned distribution of manpower. Thus, proponents of directive, supply-side planning were denied an important means of securing an allocation of labour consistent with planning objectives and one that avoided the political and social diseconomies attaching to alternative methods employing coercion.

In fact, as regards the implementation of directive, supply-side planning the government, in the immediate post-war period, tended rather to favour some of the physical/quantitative controls over scarce raw materials such as steel and timber, which it had inherited from the war. However, the use of such controls, as well as rationing, licensing of production and distribution, building licences and industrial development certificates to control location, became increasingly problematic as the period progressed. For what occurred during the years of Labour government was a dismantling of a substantial part of this wartime control structure. Thus the so-called "bonfire of controls", initiated by the then President of the Board of Trade, Harold Wilson, in 1948, continued throughout the remainder of Labour's period in office, with only a brief reversal after the outbreak of the Korean war. By 1951, therefore, many of the controls inherited from the war had gone, superseded by the more or less untrammelled operation of the market mechanism. Direct controls and restrictions, tolerable in time of war when a national government could rely on social unanimity and a sacrificial spirit in pursuing a single objective, became less so when there emerged both a plurality of competing goals and an impatience with constraints that interfered with the free enjoyment of the fruits of victory. One should not, of course, exaggerate the scale of de-control but it was sufficient to call into question many of the means by which the supporters of directive, supply-side planning would have hoped to attain their ends.

In addition, as regards planning instruments, the 1947 *Economic survey* emphasized the need for and reliance on an acceptance "by Government, both sides of industry and the people" of the planners' objectives.[5] Such an acceptance would, it was believed, induce a consequent concerted effort to attain them and to this end there were propaganda campaigns exhorting the populace to act in such ways as would further the pursuit of planning goals. However, it is generally agreed that the government's campaigns of exhortation had little effect. More importantly, as regards the use of persuasion, many Labour ministers laid great stress on the tripartite co-operation between management, trade unions and the government in organizations such as the National Joint Advisory Council (concerned with wages and conditions) and National Production Council for Industry (concerned with production). Indeed, for many in the Labour Party, such tripartite consultation and deliberation was what economic planning was all about. However, far from being a part of a planning apparatus geared to the implementation of planning directives, such organizations simply proved to be a means by which the government acquired information and sounded out both sides of industry about policy proposals.

Commentators have also identified other significant obstacles in the way of Labour's pursuit of directive, supply-side economic planning.[6] First, the considerable autonomy of the commercially orientated Morrisonian public corporations, by means of which the commanding heights of the economy were nationalized, militated against their control by a central planning authority. Secondly, the desire for consensus inherent in the government's emphasis upon tripartite co-operation made it difficult for it to act in the coercive or discriminatory manner that directive, microeconomic planning necessitated. Thirdly there was an unwillingness on the part of Labour to embark upon the substantial institutional reforms necessary to create a central planning authority having the powers and autonomy necessary to formulate and implement a National Plan. There was, in this, a definite reluctance to go down the road traversed by the French in the post-war period with the establishment of something comparable to the Commissariat Général du Plan.

It was also the case that the theoretical difficulties involved in reconciling conflicting demands for available scarce resources by way of some planned system of prioritization were never satisfactorily addressed. Indeed from the literature one can see they were often evaded in exactly those ways that characterized the work of previous generations of socialist economic thinkers who had sought to confront the technical difficulties involved in marketless planning, or at least planning where the price mechanism played a limited role. There was, for example, the ploy of simplification by analogy. Thus the 1947 *Economic survey* stated that the problem (of prioritization) was

> precisely that, only on a national scale, *which the housewife has to solve every week.* On the one side are the resources that we have to spend, on the other, are the things upon which we want to spend them. The two must be made to match. After full examination of possible means of attaining a balance, the official committee submits to ministers a report on what measures should be taken and their decisions form the basis of subsequent action.[7]

Thus the reduction of the knotty problem of providing a non-market evaluation of different kinds of output to one of housekeeping meant, in this instance, that the complex theoretical questions that it raised were simply avoided.

For all these reasons there was, therefore, a diminution in the influence and policy impact of the idea of directive/discriminatory supply-side socialist planning in the 1945–51 period while, at the same time, that of planning as macroeconomic management grew. This is reflected in a number of developments. Negatively, there was the removal of controls and the decline in the importance of manpower budgeting that can be seen after 1947. The former indicated an increasing reliance on the market mechanism and thence support for a conception of planning in which it played a crucial pricing, allocative and distributive role. The latter removed a possible basis for implementing the alternative conception of planning.

More positively, as early as 1944, acceptance by the Coalition Government of a White Paper on *Employment policy* had involved a commitment to this kind of "planning"/management; even if that document had failed to specify with any precision the instruments by which it might be implemented. Moreover, the integration of budgetary calculation with the national accounts, which had occurred during the war period, furnished a statistical basis for the economic calculation that such "planning" required. In this respect, and as the first attempt to use it to manage aggregate expenditure in the economy, Kingsley Wood's Budget of 1941 represented an important landmark.

However, as regards the conduct of fiscal policy, most commentators point to Hugh Dalton's last, emergency, Budget of November 1947, with its clear acceptance of demand management as *the* means of tackling the pressing problem of inflation, as epitomizing the triumph of this macro-management conception of planning; though it should be noted that even before that the National Insurance Act of 1946 had made provision for the discretionary contracyclical variation of national insurance contributions.[8] Certainly, by 1950, we find Cripps, as Chancellor of the Exchequer, unambiguously stressing the vital role to be played by both fiscal and monetary measures in a slump. Then, in early 1951, the second draft of a so-called Full Employment Bill aimed to give the government powers to subsidize the cost to local authorities and nationalized industries of the preparation and revision of plans to create a reserve of public works that could be introduced in a period of depression. This Bill also sought to give the government the means to stimulate private investment in similar circumstances. All these are indications of the fact that, as Cairncross has phrased it, "economic planning was [being] increasingly seen in terms of measures to maintain full employment, check inflation and preserve external balance". In other words: "demand management rather than intervention to control use of resources directly or improve efficiency, was the order of the day."[9] A Keynesian socialist conception of economic planning was in the ascendant.

Also, with respect to the increasing support for economic management as against directive, supply-side planning, it is important to note the role of economists in government. This had increased markedly during the war and the influence they wielded remained considerable in the post-war period. More importantly, such economists were often of a Keynesian, liberal socialist persuasion, seeing the primary economic responsibility of government as that of securing the full utilization of resources, rather than promoting restructuring or modernization. To the extent that such a view prevailed, so too did the macro-management as against the directive-discriminatory view of planning. In this regard the role of economists such as James Meade and Robert Hall was critical. As directors of the Economic Section of the Cabinet Office in the post-war period the influence they could exert upon government opinion was considerable.[10] In this context it should be said too that the existence of economists of a Keynesian persuasion in the government machine also provided the skills necessary to implement a policy of macroeconomic management.

Finally it can be argued that macroeconomic management triumphed because it provided the policy instruments needed to tackle some, at least, of the most pressing short-run problems that bedevilled the post-war Labour governments. Thus, as regards inflationary pressures (exacerbated by the outbreak of the Korean war) and periodic balance of payments crises, the Keynesian tool box furnished what was necessary for the kind of quick fix which, in the context of British electoral politics, is so important for political survival, even if it does nothing to tackle the underlying weaknesses in the British economy that make such fixes necessary.

Yet, if there was a growing acceptance of planning as macroeconomic management, one should be careful not to see this as synonymous with the triumph within the ranks of Labour of an unadulterated Keynesianism. In so far as the Party carried forward the banners of the Keynesian revolution they were often reluctant or at least tardy revolutionaries. Thus, as noted above, it was only in Dalton's last Budget (November 1947) that he linked increases in taxation to the macroeconomic objective of eliminating inflationary pressures and only gradually was there overt and general recognition that budget surpluses might have a vital role in this regard.[11] In addition, in the period 1945–51, there was no occasion when Labour was put to the Keynesian test of implementing expansionary demand management policies to counter the forces of deflation and depression, though it did seek to put pressure on nationalized industries and local authorities to have in the pipeline investment projects that could be used for contracyclical purposes.

That said, even if it may be questioned whether the conduct of economic policy by post-war Labour governments represented the triumph of the Keynesian revolution, by 1951 many in the Party had come to accept that fiscal policy was a fundamental instrument of macroeconomic management and also that it could prove a vital and *effective* means of securing full employment and so prevent a recurrence of the evils of the inter-war period. Thus they believed that the battle against mass unemployment could be won and capitalism reinvigorated by such means rather than by comprehensive and directive socialist planning.

What then of the other objectives to which Labour had committed itself in the literature of the 1930s and, on the eve of office, in *Let us face the future*? To begin with there was the determination to enhance social welfare provision and here the Labour government moved quickly to implement the recommendations of the Beveridge Report on Social Insurance and Allied Services of 1942. The Family Allowance Act, 1945, provided universal child allowances; the National Insurance Act, 1946, furnished a comprehensive insurance system of flat-rate contributions and benefits to cover interruptions of earnings from ill-health and unemployment; while the National Assistance Act, 1948, guaranteed a minimum subsistence income. Further, there was the creation of the National Health Service in 1948. The idea of such a service had been accepted in principle by the Coalition Government in a White

Paper of February 1944, but it was left to Aneurin Bevan to carry it through in the teeth of opposition both within the medical profession and from the civil service. While it is true, therefore, that in terms of White Papers and Reports, much of the groundwork for Labour's construction of the welfare state had been laid during the war, this cannot detract from its achievement in translating aspiration into legislation.

It was also the case that the post-war Labour Government effected a significant redistribution of wealth in favour of the poorer sections of the community. Direct personal taxation remained high in the post-war period, while price controls, food subsidies and rationing were used to implement a "fair shares" policy. Some commentators have indeed suggested that this amounted to a deleterious sacrifice of economic growth to distributive justice. However, in the light of the shift of resources in favour of exports and investment that occurred in the period and in view of the subsequent performance of the British economy in these years, such charges would seem difficult to substantiate. In any case, the heightened expectations that followed on from victory and the election of a Labour Government were imperatives demanding redistributive action that could not be ignored.

The post-war Labour governments also successfully implemented the programme of nationalization that had been outlined in *Let us face the future.* In fact, the greater part of the legislation provoked little opposition. The state and local authorities were already heavily involved in electricity distribution, coal and gas and, as regards these industries, there was general support for large operational units. Such, certainly, had been the view of a number of committees of inquiry in the inter-war period. The nationalization of the Bank of England, Cable and Wireless Ltd, civil aviation and the railways were all relatively uncontroversial: in the case of civil aviation, a White Paper of March 1945 had indicated the institutional form that public ownership should take, and as regards road transport services and road haulage, there was already a measure of state control and local authority ownership. Only in the case of iron and steel and sugar was there significant opposition and then, in the case of the former, not with respect to the need for state involvement as such, but to the proposals for outright state ownership.

The form that public ownership took did provoke greater contention and raised issues that continued to be matters of debate and concern within the Labour Party in subsequent decades. Thus it generally involved the creation of a national corporation or the management of an industry by a small number of area boards and, therefore, considerable centralization of control. These corporations were given a large measure of autonomy, in particular with respect to the day to day running of the industry. They became, in effect, industrial fiefs with rulers pursuing their own essentially commercial agenda. As a result many of the erstwhile advocates of nationalization were to be disappointed.

In fact, what became apparent in this period was the variety of often incompatible hopes vested in the extension of public ownership by its supporters. Some had seen it as a means of redistributing wealth and improving working conditions, others as the basis for national economic planning or at least macroeconomic management, while many had viewed it as providing the means of restructuring the nation's industrial base and rejuvenating her staple industries. Some had hoped it would provide opportunities for the extension of industrial democracy, with control of the means of production finally vested in those who used them. Many had also believed that public ownership would at last make possible production for social need rather than profit. However, it was the technocratic not the democratic vision that triumphed and it was commercial rather than social or moral criteria that governed public enterprise decision-making, and this was to engender much controversy, and not a little acrimony, in the years that lay ahead.

If Labour, by 1951, could therefore maintain that it had fulfilled many of the commitments with which it had entered office in July 1945, it could also claim a significant measure of success as regards its general conduct of the nation's economic affairs. The most pressing problem the Labour Government had had to confront in the summer of 1945 was that of the dollar gap – the difference between dollar receipts and dollar earnings. The Americans' ending of Lend-Lease, which had provided a substantial part of the external finance necessary to conduct the war; the diminution of invisible earnings both as a result of the war itself and also the sale of dollar-earning assets to finance it; the scaling down of export industries to release resources for the war effort and the servicing of a much expanded dollar debt all made for a problem of considerable magnitude. To close that gap and, more generally, to bring the balance of payments into equilibrium, it was estimated in 1946 that it would be necessary to raise exports 75 per cent above their 1938 level. In fact, by 1950, there had been a 77 per cent rise, while in the period 1945–50 exports rose fourfold. Thus, with respect to the country's general balance of payments performance, Cairncross has written that though "there was a fresh balance-of-payments crisis every odd year" (1947, 1949, 1951) there was also "a fairly steep underlying trend towards equilibrium; first in the overall balance, which was reached in 1948, and then in the dollar balance, which can be said to have been reached in 1952".[12]

Of course this performance was due, in large measure, to the general buoyancy of world markets in the post-war period and to the fact that Germany and Japan were initially out of the running as major competitors. Even so the Labour governments must be given some credit for what occurred. The use of direct controls (e.g. over manpower and raw materials) to steer resources in the direction of the export industries; the deliberate targeting of the US market; the restriction of imports; the dampening of consumer demand and a policy of substituting non-dollar for dollar imports and voluntary wage restraint on the part of the trade unions – all had a salutary impact.

Further, in terms of economic performance, the period 1946–52 saw industrial production increase by over a third, GNP by over 15 per cent and investment by almost 60 per cent. Most importantly, this achievement occurred in a context of full employment, despite a substantial redeployment of labour from the armed forces into the civilian workforce. Thus, in the period until (end) 1946, it has been estimated that the civilian labour force increased by some five million or over 40 per cent. Nor, during this period, although inflationary pressures certainly existed, was their any significant rise in the general level of prices. Here food subsidies, price controls, rationing, fiscal policy and the moral suasion that a Labour government could use on trade union leaders, all served their purpose.

It should also be said that such economic progress was made at a time when substantial investment was necessary to repair the destruction of social and industrial infrastructure and the depreciation of fixed capital assets resulting from a prolonged war, at a time when Britain's global military commitments were substantially out of line with her economic strength and when the sterling reserves held by countries in the Sterling Area threatened to prove the Achilles' heel of the British economy. It is true that there were failures, crises and continuing problems. The fuel crisis of 1947, the convertibility crisis of the same year and that surrounding the devaluation of 1949, all indicated just how precarious economic progress could be. In addition, as already noted, Labour Ministers were frequently unclear as to what could and what should be achieved by way of the traditional socialist nostrums of planning and management and did not always grasp the nature of the policy options open to them. Nevertheless, this should not obscure the substantial progress that was made on the economic front in the 1945–51 period. Thus Cairncross in his authoritative review of the conduct of British economic policy in these years has concluded that the Labour governments, "pointed the economy in the right direction, rode out the various crises that the years of transition almost inevitably gave rise to and, by 1951, had brought the economy near to eventual balance."[13]

In general then, it was against a backdrop of what was seen as considerable achievement that political economists in the 1950s had to consider the future of socialism and the nature of future socialist progress. At least part of the foundations of the New Jerusalem had been laid and that in itself necessitated some reconsideration of socialist means and socialist ends. Further, the Labour government had shown that a mixed economy could be run in such a way as to achieve full employment, historically high rates of economic growth, rising living standards and relative economic stability. If, therefore, so much had been achieved, what more remained to be done? Now that the commanding heights had been nationalized, into what industrial sectors and with what objectives could public ownership be extended? If the existing mixture of public and private in the mixed economy had been the agent of such material prosperity what utility was there in extending public ownership at all? What could be done to circumvent or rectify the problems that Morrisonian nationalization had thrown up? What scope remained for the redistribution of wealth and income by fiscal means and to what extent could the expansion of the welfare state be funded from the revenue sources that socialists had traditionally highlighted? More generally, as living standards rose, it was necessary to consider whether economic inequities and iniquities were what socialists should be focusing upon at all. Surely there were other, more pressing, problems that socialists should be in the business of resolving. Finally, as regards planning the question arose as to whether, given the maintenance of full employment, the macroeconomic approach had been vindicated and, if so, what value there was in socialist economic planning of a more microeconomic and directive nature.

Whither socialism? In the light of six years' experience of Labour government and in view of that government's economic and social achievements, this was the fundamental problem that socialist political economists now confronted. It is with the manner in which they did so and their consequent rethinking of the nature, objectives and instruments of socialist political economy that the next chapter is concerned.

Chapter 12
Socialism in an age of affluence, 1945–64

> Posthumously, the Webbs have won their battle, and converted a generation to their standards. Now the time has come for a reaction: for a greater emphasis on private life, on freedom and dissent, on culture, beauty, leisure, and even frivolity. Total abstinence and a good filing-system are not now the right sign-posts to the socialist Utopia: or at least, if they are, some of us will fall by the way-side."
>
> C. A. R. Crosland, *The future of socialism*, 1956

Is it capitalism?

If in the inter-war period socialist political economists were forced to grapple with the consequences of economic depression and the limitations it imposed upon socialist advance, in the two decades after 1945 they had to confront the theoretical and practical difficulties posed by the growing material prosperity and rapidly rising living standards of Western industrial nations. Thus, as one writer put it, "the capitalist system having accepted and digested the implications of Keynesianism and the reforms of the Attlee administrations has once again proved that it can operate efficiently."[1] If in the 1930s they had to come to terms with being in the political wilderness and the business of finding a way out, in the immediate post-war period they had to cope with Labour's conquest of political power and its success in implementing a significant part of the programme it had presented to the electorate in 1945. As Richard Crossman wrote in 1950, "All that talk about "capturing the bastions of capitalism and then nobody resisted . . . Those who manned the defences of Jericho could not have been more surprised than those socialists who saw the walls of capitalism tumble down after a short blast on the Fabian trumpet."[2] In the light of all this, in view of the altered economic and political circumstances they confronted, many socialist thinkers believed it imperative that they rethink and revise the political economy to which they adhered. In particular they considered it imperative to reassess the changed and changing nature of British capitalism, for only then would it be possible to consider what had been achieved and what, for the future, might prove possible and effective lines of socialist advance.

As regards the nature of capitalism most socialist writers in the post-1945 period believed that its character had, in fact, been fundamentally altered. Indeed, for Tony Crosland the social and economic arrangements that existed in post-war Britain could no longer, legitimately, be labelled capitalist at all; for all practical, political purposes capitalism no longer existed and the major problem confronting socialist thinkers was how to accommodate that fact. Some shared Crosland's view. Thus the authors of *Socialism, a new statement of principles* (1952) argued that "full employment, planning controls, housing programmes, social security, the national health service, progressive taxation, have produced a situation to which no ready-made label can be tagged".[3] Capitalism's own inner dynamic and the social and economic policies that resulted from democratic pressure had effected such fundamental changes in the economic system that it had, in its essentials, ceased to be capitalist. Roy Jenkins in *In pursuit of progress* (1953) stated that what existed in Britain, by that date, was "well-removed from capitalism in the traditional sense of the word"; what had emerged was "a managerial society controlled by a privileged elite";[4] the dream of the Fabians turned nightmare. Others were, however, convinced that something that could legitimately be labelled capitalism still existed. Yet even they accepted that the label required a qualifying adjective. Thus Richard Crossman wrote of "welfare capitalism" and John Strachey of "last-stage capitalism".[5] For them, capitalism might exist but it had been fundamentally altered, in particular by Labour's creation of the welfare state and the successful pursuit of full employment.

As well as by its dynamism and, in consequence, its capacity to furnish rising living standards for the bulk of the working population, many socialists also believed that the capitalism they confronted was now characterized by a radically altered distribution of economic power. As these writers saw it power was now dispersed; a pluralistic configuration prevailed. Power was no longer monopolized by a class of capitalist owners.[6] The state, for example, now possessed considerable authority and responsibilities in the economic sphere. Specifically, nationalization and the commitment to full employment both served to limit the power that capitalists could wield: the former circumscribing the area of the economy over which private enterprise held sway, the latter significantly enhancing the bargaining power of trade unions. Further, for many socialists, the managerial revolution had effectively taken power out of the hands of capitalist owners and placed it in those of professional managers. Thus Roy Jenkins considered the capitalist class to have surrendered their power, "partly to the state, partly to their own managers and partly to the trade unions".[7] They could, therefore, no longer play their traditional role of exploiters of labour or enemies of social progress. In addition, these professionally managed private enterprises were increasingly subject to a network of legislative controls.

Some also argued that such enterprises were driven by different motives and pursued different objectives from the traditional capitalist goal of profit maximization. In consequence, productive activity responded to imperatives radically different from those that had previously set it in motion. This was certainly the view of Crosland, who, for that reason too, believed that existing economic arrangements could no longer be denominated capitalist. For Crosland the professional manager was motivated not by the self-interested pursuit of material gain but, primarily, by the desire to enhance the "social prestige" enjoyed by the enterprise over which he exerted control, for it was that which determined his own social standing. Such an objective could be achieved in a variety of ways – "by gaining a reputation as a progressive employer" or by donations from company funds to worthy causes – but it would generally ensure that firms were run with greater sensitivity to public opinion than had previously been the case. The "new-style executive . . . subconsciously longed for the approval of society" and the "sociologist", with the result that the "aggressive individualism of the capitalist entrepreneur" had given way to "a suave and sophisticated sociability".[8] Where such motives drove the economic machine forward, capitalism, as Crosland saw it, had ceased in any meaningful sense to exist.

These views were prefigured in essays and articles written in the early 1950s but were to be most fully developed in one of the classics of post-war socialist revisionism, *The future of socialism* (1956), a book in which Crosland sought to redirect the critical thrust of British socialism and by so doing radically alter its policy agenda. For if the demise of capitalism was a *fait accompli*, then much of contemporary socialist thinking was effectively redundant, formulated as it had been in opposition to a set of economic and social arrangements and attendant iniquities that no longer existed.

However, whether, like Crosland, socialist political economists saw capitalism as dead or dying or transformed they recognized that both the critical and the constructive aspects of their socialism required revision in the light of the radically different economic, social and political circumstances that now prevailed. Opinion might differ on the degree of revision and what socialist principles and policies were to be revised but there were few who did not accept the need for some reconsideration of how the cause of socialism might be advanced. There were exceptions. There *was* a fundamentalist opposition to the many and varied forms that revisionism took. But it was small in number and, for a time at least, it was swimming against a powerful current of intellectual fashion and a rising tide of material prosperity that in itself made imperative the need to rethink the objectives of socialism and the manner in which they were pursued.

Public ownership

This rethinking is particularly evident in the discussion that took place in this period of the role and future extension of public ownership. Thus, for Crosland, the fact that capitalism had ceased to exist, that the capitalists' monopoly of economic power had been broken and that private enterprise now followed more socially acceptable objectives led him to question the central place that nationalization and municipalization had previously been accorded as regards the policy prescriptions of the Labour Party. If the extension of public ownership was to be justified it had to be on grounds other than the collective appropriation of capitalist power and its use for social purposes.

In *The future of socialism* Crosland considered three. First, he appraised the Fabian argument that public ownership was necessary to set about the conscious planning of economic activity designed to ensure that resources were allocated to the satisfaction of real social need rather than the indulgent desires of the rich. For Crosland, however, the market could now be relied upon to achieve that objective. The more equitable distribution of wealth that had resulted from social welfare legislation, full employment and the attenuation of capitalist power meant that "production for use and production for profit may be taken as broadly coinciding now that working-class purchasing power is so high. What is profitable is what the consumer finds useful and the firm and the consumer desire broadly the same allocation of resources".[9]

Secondly, it had been argued by many socialists that the extension of social ownership was required to give planners the power necessary to ensure the full and efficient allocation of economic resources. Here Crosland argued that, as regards the planning necessary to attain that objective, what was needed was the control of broad macroeconomic aggregates, and for this the requisite powers were already in the planners' hands. An extension of public ownership was not what was required to permit effective planning of this kind, but rather the political will to use the power already possessed. "If socialists want bolder planning", wrote Crosland, "they must choose bolder Ministers".[10]

Thirdly, there was the argument that nationalization was required as a redistributive measure, permitting the appropriation and more equitable distribution by the state of an economic surplus that would otherwise accrue to capitalist owners. However, this argument was rejected, first, because compensation to owners of nationalized firms would severely limit the redistributive effects of extending public ownership and, secondly, because such effects would be significant only where efficient and profitable industries were nationalized; industries whose nationalization would, in political and economic terms, be the most difficult to justify, accomplish and defend.

For Crosland, therefore, the traditional objective of public ownership had ceased to have any kind of central importance. It was certainly no longer the touchstone of socialism or crucial to distinguishing the Labour Party from its opponents. As he wrote in 1960:

> for many years past the Labour Party has not fought elections primarily on the issue of nationalization. It has fought them rather on housing, education, social services, planning, the distribution of income and foreign and colonial policy and it has found no difficulty whatsoever in differentiating itself from the Conservatives.[11]

That said, Crosland might have added that it had found considerable difficulty in winning elections.

Crosland's was an extreme position among the revisionists and one that provoked considerable opposition as evidenced by the defeat of an attempt to remove Clause Four from the Labour Party Constitution after its third successive General Election defeat in 1959.[12] Yet in the aftermath of the nationalizations of 1945–51 there were few commentators and theorists who did not have doubts and reservations about what had been achieved and what could be achieved by similar extensions of public ownership. In particular, many socialist commentators expressed concern about the consequences of the form that nationalization had assumed. Thus the public corporations created were in the Morrisonian mould (effectively autonomous as regards the day to day running of the industry) and, for some, this posed problems for the pursuit of socialist ends. Even those who, in contrast to Crosland, stressed the fundamental importance of expanding the sphere of public ownership were often critical of this autonomy, seeing it as inimical to the use of nationalized industries as an instrument of economic planning. For, to the extent that such corporations were independent of government, they ceased to be a means by which socialist planners could achieve socialist objectives. As the authors of *Keeping left* (1947) saw it, "we are prevented by it [their autonomy] from integrating their price policies into national economic planning . . . they cannot be used to influence the price mechanism according to social priorities. We thus rob ourselves of a flexible and useful tool in the task of correlating demand and supply."[13] Further, there were fears that in the absence of political and thence democratic control, nationalized industries might come to lay the basis not for socialism but for managerialism. As Bevan wrote in 1952, in *In place of fear:* "we have still to ensure that they [the boards of nationalized industries] are taking us towards democratic socialism, not towards the Managerial Society."[14]

Similar fears were expressed by Roy Jenkins, who wrote of the emergence of a "horrid managerialism" that encompassed both those public and private corporations wielding monopoly powers; while Hugh Gaitskell too wrote of the defects of "large scale management" which "have been evident in the nationalised industries".[15] In the same vein the authors of *Socialism, a new statement of principles* saw nationalized industries as a key component of "a managerial society", a society that "is in essence run by administrators out of reach of popular control. By virtue of their role and responsibility – in Government, in industry, in the social services – these rulers can easily come to treat ordinary folk not as persons but as means to an end".[16] Further, in contrast to the early Fabians, these writers did not see managerialism and capitalism as inimical. On the contrary, they could well come to "reinforce each other because the administrators virtually lean towards an alliance with the powerful representatives of the old order".[17] The "old" Fabians believed that the ideal of social service that would inspire the managers of public corporations was necessarily antagonistic to the pursuit of the self-interested objectives that drove private entrepreneurs. In fact, as these writers saw it, both public and private managers were united by a common interest in the untrammelled exercise of power.

Concern was also expressed about the insulation of autonomous public monopolies from competitive pressures. Gaitskell, for example, wrote that it was necessary "to weigh the gains from eliminating the wastes of competition against the disadvantages of destroying the competitive spirit".[18] Similarly, it was also argued, by those on the liberal socialist wing of the Party, that the public accountability of public corporations might "inhibit flexibility and experiment".[19] Such views were, of course, profoundly at odds with the argument that initiative would be inspired by the ideal of social service.

So, many had doubts about the institutional form that public corporations had assumed. However, while some, in particular those who favoured the extension of public ownership by traditional methods, argued the need for greater democratic control from the political centre, others, such as Roy Jenkins, tended to look to "far more intimate patterns of ownership and control" as a solution to the problem.[20] Jenkins advocated a greater decentralization of ownership and control and more diverse forms of public ownership; in effect, what he looked to was a move away from the Morrisonian national corporation that embraced a whole industry. Specifically, to ensure the dispersal of economic power, he argued for individual firms rather than whole industries to be taken into public ownership and for "local authorities [and] consumers' and producers' co-operatives" to be "encouraged to play a full part in the ownership of enterprises."[21] In addition, a number of writers in this period suggested the possibility of the state taking a stake in particular enterprises through the buying of shares by a national investment board. Such expedients it was believed would go some considerable way to removing the bureaucracy, the managerialist ethos and the lack of enterprise and innovation that these writers saw as likely to result when public ownership took the form of nationalization.

However, there were doubts about public ownership other than those relating to its institutional form, most of which concerned its effectiveness in attaining socialist objectives. Thus, as regards its power to redistribute wealth, Crosland's scepticism has already been noted and this was shared by a number of writers. In addition many post-war socialist political economists were convinced that its extension was not central to the pursuit and maintenance of full employment, for which the use of Keynesian demand management was sufficient. It was also argued, and with increasing force as the period progressed, that the limits of the useful extension of public ownership had been, or were being, reached. As early as 1950, we find Crosland writing that "all the industries which for the last half century have featured in our election programmes and Party manifestos . . . have now passed safely into public hands and the result is something of an intellectual void".[22] Richard Crossman too accepted that the post-war Labour government had "finished . . . some time in 1948 or 1949 . . . the job which the Fabians had laid down".[23] The obvious candidates had been nationalized and it was not immediately apparent where and how a Labour government should proceed.

For most, though, the doubts, criticisms and reservations that have been detailed were reason for a more cautious, a more selective, even a more imaginative approach to the extension of public ownership; they did not represent a case for its abandonment. Crosland was the major exception to this general proposition but in this and many other respects Crosland, or at least the Crosland of *The future of socialism*, cannot be taken as representative of even the liberal socialist wing of the Labour Party let alone the Party as a whole. Hugh Gaitskell, for example, writing in the same year that Crosland's book was published, was adamant that:

> It still remains true that nationalisation of the means of production, distribution and exchange should assist the advance to greater equality, contribute to a full employment policy, associate with the power to make important decisions a far greater sense of national responsibility, ease the development of industrial democracy and diminish the bitterness and friction in economic relationships.[24]

This was a classic statement of the case for nationalization and it was echoed by others. For Gaitskell, nationalization facilitated the maintenance of full employment because it served as an antidote to the volatility of "the expectations of businessmen – that intensely variable variable".[25] Thus nationalization provided the means of ensuring greater stability as regards the level of aggregate investment in the economy. Also, while there might be limits to the redistributive consequences of nationalization there were nevertheless gains to be made in that respect.

The point that nationalization was necessary to provide the means to ensure that crucial economic decisions were made in the public interest was articulated not only by Gaitskell but also by a number of other liberal socialists, though more often with respect to the extension of public ownership in general, than nationalization in particular. Thus Roy Jenkins wrote of the "need for a substantial extension of public ownership" to provide the "public control" necessary for "planning purposes".[26] In this context he argued that the extension of public ownership should be defended primarily on the basis of the need to "change the balance of power". "The case for public ownership", he wrote, "*is essentially a political case* tied up with the stability of the whole economy and *the transference of a great concentration of economic power from private to public control.*"[27] For that reason alone the extension of public ownership should be "substantial".

In this context too, other writers emphasized the threat that the private ownership of capital still posed to what had already been achieved, to the possibility of future socialist advance and to the maintenance of political democracy; particularly where that ownership involved the wielding of monopoly power. Thus as Strachey saw it in *Contemporary capitalism* (1956) "economic power" threatened "to submerge political power" and he cited the experience of the post-war Labour governments as providing evidence that capitalists sought to "frustrate the work of contemporary democracy to [their] own advantage".[28] Here he had particularly in mind the battles over the nationalization of the sugar industry (lost) and the steel industry (won).

This threat to democracy, posed by the concentration of economic power in a few private hands, was seen by Strachey as manifested too in the ownership of the press. It also threatened to corrupt the judicial system. Thus many courts had become "not courts of law but private courts administering rules and regulations laid down by private organisations in their own interest".[29] For Strachey, therefore, given the power still wielded by capitalists, there had arisen a "state of antagonistic balance" between "democracy and last stage capitalism" – a tension that it was vital to resolve in favour of the former by a further transference of economic power to the state.[30]

Failure to accomplish this, as Strachey saw it, would not only block socialist advance, through inability to give effect to the democratically expressed wishes of the people, but would also mean that what had been achieved, in terms of economic stability and the improvement in the economic and social position of the working classes, would be threatened. The democratic process had been used to secure such advances in the teeth of capitalist opposition. Further progress and the retention of what has been won was dependent upon the maintenance of effective democracy and that in turn required a definitive shift of economic power away from the capitalist class. Thus in 1953 he wrote that "no decisive advance to socialism can be made without breaking the class monopoly in the ownership of the means of production" by "major measures of nationalisation".[31] In this context it is also interesting to note his scathing review of Crosland's *The future of socialism*, which focused, in particular, upon the latter's dismissive attitude to the notion that nationalization was vital to the construction of socialism. Here he wrote that "if socialists", like Crosland, "lost sight of the ownership of the means of production they will cease, in a very real sense, to be socialists at all: they will subside into the role of well-intentioned, amiable, rootless, drifting, social reformers". In 1957 too, we find him writing of the need for "the rapid acquisition of ownership in *500* decisive companies."[32]

It must be said though that while, in this period, it did secure liberal socialist support, the argument that the extension of public ownership was fundamental to the social control of economic power, and thence to the building of socialism, was one that was put forward most forcefully by those on what has traditionally been termed the left or "fundamentalist" wing of the Party. Indeed, this conviction has sometimes been taken as *the* distinguishing characteristic of "fundamentalism". Hence for Aneurin Bevan there was "no way in which it is possible for anybody to carry out a plan in the modern state involving stability of employment, involving the proper dispersal of industry, involving all the things we mean by effective control over economic life, unless the power has passed from the hands of the oligarchs into the hands of the democrats".[33] Similarly the authors of *Keeping left* argued that in transferring "large basic industries and monopolies to public ownership, we are doing it not merely, to increase efficiency. We do it because *we regard irresponsible economic power as morally wrong; and we believe that a democracy can become a genuinely democratic society only when economic power has been made its servant and not its master*".[34] Effective socialist economic policy-making required a fundamental redistribution of power in favour of the state. Without that a socialist government would lack the instruments necessary to fulfil its pledges and responsibilities. That would be bad for socialism and bad for democracy.

However, questions of economic power aside, there was also the goal of equality and the role that the extension of public ownership might play in attaining it. Gaitskell, certainly, saw public ownership as a means to that end, writing that "the extension of public ownership . . . it seems to me . . . is almost certainly necessary if we are to have a much more equal distribution of wealth"[35] and while Crosland might demur there were many other writers in this period who saw it as a primary means to that end. Jenkins, for example, saw the expansion of public ownership as a means of narrowing wage differentials between the highest and lowest paid workers in an industry or firm and, if the public sector were large enough, he believed, "the effect of such a move [within it] would be widespread" because of the impact and influence this would have on wage levels in the private sector.[36]

John Strachey too emphasized the redistributive consequences of the extension of social ownership but, in contrast to Jenkins, stressed its impact on the "unearned" income derived from property ownership. Only to the extent that public ownership was extended would the flow of such "unearned" income be diminished. Strachey accepted this might be only one means of creating a society where "the labourer is paid in proportion to his work" but it was none the less important. "I for one", wrote Strachey, "cannot imagine any way of effecting [the] abolition of incomes accruing to functionless property owners, except by the transference of their income-bearing property to society."[37] In this context, he was critical of those who overemphasized the role that taxation could play. A redistributive fiscal policy was all very well but it only served to redress an evil. It did not root it out.

While, therefore, socialist writers reconsidered the contribution of public ownership to the building of socialism in the light of their post-war experience and while some questioned the traditional rationale for its extension, it was still seen as having a crucial part to play with respect to planning, economic control, the redistribution of wealth and income, the pursuit of full employment, ensuring that economic power was publicly accountable, and providing the means of defending what Labour had already achieved. Indeed the only fundamental sceptic here, or at least the only one who deployed his arguments with any degree of conviction or theoretical sophistication, was Crosland.

Planning and the price mechanism

The debate over the extent and institutional form of public ownership was only one of those that rumbled on within the Labour movement in this period. Related to it was that over planning, which was also concerned, among other things, with the extent and nature of state involvement in the economic life of the nation. At one (liberal socialist) extreme there were those who, such as Crosland in *The future of socialism* and elsewhere tended to conceive of economic planning almost entirely in terms of a Keynesian management of broad macroeconomic aggregates, that is getting the right balance between consumption, investment and government expenditure via a "skilful and determined fiscal policy".[38] Of course Crosland accepted that there were occasions when state intervention of a more specific, discriminatory, kind might be required. The market, on occasion, disseminated misleading information – in particular when private deviated from social costs.[39] However, for the most part, planning that involved the use of licences, rationing, price and physical controls to alter the allocation of resources and the distribution of the national product would infringe consumer sovereignty, reduce efficiency and make for a burgeoning bureaucracy. Crosland therefore advocated an increasing reliance on the market mechanism. Given the more equitable distribution of incomes brought about by fiscal policy during the war and in the immediate post-war period, profitability could be deemed, in large measure, to reflect the intensity of society's demands. "What is profitable is what the consumer finds useful; and the firm and the consumer desire broadly the same allocation of resources."[40] In such a situation "planning" was about the macroeconomic management necessary to keep the machine running rather than any tinkering with its construction.

Others, of course, had already made such points. For example, in *Planning and the price mechanism* (1948) James Meade had argued that "provided . . . there is not too large or not too small a total monetary demand in relation to the supplies of goods and services available for purchase and provided that there is a reasonably equitable distribution of that total monetary purchasing power, there are strong market forces at work promoting the most economic use of resources."[41] The role of the state was therefore to ensure that these preconditions were met. That was its primary planning function. For in such circumstances the market, as Meade saw it, would ensure the most efficient use of resources in relation to society's needs. There was no need then for the battery of controls that the Labour Party had inherited from the war and which some socialists saw as fundamental to the business of planning and the attainment of socialist economic objectives. Indeed, Meade wrote that if a planner:

> necessarily believes in a quantitative programme of output, employment and sales for particular industries, occupations and markets and the exercise of such direct controls by the state as are necessary to carry this out I am certainly no planner. If an anti-planner necessarily denies that the State should so influence the working of the price mechanism that certain major objectives of full employment, stability, equity, freedom and the like are achieved, then I am a planner.[42]

Even so, in the immediate post-war period, Meade clearly recognized that such would be the demand pressures on the available supply of scarce resources that control over new building and capital development as a whole would have to be exercised by the state. In general, however, he stressed the role of the market as an efficient allocator of resources.

Other writers took a similar but more qualified line. Roy Jenkins wrote of the need for an "alternative to detailed planning" that would involve "a framework of necessary strategic control" within which consumer preferences would "express themselves as forcibly as possible through the operation of the price mechanism", a "strategic control" that would ensure both full employment and a more equitable distribution of wealth. In such circumstances "the price mechanism would become no more than an accurate and sensitive device" registering the wishes of society as to the goods and services it desired and thereby indicating the optimum allocation of resources.[43] As regards the possible abuse of monopoly power by public corporations, this could be guarded against by instructing them to adopt marginal cost pricing, as many theorists in the late 1930s had recommended. Indeed with respect to his thinking on all these issues Jenkins clearly acknowledged his indebtedness to the generation of writers discussed in Chapter 10; in particular he mentions Strachey's *A programme for progress* and Douglas Jay's *The socialist case.*

However, those who conceived of planning in terms of macroeconomic management believed that state intervention in two general areas of economic life might be necessary to make it effective. Thus writers like Meade and Jenkins recognized that the attainment of full employment by Keynesian means entailed inflationary hazards. Specifically, there was the risk that trade unions would behave in such a way as to take advantage of any government-initiated expansion of aggregate demand in the form of wage or salary increases, rather than in the form of increased employment. In 1943, James Meade had expressed the hope that "the moderate wages policy which has been successfully maintained without specific state control during the active demands of war may be continued unchanged into the full employment which it is hope to provide in peace".[44] But with the enhanced trade union bargaining power that full employment brought in the post-war period and with the gradual erosion of the sense of national solidarity that the war had evoked, the possibility of such voluntary wage restraint slowly evaporated. Hence in 1953 we find Roy Jenkins among others, arguing that "it [was] nonsense . . . to believe that there can be compatibility between full employment and stable prices without some *control* over the rate at which wages as a whole . . . can be allowed to increase".[45] Opinion might differ on the form which that control should take but many socialist writers agreed with the kind of case that Jenkins made out for some kind of incomes policy as a necessary adjunct to demand management. However there were exceptions: the Socialist Union authors of *Twentieth century socialism* (1956) argued that such a policy should be rejected on the grounds that it involved "drastic inroads into personal freedom". They suggested too that an incomes policy would turn "every claim for a wage or salary increase into a nationwide political battle",[46] a prescient observation given what was to occur in the 1960s and 1970s.

The other kind of economic intervention by the state, advocated by many of those who subscribed to what might be termed a Keynesian conception of planning, was that of exchange control. This had commanded considerable support from socialist writers and from the Labour Party in the aftermath of 1931. In the 1930s, exchange control was seen as providing a Labour government with the power to stem flights of capital that would jeopardize the pursuit of radical economic policies. In the post-war period such anxieties remained and were supplemented by others. In particular, there was the fear that full employment itself might entail a level of imports that would precipitate a balance of payments crisis and threaten the international value of sterling, something rendered all the more likely by the existence of substantial external liabilities in the form of sterling reserves held by nations in the so-called Sterling Area. These represented a kind of sword of Damocles, suspended above the neck of the British economy and threatening to drop whenever Britain experienced balance of payments difficulties and international confidence in sterling ebbed. Further, in the immediate post-war period, as we have seen, there was the pressing problem of balancing dollar earnings and dollar receipts. In *Planning and the price mechanism* (1948) Meade was therefore adamant that "steps must be taken to control the export of capital".[47] Gaitskell too, in 1953, argued forcefully for foreign exchange control, as central to the successful pursuit of full employment policies. The authors of *Twentieth century socialism* also, in 1956, emphasized the need for the continued control of "foreign exchange and currency movements",[48] while John Strachey wrote in 1954 that although exchange control might seem a "narrow and technical" matter it was a vital one for any Labour government, for "behind the façade of financial technicalities, what is at issue . . . is power . . . Power progressively to remould the economy to any desired extent". Strachey even went so far as to say that "the life and death of British social democracy depends on the issue" and that in his view "it transcends in importance even the question of how much more nationalisation we ought or ought not to do".[49] Control over the foreign exchange transactions of British citizens was generally seen, therefore, as a fundamental prerequisite for the success of any Keynesian strategy that aimed to maintain a high and stable level of employment and for any egalitarian strategy that aimed at the radical redistribution of wealth.

So far we have been concerned with socialist political economists who, for the most part, saw planning in terms of an extension of Keynesianism, who also, while recognizing its failings, wrote positively about the role the market could perform and who stressed the importance of private enterprise and the dangers of a situation where the state, either directly or through its agents, monopolized or sought to monopolize economic decision-making. However, there were others whose conception of the political economy of socialism was markedly different – specifically, those who had considerable doubts about the market as a pricing, allocative and distributive mechanism and who therefore placed much greater emphasis on the constructive socialist role that the state or its intermediaries must necessarily play.

To begin with, these writers were concerned with the limitations of Keynesianism as a means of socialist advance and, therefore, with the dangers involved in reducing socialist political economy to a fusion of demand management, a redistributive fiscal policy and a few interventionist trimmings such as building licences. The authors of *Keeping left* were among a number who voiced such fears. "The attitude of some members of the Labour Party", they wrote, "raises anew the fundamental question of whether we are determined to reshape the character of the British economic and social system or whether we are going to be satisfied with the coalition Government's doctrine of relying on intermittent budgetary policy to counteract the instability and injustice of an uncontrolled market and price system."[50] Richard Crossman was to make the point again in *Labour in the affluent society* (1960), when he argued that if socialist political economy shackled itself to an economic programme simply designed to manage capitalism better, such as that provided by Keynesianism, then Labour would be transformed from an "anti-Establishment Party" to one that advanced "an alternative style of management *inside* the Establishment". For Crossman, this would be disastrous; both because the Labour Party would cease to have furnished an ideology "for interests and social groups denied justice under the status quo" and also because such a stance on economic management would preclude the pursuit of those policies necessary to effect a socialist rejuvenation of the British economy.[51]

G. D. H. Cole highlighted similar dangers in *Socialist economics*, a work published in 1950, when he wrote about the manner in which the new Keynesian economics had deeply affected the thought of Socialists:

> Hitherto most socialists had contended that the disease of unemployment was incurable except by socialisation . . . But now it appeared, if Keynes was right, that full employment could be maintained without socialisation, merely by manipulating the correct levers at the centre in the money and investment markets. There might be a case for socialising this or that industry on other grounds . . . but not in order to cure unemployment.[52]

The message was clear, the infusion of Keynesianism carried with it the danger of a fundamental dilution of socialism or at least of socialist intent.

For Cole, Crossman, the authors of *Keeping left* and others, those who believed that socialism might be advanced by macroeconomic management *tout seule* were relying on means that were not sufficient to attain the ends they sought. More than Keynesian style planning was required to reshape the character of the British economic and social system and Keynesianism itself would only prove successful if pursued as part of a much broader economic strategy. Thus, although Cole shared the concern of the Keynesian socialists about the inflationary tendencies that might emerge where full or near full employment existed, he believed, in marked contrast to them, that to prevent the emergence of inflation as a substantial problem, it would be necessary for the state to "control, broadly, what is to be produced and when and what is charged for it".[53] It would also be necessary for it to determine the general distribution of purchasing power by way of an incomes policy. In addition, in order to secure a balanced distribution of employment, it would have to "control the location of industry". Further, "to enable export industries to hold a satisfactory place in the world markets" and maintain employment in them it would be imperative "to manage and regulate their costs." To implement such a strategy of course "the Keynesian apparatus for maintaining economic equilibrium at a high level" was necessary but insufficient. Such comprehensive planning of economic activity could only take place "through some publicly responsible agency – or rather through many such agencies – *which own[ed] and conduct[ed] a large part of the apparatus of production*".[54]

Barbara Wootton took a similar line in *Freedom and planning* (1945) but went further than Cole in arguing that "full employment [was] incompatible with any system . . . in which production is left to follow the dictates of market purchases".[55] Cole's faith in the market mechanism might not have been great but, as we shall see, it was greater than that. Indeed, in her distrust of consumer sovereignty and her consequent misgivings as to the allocative role that the market performed, Wootton carried into the post-war period more than a little of the spirit of Webbian Fabianism. For Wootton, like Cole, socialist economic planning must involve more than managing macroeconomic aggregates. In contrast to writers such as Meade, Gaitskell and Crosland, she believed that, even with a more equitable distribution of wealth, the market mechanism and consumer sovereignty could not be relied upon to effect a socially optimal allocation of resources. It would therefore be incumbent on planners to play the directive role necessary to attain this objective. They, not consumers, must assume responsibility for resource allocation. Indeed, the whole concept of consumer sovereignty came in for some rough handling from Wootton and, unlike many socialist political economists of this period, she was quick to dismiss the notion that it was an integral element of the kind of freedom that socialists sought. Rather she stressed its dangers, in particular the threat to economic stability and thence full employment posed by consumer caprice. She also cast doubt on whether, in any case, the loss of consumer sovereignty could be perceived as an erosion of economic freedom. "Liberty of consumption", Wootton wrote, "is a highly sophisticated concept. It can hardly be said that people greatly prize a freedom the nature of which they do not fully understand and the presence or absence of which they would not even recognise."[56] Here speaks the voice of "old" Fabianism with its distrust and disparagement of the private consumer. This was an attitude that contrasted markedly with the views of a liberal socialist such as Crosland and was not shared even by some of those who emphasized the importance of comprehensive and directive planning. G. D. H. Cole, for example, in *Socialist economics*, stressed the importance of free consumer choice in the context of a market economy, which, "given a reasonably satisfactory distribution of incomes . . . is obviously the most suitable instrument for ensuring that each individual gets what he wants, subject only to the insistence of the State that he shall have some things (such as education) whether he wants them or not".[57]

With respect to resource allocation, Wootton was particularly emphatic that the distribution of labour could not be determined by uncontrolled market forces if planning was to be effective. Labour could simply not be left free to respond to the levels of remuneration that the market determined. Here a wages or incomes policy was argued for strongly: one that would establish the rates of pay required to provide the supply and distribution of labour necessary to fulfil the objectives of the planners. As Wootton put it, "the conscious determination of production priorities implies conscious regulation of relative wage rates". This ruled out free collective bargaining and ruled in the use of some system of compulsory arbitration,[58] something also favoured by G. D. H. Cole. It should be said too that Wootton saw an incomes policy as an antidote to the kind of corporatism that involved trade unions, "marching hand in hand with employers to exploit monopolistic positions".[59] As she saw it, such an unholy alliance would entail the exploitation of the consumer and could precipitate an inflationary spiral with wages chasing prices inflated by the exercise of monopoly power.

Here, in passing, it is worth remarking upon the significant degree of unanimity regarding incomes policy that characterized the Labour Party in the immediate post-war period. Advocacy of such a policy was just as much a feature of the political economy of those regarded as being on the left of the Party as of those considered to be on the right. Thus, like Wootton, the authors of *Keeping left* believed that "economic planning in a democratic socialist economy" could not "operate successfully if wage-fixing is left . . . to the accidents of *uncoordinated sectional bargaining*."[60] However, it is also important to stress that this unanimity was, in most important respects, a superficial one. For writers such as Meade, Gaitskell and Jenkins, an incomes policy was seen as a means of ensuring that the advantages of full employment were attained without precipitating inflation; for Wootton, Cole, Bevan and others it was fundamental to the more detailed and directive planning involved in the selection of "production priorities". Both groups sought to curtail free collective bargaining, the first because such freedom might undermine the liberty to labour and the second because it stood in the way of that conscious social control over the nation's economic affairs which, if labour but knew it, was in its own best interests.

As regards her general conception of planning and the instruments by which it might be given effect, Wootton recognized that there might be major political obstacles to what she was proposing. Thus an incomes policy and a significant infringement of consumer sovereignty would "involve encroachments on existing liberties", which, however illusory, "would be widely thought to be intolerable".[61] There was also the whole question of the feasibility of long-term planning in the context of the kind of adversarial, class based, two party, political system that characterized Britain. Planning for Wootton was only possible where there existed some shared notion of the common good and thence a measure of consensus on the existence of social and economic objectives that transcended traditional political divisions. In the absence of this, the continuity fundamental to successful planning "could only be maintained by tying the hands of an Opposition",[62] that is by the suppression of at least some political liberties. Yet, for Wootton, securing the requisite consensus really presented an insuperable difficulty *only* for those who adhered to the notion that politics was necessarily class based; for those who believed "that every political party is based upon a particular economic interest or class" must deny any possibility of the emergence of the consensus that planning required. Either that or they must accede to the view that "any continuous planning without sacrifice of political freedom was simply not possible";[63] that any dissent being suppressed in the interest of planning continuity.

Wootton did not share the view that politics was invariably class based and therefore characterized by irreconcilable antagonisms, and in consequence she was optimistic about the possible emergence of common ground on the basis of which planning might proceed. She did not share it because of what she saw as the growing complexity of social stratification in Britain. "More and more", she wrote, "ours is a world of many little coteries, combining and recombining in complex patterns of harmony and discord; and less and less is it a world of large groups in clear and permanent conflict with one another."[64] The full implications of this conception of an emerging social pluralism for the political economy for those who adhered to it will be discussed below but for Wootton it meant that "the traditional battle-cries" and the traditional adversarial politics that went with them no longer reflected the underlying social reality. That social reality did not signal the end of conflict but it did render social conflict a more complex phenomenon. It also rendered more likely the emergence of some kind of consensus as to economic objectives which would provide the continuity that successful planning required, even if that consensus amounted only to a common commitment to adequate nutrition, good housing and full employment. Indeed there were signs that such a consensus was already emerging for "no Party upholds or condones hunger, slum living or unemployment. Either there is now general agreement that these are elements in the common evil or someone is telling a crashing load of lies". That said Wootton recognized that a significant modification of political attitudes would still "be necessary if democratic governments are to undertake extensive [long-term] economic planning".[65]

Wootton's whole position shows clearly the longevity of "old" Fabian influences on socialist political economy in Britain. Her work is suffused with the belief that planned economic decision-making must be seen as preferable to unplanned reactions to market stimuli and, above all, that intelligent, rational, knowledgeable individuals, uncorrupted by vested interests could, after a suitably rigorous, scientific investigation of problems, agree how a nation's resources might best be allocated among competing ends so as to maximize social welfare. It was that positivist faith, in fact, which in some measure underpinned her view that the consensus necessary for successful economic planning was possible. Social science would provide right answers to which all would subscribe, not class answers that must prove divisive.

Richard Crossman was also profoundly critical of Keynesianism, in particular with respect to the capacity of its policy prescriptions and policy instruments to improve Britain's general economic performance, as opposed to simply ensuring that all available resources were fully utilized. Thus in *Labour in the affluent society* (1960) he argued strongly that the acceptance of a Keynesian socialism and the style of economic management it dictated would ensure that communist economies continued to outperform those of the Western democracies. "I am convinced", he wrote, "that the kind of Keynesian managed capitalism which has evolved since the war, is intrinsically unable to sustain the competition with the Eastern bloc."[66] Of the communist achievement he wrote: "in terms of military power, of industrial development, of technological advance, of mass literacy and eventually, of mass consumption too, the *planned socialist economy* as exemplified in the Communist states, is proving its capacity to outpace and overtake the wealthy and comfortable western economies."[67] Central planning and the powers that planners wielded made this possible because they allowed the prioritization of resource use; in effect they permitted planners to act directly on the economy's supply side. In such circumstances, consumer choice did not, as in a market economy, damage the nation's long-term economic interests by skewing resource allocation in favour of consumption at the expense of capital investment and "vital public services".

In an unplanned market economy the citizen, as consumer, was also seen by Crossman as the dupe of mass advertising, which dulled "the critical faculties which would normally have been stimulated by the improvement of popular education since 1945".[68] A deluded consumer sovereignty resulted in an intertemporal preference skewed in favour of the now, with consequent adverse repercussions for investment and thence future economic growth; skewed too in favour of private as against public consumption. John Strachey had also argued on these lines in *The end of empire* (1959) and both he and Crossman were pursuing a path already mapped out by the American economist J. K.Galbraith in *The affluent society*, with its identification of private wealth in the midst of public squalor as a characteristic feature of post-war Western capitalism.

For Crossman Labour must therefore refuse "in any way to come to terms with the Affluent Society".[69] On the contrary the Party should formulate and advance measures that would ensure that social objectives should be prioritized over private ambitions and wealth-getting. This was a reason for the rapid extension of public ownership and it was also a reason for the Party embracing central economic planning. As he wrote: "a socialist programme . . . will involve transferring gigantic powers, which are now dispersed amongst the oligopolists, to the central Government and the planning authorities which it would have to establish."[70] This was a vision of the political economy of socialism radically different from that of the Keynesian socialists.

However, those writers who favoured directive economic planning rather than economic management also did so because they saw the former as a means of attaining socialist objectives of a non-economic kind. Aneurin Bevan, for example, saw the kind of planning made possible by extensive public ownership as allowing economic decision-making to be impregnated with ethical considerations. It was, in effect, a means of ensuring that the economic system served a "social aim". He looked to a situation in which, under socialist planning, "moral considerations [took] precedence over economic motives" with decisions being made, for example, on the "worthwhileness of different forms of consumption" according to what he termed "an order of values", by which he clearly meant an order of moral values. It was the absence of this in an economy directed by market forces that made for the moral shallowness of capitalism, that allowed, among other things, the emergence of public squalor in the midst of private affluence.[71]

Linked with this also went the view that planning might be used to effect a general inculcation of socialist attitudes. Thus, like socialist writers going back to the early nineteenth century, Bevan saw the market economy as one that encouraged a socially destructive possessive individualism. Socialists should therefore be in the business of eroding the influence of the market on economic behaviour. "The more and more things that we are able to enjoy without their having to pass through the price system", he wrote, "the more civilised and less acquisitive society becomes"; "the more of the world's goods that reach the individual in some other more civilised way than by the haggling of the market, the more progress that society is making towards a civilised standard."[72] Such views had a long pedigree and there can be little doubt that they were still widespread on the left and within the Labour Party in the post-war period.

Finally there was the international dimension of the comprehensive and directive approach to planning, with G. D. H. Cole, in *Socialist economics*, viewing the matter in this way: "Just as each society needs to plan its own essential production in accordance with its conception of wants, so the economic intercourse between different societies needs to rest on a basis of concerted planning." For Cole this should take the form of "international discussion" to establish international needs "in order to enable each country to plan its national output with assured markets for its surpluses in view, and with foreknowledge, of the imports it can expect to receive, and to be able to pay for". Again the objective was to avoid the uncertainty, the anarchy and the waste that characterized unplanned or "free" international trade. In place of this Cole envisaged trading agreements committing countries to purchases over a long enough period of time to permit the "effective planning of production" in relation to demand. Such planning would also allow exchange on a basis and at a price that effected an international redistribution of wealth in favour of those whom Cole refers to as "peasant or native producers".[73] Thus he argued that "an advanced socialist country" would be "prepared to revise its valuation "of their products "in terms of its own goods as part of an effort to raise standards of living throughout the world even if this revaluation reacts to some extent to its own disadvantage". Cole also believed that, where possible, "investment and development policies, as well as trade, should be planned on a supra-national basis"; planning that would involve "more advanced countries" helping "less advanced countries" with loans for purposes of capital investment.[74]

As in the 1930s, therefore, there were different and competing views of what planning entailed and the instruments by means of which it would be rendered effective. All might be planners, all might subscribe to the rhetoric and virtues of planning but that merely concealed fundamental differences within the socialist camp and within the Labour Party over what and how to plan. These differences related to the place of the market in a socialist economy, the extent of public ownership required for effective planning, what economic freedoms should be prioritized by planners, the need to establish production priorities as against simply controlling macroeconomic aggregates, the extent to which production should be driven by moral or social as opposed to narrowly economic imperatives, and the economic priorities that planners should establish. In short, among democratic socialists, there was no generally accepted conception of what economic planning was and how it should be implemented.

Redistribution

If public ownership and planning came in for critical scrutiny in the post-war period so too did the traditional socialist objective of redistributing wealth and incomes, and again it was Crosland who proved the most radical of those who sought to rethink the socialist position. His view was that "saturation point" had been reached "so far as the taxation of income is concerned", something that, in itself, constrained the effectiveness of redistribution as a means of securing the socialist goal of equality. "Selective measures of redistribution towards small groups" might be possible and efficacious but it was no longer possible to secure significant redistribution of income between classes.[75] In this period other writers also queried the scope for the redistributive taxation of earnings but Crosland went further and actually questioned whether in any case a further levelling of incomes would actually achieve what socialists sought. Thus, as he saw it, "despite the levelling of incomes since the war we still retain in Britain a deeper sense of class, a more obvious social stratification and stronger class resentments than any of the Scandinavian, Australasian or North American countries."[76] Even if it were feasible, therefore, Crosland believed "the classless society" would "not be reached simply by more redistribution of wealth".[77]

Rather, to attain this goal, it would be necessary to remove what Crosland saw as the profoundly divisive social effects of occupational prestige, accent and vocabulary and differing "lifestyles". The first could be eliminated by the adoption, in Britain, of what he saw as the inherent egalitarianism of American management practices, with their dissolution of status divisions in the workplace; the socio-cultural divisiveness of accent and vocabulary would be removed by the widening of educational opportunity; while greater uniformity of lifestyles could be expected to emerge in the wake of the rising tide of contemporary affluence. As regards the last point, Crosland believed that "the higher the average level of real income, *whatever the distribution*, the greater the subjective sense of social equality."[78]

As Crosland saw it, the classic socialist objective of redistribution had lost its importance. The advantages it was expected to yield could now be attained in other, more effective, ways. This was certainly Crosland's position in *The future of socialism*. It must be said though that in some of the pieces that were published as *The conservative enemy* in 1962 he was to take a different and less sanguine view. There he argued that "we are evidently *not* . . . up against the limit of personal taxable capacity" and emphasized "the importance of increased taxation on capital gains, distributed profits, gifts and inherited wealth." Further he argued that: "we want a more equal distribution of wealth, not because redistribution to-day will make all the workers rich, but to help create a more just, united and humane community."[79] Hence social legislation, a change in social attitudes and an all-engulfing affluence were not enough. The traditional *economic* policy of redistribution was very much back on the agenda. It had a vital role to play in the pursuit of social equality.

Yet others, in this period, shared many of Crosland's "future-of-socialism" views on the scope for further taxation of earnings. Meade for example was concerned about the impact on the incentive to work and stressed the need to "find alternative means which will reduce inequalities without . . . discouraging effects upon incentives". Indeed Meade argued that if such alternatives could be found "there should be an appreciable reduction in the progressiveness of direct taxation on earnings". As regards alternatives, Meade suggested a range of measures to tax unearned incomes and the sources of unearned incomes, including an increased inheritance tax, a gift tax and a capital levy. Jenkins, similarly, believed that there was still considerable scope for revenue raising by means of "the stiffer taxation of property",[80] while Gaitskell also expressed concern about the burden of direct taxation and, like Meade, its impact on the propensity to save and so the level of investment in the economy. He believed that a redistributive fiscal policy could, in this way, adversely affect economic growth and thence employment opportunities and living standards.

Of course one fundamental means of securing a more equal distribution of wealth was not to tax the "unearned" income derived from property ownership but simply to cut it off at source by taking that property into public ownership. However, in line with his less than sanguine views on what the further extension of public ownership might achieve, Crosland denied the efficacy of this. The compensation attendant upon the extension of public ownership would inevitably limit its redistributive impact. Further, if such a strategy were to prove effective it would have to involve efficient and profitable industries, otherwise the dividends would not represent a substantial flow of revenue into the nation's coffers. In fact, the public ownership of loss-making industries, from a distributional perspective, would be counterproductive. On the other hand, the public ownership of efficient and profitable enterprises on purely redistributive grounds would be difficult to defend and therefore to effect. Either way, there was not much scope for advance in this direction.

However, many socialist writers in this period took a radically different view. Roy Jenkins, for example, while he questioned the efficacy of *nationalization* as a means to achieve this end was equally clear, in his contribution to *New Fabian essays*, that "a substantial extension of public ownership is . . . an essential prerequisite of greater equality of earned incomes".[81] In fact, he went so far as to suggest that, for the future, public ownership would be justified largely on egalitarian grounds rather than on those of efficiency and even more than on the basis that it was necessary for effective planning. Gaitskell was equally emphatic, arguing that "the extension of public ownership . . . it seems to me . . . is almost certainly necessary if we are to have a much more equal distribution of wealth".[82]

It was John Strachey, however, who was one of the staunchest defenders of extending public ownership on the grounds of its redistributive impact, writing in 1953 that the primary objective of further "socialisation" was "to secure the proper distribution of the net national product amongst those who created it". It was, as he saw it, the only way of eliminating the source of unearned income. Taxation had its place in the business of redistribution but, like Crosland, Meade and others, he was convinced that, as regards earned income, the limits of what could usefully and easily be taxed had already been reached, while as regards unearned income, he believed taxation obscured its indefensible nature by ignoring "the profound social, historical and moral issue of who it is has a right to the product of modern industry".[83] Such redistributive arguments in favour of public ownership continued to be advanced by Strachey throughout the 1950s and, in *Contemporary capitalism*, he was to write that he could not "imagine any way of effecting [the] abolition of incomes accruing to functionless property owners, except by the transference of the income-bearing property to society".[84]

There were also socialist writers who challenged the Croslandite view that the scope for further redistribution was limited. Thus Douglas Jay, while accepting that the Labour governments of 1945–51 had undoubtedly been successful in reducing income inequality, also argued that since 1951 "property owners and the rich generally [had] greatly improved their position".[85] For Jay, the 1950s and the years of Conservative government had witnessed a counter-attack of the rich to recover the ground that had been lost and here he singled out, specifically, "the growingly important phenomena of steady long-term capital gains and rising dividend incomes". To drive home these general points about what had occurred Jay drew in particular on the work of Richard Titmuss, Peter Townsend, Brian Abel-Smith and others whose work in the 1950s and 1960s cast grave doubt on the idea that a more equitable distribution of income and wealth (courtesy of fiscal policy and the welfare state) and the rising tide of affluence were rapidly eliminating the problem of poverty.[86]

These writers, with respect to both the taxation system and social welfare provision, made clear that it was a middle-class – literate, articulate and skilled in negotiating the labyrinths of public bureaucracies – that had proved the main beneficiaries. In particular, it was this class that had proved adept at lightening its fiscal burden by means of tax avoidance and making full use of the welfare services that the state now provided. Thus the work of these writers exposed the myth of greater equality and established the reality of continuing, crushing and widespread poverty in the midst of "affluent" Britain. It represented too, a fundamental attack upon Croslandite optimism and the attendant notion that little mileage was left in pursuing the traditional socialist objective of wealth and income redistribution by fiscal means.

For Jay the evidence they furnished suggested the existence of strong natural forces intrinsic to unconstrained capitalism that made for substantial inequality in the distribution of income and property; a distribution that, whatever its economic justification, had no defensible, ethical basis. As he phrased it "the simple truth is that the scale of rewards and incomes thrown up by the uncontrolled economic forces, operating even in theoretical circumstances of complete competition have no moral validity whatsoever". For Jay therefore, the moral imperative that demanded a more equal distribution of income and wealth remained as well grounded and compelling as in 1937. Thus it continued to be the case that "because market forces throw up rewards which have no moral validity and tend towards growing inequality in incomes and property . . . *massive redistribution* is necessary if political freedom and other civilised values are to be preserved".[87] Powerful redistributive measures were required and, in marked contrast to the Crosland of 1956, Jay believed there was considerable scope for action of that kind, action that would in no way adversely affect economic motivation and thence the dynamism of the economy. Thus he stated that "if we consider the actual living standards maintained by capital gains, by non-return [tax return] of incomes, by business expenses and so forth, in addition to higher incomes, *there appears no evidence at all that the resources available for redistribution, even in Britain to-day, are negligible*".[88]

In contrast to Strachey, therefore, Jay favoured the fiscal route over that of extending public ownership. As he saw it, "it is the process of free exchange and the institution of private inheritance, not the ownership of productive assets, from which the main tendency to cumulative inequality springs". Standing Strachey on his head, he believed that it was "almost true to say that *progressive taxation* can transform society while transfer of ownership merely tinkers with property claims".[89] The one significant qualification to this was his emphasis on public share ownership, which could be used to allow society to tap into the growth in the capital value of private enterprises.

So the redistributive objective was also reconsidered and revised in the light of the social and economic realities that presented themselves in the post-1945 period. With the highest rate of income tax standing at 97.5 per cent (1951) it is not surprising that some were convinced that little could now be done by way of direct taxation. However, many disagreed and considered that, even as regards earned income, the elimination of tax loopholes and the fiscal privileges enjoyed by the rich would serve a useful redistributive function. Further, as regards income derived from accumulated wealth, most accepted that much could still be achieved either by fiscal policy or by the extension of public ownership. Opinions might vary as to how unearned income could best be appropriated by the state but few dissented from the view that there was both a moral and an economic justification for such a course of action.

Class conflict

Along with the belief that capitalism had been stabilized and/or transformed by a combination of Keynesianism, welfarism and selective public ownership went the view that, in consequence, social conflict had, and would increasingly assume, a form qualitatively different from that which had characterized Western societies in the previous 150 years. In turn, those who adhered to such a view recognized that it had profound implications for the manner in which a socialist transformation of society might be effected.

Specifically, many writers detected an embourgeoisement of the working class. As early as 1940, in *The politics of democratic socialism*, Evan Durbin had written of "the proletariat" having acquired "many of the characteristics . . . typical of the petit-bourgeoisie" and, in the 1950s and 1960s, others were to echo these sentiments. Crosland, for example, wrote of the "spread of a middle-class psychology",[90] and Wootton's remarks on the growth of an increasingly "numerous and very heterogeneous" middle class have already been noted. Such developments were seen as having important implications for socialism. In particular, they implied that there no longer existed a social basis for that class conflict *à outrance*, which some socialist writers had previously seen as the necessary prelude to socialist advance. "The militant language of class war, the terminology of revolt and counter-revolt" were now redundant.[91] The old battle cries no longer had a popular resonance.

One aspect of this embourgeoisement was the emergence of bourgeois consumer tastes among a significant section of the working population. Some came to believe, therefore, that henceforward the advance to socialism would be judged by reference not just to the liberty, equality and fraternity but also to the material affluence that it engendered. At any rate an embourgeoised proletariat had more to lose than its chains and would not take kindly to those who proposed measures that threatened to deprive it of what, in material terms, it had come to possess. A certain cross-class, aspirational consensus was seen by some as having emerged, something that militated against class conflict and thence the kind of policies that such conflict had previously implied. Consistent with this was Crosland's view that increasing affluence, regardless of any relative impoverishment, would progressively erode the material basis of social antagonism.

If the nature of the working class had changed in a manner that eroded the basis of conflict, so too had the nature of capitalist enterprise. Here, the most radical revision of the socialist position was, as so often, articulated by Crosland. The managerial revolution, with its increasing divorce of ownership from control had entailed the emergence of a new breed of industrial leaders whose priority was the maximization of the social prestige of the enterprise over which they had charge, rather than the maximization of profits. This pursuit of social-approbation-by-association necessitated a more humane and socially enlightened management style and that too went a long way to unearth the roots of class conflict. Here Crosland agreed too with the authors of *Twentieth century socialism*, who argued that the existence of "full employment

[had] undermined . . . old [management] methods. As consent cannot be so easily enforced it must be won by persuasion".[92]

The achievements of the post-war Labour governments were also seen as having had an impact on the nature and likely longevity of class antagonism; such was the extent to which they had transformed British capitalism, some argued, that the possibility of a capitalist counterattack of either a parliamentary or extra-parliamentary kind lay only in the realms of left-wing paranoia. "No one", wrote Crosland, "supposes that the Conservatives will now suddenly dismantle the welfare state or utterly neglect the claims of the socially underprivileged."[93] Similarly, as Strachey, Crosland and other socialist writers argued, no Conservative government could, in the aftermath of the Keynesian revolution, renege on a commitment to full employment. Keynesian remedies might be opposed by devotees of the free market within Conservative ranks but political survival dictated their application. Thus Strachey was adamant that "the re-appearance of marked symptoms of either slump or secular stagnation would be . . . fatal for a democratic government in Britain".[94] Retreats and reverses there might be but, as Jenkins saw it, "these retreats will stop at a point far short of the line from which the previous Labour government made its advance . . . the following Labour government will not, therefore, find itself fully occupied in repairing the damage."[95] So opposition to the advance of socialism would not be of a kind that would engender fundamental conflict. It might retard but it could not halt, still less reverse it. In the post-war period, therefore, many socialist political economists subscribed to a Fabian faith in a non-conflictual, incremental progression towards socialism. The inevitability of gradualness was back in fashion. Admittedly a few did see things differently; but on the non-Marxist democratic left they were few indeed.

The de-prioritization of the economic

This chapter has been concerned with the way in which socialist political economists reacted to the changed and rapidly changing economic and social circumstances that confronted them in the two decades after 1945. It has sought to consider the rethinking that those circumstances prompted both as regards the economic objectives that it was believed socialists should pursue and the instruments that they should use to pursue them. However, one interesting aspect of this rethinking has yet to be touched upon, namely what may be seen as a tendency to de-prioritize the economic dimension of socialism.

There are a number of reasons why such a de-prioritization should have occurred. To begin with, it seemed to some that while significant progress had been made by the post-war Labour governments, towards implementing the key components of a socialist economic programme, a genuinely socialist society was as far away as ever. As Richard Crossman saw it, while the Labour government had "finished the job which the Fabians laid down for it in the previous 30 years . . . sometime in 1948 or 1949 . . . the ideal, *the pattern of values*, has not been achieved."[96] For some, of course, this indicated the deficiencies in an economic programme based on Morrisonian nationalization or the absence of comprehensive planning, but others, Crossman included, drew the lesson that socialist economics would take society only part of the way to the New Jerusalem. The social ownership of the means of production, distribution and exchange and the more equitable distribution of wealth were necessary but not sufficient conditions for the emergence of socialism. As Crossman put it in *New Fabian essays*, "social morality, freedom and equality do not grow by any law of economics".[97]

As has been noted, the post-1945 period also witnessed the emergence of a full-employment capitalism, which seemed to have been permanently stabilized using the instruments of Keynesian demand-management, a capitalism too which, in the 1950s and 1960s, clearly displayed a capacity to sustain historically high levels of economic growth. In these circumstances some expressed the view that it was increasingly difficult to argue the case for socialism in terms of the superior economic performance that it would permit. As the writers of *Twentieth century socialism* asked, "if increased production is to be the criterion, can we really prove that socialist policies will be more effective than the capitalist policies which set the pace in the US to-day?"[98] If the answer was in the negative, as they suspected, then the case for socialism must henceforward be argued in other than economic terms; or, at least, economic arguments for socialism became considerably more problematic than they had previously been. As these writers saw it, the case for socialism must become essentially ethical: "we should take to socialism", they wrote, "because it is ethically right, otherwise we shall stop short at collectivism . . . We share Kier Hardie's view that socialism is, at bottom, a question of ethics or morals. It has mainly to do with the relationships which should exist between a man and his fellows."[99] This did not mean that socialist economics was redundant but it did mean that economic questions had to be considered with respect to other than narrowly economic goals. Socialism was not just about the creation of material abundance: it was about what kind of society, embodying social and moral values, socialists hoped to create. In this context, the democratization of industrial power, the purposes for which economic power was used, the rights and responsibilities of workers and citizens all became of central importance, and to formulate a coherent socialist position on such issues required a socialist moral economy rather than a socialist economics. For to change the values by which people lived was what was wanted and that was a task that transcended the competence of socialist economists, however sophisticated their economic thinking.

Doubts of another kind as to the centrality of economics in the creation of a socialist society were also expressed in this period. Increasing prosperity progressively diminished the intensity of economic discontent that had previously persuaded many of the imperative need for a socialist transformation of society. More generally, affluence, or relative affluence, was seen as reducing the importance of material concerns in many people's lives. That, certainly, was the view of the authors of the Socialist Union's *Twentieth century socialism*, who argued that "if socialists are to continue to think only in material terms theirs will be a limited appeal . . . the goal of material equality is no longer sufficient to inspire a generation which has all the jobs it wants and more money in its pockets to spend on pleasure than its parents had to live on for weeks."[100] If support for socialism was to be maintained or increased, if socialism was to retain its inspirational character, it had to offer more than a refrigerator in every kitchen and a car in every garage. "Material values no longer provide satisfaction or incentive or social purpose. They can no longer even provide a political programme. For a basis of material welfare is only a condition for the enrichment of the human personality; it is not the decisive cause. An empty belly is a wretched possession but a full one can go with an empty life."[101] Of course such arguments had a long pedigree – Tawney's remark on Fabianism's failure to open windows in men's souls springs immediately to mind – but in the "golden age" of Western capitalism they did acquire an unprecedented force.

This line of argument was also to be developed in *The future of socialism*. For Crosland, what he termed an "economic politics" was "characteristic of any country or situation to which a Marxist analysis might plausibly be applied. Thus they are typical of periods of growing pauperisation, depression and mass unemployment, falling real wages and sharp polarisation of classes". In such circumstances "*economic issues are the main determinants of political attitudes*". However what he termed "social politics" was "characteristic of periods of prosperity, rising incomes, full employment and inflation, *when attention is diverted from economic to social issues*". Such was the post-1945 period. In consequence, previously legitimate reasons for emphasizing the economic dimension of socialism no longer held good. "The pre-war reasons for a large economic orientation are . . . steadily losing their relevance and we can increasingly divert our energies into more fruitful and idealistic channels and to fulfilling earlier and more fundamental socialist aspirations." Elsewhere Crosland was to write of the "sociological and cultural issues which [one hopes] will come increasingly to the forefront as the traditional economic problems recede".[102] Here again there are echoes of Tawney.

If rising prosperity reduced the urgency of economic issues, it also allowed discussion of what on the surface were economic questions, without acceding to the assumption that economic considerations must be paramount when it came to furnishing answers. Crosland believed that "we could . . . when arguing about taxation, the location of industry, labour mobility and the status of the worker in his factory, give precedence to social and psychological needs instead of treating efficiency as the sole criterion."[103] Where economic growth was assured, society had the luxury of seeing it as a subsidiary objective.

What is also apparent in this period, and bears upon the de-prioritization of the economic within socialist thought, is the continuation of that "professionalization" of socialist political economy that has already been remarked upon in a previous chapter. This development not only proceeded, it was reinforced, in particular by the seeming success of the stabilization policies that writers such as Meade, Durbin, Gaitskell, Jay and others had advocated. Thus, for example, discussion about the use and means of using the Keynesian instruments of economic management was, manifestly, a matter for the professionals, something that the increasing use of economists in the Treasury and elsewhere in government appeared to make plain. In consequence, the sphere of *economics* – characterized by an essentially technical debate conducted almost exclusively by the accredited practitioners of a social science – was enlarged, while that of socialist *political economy*, where no such professional exclusivity prevailed, was correspondingly contracted. In such circumstances it is understandable that the belief should grow that what distinguished the socialists was not their stance on economic issues, now the preserve of ideologically untainted technicians, but their position on moral, social and political questions.

Yet the downplaying or de-prioritization of the economic was something that characterized the work of only some socialist writers. Most continued to see economic arguments as vital in making the case for socialism and specifically economic policies as crucial to socialism's realization. These continued to insist that a fundamental redistribution of *economic* power was necessary to effect radical social and political change and that that was something which socialists must continue to strive to achieve. Socialism might be a question of ethics or morals, as the writers of the Socialist Union believed, but, as Bevan for one recognized, there was no hope of constructing a moral economy until economic power had been won for the Labour movement. Only then would there be any possibility of "moral considerations [taking] precedence over economic motives".[104]

Chapter 13
Party thought and party policy, 1951–70

> The one lesson of the past few years is that you won't make sterling strong by making the economy weak. We condemn attempts to solve our export–import problem by holding production down below the level of our industrial capacity. The key to a strong pound lies not in Britain's finances but in the nation's industry. Finance must be the index not the determinant of economic strength.
>
> H. Wilson, *The new Britain*, 1964

Party thought

Many of the salient ideological characteristics of the post-war rethinking of socialist political economy were reflected in the Labour Party's economic literature of the 1950s and early 1960s. To begin with, much of it called into question the utility of further extending public ownership in the manner adopted by the post-war Labour governments. Thus, while recognizing that in certain circumstances it could be used to enhance efficiency and competitiveness, the nationalization of entire industries was no longer seen as the primary means of securing such objectives. As it was phrased in *Industry and society* (1957), "the advantages of unified control . . . will be *frequently outweighed* by the advantages of *autonomy* and *competition*". Given this, what the pamphlet proposed was "competitive public enterprise" to "break production bottlenecks" and "*restore competition* in industries characterised by monopolistic practices",[1] such enterprises being created either by the nationalization of particular firms or by the formation of new public companies. This latter proposal had also been put forward in the 1951 and 1955 election manifestos, which both stated Labour's intention "to start new public enterprises".[2] The idea of extending social ownership by way of public share ownership was also mooted but, as will be indicated below, the primary purpose here was redistributive and not that of controlling decision-making. Indeed *Industry and society* specifically stated that public share ownership would "not . . . call for the exercise of more control *than is at present exercised by private shareholders*", that is such control would be negligible.[3]

As regards enhancing efficiency, the literature of the period made clear that that need not entail recourse to public ownership at all. Thus "industries where units of production are too numerous and too small to face effectively the challenge of modern technology and overseas competition" could be rendered more cost efficient by the provision of central services by Development Councils and the use of "special Finance Corporations" to ensure an adequate supply of new capital. In addition, where competitive pressures making for efficiency were blunted, as in "industries dominated by large and powerful corporations", and where "trading, pricing and profit policies" were "not attuned to the public interest", further legislation along the lines of the Monopolies and Restrictive Trade Practices Act of 1948 could be relied upon to increase the potency of market forces. That would, in the words of *Plan for progress* (1958), "release the forces of change in the British economy" by "breaking down restrictions and reviving competition in British industry."[4]

In general though, *Industry and society* argued, private firms under their "increasingly professional managers" were "as a whole, serving the nation well" and the Party had "no intention of intervening in the management of any firm which is doing a good job". Certainly, "in the host of medium and small businesses which exist, the traditional sanctions and rewards of capitalism can still operate and, as we have seen with respect to large companies, the legislative destruction of restrictive practices would ensure that they operated there as well."[5] There has (until recently) rarely been such a strong attestation of faith in the virtues of the competitive market, private enterprise and the mixed economy in the literature produced by the Labour Party. Given this, it is understandable that the only specific proposals for the "extension" of public ownership were those relating to the renationalization of steel and long distance road haulage, proposals reiterated in *Britain belongs to you* (1959). This latter document also specifically stated that the Party had "no other plans for further nationalisation".[6]

With respect to the redistributive function that public ownership might serve the literature was, once again, circumspect. *Industry and society* accepted that private ownership was productive of major inequality in the distribution of income and wealth. Further, the dividends that accrued to the owners of share capital represented "unearned" income, unwarranted by either risk or effort. Contemporary capitalism was characterized by the "the paradox of a substantial sector of industry in which private ownership has ceased to be necessary and yet is still a major bulwark of inequality of wealth in our society". In addition, "in the case of large firms, no difficulties of finance, incentive or management stand in the way of a transfer from private to public ownership, [while] at the same time such a transfer would contribute powerfully towards a better distribution of wealth."[7] However, while all this might seem to point to the need for a substantial extension of public ownership for redistributive purposes, it was, in fact, used only to argue in favour of considering ways in which the "community may become the owners of industrial shares". To this end a proposal was put forward in the 1959 election manifesto, which advocated the "purchase of shares by public investment agencies"[8] while, in addition, the pamphlet indicated that part of the gains enjoyed by shareholders could, in any case, be appropriated for social use by fiscal measures such as a capital gains tax. So although the critical analysis, or more accurately the rhetoric, of *Industry and society* sometimes assumed a fundamentalist tone, the policy prescriptions were undoubtedly of a liberal socialist hue.

Nor did economic planning and the powers necessary to pursue it require any extension of public ownership, for it was largely conceived of in terms of macroeconomic management. This comes across with particular clarity in *Plan for progress:* "planning should . . . be concerned with the larger decisions – matching savings with investment, imports with exports, spending with production and jobs with workers. The object of planning will be to provide a broad framework within which the creation of new wealth can go smoothly ahead", something which would also involve a stabilization of the general price level. In this context the key instruments of economic planning were the budget and, to a lesser extent, monetary policy. The budget would be used to bring "the spending of the community as a whole . . . into balance with its total output".[9] In addition, fiscal measures could be used to influence the level of savings and investment with a view both to securing a balance between the two and to raising the overall level of the latter, though investment could also be expected to rise to the extent that macroeconomic "planning" was successful in securing and maintaining full employment.

With respect to the planning of investment *Plan for progress* also suggested the, by then, very hardy perennial of a National Investment Board. Its role was, however, to be considerably less interventionist and directive than its inter-war ancestors; it was to "re-view and co-ordinate all forms of capital expenditure . . . examin[ing] the general level of investment programmes in the light of available physical and financial resources . . . point[ing] up under and over-investment in particular industries and . . . draw[ing] attention to inconsistencies in investment plans."[10] Essentially, therefore, its function was that of an information disseminator, facilitating and encouraging greater rationality and foresight in the economic decision-making of others. It was to supplement rather than supplant the market mechanism.

Plan for progress did recognize that, as regards private investment, "the key role . . . [was] played by a few hundred dominant firms. The firms not only undertake the bulk of the new investment themselves but directly influence investment projects in the rest of the private sector."[11] Like *Industry and society*, (which drew on the work of the American A. A. Berle[12]) it highlighted here the fundamental and growing importance of large companies. But again, the emphasis was placed firmly on *influence* and *control*, rather than public ownership, as the means of securing investment decision-making in harmony with the national interest. To this end the pamphlet suggested the use of building licences "as a strategic *control* over industrial development"[13] and the use of investment grants and depreciation allowances to expand investment in those areas, particularly export-oriented industries, whose growth was deemed to be of national importance. Thus financial carrots and sticks, not the shotgun of nationalization, were what was on offer. In the words of *Britain belongs to you*, it was to be by means of "investment grants" that the government would ensure that "firms *plan* their operations in accordance with our national objectives of *full employment and maximum efficiency*".[14] It is to be noted too that it was in such aggregate terms that "planning" objectives were articulated, while the government's role with respect to industry was seen as that of providing "a watching brief" and "creat[ing] the *general* conditions in which industry can be expected to prosper".[15]

As regards the goal of stabilizing prices, it was fiscal policy that was seen as playing the crucial role. First, it could mitigate upward or downward pressure on prices through its impact on aggregate demand. Secondly, fiscal policy would be used to implement "policies of social justice", "fair shares" that would create "the economic and social climate in which moderation [with respect to pay claims] would prevail". The creation of such a climate was seen by the Party as crucial to the business of keeping "the growth of money incomes . . . broadly in step with higher productivity", for in such circumstances a Labour government had "the right to rely on the goodwill and co-operation of the trade union movement".[16] Not for the first time, and certainly not for the last, the Labour Party was to place its faith in buying union goodwill as the means of securing non-inflationary wage settlements.

With respect to the redistribution of income and wealth, much of the literature in the mid and late 1950s indicated some recognition of the growth in inequality that had occurred since 1951. "The Tories", it was argued, had "reduced taxes on profits and unearned income and granted tax reliefs which give most help to those who need help least". In addition, it was stated, "dividends have gone up much faster than wages or salaries" and so, in consequence, "the contrast between the extremes of wealth and poverty is sharper than eight years ago".[17] Thus the need and moral imperative to redistribute had strengthened. But to this end all that *Britain belongs to you* had to propose was a capital gains tax, an increase in inheritance tax, the tightening up of tax allowances on business expenses and the closing of tax loopholes. In short, therefore, although there was a recognition of the growing material inequality that had characterized the previous period of Conservative rule, this produced relatively mild fiscal policy prescriptions. Further, as regards the financing of Labour's proposals for increased social expenditure on housing, health and education, *Britain belongs to you* stressed that the cost would be covered by the nation's "steadily expanding national income . . . *without increasing the present rates of taxation*",[18] a display of electoral sensitivity, as regards fiscal matters, which was to be replicated many times during the next four decades and one that may have derived, in part, from a growing belief that an increasing part of Labour's constituency had now joined the ranks of the tax-paying bourgeoisie.

Many of these policy themes were to re-emerge in the literature produced by the Party in the run up to the 1964 election, particularly in *Signposts for the sixties* (1961). However what came much more to the fore in that and the Party's subsequent documents was an increasing awareness of the extent of Britain's relative economic decline and, in the light of the failure of macroeconomic management to reverse it, a growing determination to use "planning" as the primary means of doing so. This also went hand in hand with an emphasis on the need to make the key economic decision-makers in the private sector more accountable to the community, where their actions had a bearing on national economic interests. Discussing the power wielded by "the directors of a few hundred great combines", *Signposts* argued that "the greatest single problem of modern democracy is how to ensure that the handful of men who control these great concentrations of power can be made responsive and responsible to the nation"; for, at that juncture, they were in effect "usurping the functions of a Government which is theoretically responsible to the whole people".[19] There are echoes here of both Bevan's *In place of fear* and Strachey's *Contemporary capitalism.*

It was therefore to render such power "responsive and responsible", and so to give government the means of reversing the relative economic decline that Britain had suffered since 1945, that the idea of a National Plan was vigorously advanced by the Labour Party in this period.[20] In fact, it should be said that in the early 1960s the call for planning enjoyed a vogue and a cross-party support that it had not had since the 1930s, and the first "plan" was formulated by the National Economic Development Council in 1962–3, while the Conservatives were still in office. Macroeconomic management was seen as having failed to eliminate the structural weaknesses that had plunged the British economy into periodic balance of payments crises and clearly other expedients had to be tried.

The primary objectives of the National Plan were to raise the level of investment in the British economy and accelerate the pace of technological innovation. As regards the latter objective the Party suggested "reconstruct[ing] and greatly enlarg[ing] the existing National Research Development Corporation", which "would be able to advance the public sector . . . where it was most needed . . . at the growing points of the British economy and in new industries based on science". This it would do by way of its "own establishments" or through "joint enterprises" with the private sector.[21]

To secure the requisite rise in investment and a consequent acceleration in the growth of output, fiscal incentives and disincentives would be used to ensure that "targets for individual industries", worked out with a National Planning and Investment Board, were met. Further, where private enterprise was unable to meet planning targets, the possibility was mooted of "new publicly owned undertakings", either by way of nationalization or their creation *de nouveau*. As regards the former expedient, Harold Wilson in "A four year plan for Britain", a piece published in the *New Statesman* in March 1961, suggested that "where a firm or industry refuse[d] the demands placed on it" in a national plan "there [was] a clear case for public ownership." Indeed, he argued that henceforward this should be the key criterion by reference to which the extension of public ownership should be decided. He was also emphatic that if planning was to be effective, if investment were to be raised and the pace of technological advance accelerated then there must be "an expansion of common ownership substantial enough to give the community power over the commanding heights".[22] In this context too, *Signposts for the sixties* once more stressed the need for "competitive public enterprise to spur on the private sector in the required direction".[23] All that said, the only specific proposals for nationalization were, once again, steel and road haulage, though "the transfer to public ownership of the freehold of the land on which building or rebuilding is to take place" was also put forward and noises were made too about reviewing "the position of industries which are largely dependent on State purchasing programmes" (e.g. pharmaceuticals and aircraft), with a view to the public provision of such products.[24]

In relation to the planning of income growth, the idea of moral suasion through greater equity was the means preferred. This had already been articulated in *Britain belongs to you*, which had insisted that "only a Labour Government [was] ready to use the necessary controls and able to win full co-operation from the unions by such measures as a " 'fair shares' Budget policy and the extension of the Welfare State". Similarly, in *Signposts for the sixties*, it was a redistributive fiscal policy that was seen as laying the basis for "the high degree of political maturity and self-discipline" necessary for planned "economic expansion without inflation".[25]

In summary, therefore, *Signposts for the sixties* embodied a strong emphasis on planning, a concern with influencing the investment decision-making of large companies in the context of the planning process, a commitment to harness science to the needs of industry in such a manner as to accelerate the pace of technological change and a general determination to use the public sector (expanded if need be) to both raise investment and foster innovation. There were, as well, distinctively Fabian allusions to unleashing the creative energies of a new generation of scientifically trained technocrats: "if the dead wood were cut out of Britain's boardrooms and replaced by the keen young executives, production engineers and scientists who are at present denied their legitimate prospects of promotion, our production and export problems would be much more manageable."[26]

This stress on science and planning and on a meritocratic technocracy were also the key themes of Labour's Manifesto and the election speeches of Harold Wilson in the run up to electoral success in 1964. It was in the "white heat" of a planned technological revolution that the "New Britain" was to be forged and the language used to conjure up this vision was equally the language of revolution and science. This revolution would see the triumph of a new class: the "sweeping away" of the "grouse-moor", the "Edwardian Establishment, the small minority of . . . British people" who in consequence of "their family connexions and educational background" saw themselves as having "a unique right to positions of influence and power" and whose incompetent "amateurism" was at the root of the nation's economic failings. Their place would be taken by "those previously held down", namely "the millions of products of our grammar schools, comprehensive schools, technical schools and colleges". It was the "thrusting ability and even iconoclasm" of "technicians, scientists and production men", their implementation of planning and their "purposive application of science to Britain's industry" that would transform the nation's industrial fortunes.

For Wilson, socialism was very much about "applying a sense of purpose to our national life", with purpose, significantly, being defined as "*technical skill*". As to the "motivation" of such men and women, this would be "not private profit and the aggrandizement of personal fortunes" but the recognition of a need for "national effort and national purpose". What would be created, therefore, was a "Britain based on *public service*, not a commercialized society where everything has its price".[27]

So the spirit of the Webbs once again suffused the economic literature of the Labour Party. The rhetoric of science, expertise, planning, purpose and public service was in the ascendant. This was Fabian revivalism and like all revivalism there is about it an intoxicating exuberance that in some measure explains the enthusiasm with which Wilson's speeches were received by the Party faithful and, to a lesser extent, by the electorate. There was too the nature of the language used to conjure up his vision of the "New Britain". It was a language of social revolution that thereby engaged the sympathies of the left; but it was the language of modernization, dynamism and progress and that gave it a more general appeal both within and outside the Party.

For all that, the inspirational rhetoric cannot conceal the prescriptive fragility of the basis on which the vision rested. There was, for instance, little of substance in Harold Wilson's *The new Britain* on the instruments of planning. Wilson spoke of "planning with teeth" assuring his audience that planning did not mean just "the publication of academic statistics and blueprints". Yet with the exception of allusions to what might be done by way of the tax system and vague references to the extension of public ownership, it is not immediately apparent what would make planning bite. These were supposedly the tools by which what Wilson referred to as a "ruthless" discriminatory intervention was to be practised. In fact, one senses Wilson believed that once the "government [had] pick[ed] the best brains in the land and harnessed them to the task of national regeneration", solutions to the problems of economic planning would inevitably be forthcoming. If he did so, then again he was very much at one with the Webbs.[28] The consequences of this absence of a clear specification of planning instruments and the failure to address the central question of the economic powers necessary to render planning decisions effective will be considered below. It suffices to say at this juncture that Wilson's and Labour's relative silence on these matters was distinctly ominous.

As regards the "planning" of incomes too, the old formulae found expression in Wilson's speeches. He spoke of a "planned *growth* of income related to national productivity" and "the essential unity of social policy and incomes strategy", the latter entailing control of "profits, dividends, prices and rents".[29] In short, growth, plus greater social and economic equity, would create the climate in which the requisite voluntary restraint could be anticipated. However, all too rapidly, subsequent history was to show the woefully inadequate nature of such position.

Labour in power, 1964–70

The revivalist rhetoric of planning and science was undoubtedly crucial to Labour's electoral success in 1964 and on coming to power the government moved swiftly to translate the vision into reality and put in place the institutional structures within which planning could be pursued. To this end the Department of Economic Affairs (DEA) was established in October 1964 under the ebullient leadership of George Brown and given responsibility for long-term economic planning. It was seen as providing a vital counterweight to the Treasury and thence an antidote to the short-termism that derived from a concern with the day-to-day conduct of fiscal and monetary policy. Its primary objectives were: to raise the level of private investment by creating a long-term expansionist perspective and thence more optimistic expectations as to future profitability within the business community; to engender a process of consultation involving industry, government and the trade unions, for example through the Economic Development Councils ("little Neddies"), which would aid both the formulation of a plan and its implementation;[30] to add to the flow of information necessary for rational and informed decision-making both by way of consultation and through the formulation of an indicative plan; to identify where private enterprise and the market had failed to rectify structural deficiencies in the British economy, or had allowed such weaknesses to emerge, and suggest appropriate action. It was, then, with these goals in mind and with the assistance of the Ministries of Power, Technology and Transport, research organizations, trade associations and the "little Neddies", that the DEA formulated Britain's first National Plan, which was published in September 1965.[31]

Of importance too in the planning process was the National Board for Prices and Incomes, which was established in September 1965. On the prices side, the aim was to prevent the emergence of supranormal profit as a result of the exploitation of monopoly power and also to use price control to put pressure on firms to increase productivity and reduce unit costs. On the incomes side, it was to have responsibility for "planned growth" (the allusive and anodyne manner in which the possibility of an incomes policy had been mooted in Labour's pre-election literature). On both counts it was, therefore, to be a key institution in fostering that improvement in competitiveness and efficiency which was seen as vital for the long-term, economic rejuvenation of Britain that the planners sought.

With respect to the structural dimension of planning, the crucial institution was the Industrial Reorganisation Corporation (IRC), set up in January 1966 to promote the rationalization and reorganization of industries with a view to reaping economies of scale. It was also given the power, "if requested" (by the DEA), to "establish or develop or promote or assist the establishment or development of any industrial enterprise".[32] At the same time, though, the government gave new powers to the Monopolies Commission by the Monopolies and Mergers Act of 1965. Specifically, the Board of Trade was given the power to refer proposed mergers to the Commission and if necessary delay or even dissolve them. Thus, on the one hand, the government sought to reap the economies of scale associated with industrial concentration; on the other, it sought to prevent the abuse of the monopoly power that a concentration of ownership bestowed.

To intensify the white heat of the technological revolution and thereby quicken the pace of technical change the National Research and Development Corporation was expanded, while a Ministry of Technology (Mintech) was established with powers, augmented by the Industrial Expansion Act of 1968, to use loans, grants and guarantees to encourage industrial development where that would "promote or support technological improvements". Its primary aim, as this indicates, was to accelerate the pace of technical change and facilitate the structural adjustments necessary to achieve this. In many ways Mintech embodied the spirit of Wilson's New Britain: the ideal of an economy driven forward by scientifically knowledgeable, technocratic public officials who, in co-operation with the private sector, would promote the restructuring, technological advance and general modernization of Britain's manufacturing base.

The fundamental objective of the National Plan was clearly stated. It was "to achieve a 25% increase in national output between 1964 and 1970; an objective chosen in the light of past trends in national output and output per head and a realistic view of the scope for improving upon those trends." This, in turn, would involve "achieving a 4% annual growth rate of output well before 1970 and an annual average of 3.8% between 1964 and 1970".[33] In the event, achievement fell well short of aspiration. Over the period 1964–70 the economy grew by 14 per cent, as against the 25 per cent projection of the Plan; investment grew by 20 per cent as against a projected 38 per cent; while private sector investment grew at less than half the projected rate. Of course statistical evidence can be cited that somewhat lightens the picture. For example, there is evidence to suggest that, as regards the increase of labour productivity, Britain's economic performance 1964–8 was superior to that in the period 1960–4. However, the extent to which policy and planning contributed to this improvement is very much open to question and, in general terms, the attempt to translate inspirational rhetoric into solid economic achievement must be considered a failure.

As to why that proved to be the case a number of points can be iterated. To begin with the charge has been that "the Plan had no teeth", that "far from being directive, or even indicative, it was merely subjunctive".[34] That is, it was formulated in the manner – if *a* happens then *x*, *y* and *z* will be the implications for industry and the economy – without the DEA possessing the power to ensure that *a* occurred. In large measure such a categorization of the Plan is warranted. If it was not altogether toothless the gaps were none the less as considerable as those in the mouth of an Irish hurley player. Further, what teeth there were often lacked effective bite and too often ground to little purpose. Thus crucial to the business of attaining the growth targets was a rise in the level of domestic investment, but aside from moral suasion and an indicatively induced optimism as to future profitability, the government deployed few instruments to achieve this. Investment grants were substituted for tax allowances but with little obvious effect. Corporation tax was introduced (April 1966) with a view to encouraging the retention of profits and discouraging overseas investment: again with little significant impact upon the overall level of investment.

The primary fiscal means of attempting to induce structural change was the selective employment tax (SET). This was a tax levied on the employment of labour of £1.25 a week for men, 62.5p for boys and women and 40p for girls. However, while all employers paid, those in manufacturing received a refund of 130 per cent while those in the public sector and transport received a 100 per cent rebate. This measure, advocated by Nicholas Kaldor, the Chancellor's special adviser on taxation, represented in effect a subsidy to manufacturing enterprise and, it was believed, also furnished an inducement to the service sector to use labour more efficiently. The productivity benefits would therefore be twofold. Productivity would rise in manufacturing, for Kaldor believed that productivity growth in that sector would increase in line with the acceleration in the growth of employment and output that SET induced. It would rise too in the service sector as a result of the more sparing use of labour that a tax on its employment encouraged. However, increasingly, this tax came to be seen, and to be used, as a convenient means of revenue raising and thence as a deflationary instrument of demand management, rather than as an effective means of promoting structural change. In that respect it epitomized a fundamental and more general tendency, discussed below, to allow the imperatives of short-term macromanagement to triumph over longer-term planning objectives.

As regards the role of the IRC in promoting structural change, it was initially given resources amounting to £150 million and its activities largely took the form of expediting takeovers and mergers, most obviously in the electronics and car industries. In the former it promoted the takeover of AEI by GEC and then the merger of GEC with English Electric. In the car industry it promoted the merger of British Motor Holdings and Leyland Motors to establish British Leyland. Such promotion took the form of loans, financial incentives, the direct purchase of equity and most importantly persuasion and proceeded on the underlying assumption that big must necessarily be beautiful, at least in terms of productivity gains. However, there is little evidence that this was the case. Certainly with respect to the car industry concentration did little to reverse growing import penetration, with foreign cars taking 14 per cent of the domestic market in 1970 as against 5 per cent in 1965. As one commentator has put it, all the policy seemed to have done was "encourage firms to grow by acquisition rather than by investing in modern plant and finding new markets".[35] This might be good for those who wielded boardroom power in the enterprises that emerged but it was hardly the way to reverse Britain's declining industrial fortunes.

This policy of industrial concentration also sat uneasily beside Labour's determination to curb the abuse of monopoly power and eliminate restrictive practices. As it was, the powers given by the Monopolies and Mergers Act to the Board of Trade were sparingly used: of 350 mergers (1964–70) that fell within the scope of the Act, only ten were referred to the Monopolies Commission and of those only four were found to be against the public interest. It would seem, therefore, that the Labour Government, through the IRC, was fostering a concentration of industrial ownership that enhanced the growth of monopoly power, while at the same time putting legislation in place which, in theory, subjected the process to critical scrutiny. Of course there was no necessary inconsistency here. It was not a case of the left hand not knowing what the right was doing. But there were, none the less, the problems involved in the two hands attempting to play separate tunes.

In the case of Mintech too a number of problems emerged. Attempts to restructure the shipbuilding, machine tool and car industries proved less than successful as did its involvement in certain aircraft industry projects.[36] In part these failures were due to the absence of the powers and instruments necessary for effective intervention and in part to lack of resources in relation to the magnitude of problems. There was, as well, an antipathy on the part of private industry to anything that smacked of coercive intervention and also, on occasion, a confusion of Mintech objectives when intervention did occur. However, most importantly of all, for much of its life Mintech was running up hill, seeking to stimulate innovation and raise productivity in a context of deflationary macroeconomic policies.

Here it should be said that what was fatal to Mintech was what was fatal to the National Plan as a whole. If the requisite planning instruments were absent and if there was inconsistency in the application of those that were available, what nonetheless proved decisive to the destruction of the National Plan was the conduct of macroeconomic policy and the prioritization of the essentially short-term, balance of payments, considerations that governed it. Certainly, when it came to the economic crunch, it was those considerations that prevailed over the longer-term objectives of the Plan. That this was so might come as no surprise to the political realist, but there had, after all, been a clear pre-election commitment on the part of Labour that that would not be the case. Thus Labour politicians prior to the 1964 election had shown themselves aware of a possible conflict between macroeconomic management objectives and radically transforming Britain's growth performance by way of economic planning. They were also adamant that should such a conflict arise the objectives of the planners must prevail. This was specifically stated by both James Callaghan and Roy Jenkins, in the early 1960s, prior to Labour's accession to power. Jenkins, in 1961, was insistent that "we should be prepared to go through a period of weak balance of payments . . . a period of losing reserves if necessary, *in order to get over the hump of stepping up our rate of growth*". Similarly, in 1962, Callaghan posed the question as to whether the Conservative Government wanted stagnation and a firm balance of payments or whether they wanted "growth, and to handle the difficulties that would arise on the balance of payments as they occur". His own answer to the question was emphatic – "I would choose the second".[37] Key Labour Party figures were aware, therefore, that in the short run, until the fruits of economic planning could be gathered, there might well be difficulty in adhering to the traditional objectives of demand management. Nevertheless, they were insistent that planning objectives must be given priority.

As it transpired, the opposite occurred. With pressure mounting on sterling in the early summer months of 1966 the Labour government, in an effort to avoid devaluation, implemented a deflationary package (July 1966) that put paid to any possibility of achieving the growth objectives set out in the National Plan. In effect the traditional, short-term concern to defend sterling's international value triumphed over the radical, longer-term goals of the planners. Deflation, with its inevitably adverse repercussions for economic growth was preferred to devaluation, which, whatever its knock-on effects upon inflation and thence wage demands, might at least have kept alive the hope of attaining some of the National Plan's objectives. Why this choice was made and deflation favoured is something that has been keenly debated in the secondary literature. Certainly there was strong pressure from both the Treasury and the Bank of England and, historically, Labour governments have been notoriously vulnerable to the influences emanating from such sources. Yet there was also a strong body of opinion among economists and economic advisers that preferred devaluation to deflation, so susceptibility to the pressure of putative expertise does not entirely explain the choice.

Wilson himself was undoubtedly a key variable in the equation, determined as he was to adhere to commitments given in manifestos and speeches to maintain sterling's international value and believing, as he did, that the government's credibility was dependent upon this. Yet it should be said that the decision to deflate rather than devalue represented not so much the adherence to manifesto commitments as a choice of which commitments would be sacrificed. Further, as regards Wilson, he had been President of the Board of Trade the last time Britain had devalued in 1949 and the scars of that experience may have predisposed him against any repetition. In this context, the great fear was that Labour would be indelibly branded the party of devaluation. It has been argued too that Wilson's experience of the Board of Trade left him with a faith in the efficacy of controls as against purely monetary manipulation. On the positive side this may be seen as an adherence to the notion that a quick fix was no substitute for fundamental adjustments. However, the problem at this juncture was that a refusal to devalue and a determination to deflate effectively destroyed the opportunity to set about making the fundamental adjustments required. Finally there is the view that the decision not to devalue was the *quid pro quo* of an agreement with the United States that involved American financial support for sterling. In that respect 1966 may be seen as a dress rehearsal for the crisis of 1976 when, as we shall see, a Labour government once again handed over the reins of economic management to the US Treasury and the US Federal Reserve – a willing acceptance of powerlessness in the face of impending economic catastrophe.

Whatever the reasons for preferring a deflationary course, the question of whether devaluation in July 1966 would have saved the Plan is also debatable. Thus even had the Labour Government opted for devaluation, it would have had to be accompanied by some kind of deflationary package to release the resources necessary for export growth. Further, a strong case has been made out for the view that only if Labour had acted immediately on coming to office in March 1964 would the preconditions have been established for the sustained growth that the Plan envisaged; that is, it was the failure to deal swiftly with the pre-election boom unleashed by the Conservative Chancellor Reginald Maudling in 1963–4, which postponed the taking of the unpalatable medicine of deflation to a date when it was guaranteed to undermine the National Plan. Yet it must be said that the political ammunition that would have been given to the Opposition by such speedy deflationary action, with another election obviously imminent, would automatically have ruled it out as an option.

Whatever the pros and cons of timing, the fact remains that the decision not to devalue in July 1966 represented the triumph of short-term over long-term considerations. It represented the victory of the Treasury over the DEA. It showed that where the objectives of macroeconomic management and planning clashed the former were to be preferred; that economic policy would not be subordinated to planning objectives. It made plain too that traditional Treasury and Bank of England goals were still in the ascendant and that, at root, Labour still craved respectability in the eyes of the City and those whose economic interest lay in the maintenance of sterling's international value. As it was, even Labour's defence of sterling was to prove ineffectual with a devaluation of 14 per cent being forced upon the government just over one year later in November 1967.

Of course in the long run we are all dead. Governments must cope with immediate crises and cannot afford to have their gaze perpetually fixed on the distant horizon. Yet it is also incumbent on them to assess the range of short-term expedients available and choose those consistent with their vision of how things might be. The essential failure of Labour in the 1964–70 period was the failure to do just that. To borrow another of Keynes's dicta, they were unwilling to try the possibilities of things, though the unwillingness itself was very much a function of that failure, already remarked upon, to take the powers and wield the instruments necessary to make planning decisions effective. Instead short-term survival became an end to which all else was subordinated and, along the way, the Wilsonian vision of a technologically dynamic and economically rejuvenated Britain was lost.

As regards this triumph of short-termism a number of illustrative points can be made. For example, the Selective Employment Tax, introduced originally as a means of facilitating structural adjustment in favour of the manufacturing sector, was increasingly used as a convenient method of deflating the economy. More importantly incomes policy that had been seen as an integral element of planning assumed a comparable, deflationary, crisis-management role. Thus as part of the July 1966 package, what had previously been a policy of voluntary wage restraint became a wage and price freeze and then, from November 1966 until July 1967, one of severe (wage and price) restraint with statutory backing. In effect, therefore, the National Board for Prices and Incomes, conceived originally as an integral part of the planning process (concerned with the "planned growth of incomes" and ensuring prices that both encouraged efficiency gains and precluded the exploitation of monopoly power) increasingly assumed the role of implementing a demand management strategy geared to the short-run objective of preventing devaluation and, after 1967, to that of making devaluation work. In this context too, the Labour Government's abortive and disastrous attempt at trade union reform embodied in *In place of strife* (1969) can be seen as driven, in some considerable measure, by a concern for the immediate benefits of controlling income growth.

By way of mitigation it can be said that if there was no transformation of economic performance, if the major growth objectives that Labour set itself were not attained, the years 1964–70 did see progress as regards the diminution of inequality. To quote one commentator there exists "powerful evidence of an improvement in income distribution as a result of the Labour government's policies".[38] Rises in national insurance and supplementary benefits and a rapid increase in the provision of health and educational services were crucial here. There was also a narrowing of regional disparities as regards unemployment , which may in part have been the result of government policies.

Even so, if the term failure must be applied in a qualified manner to the economic policies of the Wilson governments, it is none the less applicable. The Plan, keystone of the strategy arch, disintegrated in July 1966. The inspirational images conjured up by Wilsonian rhetoric proved, in the end, evanescent. Labour's long-term economic strategy was hamstrung by the macroeconomic constraints that had for so long bedevilled the British economy. There was no reversal or appreciable slowing of the long-run tendency to relative economic decline. The targets set were not even nearly attained and the expectations raised were dashed, the latter tarnishing the whole idea of indicative planning in a manner that, if it did not preclude its future use, certainly rendered its future implementation considerably more problematic. For indicative planning of the kind embodied in the National Plan is, in part, about inducing a certainty of expectation that in itself produces the decisions that ensure that expectations are realized. Success in large measure derives, therefore, from the Plan's and planners' credibility among the business community and once lost such credibility is mighty difficulty to retrieve.

What then were the implications of this experience for the evolution of socialist political economy in Britain? In large part this is a question that is best considered in the next chapter but it is useful here to make some general observations. To begin with there were grounds for arguing, and there were those within the Party who believed, that the traditional tools of macroeconomic management still worked. They had, during the years of the Wilson governments, taken longer to work than expected but, by 1969–70, the balance of payments had come round, a prices and incomes policy had slowed the level of wage increases, growth had proceeded and unemployment while higher in 1970 than in 1964 was still not much above the 2 per cent mark. Assuming for the future an effective prices and incomes policy, there was no reason to doubt therefore that macroeconomic management could still provide the basis of Labour's economic strategy.

Yet, for many, the experience of the Wilson governments suggested that such a view was manifestly untenable. The fundamental problems of the British economy had not been addressed and would continue to act as an increasing constraint upon Labour's pursuit of its egalitarian and other objectives. Macroeconomic management might deal with, or more accurately suppress, some of the symptoms but it clearly could not touch the underlying causes of Britain's economic malaise. Also the symptoms were increasingly suppressed in a manner that threatened working-class living standards and a rise in unemployment. As regards planning, the problem was not that it had failed but that it had not really been tried. More specifically, it was argued that planning had occurred in a context where those responsible possessed neither the power nor the institutional framework necessary to implement it effectively. It was what was required in these respects to make future planning work that increasingly engaged the attention of many within the Labour Party in the late 1960s and early 1970s and it is to their deliberations that we now turn.

Part four

1970–95

Chapter 14
Rethinking socialism: left-wing revisionism in the 1970s

> . . . recent acceleration in the trend to monopoly and multi-national capital has eroded Keynesian economic policies and undermined the sovereignty of the capitalist nation state. The trend has resulted in a new mesoeconomic power between conventional macroeconomics and microeconomics. In compromising Keynesian economic management, the new economic power has compromised the gradualism of Keynesian social democracy.
>
> S. Holland, *The socialist challenge*, 1975

For many within the Party the record of the 1964–70 Labour governments demanded a fundamental reappraisal of the political economy that had underpinned its policies. The failure to arrest Britain's relative economic decline, a deflationary response to sterling crises that destroyed any possibility of meeting the ambitious growth targets set by the National Plan, periodic public expenditure cuts, the failure of the Industrial Reorganisation Corporation to effect a restructuring of British industry that would enhance its international competitiveness, a 60 per cent rise in unemployment, an increase in Britain's international indebtedness and a rate of price inflation that rose from 3.3 per cent in 1964 to 6.4 per cent in 1970, all clearly indicated that there had been no forging of a "new Britain" in the white heat of a technological revolution. Indeed for many it seemed, in this period, that the only new development was the virulence with which old problems asserted themselves.

In this context, reappraisal was seen as imperative – all the more so as the late 1960s and early 1970s were characterized by what seemed a more general failure of Keynesian demand management even to secure the traditional trade-off between inflation and unemployment, for both rose simultaneously. The old certainties were evaporating and the policy-making consensus that they had underpinned was, in its turn, disintegrating. This seemed particularly so in the early years of the Heath Government as it articulated the need for a diminution in state involvement in the economy and increasing reliance on the imperatives of market forces. And if Keynes was dead, what of the health of Beveridge? If full employment could no longer be secured by traditional techniques then the guarantee of rising levels of social welfare provision, to which both political parties had adhered, could no longer be taken for granted. The left had always argued that Keynes was not enough; now events seemed to have proved them right.

However, if Keynesian social democracy had failed, there could be no easy retreat into a traditional fundamentalism of planning and nationalization. The failure of the National Plan showed clearly that some hard thinking had to be done about what planning entailed and how it could be implemented. Further, while the nationalized industries had, in fact, performed much better then many of their critics allowed, a further extension in its Morrisonian form was problematic. The creation of more autonomous national industrial corporations covering entire industries was unlikely to rejuvenate an ailing economy. Such corporations had not effected a transformation in the attitude of their workforce to the tasks that they performed; they could not easily be used by government to restructure or to plan the economy and, in addition, considerable political and financial costs attended their formation. Consequently in the early 1970s a revision of traditional doctrines and attitudes was as vital for those on the left as for those on the right of the Party.

To the forefront, as regards the left, were figures such as Stuart Holland and Michael Barratt Brown and organizations such as the Institute for Workers' Control; it was their ideas that played a fundamental role in the formulation of what came to be known as the Alternative Economic Strategy: a strategy that to a greater or lesser extent left its imprint on many of the policy documents produced by the Labour Party in the 1970s and early 1980s. It is with the salient elements of this strategy and the work of some of those who contributed to it that this chapter will therefore be concerned.

Stuart Holland

For Stuart Holland, Labour's record in office showed clearly that the fusion of Keynesian social democracy and indicative planning, to which the Wilson governments adhered, was manifestly unsound. It was so, he argued, because it failed to comprehend the manner in which capitalism had changed since the Second World War. Specifically, those 25 years had witnessed a considerable concentration of ownership of capitalist enterprises and thence of economic power. Thus Holland cited the 1968 Industrial Census to show that the top 100 firms in Britain "commanded half or more of the key macroeconomic aggregates of the economy . . . output, industrial employment and assets . . . and [the] direct or visible export trade."[1] Oligopoly or monopoly, not competition, were what now characterized not just the British but all Western capitalist economies and the salient entity here was the large multinational corporation – a firm that embodied an international division of labour with subsidiaries spanning the globe. As Holland saw it, in the 20 years 1950 to 1970 "there had been a change from predominantly national to predominantly international capital". Thus by 1970 all of the top 100 companies in Britain had "a sizeable number of subsidiaries outside Britain".[2]

It was these firms that now represented the commanding heights of the economy, wielding, as they did, enormous economic power. Further, it was the use of that power which, for Holland, had emasculated the monetary, fiscal, exchange rate, regional and other policies that governments sought to pursue. It effectively destroyed national sovereignty as regards the conduct of economic policy and in so doing destroyed the basis of Keynesian social democracy; for that had assumed the possibility of managing the level of economic activity and thence employment on a national basis, by an appropriate combination of fiscal, monetary, exchange rate and exchange control policies.

As regards the conduct of monetary policy, the size of these corporations gave them privileged access to finance of a kind and at a price that was relatively uninfluenced by the policies that national governments pursued. Use of Eurodollar and Eurobond markets in particular allowed them to circumvent a restrictive monetary policy. In effect, it was they and not governments that determined when they would increase the level of their activity. With respect to fiscal policy, these corporations again enjoyed a comparable autonomy. The fact that the focus of multinational corporations was the *international* market and a large part of their trade was with their own far-flung subsidiaries meant that the use of fiscal policy to expand or dampen down demand *in the domestic economy* would be unlikely to have a significant impact on the level of a multinational firm's imports and exports. In addition, because "corporate planning for the big league spans at least five years and often more" and because this was "longer than the full parliamentary term of any government", the level of investment of large corporations would be determined independently of the manipulation of aggregate demand, which in Britain was usually focused on the short-term objectives that could be attained within the lifetime of a Parliament. As Holland phrased it, "a divorce has arisen between the demand management . . . of governments and the supply management cycle of big business."[3] Again this eroded the efficacy of Keynesian economic management.

For Holland the power of these corporations also impinged on the conduct of fiscal policy in another way. Because of their *multinational* nature they had the power to arrange "intra-company payments between subsidiaries in such a way as to minimise declared profits and maximise undeclared global profits".[4] In effect, they used the prices on the basis of which subsidiaries made exchanges to massage down taxable profits in countries with a relatively progressive tax system and increase the profits of subsidiaries operating in countries where company taxation was relatively low. This "transfer pricing", as it was called, therefore allowed companies "to declare what profits they want to declare" and, in particular, to "declare lower profits than they actually make" in high-tax welfare state countries.[5] In so doing, of course, they could hinder the pursuit of redistributive fiscal and social welfare policies by reducing the government's tax revenue.

In so far as it artificially inflated or deflated export and import prices, "transfer pricing" also had a bearing on trade performance that might be further amplified by the impact that the behaviour of multinationals could have on exchange rate policy. Thus the movement of funds across national boundaries between subsidiaries could be on a scale sufficient to exert upward or downward pressure on exchange rates independently of the wishes of a national government. This had occurred, as Holland saw it, in 1967, when part of the downward pressure on sterling was a consequence of companies delaying foreign currency payments to British subsidiaries and delaying sterling payments to foreign subsidiaries in the expectation that the pound would be devalued.

In addition, the self-interested behaviour of multinationals could reduce the impact of an exchange rate policy designed to enhance trade performance: cartel-like arrangements between multinationals often meant that they did not lower their prices by the full extent of a currency devaluation for fear of touching-off a damaging price war. In such circumstances the impact of devaluation on price competitiveness would not be on the scale expected by policy-makers and the anticipated, favourable impact on the balance of payments would fail to emerge.

Economic sovereignty was also eroded by multinationals in other ways. First their size meant that threats to relocate had to be taken seriously in the light of the potential impact on regional economies. Governments might therefore be coerced into providing more favourable tax and other concessions than those available to other, even indigenous, firms. Secondly, multinationals could extend their activities deliberately to pre-empt the growth of indigenous firms and in that way damage national economic development. Thirdly, the monopoly power of multinationals gave them a significant influence over the level of prices in a national economy, which they usually asserted, with considerations of profitability in mind, in an upward direction.

Holland's general conclusion was, then, that the "recent acceleration in the trend to monopoly and multi-national capital has eroded Keynesian economic policies and undermined the sovereignty of the capitalist nation state. The trend has resulted in a new mesoeconomic power between conventional macroeconomics and microeconomics. In compromising Keynesian economic management, the new mesoeconomic power has *compromised the gradualism of Keynesian social democracy*."[6] Keynesian social democracy was doomed because the power of national governments to achieve objectives such as full employment, the increase of social welfare expenditure and the redistribution of wealth had been seriously eroded. Policy-makers simply lacked the institutions and the instruments to counter the mesoeconomic power of the multinationals. Demand management was not enough; nor had nationalization to date provided governments with alternative sources of economic power. Nationalization had not been on the requisite scale. It had also been focused either on basic (often declining) "passive or growth dependant" industries, requiring major public support for purposes of rationalization and restructuring, or on advanced technology ventures whose high risk discouraged the involvement of private capital. As Holland phrased it: "public ownership in the mature capitalist countries is not represented on any scale . . . in profit-making sectors. It is classically concentrated at two loss-making extremes: basic industries and services and advanced technology industry."[7] In addition Holland argued that nationalization had also created corporations whose autonomy precluded their use by government to achieve socialist objectives. If British governments no longer possessed the powers necessary for effective macroeconomic management, then nationalization had also failed to give them the power "to implement the broad range of objectives which should characterise *a comprehensive national plan*".[8]

It was this impotence that lay at the root of the failure of Labour's National Plan. For Holland the problem with the Plan was that it was purely indicative – "an econometrician's dreamworld". There were no instruments for turning the dream into a reality. "It attempted no major change in the balance of public or private power."[9] It had no teeth. Supposedly replicating the indicative planning that had proved successful in France, Labour's policy-makers had failed to understand that, in France, success was in large part due to the fact that planners had the power to be both "bully and banker", as well as guide and counsellor.

For Holland, the way forward was clear. A Labour government must shelve the agenda of Keynesian social democratic gradualism that had guided its actions since the war and challenge the centres of mesoeconomic power by the selective nationalization "over a parliamentary term" of 20–25 leading companies in the high growth sectors of the economy. These firms, primarily involved in what Holland termed "intermediate manufacturing", constituted the commanding heights over which Labour had now to extend effective control. Through the medium of a State Holding Company (the National Enterprise Board), a Labour government should therefore purchase shares "to ensure direct control of the strategic decision-making in a range of leading companies", thereafter exploiting the power that this gave to pursue a co-ordinated, planned programme of expansion that would reverse the decline of the British economy and lay the basis for a significant improvement in the material lot of the working population.[10]

Drawing on his knowledge and experience of comparable continental holding companies, in particular the Italian IRI (Institute for Industrial Reconstruction), Holland envisaged the National Enterprise Board using its power in a number of ways. To begin with, it could act to stimulate investment and accelerate the pace of technological innovation in those sector-leading firms over which it had direct control. Also, these firms could be used to "maximise [the] direct promotion of exports and domestic import substitution", thereby enabling Britain to circumvent the constraints previously imposed by her parlous balance of payments position. Such firms could also be used to spearhead an effective regional policy. Thus "further social dislocation in mining, steel and shipbuilding [could be] . . . largely avoided", through "the extension of regionally mobile new public enterprise in manufacturing." Moreover, as the firms over which the Board took control were in the dynamic, profit-making sectors of the economy, as they represented the real commanding heights, their control and use to achieve the social and economic objectives of the Labour Party would go a long way to dissipate the "disillusion which followed the first-generation nationalizations".[11] Hence the popular support engendered would help ensure that nationalization was once again perceived as an electorally attractive policy option for the Labour Party.

Such an extension of public ownership and control could also be used to establish an effective counter-inflationary policy, for it would be possible to impose price restraint through public sector leadership. The dominant position of these new public enterprises would be used to ensure that truly competitive prices prevailed in the sector in which they operated. In effect, public enterprise would operate to countervail the price-setting power previously wielded by the multinationals, which had allowed them to reap supranormal profits while exacerbating inflationary pressures. More generally, Holland saw the State Holding Company, through the enterprises it controlled, as providing a means of countering those actions of multinationals deemed to be harmful to the national economy. So where multinationals threatened to pre-empt the growth of indigenously owned companies in modern and advanced technology sectors (perhaps by buying them out, perhaps by a pricing policy that undermined their competitive position) the State Holding Company would act either through the enterprises it already owned or through its share-buying powers to counter such actions. In this context Holland also envisaged state firms being used to influence the scale, rate and location of private investment; private firms, to survive, having to react to the investment strategies of sector-leading public enterprises.[12] Thus the State Holding Company and the enterprises it owned would provide planners with the means of ensuring that particular sectors of the economy developed in the way and in the areas that were deemed to be in the national interest.

However, in addition to this kind of influence on the behaviour of private sector firms, Holland also put forward the idea of "planning agreements" between a National Enterprise Board and major private companies, in "the key industries and services on which the viability of the economy depends"[13]. As he envisaged them, these agreements could be used both to furnish the information necessary for the formulation of a comprehensive, purposive national plan and to provide an effective means of ensuring that all major enterprises acted in accordance with the strategy and objectives of the planners, once these had been established. They would be "written agreements" that would secure "up-to-date information on a systematic and continuing basis from all companies and enterprises" which signed them: information concerning "present and future investment, prices, product development, markets [and] export and import requirements". This information would be used in the formulation of a national plan and firms would then, in return for "selective government assistance . . . help governments to meet clearly defined planning objectives". So as Holland saw it, "the Planning Agreements system" would "be less than wholly imperative but more than indicative".[14] It would provide the means of making those companies wielding mesoeconomic power accountable for its use and, if they failed to adhere to the agreements that they signed, competitive public enterprise, public purchasing power and selective assistance could be deployed to bring them into line. In this way the capacity of large corporations and, in particular, multinationals to obstruct or undermine the economic strategy of a future Labour government could be considerably reduced where it was not altogether eliminated. Thus planning agreements, underpinned by the threat of coercive or punitive economic action by a State Holding Company controlling a much extended public sector, provided the teeth that were so manifestly lacking in the 1965 National Plan.

In addition, and crucially for Holland, such agreements provided scope for the extension of industrial democracy, enthusiasm for which enjoyed a resurgence within the Party in the late 1960s and early 1970s. As Holland saw it, unions would play a vital role in the shaping of planning agreements, "negotiat[ing] with governments and management . . . the main features of their companies' programmes over the medium term."[15] This process of negotiation would have a dual socialist function. On the one hand "tripartite bargaining in the mesoeconomic sector between workers' representatives, management and government can bridge the gap between overcentralised and undercentralised planning". In particular, it could operate as a counterweight to the concentration of power in the hands of an authoritarian bureaucracy. On the other hand it gave workers a crucial input into the formulation of the economic strategies of major private companies. In this way, at both company and national level, unions could make a fundamental contribution to the planning process.

This involvement of unions in planning was to be part and parcel of their wider involvement in helping the next Labour Government to achieve its economic objectives. In short, it was to be part of a "social contract" between the Party and the unions that would embrace commitments by the former to the redistribution of wealth, increased social welfare expenditure, a transformation of "the viciousness of the capitalist labour market by undertaking the provision of alternative employment in cases of major redundancy" and a shift in the balance of economic decision-making power in favour of working people.[16] It would be as part of this kind of broadly conceived social contract that a sustained, non-inflationary rate of wage increases would be determined and enforced. An incomes policy could only be successful as part of this wider agreement. If, therefore, a non-inflationary, full employment, Keynesian strategy was to work it must be in the context of extended public ownership, industrial democracy and purposive economic planning. Ironically, the macroeconomics of the Keynesian liberal socialists only became viable as part of a radical-left economic programme.

Michael Barratt Brown

Other writers in the late 1960s and early 1970s also focused on the power wielded by multinational corporations. Michael Barratt Brown's *From labourism to socialism* (1972) discussed at length the nature, causes and consequences of their phenomenal growth since 1945 and the implications that had for the pursuit of a socialist economic strategy. For Barratt Brown, economies of scale, control over diminishing raw material inputs and markets, the scale of the expenditure on modern research and development that only large corporations could accommodate, state support for mergers and takeovers (in Britain through the Industrial Reorganisation Corporation), the rapid increase in defence expenditure on products furnished in large part by the multinationals, and the accelerating pace of technological change that these corporations fostered and which allowed them to outstrip and absorb their rivals, had all played a part in a dramatic growth in their size and thence the economic power they wielded – a power that had already eroded, and threatened to erode further, national economic sovereignty.

To a significant extent this erosion of national sovereignty was a simple function of the size of multinationals but there were a number of other characteristics that these corporations had acquired, largely in the post-1945 period, which also had an important bearing on this development. First there was their marked and growing reliance on overseas markets and subsidiaries, which rendered them less responsive to the policy imperatives of national governments, where those imperatives were not in their interests. Secondly, as a result of this global diversification, there was the growing importance of trade *within* what Barratt Brown denominated "trans-national corporations" – trade conducted on the basis of "transfer prices", "fixed at a level to show no profit in countries with high rates of taxation and likewise to attract minimal import duty when entering countries with high tariffs".[17] This in itself was sufficient to subvert government policy, but added to that the manipulation of prices at which goods exchanged between subsidiaries meant that "the nation state government" had a real problem in simply determining "what companies are up to".[18] Thirdly there was an increasing interdependence of the state and transnationals as a result of the growth of military and semi-military orders that had implications for the autonomy of the state. Finally, just as the movement of goods within transnational corporations could be conducted in a manner inimical to the economic objectives of governments so could the transfer of funds within these organizations. Thus Barratt Brown quoted a *Times* report which indicated that the main cause of the pressure on sterling and the franc, in late November 1968, was the movement of funds to accounts in Bonn by Unilever, ICI, British Petroleum and British American Tobacco.

Transnational corporations therefore had the power to constrain or negate government economic policy. Indeed such was their power and their importance to individual national economies that pressures could be applied to ensure that policy was conducted in a manner consonant with these corporations' interests. Thus governments could be "persuaded" to provide "a favourable environment" for their development. This might include "national prices and incomes policies that make possible long-term cost control . . . ; national education and training arrangements that provide reserves of skilled and qualified labour at all levels; national industrial relations systems that ensure a dependable labour force at all times; national policies designed to ensure steady growth of consumption and investment expenditure."[19] In addition, they could and did use their influence to persuade governments to treat them, in terms of legal status, taxation and access to capital markets, as favourably as indigenous companies. In this way the power and economic importance of transnationals often meant that policy was made with their best interests in mind. In short, as Barratt Brown saw it, "the trans-national company has now reached a size where it can challenge the power of all but the largest nation states" and this, inevitably, raised the question as to whether the nation state could, any longer, be used to provide an effective economic framework for socialism or whether the existence of transnational corporations vitiated that possibility.[20]

For Barratt Brown there was indeed a way forward. In the short run this would involve countering the power that transnationals wielded, where it threatened the pursuit of immediate objectives; in the longer term, it would entail eroding and destroying it altogether. As regards immediate objectives, Barratt Brown was adamant that "governments [could] maintain full employment at least for most of the trade cycle" and an incoming Labour government could be expected to do this by conventional Keynesian means. Inflationary pressures were not a significant constraint, Barratt Brown dismissing any notion of an inevitable trade-off between unemployment and inflation. As he saw it, a return to full employment would result in an increase in output to match any increase in expenditure and incomes, while the National Board for Prices and Incomes had shown that price controls "on many types of goods and services" could be successfully implemented. Such an effective price control policy would necessarily involve clipping the wings of transnational corporations, while it was also seen by Barratt Brown as a basic prerequisite for a successful incomes policy.

As regards the balance of payments and exchange rate repercussions of such a full employment strategy, Barratt Brown accepted that while the existence of transnational corporations made life difficult, the potentially destabilizing impact of the capital flows and transfer pricing that an expansionary strategy might precipitate, could be countered by exchange and import controls. More generally, what he envisaged was a "foreign trade plan drawn up with major trading partners" that would guarantee those imports vital to the planned growth of the domestic economy. He accepted, though, that such a course of action would require both "a government determined to stand up to the giant companies" and one prepared to "eschew totally the 'freeing' of trade in manufactures . . . involved in membership of the EEC."[21] Thus, like most on the left in the late 1960s and early 1970s, including Holland, Barratt Brown called into question the compatibility of continued EEC membership and a socialist or even a radical economic strategy.

It was not a question, therefore, of whether a non-inflationary, full employment strategy was feasible but rather whether politicians were prepared to prioritize its pursuit and implement the full range of necessary measures. As Barratt Brown put it, "The question [was] not one of feasibility but determination";[22] a determination which, among other things, involved a preparedness to counter, where necessary, the power wielded by the transnational corporations.

In the longer term, though, the power of the transnationals had to be more directly addressed. Here, as he saw it, the way forward lay less in a frontal assault by way of public ownership, as envisaged by Holland, and more through what might be termed "encroaching control". This had two dimensions. First there was the encroaching control of state intervention. Thus Barratt Brown believed the state's assumption of responsibility for full employment, social welfare provision, education and housing all served to extend the range of those goods and services that were supplied on the basis of social need rather than private profit. This, in turn, highlighted "the political possibility of establishing an economy without capitalists" – with economic decision-making proceeding by reference to non-capitalist or even non-monetary considerations. Further, "the more . . . the state [had] to step in to meet social needs and prevent social abuses . . . the more needs [came] to be formulated socially", that is the less wants would be signalled individualistically in the market and the more they would be determined democratically and collectively.[23] Here again capitalist imperatives and capitalist power would be eroded.

The second dimension of encroaching socialist control, as it was envisaged by Barratt Brown, was implicit in the extension of industrial democracy. Such an extension not only constrained capitalist power but was to be welcomed too because it laid the basis for a truly socialist economy, a salient feature of which would be worker managed industrial companies. The growth of workers' control necessarily entailed increasing "checks and vetoes over the arbitrary and centralised decisions of the managers of capital. From control over pay for the job, and hours of work, it moves forward to control over manning the job, over hiring and firing, over redundancy and work sharing, to raise questions about what is produced and where and when investment should take place."[24] Hence in this period Barratt Brown and others associated with the Institute for Workers' Control breathed new life into the old syndicalist and guild socialist idea of eroding the prerogatives of management to the point where the workers assumed actual control of productive enterprises.

In fact, in *From labourism to socialism*, Barratt Brown traced his ideological pedigree back to just these roots. However, he stressed too that developments since the high tide of guild socialism and syndicalism in Britain had made "encroaching control" a potentially more powerful weapon. Increased public sector employment, a more educated workforce, the self-confidence of trade unionists after two decades of increasing trade union membership and, in a climate of full or near-full employment, growing union power, all combined to enhance the viability of a socialist strategy based on workers' control. Most importantly, the "work-ins" and "sit-ins" of the early 1970s associated, in particular, with Upper Clyde Shipbuilders, the River Don Steel Company in Sheffield and Fisher Bendix in Liverpool, all provided evidence of the capacity of workers to manage their own enterprises.

For Barratt Brown the trade unionists involved in these had also raised questions about the wider social costs and benefits of particular plant closures and, in so doing, had highlighted the need to broaden the basis of economic decision-making to accommodate considerations other than the narrow commercial ones of profit and loss with which capitalist enterprises were usually concerned. Such episodes focused critical attention on the rationality of economic calculation under capitalism, emphasizing by implication that there was a pressing need for an alternative socialist basis for economic computation, one that started from the democratic expression of social needs. For Barratt Brown, therefore, the extension of industrial democracy led on logically and imperatively to democratic socialist planning.

Drawing on the work of the Institute for Workers' Control, Barratt Brown showed how this idea might be developed further. At the time of the Upper Clyde Shipbuilders "work-in", Brown had proposed that if, after all considerations had been taken into account, it was decided that there was no economic *or* social utility in retaining a shipbuilding capacity on the Clyde, then the government should assume responsibility for the provision of alternative employment in state factories – factories that would provide directly for a range of social needs that the community would have a vital role in formulating. In effect, what was proposed for Scotland was that

> all kinds of bodies should be called upon to draw up an inventory of social needs and priorities; universities and colleges, trade unions and industrial research bodies should at the same time inventory the resources of man power, education and training facilities, plant and equipment existing inside Scotland and available from outside in exchange for Scottish products. In this way an emergency plan might be drawn up leading to a long-term plan for economic development.[25]

Democratic planning on the basis of need and physical resources would therefore replace profit maximizing decision-making on the basis of price. Democratic control of enterprises would replace the self-seeking capitalist exercise of power and along with this would go the "sometimes slow, sometimes rapid diminution of the power of the market and the role of money". "Production for use instead of profit, for socially formulated needs in place of privately managed markets"[26] – that, for Barratt Brown, was the ultimate objective.

There are marked similarities with respect to both the critical analysis and socialist vision of Barratt Brown and Holland. Both focused on the monopolistic and transnational nature of contemporary capitalism. Both saw it as vital that the powers of multinational and transnational corporations should be circumscribed and/or appropriated and used by a Labour government for socialist purposes. Both saw the extension of industrial democracy as a socialist goal in itself and as a means of destroying capitalist power. However, there was a difference in emphasis as regards the agencies of socialist transformation. Here Holland's views were altogether more statist, with the extension of public ownership and the activities of the State Holding Company playing a central role. Of course there was, in his political economy, an important place for the extension of workers' control, particularly with respect to the formulation of planning agreements, but it is clear that Barratt Brown envisaged a more proactive role for trade unions and workers' organizations in the process of transforming capitalism. Certainly the influence of the Institute for Workers' Control, while apparent in the work of Holland, looms much larger in that of Barratt Brown. And as regards planning, Holland's views, in addition to being more precisely formulated, establish a central and clearly defined role for the state and state institutions. Barratt Brown's views on planning are altogether more nebulous, more difficult to translate into specific policies and are less clear on the functions the state would perform, at least in the long run. As he wrote in *From labourism to socialism:* "a different system of political economy will . . . be required in the end and will involve the expropriation of the giant companies *and the capture of the state apparatus, but the way forward and what will follow can only be decided as and when the situation arises.*"[27]

Institute for Workers' Control

As we have seen, industrial democracy had an important place in the political economy of Stuart Holland and Michael Barratt Brown and their incorporation and development of the idea in their work was indicative of an intensifying interest in workers' control within the Labour movement in the late 1960s and early 1970s. There were a number of reasons for this. To begin with, the full employment and the increasing trade union membership that characterized the 1950s and 1960s had created an upsurge of trade union confidence which, in turn, encouraged trade unionists to think in other than defensive terms. Further, there had been an increase in grass-roots activity and, in particular, "a growth of shop stewards' control and bargaining influence . . . at a time (1950s and early 1960s) when national union bargaining was achieving only very modest gains".[28] These developments made for an interest in, and enthusiasm for, what could be achieved, in terms of decision-making and control, at a grass-roots level.

There was also, within nationalized industries, a growing dissatisfaction on the part of trade unionists with what had been achieved within a Morrisonian scheme of things, disgruntlement that frequently focused on the exercise of power by an authoritarian management distanced from the workforce. Thus by the 1960s "the largest concentrations of low paid workers [were] to be found in direct government and local government service and in nationalized industries".[29] Inevitably, then, the view grew that the extension of public ownership on traditional lines was simply not enough to effect a substantial improvement in the position and conditions of labour.

The rapid growth of multinationals in the post-1945 period also entailed the emergence of enterprises whose decisions were made in boardrooms at a considerable distance, institutionally and geographically, from their employees. In consequence, as power became increasingly concentrated at the top of the industrial pyramid, so resentment intensified at its base and again, as in the nationalized industries, this resentment manifested itself constructively in an increasing desire, on the part of the workforce, for a say in the decisions that materially affected their working lives.

The disaffection produced by the increasing separation of an anonymous management from a powerless workforce was further exacerbated by the alienation that rapid automation and the increasing use of production-line techniques across a wide range of industries precipitated in the post-war period. The "subordination of . . . personalities and talents to the mechanical needs of the manufacturing process"[30] and the boredom and mental atrophy inherent in mindlessly repetitive tasks produced a level of frustration that was reflected in waves of industrial unrest in mass production industries. Once again, this raised the question of control, for it was the absence of control that demeaned labour, making it the servant not the master of technology.

One other factor increased the fertility of the soil in which the idea of workers' control was to take root and that was the seeming impotence of the Labour governments of 1964–70. For many, their failure lay in their inability, or unwillingness, to effect a decisive shift of power in favour of the working class. For many too, the lesson to be drawn from this was that there could be "no conceivable [socialist] alternative" other than one that involved the rapid "dismantling of the industrial authoritarianism" that otherwise would continue to obstruct any attempt by a future Labour government to improve economic performance and create a more just society.[31] Workers' control was the obvious means of achieving this: an extension of workers' control to be effected by the industrial muscle of the trade union movement in alliance with the legislative authority of a Labour government.

It was against this kind of background that the Institute for Workers' Control was established at the Sixth Conference on Workers' Control in 1968, one of a series of such conferences involving trade union activists and academics that had originated in 1964. The role of the Institute was to "service existing groups" of trade unionists who had "already arrived at the stage of producing publishable schemes" for workers' control of the particular industries in which they were involved and "to foster the formation of new groups wherever possible".[32] What followed was a spate of publications concerned with the theory and practice of such control, which were to have a significant influence on the economic and political thinking of many within the Labour Party. The Institute was, therefore, in its own right, an important factor fuelling the growing interest in and support for workers' control and industrial democracy generally in this period. In this context it is interesting to note the view of Tony Crosland, expressed in 1973, that while "ten years ago scarcely a whisper was heard on this subject (industrial democracy) at Labour or trade union conferences . . . to-day there is a dramatic upsurge of interest".[33]

It is not possible in a publication of this length to do justice to the work of all those connected with the IWC. However, to appreciate the political economy of workers' control articulated in this period it is useful to look briefly at one of its more extended expositions: that to be found in Ken Coates and Tony Topham's *New unionism, the case for workers' control* (1974). Both were IWC members.

For Coates and Topham there were four key components of the extension of workers' control – an end to managerial secrecy; adequate levels of representation on decision-making boards at plant, enterprise and, where appropriate, industry level; workers' powers of veto over the appointment of managers; and the power to scrutinize management decisions. As regards secrecy, information on profitability, dividends, unit costs, investment plans, labour requirements, productivity, directors allowances, etc. was crucial for any informed participation of trade union representatives in decision-making at enterprise level. On a national basis it was also crucial to trade union participation in the business of economic planning. Thus, if support was to be forthcoming for the planning of incomes and income growth, it could only be on the foundation of trade union access to information on profitability, rents, dividends, managerial perks, etc. After all, accurate information on wages was available to government and employers and there was, therefore, "a danger that with information on other categories of income being less accurate or even non-existent, the weight of any restrictive measures (on income growth) may fall on wages".[34]

With respect to representation, it was crucial that this was sufficient and at such a level as to allow worker representatives to make a significant input to decisions on such matters as "the right to hire and fire, the control of redundancies, the enforcement of industrial safety, investment decisions, industrial health and welfare, the decisions about product mix and rationalisation".[35] What Coates and Topham envisaged here was a capacity, in terms of representation, for a continual encroachment by workers on those areas of decision-making previously regarded as the exclusive preserve of management. Trade unionists could and should no longer rest content with the representative power to negotiate solely over wages and conditions. They "should not rest content with a merely oppositional role in industry".[36] They had to be able to act and act decisively to erode the prerogatives of management. As regards the veto on managerial appointments and the power to scrutinize management decisions, these were seen as vital to curbing the arbitrary and authoritarian nature of much management in both the public and private sectors. It was essential for the democratization of economic life that managers were made accountable to the workforce for their actions.

Once established on these four pillars industrial democracy would raise further questions, whose resolution, for the authors, led inevitably in the direction of socialism. First, where workers were able to play a decisive part in determining the key decisions of an enterprise, this would call into question the function of professional managers operating on behalf of capitalist owners and thence the rationale of capitalism itself. Secondly, this extension of workers' control would at the same time move decision-making away from an overriding concern with profit. Specifically, it could lead, for example, to a consideration of the full costs to workforce and community of decisions to contract or alter the structure of production. In effect, decision-making would proceed on a broader computational basis than that which characterized contemporary capitalism. It was on such a foundation that the idea of a "social audit" rested, an idea already noticed above in the discussion of its suggested use by Barratt Brown at the time of the "work-in" at Upper Clyde Shipbuilders. The purpose of a social audit was, in the words of Coates and Topham, to take stock of the "*full costs* of adverse social decisions"[37] and this was seen by them and others as an exercise that contained the potential for full-scale, democratic, socialist planning, with "economic" decisions being made on the basis of need and welfare rather than commercial considerations.

Ultimately what Coates, Topham and many others associated with the Institute looked to was a "socialized, democratically planned system of *self-management*", in which socially owned enterprises were controlled by managers appointed by and answerable to the workforce. In the words of Jack Jones, general secretary of the Transport and General Workers' Union in the late 1960s and 1970s and a Vice-President of the Institute: "units of industry [would] eventually be seen as a series of self-governing communities within which working people [would] assume the role of policy-making and controlling."[38] This was the vision of a decentralized, democratic socialism that inspired much of the work of those associated with the Institute for Workers' Control and that left its imprint on writers such as Stuart Holland, Michael Barratt Brown and, as we shall see, Tony Benn. It also percolated into the policy documents produced by the Labour Party in the early 1970s, and the concern with industrial democracy, which the Institute helped to instil in the Labour movement, became a central component of the so-called Alternative Economic Strategy, supported by many on the left of the Labour Party, which will be considered in a later chapter.

New Cambridge School

The notion of import control played a part in the economic strategy advanced by such writers as Michael Barratt Brown and Stuart Holland and, in the

1970s and early 1980s, it became an integral element of the left's rethinking of its position on the pursuit of an expansionary, full-employment strategy. However, in terms of fleshing out the theoretical underpinning of this protectionist component, the work of the Cambridge Economic Policy Group (economists such as Wynne Godley and Francis Cripps) should also be noted.

The work of the Group, or New Cambridge School, directly addressed the constraint that the balance of payments imposed on the conduct of policy. It took its theoretical stand on the accounting identity which stated that the Public Sector Deficit = Private Sector Surplus + the Balance of Payments. Working on the assumption that the private sector surplus could be deemed to be roughly constant, they arrived at the conclusion that the public sector deficit determined the size of the balance of payments deficit. On this reasoning, and in contrast to Keynesian orthodoxy, changes in the public sector deficit impacted on the balance of payments, not on the level of aggregate demand, while changes in the latter could be effected through alterations in the exchange rate, with a fall being used to stimulate demand through the rise in exports and the reduction in imports that it produced. Of course, this could also be achieved by import controls and that was the position eventually adopted by the New Cambridge School.[39] For New Cambridge, therefore, the reflation of the British economy necessary to return to full employment could only be successfully pursued by means of appropriate protectionist and/or exchange rate policies.

In the short run the New Cambridge School recognized that the import substitution involved might adversely affect the exports of Britain's trading partners. However, they argued that a more prosperous and competitive British economy would ultimately allow for a "planned *growth* of imports" more rapid than would be the case if it continued to lurch from one balance of payments crisis to the next with attendant periodic bouts of deflation. The School stressed, therefore, that the purpose of import controls was not to reduce the level of imports but to allow the economy to operate at a higher level of activity for any given quantity. So what was proposed was a fixing of import penetration ceilings for the key sectors of manufacturing industry in order to match imports with available foreign exchange. Thereafter, they could be raised in line with economic growth. Ultimately of course they might be removed altogether as a higher level of activity had its salutary impact on investment, innovation, productivity and international competitiveness.

Such an insulation of the British economy had definite attractions for left revisionists and these ideas certainly influenced some of their thinking. As they saw it, it could remove the balance of payments and exchange rate constraints from the pursuit of an expansionary full employment policy and it also permitted the kind of socialist economic planning they proposed to proceed relatively free from the exogenous shocks that might blow it off course. In that respect they wanted no repeat of 1966–7. New Cambridge thinking therefore proved influential, and adherence to protectionism, exchange rate flexibility and a concomitant determination to abandon the EEC became prominent features of left political economy in this period, though it must be said too that a visceral antipathy to the EEC was by no means a position monopolized by the Left of the Party.

The substantial extension of public ownership, socialist economic planning with planning agreements and the use of other powers to make it effective, the extension of industrial democracy and the immediate reflation of the economy with the aid of appropriate commercial and exchange rate policies: this was the substance of left revisionism and what came to be termed the Alternative Economic Strategy that was advanced by the Left both within and outside the Labour Party in the 1970s and early 1980s. Its impact on Labour Party policy and ultimate fate will be considered in Chapter 16. However, before embarking on such an assessment, it is necessary to consider the manner in which Keynesian liberal socialists sought to respond to this and other ideological challenges to their dominance of Labour Party economic thinking in the 1970s.

Chapter 15
Liberal socialism revised, the 1970s

> It is now clear that techniques for managing the whole economy cannot solve detailed problems – even when the problem is that of a whole region rather than a single firm. General demand management must be supplemented by more rigorous policies of direct intervention than those which we used between 1964 and 1970.
>
> R. Jenkins, *What matters now*, 1972

The economic failures of the Wilson governments, in particular the failure to effect any significant improvement in Britain's economic performance, posed more profound problems for the liberal socialist wing of the Party than for the revisionist Left. After all, it was the policies of indicative planning and Keynesian demand management that had been applied and found wanting, the National Plan disintegrating soon after publication and conventional macroeconomic management failing to circumvent the constraints of rising inflation and balance of payments crises. Further, the Left could claim to have both identified the deficiencies and predicted the fate of "planning" without power. So, while the liberal socialists had to set about the task of explaining what had gone wrong with what *they* had proposed and how it might be set right, the Left had the advantage both of a clear explanation of past policy errors and an alternative approach to a Keynesian socialist conduct of the nation's economic affairs. In this period they occupied the high ground reserved for those able to declaim "I told you so".

These things must, in part, explain the extent to which in the 1970s and early 1980s it was the Left that made the running in terms of economic ideas. It is, after all, more difficult to set about the business of refurbishing what has been tarnished in practice than to furnish blueprints for what has yet to be tried. However, three writers who did set about the former task in the early 1970s were Crosland, Jenkins and Meade. All, as we have seen, had made a fundamental contribution to the rethinking of socialist political economy, both in the late 1930s and in the post-war period, and all now accepted the need, once again, to revise their liberal socialism in the light of the changed economic circumstances that now confronted Britain. Thus Crosland, in his long essay *Socialism now* (1974), took as his starting point *The future of socialism* and posed the question, "where stands the revisionist thesis [which it contained] in the light of the last ten years of experience?" Similarly, James Meade saw his *Intelligent radical's guide to economic policy, the mixed economy* (1975), as "a sequel to my *Planning and the price mechanism*".[1]

Crosland and Jenkins in particular had to confront directly the failure to deliver the New Britain that had been promised in 1964. Both had occupied Cabinet positions in the Wilson governments and Jenkins had, in the late 1960s, been Chancellor of the Exchequer. Both were therefore implicated in what many saw as the inability of these governments to make a combination of welfare Keynesianism and indicative economic planning work. Their response was similar. Neither denied what Crosland termed "the central failure of economic policy".

> In 1970 unemployment was higher, inflation more rapid and economic growth slower, than when the Conservatives left office in 1964. The growth performance in particular was lamentable; GDP, in real terms, rose by an average of only 2.3% p.a. compared with 3.8% in the previous six years. Growth was consistently sacrificed to the balance of payments, notably to a fixed and unrealistic rate of exchange.[2]

But both were adamant too that, even so, much had been achieved in consequence of the policies pursued. Expenditure upon education, health and social security benefits had all increased as a percentage of the National Product, while pensions, supplementary benefits and family allowances all rose faster than incomes generally. There had also been the introduction of redundancy payments and earnings-related unemployment benefits. Despite the failings much had been accomplished. What was required, therefore, was not a fundamental reappraisal of the political economy to which the Party had adhered, such as that provided by what Crosland termed the "refurbished Marxism" of Holland, Barratt Brown and others; what was wanted was a careful and selective revision of the tenets of liberal socialism in the light of the experience of the 1960s.

What, then, were the aspects that needed revision? The liberal socialist political economy articulated by these writers in the 1950s and early 1960s had been rooted in Keynesianism and the expectations and hubris that Keynesianism had created. But Keynesianism, in a British context, now seemed to deliver balance of payments deficits and, increasingly, inflation rather than full employment and sustained economic growth. Inflation in particular was seen as a growing obstacle to the progress of social reform. Crosland, writing in the early 1970s, saw it as "rampant" producing "a menacing insecurity about the future, threatening to erase all our familiar benchmarks" and "inducing a mood of anxious yet militant resentment". As he saw it, "inflation is becoming more and more our *central* problem".[3] Thus it redistributed wealth in an inequitable fashion, created a confrontational climate of industrial relations through its erosion of real wages and induced a level of wage demands that further exacerbated inflationary pressures.

For the liberal socialists of the early 1970s the favoured solution to all this was an incomes policy, despite the manifold difficulties involved in its effective implementation, which had been all too apparent during the years of the Wilson government. Crosland, in particular, was unambiguous: "I have no doubts in my mind that we must have a prices and incomes policy. We must have it because the only alternative will be squeeze and deflation . . . and unemployment. I personally . . . believe that a prices and incomes policy is also necessary for reasons of social justice, and reasons of social equality." However, Crosland recognized too that if it were to secure the support of the trade unions, and such support was integral to its success, then it must not be pursued "against a background of reactionary social policies", as would be the case under the Conservatives.[4]

Jenkins took a similar line. The problem with the incomes policy pursued by the previous Labour Government was that the sole objective had been the short-term one of circumventing a balance of payments crisis. Inevitably, therefore, it had been seen by the trade union movement as a sacrifice made by the workers, to ensure the survival of British industrial capitalism. An incomes policy was necessary to secure the macroeconomic objectives of full employment and price stability but it must also be part, *and be seen to be part*, of "a longer term contribution to social justice".[5] Indeed Jenkins went so far as to argue that that should be its "central objective". It should prevent the strong collective bargainers triumphing at the expense of the weak and, in so far as it proved successful in stabilizing prices, it would also make a contribution to social justice because inflation invariably penalized those with little economic muscle. Additionallly, it should be possible under its auspices to introduce a national minimum wage.

Jenkins was also clear that it should be a *prices* and incomes policy. Prices, in general, would be stabilized by an effective incomes policy but they must also, in particular instances, be subject to control by the government. "We must . . . be prepared to establish controls over key prices which significantly affect the real income of wage earners, particularly the low paid."[6] On grounds of political expediency, such a policy was imperative in order to secure the support of the trade union movement but is was also an important means of promoting greater social justice. In this context, Jenkins defended and praised the work already done by the National Board for Prices and Incomes and saw it as having the necessary technical expertise to implement an effective prices and incomes policy.

For Jenkins and Crosland, a prices and incomes policy was one that was to be executed by way of government regulations and controls. For Meade, this was simply not practical economics. "It is inconceivable", he wrote, "that bureaucratic regulations could be devised which over any considerable period would keep the myriads of prices, costs and incomes at a stable average level but with sufficient relative flexibility to preserve both efficiency and equity as conditions changed in various sectors of a complex economy." Lack of knowledge set limits to what could be intelligently done here. Not enough was known about the dynamic relations between the "movement of prices, costs, profits, wages, tax payments, savings, consumption, investment, output, employment, amounts of money, interest rates, imports, exports, foreign capital movement, foreign exchange rates and so on . . . to be certain about the precise effect of particular stabilising devices."[7]

How then could governments influence prices and incomes in such a way as to permit the pursuit of a non-inflationary full employment policy? First, as regards price stabilization the problem should be tackled at a macroeconomic level. Meade suggested, therefore, the creation of a Stabilization Committee which "would be given the power to impose, within prescribed limits, positive or negative surcharges on certain specified direct and indirect taxes and to determine week to week changes in the supply of monetary funds to the capital market". This it would do with the object of keeping a "designated price index at its stable pre-determined level."[8] Thus fiscal and monetary policy could be utilized in the pursuit of price stability.

Meade recognized, however, that the growth of monopoly power in the form of "giant industrial concerns" and what he termed "labour monopolies" had profound inflationary implications because of the market power that they wielded. What Meade also looked to, therefore, were measures which both curbed that economic power and dispersed it "over many relatively small units".[9] Thus there should be measures to encourage small-scale enterprises – the replacement of corporation tax by taxes on numbers employed, the creation of special sources of finance for small businesses, and anti-monopoly legislation. These measures that Meade advocated would promote price competition as an antidote to inflation. Along these lines he also argued for the prohibition of various restrictive practices (e.g. price agreements), the "completely free import of products from foreign suppliers" and a "substantial tax on advertisement" – the latter being an attempt to "increase the incentive for firms to seek markets by cutting prices rather than persuasive bamboozlement".[10] Meade's aim was to use the market rather than the bureaucrat as the primary means of price restraint, though he recognized that on occasion direct state intervention would be needed to curb monopolistic pricing. Also, as a last resort, he was prepared to contemplate the use of social ownership with prices determined by reference to "demand-needs" and "supply costs".[11]

But what of labour monopolies and the lack of responsiveness of wages to market forces that they induced? Again Meade rejected the bureaucratic solution to the problem. A statutory incomes policy might work in the short run, as an emergency measure, but in the longer term it was almost inevitable that it would impinge on the objectives of fairness, efficiency and economic dynamism. A voluntary incomes policy was also rejected on the grounds that it would be determined by two private monopolistic organizations – the TUC and the CBI – rather than by the democratically elected government. On political grounds alone this was indefensible.

However, if an incomes policy of the kind envisaged by Jenkins and Crosland was ruled out, Meade none the less believed that the state could influence the level of wage settlements. What he put forward was the idea of wage-increase norms, established in the light of information about profitability, productivity and the demand for and supply of labour in a particular occupation. Once established, penalties would be applied to curb the bargaining power of trade unions where they pressed claims that were in breach of those norms, penalties that might include loss of accumulated rights to redundancy payments and the charging of social benefits received by the families of those on strike to the trade unions of which they were members. The objective was to establish a kind of social control over labour monopolies that parallelled the control over industrial monopolies to be exercised by market competition and the state. The setting of the norm would be a vital means by which the government could pursue its objective of price stabilization, while at the same time creating a system of wages that was more responsive to conditions of demand and supply than one dominated, as at present, by the combative exercise, on both sides, of monopoly power. Here also, Meade emphasized the need for measures that would eliminate "unnecessary restrictive practices by industrial or professional workers", practices that inhibited the free movement of labour into and out of occupations.[12]

Meade claimed to provide a guide for the intelligent *radical*. However, much in that "guide" was in harmony with the liberal *socialism* that he had been professing for more than three decades. The 1975 work also mirrored certain aspects of liberal socialist opinion that found expression within the Labour Party in this period. First, there was what might be termed the "small is beautiful" theme, which runs through *An intelligent radical's guide*: the belief that an economy characterized by a multiplicity of relatively small-scale enterprises, subject to competitive pressures, would produce an economic outcome more efficient and equitable than one distinguished by a concentration of ownership. Such enterprises would also, Meade argued, be the kind that could be safely given over to workers' self-management, in contrast to large-scale concerns where "labour management . . . carrie[d] with it grave dangers of restrictive action . . . the great argument against guild socialist or syndicalist solutions to the social problem".[13] Such views were in accord with a general concern within the Party about the exploitation of monopoly power by large corporations and consonant too with the opinions of those within the Party who feared the abuse of power by overmighty trade unions. They were also in harmony with anxiety over the burgeoning of a coercive state bureaucracy[14] and, consistent with this, the predilection for industrial democracy that existed within the Party in this period. There ran through Meade's work too a general concern with freedom and the dispersal of power that was to be a salient theme in the writing of Shirley Williams and Bill Rodgers, who were soon to exit to form the Social Democratic Party, and also, as we shall see, in the work of prominent figures within the Labour Party in the 1980s. In all these respects *An intelligent radical's guide* can be taken as representative of currents of thinking within the Labour Party in this period.

Returning, however, to the work of the other liberal socialist revisionists: in addition to their proposals for some kind of incomes policy as a necessary adjunct to a non-inflationary Keynesianism, both Crosland and Jenkins confronted the balance of payments constraint upon the effective use of demand management. Here they suggested the need for greater exchange rate flexibility. As Crosland saw it, the failure of the economic strategy pursued by the Wilson governments was in large measure "due to the deflationary policies which stemmed inexorably from the Labour government's obsession with a particular parity for sterling".[15] Greater exchange rate flexibility would, for the future, allow such a pitfall to be avoided.

So, given the apposite prices and incomes and exchange rate policies, these writers believed that demand management could still deliver the goods or, at least, many of the goods that socialists desired. Obituaries for Keynesianism, whether written by the Labour Left or the Conservative Right, were therefore premature. Yet Crosland and Jenkins were also clear that a revamped Keynesianism, while a fundamental, was no longer a sufficient condition for the successful pursuit of full employment, sustained economic growth and rising living standards. In this fundamental respect they did shift their ground from the position that they occupied in the late 1950s. Jenkins characterized their erstwhile position thus: in that period they had believed that: "Keynesian techniques . . . could maintain full employment; and indicative planning could ensure balanced growth. Public ownership would no doubt be used from time to time, as one instrument amongst many; but its role in future would be much less central than it had been between 1945 and 1950 or than the pioneers of the Labour Movement had imagined." However, it was "now clear that techniques for managing the whole economy cannot solve detailed problems – even when the problem is that of a whole region rather than a single firm.

General demand management must be supplemented by more rigorous policies of direct intervention than those which we used between 1964 and 1970."[16]

To supplement the tools of macroeconomic management, therefore, Jenkins mooted the need for a substantial extension of public ownership, the case for which is spelt out powerfully in *What matters now* (1972). As he saw it,

> [the] Government, acting through the public sector, can adopt a broader perspective than that of any board of directors nominally responsible to its shareholders. It can view an investment in a much longer time scale. It can estimate the benefit of an industrial development to the community as a whole, in terms of new jobs and better use of social capital. It can assess the profitability of any single project in the context of other linked developments. Often the scale of development required to provide the base for a new industrial complex is too great for any individual firm to take the risk. Perhaps, most important of all, the Government alone can estimate the costs of inaction as well as action. The problem of the regions will not be cured without more direct Government involvement and a greater use of public enterprise.[17]

Seldom has the case for a substantial extension of public ownership been better put and, indeed, Jenkins was adamant that "we should seek to hive *on* parts of the private sector to the nationalized sector and to encourage the nationalized sector to diversify wherever it sees the opportunity." To this end he supported the creation of a State Holding Company, financed by its own profits, government grants and borrowing from the capital market, which would take a public stake across "a broad spectrum of industry".[18]

Here there would seem, on the surface, to be a remarkable parallel between Jenkins and those whom I have labelled the left revisionists and it is interesting to note that, for a time, Stuart Holland was adviser to Jenkins and others on the liberal socialist right of the Party. There were, however, a number of crucial differences in their respective conceptions of the role of the State Holding Company; specifically, with respect to the scale upon which it would operate and the central objectives it would pursue. For Jenkins, the key issue was not the radical transference of economic power but the elimination of regional disparities and the general enhancement of performance within an essentially Keynesian structure of macroeconomic management. For Holland et al. the State Holding Company was about an "irreversible shift in power in favour of the working classes" and the creation of a foundation for extensive economic planning that would, increasingly, proceed on a non-market basis, with non-commercial objectives.

Crosland too accepted the need for the extension of social ownership by means, among others, of a State Holding Company, but took some pains to distance himself from what he saw as both the flawed analysis and the overall policy stance of those whom he described as the "semi-Marxists". Thus, while Crosland agreed there had been a significant concentration of industrial ownership over the previous two decades, he did not consider that that had produced a substantial shift in the balance of power in favour of capitalist enterprise relative to the power wielded by the state and trade unions. Public expenditure as a percentage of GNP *had* risen significantly in the late 1960s and early 1970s, the government *had* extended its control over the activities of the private sector by means of legislation on prices, pollution, factory and office location and by corporate taxation. In general, then, the economy had become a more managed one than at any time since 1945. Further, no one could argue, given the experience of both the Wilson and Heath governments, that the power of the trade unions had diminished. On the contrary "some of the commanding heights of the economy are now to be found in union headquarters in Euston Road".[19] Also, the marked fall in profits experienced by British industry in the late 1960s hardly suggested a capitalist class whose power had been enhanced. For Crosland, then, one of the central propositions of *The future of socialism* still held. Economic power remained dispersed between trade unions, the state and private enterprise. The left revisionist view of things was, in that respect in particular, fundamentally distorted.

More specifically, as regards the activities of multinationals, Crosland rejected the idea that, for the most part, they were either economically pernicious in relation to their host countries or that they undermined the economic policies pursued by host governments. On balance the inward investment of multinationals had favourable consequences: estimates suggested that, in Britain, it had increased real income by some 2 per cent. Nor had studies on the behaviour of multinationals produced any evidence of loss of national autonomy. Transfer pricing was a potential problem but the government had the necessary powers "to legislate, to tax, to police, to embargo", to prevent any substantial damage to the British economy. For Crosland, then, there had been no drastic or deleterious "transformation of power relations";[20] the extension of public ownership had therefore to be justified on other grounds.

In *The future of socialism* the extension of social ownership had been relegated to playing a subsidiary role as a means to socialist ends. By the early 1970s, Crosland's position had altered and it had changed, primarily, because events had dissipated the economic optimism with which the 1956 work was imbued. In 1956 Crosland had held out the prospect of inequality and the tensions it bred being drowned in a rising tide of affluence while apposite social reforms eroded class consciousness and class distinctions. However, stagflation and

Britain's rapid relative decline in the 1960s and 1970s had rendered such a vision illusory. As Crosland himself accepted, "extreme class inequalities remain, poverty is far from eliminated, the economy is in a state of semi-permanent crisis and inflation is rampant. All this undoubtedly belies the relative optimism of *The future of socialism*."[21]

Britain's difficulties once again prioritized an economic rather than a social politics and it was as a means of arresting Britain's economic decline and laying the basis for future socialist advance that Crosland, in marked contrast to *The future of socialism*, now advocated the extension of public ownership and state involvement in the economy. What he proposed was "an active policy of competitive public enterprise" or "aggressive public competition", pursued through state companies set up from scratch or established by way of take-overs and joint public/private ventures. These public enterprises would be controlled by a State Holding Company, "a roving body with money of its own and a high degree of independence".[22] In addition, their activities would be backed and strengthened by a State Investment Bank; an institution – (mooted in Edmund Dell's *Political responsibility and industry* (1973)) – whose function would be to foster competition, "redeploy management, back sensible but risky investment projects, restructure industry . . . and give advice on the inevitable periodic rescue operations". Its role would, however, be less that of saving lame ducks than that of breeding industrial eagles that would prove "price-leaders, pace-setters" and "yardsticks of efficiency".[23] In this respect, they would perform a galvanizing role similar to that which Holland and others envisaged public enterprise playing, though, as with Roy Jenkins, Crosland's conception of the role and objectives of the State Holding Company was radically different from that of the left revisionists. It should also be mentioned here that this idea of competitive public enterprise, subscribed to by both Jenkins and Crosland, was one that had been advanced by both writers in the early 1950s. It was not in any sense, therefore, a notion appropriated from the left.

So, like Jenkins, Crosland believed that Britain's relative economic decline could only be reversed and the forward march of socialism resumed, through a rejuvenated Keynesianism pursued in conjunction with a public assumption of the economic power necessary to effect a restructuring of Britain's industrial base. For, if Keynesianism could still be used to ensure a full-employment level of aggregate demand, the selective extension of public ownership over individual firms was a necessary adjunct to reinvigorate the supply side.

Crosland and Jenkins also emphasized the importance of extending industrial democracy: as Crosland saw it, part at least of the industrial and social unrest that increasingly characterized British society could be put down to a growing intolerance of authoritarian management, "the boredom of dull and monotonous jobs" and "the exigencies of the production line".[24] Industrial democracy would provide an apposite antidote to such coercion and alienation. What he proposed, therefore, was the extension of "the principle of collective bargaining – from plant bargaining over wages and work to bargaining at company level over the whole range of management functions, including the formulation and application of the company's corporate plan".[25] In that way trade unions would come to negotiate over the structure, organization and environment of work, as well as traditional wage questions, while worker directors would have an input to decision-making at the highest level.

For Jenkins, workers should be given the opportunity to *participate* "in the detailed design of their own jobs" and should be given greater "*influence* . . . on matters which concern them as individuals or in small work groups and on matters of company policy in general".[26] Participation in, and influence on, decision-making at shop floor and management board level would furnish greater work satisfaction and would help dissipate the corrosive frustration that soured the climate of industrial relations, with disastrous consequences for performance and inflation, labour alienation being seen by Jenkins as an important reason why what he termed "the will o' the wisp of rising money wages . . . [was] so superficially attractive".[27]

Yet again there are echoes of the more stridently articulated proposals emanating from the left in this period. But they were only echoes. Both the objectives that Crosland and Jenkins sought and the degree of industrial democracy they were prepared to propose to attain them were very different. Their primary aim was to eradicate individual alienation, not to effect a fundamental shift in the balance of decision-making power from the capitalist to the working class in order to give the latter victory in the class struggle. Nor were their proposals seen as an "encroaching control" route to self-management; still less were they linked to any overall conception of democratic economic planning. The key words are those of Jenkins – "participate" and "influence".

If, for Crosland and Jenkins, more concerted and vigorous action was required with respect to the extension of public ownership and industrial democracy, they were in agreement too that the attack on poverty had also to be pursued more energetically. Here again the optimism of *The future of socialism* had been vitiated. The problem of poverty had proved to be of greater magnitude, more complex and more intractable than had been envisaged, certainly by many liberal socialists in the 1950s. The work of such writers as Titmuss, Townsend and Abel-Smith continued to make clear just how little had been achieved. As Jenkins wrote, "the social forces which bolster inequality are immensely powerful and immensely persistent . . . In the 1950s many of us thought the inequalities would diminish as society became more prosperous. It is now clear that this view was at least oversimplified and at worst just wrong."[28] This had certainly been Crosland's view though not, of course, that of Douglas Jay.

Jenkins stressed, in particular, that the policies that derived from the "pocket of poverty" conception of the problem were completely inadequate. "Our approach has been too limited . . . we have underestimated the scale of poverty in Britain." Absolute poverty was still widespread, relative poverty was, if anything, increasing, so policies that sought to target benefits by means testing were always "in grave danger of helping the very poor at the expense of the not quite so poor"[29] and that, in many respects, had been just what had occurred. For Jenkins, poverty could only be eradicated by broadly based policies that aimed at the general objective of social equality. What he proposed, therefore, were substantial changes "in our tax and social security systems to improve the economic security of *that fifth of the population who are near the poverty level*",[30] with the general objective of a minimum level of income for all. This would involve considerable increases in retirement pensions, family allowances and national insurance benefits. It would require the allocation of substantial human and financial resources to provide better health care, education and housing, in particular to "deprived areas". It would also necessitate an improvement in "the standards of our social services generally". This might prove costly but it was necessary to transform a "morally unjust and damagingly insecure society".[31] Further, while the cost could, of course, be more easily met if the economy was growing rapidly, it should still be met even if that were not the case. This, Jenkins recognized, would involve a significant redistribution of wealth but the bullet had to be bitten. Socialists must not eschew the notion of sacrifice. "The more prosperous *half* of us will have to sacrifice some of the material prosperity which we would otherwise enjoy . . . to pretend that resources can be somehow redistributed in favour of the poor at no cost to the *majority*, is to pave the way for demoralisation and disillusionment once the attack is launched."[32]

More generally, in this vein, we find in Jenkins's *What matters now* a powerful articulation of an ethical socialism that had certainly not been in vogue since the triumph of the technocratic discourse of Wilson's "New Britain" in the 1960s. The emphasis on social justice as the primary objective of an incomes policy has already been noted. But further, Jenkins argued for the Labour Party to replace "the politics of envy" with "the politics of compassion" and the "politics of cupidity" by the "politics of justice".[33] Not for the first time, when the economic road ahead seemed fraught with difficulty, the Labour Party was reminded that its members should not seek to live by bread alone, or forget that their goals should be moral not material.

Meade too stressed the importance of fiscal reform with respect to the more equal distribution of wealth and income. Indeed he argued strongly that the "appropriate fiscal measures, determined by democratic, parliamentary procedures", not "wage-bargaining determined by industrial action", should be seen as *the* means of ensuring that the working classes secured an equitable share of the wealth that they produced. He also made the point that the pursuit of "a more equal distribution of what we . . . produce",[34] rather than producing more, with all the environmental and other costs which that entailed, was the best means of raising the living standards of the population. To this end, he proposed measures to simplify the administrative muddle and inequities involved in the existing system of personal taxation and social benefits, the centrepiece of which was the "social dividend". This would be based on the existing supplementary benefit scale, with the size of the dividend dependent on the composition and size of a family. It would be tax exempt and would replace all other social benefits, and it should be sufficient "to keep . . . [a] family out of poverty and . . . give it a decent standard of living".[35]

For Meade the social dividend could be used as a means of "extensive redistribution";[36] though the extent of that redistribution would naturally be dependent upon the system of taxation that was used to raise the necessary finance. Here his major proposals were the imposition of a standard rate of VAT on "all goods and services for consumption" (replacing the standard rate of income tax), a surtax on high levels of consumption and an annual, progressive wealth tax. Meade also saw the social dividend as a means of enforcing compliance with the wage norms, which he believed could be used to check inflationary wage bargaining. Thus the social dividend would not be paid to the families of strikers engaged in industrial action aimed at securing wage increases deemed to be in breach of those norms. It was to be used, therefore, as a means of exerting control over powerful labour monopolies, where their actions were seen to run contrary to the national economic interest.

To summarize. For Crosland and Jenkins what was required was a significant increase in public ownership, a substantial redistribution of resources in favour of the poor at the expense, if necessary, of the majority of the population and the extension of industrial democracy. Confronted in the early 1970s by an economy in crisis and intensifying social conflict, these liberal socialists therefore gave at least a passing nod in the direction of left fundamentalism. Of course, as with the form in which the extension of public ownership was proposed, it is possible to see a measure of continuity with the revisionism of the 1950s, but that said, what is most striking – certainly in the case of Crosland – is the extent to which liberal socialism had shifted its ground.

This is not surprising. In the 1950s, liberal socialists were formulating their economic philosophy against a background of relative economic success; in the late 1960s and early 1970s, they wrote in the context of perceived economic failure. In the 1950s, the Keynesianism that they espoused and that underpinned their position was the accepted wisdom; by the later period it was under substantial critical fire from the monetarist, free-market Right and the Marxist and semi-Marxist Left. In the 1950s, Crosland and others could assume, or at least claim, that their political economy rested on a positive basis that it had the authority of science. However, by the late 1960s and early 1970s, positive economics had disintegrated into a free-for-all of competing and ideologically tinctured paradigms. As one perceptive commentator eloquently phrased it, "the spanners from the economists' toolkit" had begun to "bang on the dissonant drums of political ideology"[37] – something that may explain the sharper ideological bite in what writers like Crosland and Jenkins now offered.

However, they were clearly swimming against the general flow of economic opinion even within the Labour Party. For now it was not their ideas but those of the left revisionists that were making the running. They were engaged in an attempt to buttress a crumbling edifice rather than, as had previously been the case, sweeping away the socialist shibboleths that increasing affluence had rendered redundant.

Of course Meade's position was different from that of Crosland and Jenkins. Like them he sought to establish the conditions necessary for an effective non-inflationary Keynesian pursuit of full employment. But these conditions were to be established not by a formal incomes policy or the creation of competitive public enterprise but by constraining the activities of those who wielded economic power in a coercive, exploitative or socially irresponsible fashion. In effect he sought to create, or re-create, the conditions necessary for the free and effective operation of the market mechanism in a non-inflationary, full employment, welfare state context. In that respect, as Meade himself pointed out, his general economic philosophy had changed little from that embodied in *Planning and the price mechanism.*

Chapter 16
The alternative economic strategy and after, 1972–84

> It is necessary to reject both the work-centred fatalism of the orthodox Marxists and the myopia of reformed socialism. The fudging, consensus politics that has predominated in the West has broken down. The future is in the hands of the radicals and visionaries.
>
> G. Hodgson, *The democratic economy*, 1984

It was in the context of an ideological conflict between the political economies of the Left and liberal socialist revisionists that Labour Party economic policy was formulated in the early 1970s. It is apparent, however, that for a time it was the school of Holland and others that had the upper hand, Holland, in particular, exerting considerable influence through the Party's Public Sector Group and Industrial Policy Committee. Further, the voice of liberal socialism in the key policy-making committees was considerably muted when Roy Jenkins resigned as deputy leader of the Party in early 1972 over Labour's position on Europe; a resignation that meant he ceased to be chairman of the key Finance and Economic Committee.

The growing ascendancy of the kind of socialist political economy embodied in the Alternative Economic Strategy (AES) was apparent in, for example, *Programme for Britain*, which was launched in July 1972 as a consultative document. A kind of Green Paper, to be presented to the next Labour Party Conference as a basis for discussion, it was described by Tony Benn as "the most radical and comprehensive programme ever produced by the Labour Party".[1] This ascendancy was, however, to be even more evident in *Programme 1973* (June 1973), a document produced by Labour's National Executive, whose very formulation precipitated a major confrontation between Left and Right within the Party. Central to that policy statement, as it finally emerged, were proposals on industrial strategy and economic planning. These involved, in particular, a commitment to plans for long-term capital investment in a much expanded public sector. In the words of the *Programme*, there would be

> a substantial addition [to the public sector] of companies from the present private sector . . . spread across leading firms throughout the different sectors of industry . . . For the range of tasks suggested some twenty-five of our largest manufacturers would be required . . . we need this new tool if we are to match the rapidly changing structure of modern capitalism with new means of intervention. Unless we face these implications, the next Labour Government will preside over an economy where power of decision rests with leading private companies.[2]

In addition specific commitments were made to the nationalization of development land, mineral rights, North Sea oil, shipbuilding and ship repairing.

All this would be accomplished under the auspices of a State Holding Company – the National Enterprise Board – which would not only "establish a major [public] stake in manufacturing industry" but also exercise control over the plans of the public and private sector through a system of planning agreements (of the kind discussed above) embracing at least the largest 100 industrial companies. This would entail the provision of information by such companies on "investment, prices, product development, marketing, exports and import requirements" and close co-operation with the NEB in meeting planning goals. To give teeth to these agreements, a number of expedients were suggested. Thus the planning agreements themselves would "provide a basis for channelling *selective Government assistance directly to those firms which agreed to help . . . meet the nation's planning objectives*".[3] As well as selective financial aid the *Programme* suggested "directives", if it was considered necessary, in relation to company decisions affecting prices, profits and investment. It also advocated "reserve powers" to remove recalcitrant directors, and put forward the idea of an "Official Trustee" to take control of a company if it were deemed to be acting contrary to government objectives;[4] in the words of the document, when it was seen as having "fail[ed] to meet its responsibilities to its workers, to its customers, or to the community as a whole". When it came to nudging firms in the direction in which planners wanted them to go, it was suggested that they could also use the power of public purchase and, as a last resort, there was the sanction of nationalization – "preferably with agreement" but "if necessary, in the national interest, by Statutory Instrument".[5]

As regards the implementation of this strategy the National Enterprise Board, operating "under parliamentary control", was to be the key institution. Its responsibilities would be wide and its powers correspondingly so. It would be responsible for: "job creation, especially in areas of high unemployment; investment promotion; technological development; growth of exports; promoting government price policies; tackling the spread of multinational companies; the spread of industrial democracy; import substitution."[6] Given the powers listed above, and the economic leverage derived from ownership, it would, in contrast to the fiasco of the 1960s, have all the necessary authority to fulfil those responsibilities and, in so doing, make socialist economic planning a reality. The "arbitrary exercise of economic power" by monopoly capital would not be allowed "to frustrate the national will". Thus the *Programme* sought "to provide a systematic basis for making large companies [publicly] accountable for their behaviour and for bringing into line those who refuse to co-operate".[7] The tone, rhetoric and analysis was clearly that of the left revisionists.

It is true that the final version of *Programme 1973* did involve less direction and compulsion of the private sector than had been the case in earlier drafts of the document. The emphasis was more on planning *agreement* than planning compulsion. Nevertheless, the threat of the latter was obvious, as was the determination to effect "a fundamental and irreversible shift in the balance of power and wealth, in favour of working people and their families", which was now highlighted as the fundamental prerequisite for the attainment of socialist objectives. It was no longer possible to "rely on indirect measures to control the economy – whether these be fiscal or monetary measures, or generalised handouts and tax concessions . . . we must act *directly* at the level of the giant firm itself".[8] Of course contracyclical demand management had its place. "A Labour Government will always be ready to act on the level of demand, stimulating it where necessary not only through consumers' expenditure, but through bringing forward public expenditure plans."[9] However, it was only in the context of a radical socialist strategy that Keynesian techniques could prove successful. In any case "the surest guarantee of full employment is the resolute pursuit of policies for sound and steady economic growth".[10] Clearly, as regards this central aspect of the policy document, the ideas of Holland and company had carried the day.

As might be anticipated, this radical industrial strategy, founded on a substantial extension of public ownership and control, provoked the ire of liberal socialists such as Crosland, Jenkins, Edmund Dell and Shirley Williams. For them this was old-fashioned, Clause IV socialism of a kind that proceeded upon the fallacious equation of socialist advance with nationalization. Further, it was guaranteed to provide political ammunition for the Conservative Party, thus obscuring the more constructive aspects of Party policy such as fiscal reform. Specifically, it was argued, much damaging political mileage would be made out of the proposal to take 25 leading industrial companies into public ownership, both as regards the threat it posed to industrial confidence and the massive expansion of the state bureaucracy that would ensue. In addition, these writers contended that, if acted on, *Programme 1973* would entail the creation, in the form of the NEB, of an enormous national conglomerate, that would in large measure be independent of ministerial control. It would not, therefore, as claimed by its supporters, give a Labour government direct access to the levers of power. Edmund Dell in particular was concerned by its size and quasi-independent status, critically highlighting these features in ways already well rehearsed in *Political responsibility and industry*, where the whole question of the democratic accountability of industrial policymakers had been discussed. Above all, though, *Programme 1973* was condemned for its explicit abandonment of the kind of Keynesian social democracy to which Crosland and Jenkins in particular had subscribed since the early 1950s.

The economist Wilfrid Beckerman also contributed to the critical fire to which the *Programme* was subjected, most obviously in an exchange with Stuart Holland in the pages of the *New Statesman*. Specifically Beckerman challenged Holland's central contention that industrial corporations had emerged whose power was sufficient to frustrate the will of national governments. Thus he argued that foreign competition, for example, imposed constraints upon the economic power that those corporations wielded, particularly in relation to their capacity to pursue pricing policies that enabled them to reap monopoly profits. Further, it was difficult to see how the activities of individual companies, however powerful, could frustrate that manipulation of broad macroeconomic aggregates which was the essence of Keynesian demand management. Holland responded by a reassertion of the view that the multinational corporations' control over prices and investment fundamentally damaged the efficacy of Keynesian policies, and the exchange progressed in an acrimonious manner all too often replicated in the debate that now raged within the Party.[11]

On "prices and pay", *Programme 1973* was long on aspiration and short on specifics. As regards pay, mention was made of establishing a "new social contract" between a Labour government and both sides of industry. This would be formulated in a context of accelerating economic growth, socialist economic planning, rising social welfare expenditure, a strongly redistributive fiscal policy and tight control over the prices of key elements of the cost of living. In such circumstances, it was argued, "the way will be open for a Labour government to sit down with both sides of industry to hammer out an agreement for *the orderly growth of incomes* with stable prices."[12] Further, any agreement on incomes was to be voluntary; a statutory policy was ruled out. This was clearly a counter-inflationary strategy designed more for travelling in hope than arriving.

With respect to industrial democracy there was a commitment to "a major move". There was a need, stated the *Programme*, "to go considerably further than previous proposals [made in 1968] for joint regulation and joint determination". Here it noted favourably the consideration being given by the Party to "the provision of *direct* representation for workers" (through the trade unions) on new "Supervisory Boards" that would "be responsible for overall company policy and practice" and also to the creation of "joint control committees" made up of management and worker representatives.[13] Such proposals again illustrate the influence of certain elements of left revisionism.

What followed the publication of *Programme 1973* was a counterattack from the Right, which aimed to dilute or excise many of the policies that it contained: an attack that, in many respects, was to prove successful. In particular there was concern on the Right, and within the leadership of the Party, over the specific commitment to take 25 leading companies into public ownership and over some of the coercive powers that it was proposed the NEB should wield. At the Labour Party Annual Conference of October 1973 motions were passed on industrial policy that deliberately made no mention of specific numbers and which left the NEB role, *vis-à-vis* the profitable private sector, ill defined. Moreover, when the Party's Manifesto, *Let us work together*, appeared in January 1974 there was again no mention of the famous 25. That said, the Manifesto did commit the Party to a substantial extension of public ownership. "North Sea and Celtic oil and gas reserves" were to be taken into "full public ownership" and "the operation of getting and distributing them" put "under full public control, with majority public participation".[14] Further, "land required for development will be taken into public ownership" while "shipbuilding, shiprepairing and marine engineering, ports, the manufacture of airframes and aeroengines" would also be brought "into public ownership and control".

> We will also take over profitable sectors or individual firms in those industries where a public holding is essential to enable the Government to control prices, stimulate investment, encourage exports, create employment, protect workers and consumers from the activities of irresponsible multinationals and to plan the national economy in the national interest.

The document also proposed public ownership of the road haulage industry and parts of the pharmaceutical, construction and machine tool industries. As regards the NEB, though, there was no specific mention of coercive powers; but the commitment was to a "powerful" institution "*with the structure and features set out in Labour's Programme 1973*".[15] Not since the immediate post-war period had the Party committed itself to such an extensive programme of nationalization, a programme that contrasts markedly with the tentative stance on public ownership in 1964 and 1966, to say nothing of Gaitskell's attempt to expunge Clause IV from the Labour Party constitution in 1959. The fact was that despite all attempts at dilution it was quite clearly the industrial strategy of the "left revisionists" to which the Party now adhered.

The nature of the social contract proposed in the Manifesto also bore the hallmarks of left influence. The emphasis was on creating "the right economic climate *for money incomes to grow.* That is the essence of the new social contract which the Labour Party has discussed at length with the TUC and which must take its place as a central feature of the new economic policy of a Labour Government."[16] To this end, the government would exert downward pressure on food prices by way of subsidies, bulk purchase arrangements and a renegotiation of the Common Agricultural Policy. It would also pursue a strongly redistributive fiscal policy by measures such as a wealth tax and a tax on property speculation. In addition, local authority powers to fix rents would be restored and there would be an increase in pensions and sickness and unemployment benefits that would henceforward "be increased annually in proportion to increases in average national earnings". It was the fairer distribution of wealth that such measures would bring about that would create the "climate" necessary for future voluntary exercise of wage-claim restraint.[17]

Such was the insipid and toothless nature of the social contract put forward for the electorate's approval in February 1974; but insipid or not it did prove sufficiently attractive to convince them that Labour had the kind of relationship with the trade union movement necessary to bring to an end a period of industrial unrest that, under the Conservatives and Edward Heath, had culminated in a national miners' strike and a three-day week. Labour formed a minority government in February 1974 and one with a small overall majority after another election in October 1974. Tony Benn became Secretary of State for Industry with responsibility for giving legislative embodiment to Labour's industrial policies. In addition, he had two left-wingers in Eric Heffer and Michael Meacher as Ministers of State and utilized the services of left-wing economists such as Francis Cripps and Stuart Holland. However, if the Left, with minor setbacks, had hitherto proved triumphant as regards the formulation of policy, the Right still dominated the Cabinet and thence held the levers of political power. In the event, as might be expected, this proved decisive.

This power was used in particular to shape the content of the White Paper brought forward by the Department of Industry, prior to the drafting of an Industry Bill. Fears were raised by the CBI about the loss of industrial confidence that would result from the emergence of a powerful and interventionist NEB; suggestions emanated from the Treasury that the proposed extension of public ownership would prove inflationary and a climate of opinion was created that made possible significant modifications to the position taken up in previous policy documents. Thus the compulsory dimension of planning agreements was absent from the White Paper as it finally emerged. Also, it was made clear that planning agreements would "not be an agreement in the sense of a civil contract enforceable by law".[18] Further, the compulsory disclosure of information was no longer seen as a necessary part of planning agreements, while the idea of an "Official Trustee" was abandoned and the interventionist powers of the NEB were generally reduced. In the words of one commentator, "the moderates led by Wilson and Healey" had, in effect, crushed "any attempt to have the Government's industrial strategy so demonstrably interventionist that the confidence and co-operation of industry would be lost".[19] Not for the first time, nor the last, the CBI and the Treasury had a greater influence in shaping Party policy than the resolutions and views of Conference. While, therefore, the Left may have won the pre-election policy documents battle, it was the Right that was triumphant in the policy implementation war, a victory rendered complete when first Eric Heffer and then Tony Benn were removed from their posts during the course of 1975.

In the circumstances the scene might seem to have been set for a reassertion of Keynesian liberal socialism. However, in terms of both circumstances and ideas, Keynesianism found itself increasingly embattled in the Britain of the mid-1970s. On the one hand, it seemed to have lost its explanatory power. Thus while most Keynesians had come to believe in the existence of a trade-off between unemployment and inflation (with the former remediable at some inflationary cost and the latter at the expense of an increase in unemployment),[20] the late 1960s and early 1970s saw inflation and unemployment increase in tandem. In fact, by 1975, Britain could boast a 25 per cent rate of inflation and a post-war high, as regards the rate of unemployment, of 5 per cent. Such a state of affairs called into question both the efficacy of traditional macroeconomic policy instruments and the theoretical justification for their use.

A theory, seemingly inconsistent with the facts, created an opportunity for those who purveyed an alternative view of things. Foremost here were the proponents of monetarism. Milton Friedman and the Chicago School had long attacked the notion of a trade-off and the associated idea that an increase in government expenditure could effect a permanent net increase in numbers employed. They argued, rather, that such an increase, while producing a favourable short-run impact on the level of employment, would in the longer term simply precipitate a rise in the general price level with unemployment inevitably gravitating to what was termed its "natural rate", a rate determined by the degree of imperfection that prevailed in the labour market. Reducing unemployment permanently should, therefore, be about removing such imperfections, many of which were seen as being a consequence of excessive trade union power.

In this view of things, increasing inflation was a result of misguided attempts on the part of governments to reduce unemployment below its natural rate and stagflation had emerged as a consequence of the adverse impact on investment intentions of the generalized uncertainty that such a situation had created. As David Laidler, one of the leading British monetarists, summarized it in 1976, "The basic error committed has been to neglect to control the money supply while pursuing an unrealistically low unemployment target, primarily by fiscal means. Monetary expansion, largely a by-product of full employment fiscal policies, has been responsible for the high British inflation rate in the early 1970s."[21]

Monetarists also believed they could explain the chronic balance of payments problem that simultaneously afflicted the British economy. Again, like inflation, the problem had monetary roots. As one writer saw it, if monetary expansion caused "an open economy [to] maintain a lower than 'natural unemployment' rate this [would] result in a higher inflation rate than that ruling in the rest of the world and hence in a secularly worsening balance of payments situation", as competitiveness declined.[22] This was what had occurred in Britain, where expansionary policies had resulted in a rate of inflation that eroded Britain's competitive edge and created chronic balance of payments problems. Again, Keynesianism was viewed as the disease not the cure.

As the roots of Britain's difficulties were monetary they might be tackled by an apposite use of monetary policy. This would involve control over the rate of growth of the money supply and that, in turn, implied adherence to the principle of balanced budgets and thence control over the rate of increase of public expenditure. Without such control, a positive public sector borrowing requirement (PSBR) would continue to fuel monetary growth and inflation. In addition, the economic philosophers of the Right argued that greater control of government expenditure was necessary because of a strong and growing tendency for increasing public expenditure to crowd out private enterprise, both with respect to available resources and also financially by way of higher interest rates. A tight monetary policy, fiscal self-discipline and a growing reliance on private initiative in a context of competitive market forces – this was the way forward that monetarists exhorted governments to take, over the corpse of Keynesianism.

It was in such a context that the leadership of the Labour Party seemed, if not to succumb to the siren call of monetarism, to be tainted both by its scepticism as to the efficacy of Keynesian policies and to take on board some, at least, of its prescriptions. As regards the latter, this taking on board was determined as much by political expediency as by intellectual conviction, but that a measure of such conviction did exist there can be little doubt. Both utterances and actions made that all too clear. Harold Wilson in a speech to the National Union of Mineworkers in 1975 had stated that "it is not a question to-day . . . of choosing between inflation and unemployment. Inflation is causing unemployment". James Callaghan gave classic expression to the scepticism, stating in September 1976:

> For too long we postponed facing up to fundamental choices and fundamental changes in our society and in our economy . . . The post-war world we were told would go on forever, where full employment could be guaranteed by a stroke of the Chancellor's pen . . . We used

> to think that you could just spend your way out of recession . . . I tell you in all candour that that option no longer exists and in so far as it ever did exist, it only worked . . . by injecting a bigger dose of inflation into the economy, followed by a higher level of unemployment.[23]

In some measure, of course, this obeisance to monetarism represented the chanting of a mantra to propitiate the Washington gods whose benison and whose gold were desperately needed at this juncture. Thus a sterling crisis that had been staved off in the summer of 1976, with cuts in government expenditure and standby credits of $5.3 billion furnished by central banks of the Group of Ten and the Bank for International Settlements, erupted again in the autumn of that year. In consequence the Labour Government had to look for further support from the IMF and the price demanded was that of surrendering into the hands of others – the IMF and representatives of the US Federal Reserve Board and US Treasury – the conduct of the nation's economic affairs. What therefore became important, as regards Labour's conduct of economic policy, was not so much the political economy of the Labour leadership, still less the Labour Party, but the political economy of those who in fact held the levers of economic power. Thus, in order to secure an IMF loan ($3.9 billion) sufficient to bolster international confidence, rescue sterling and honour previous loan commitments (particularly those entered into in July), the government had to make a Declaration of Intent to that body in which it agreed to cut expenditure by a further £1 billion in 1977/8 and £1.5 billion in 1978/9. In addition, it accepted the need to adhere to a planned series of reductions of the PSBR for those years. The government also acquiesced in the setting of targets for domestic credit expansion, to achieve which it agreed to a reintroduction of a "corset" to regulate the increase of bank lending.[24] However, it should be noted that, as a concession to market opinion, money supply *forecasts* had already been enunciated as early as July 1976. Then they had been part of the emergency package of measures that had been put together to tackle an earlier run on sterling. Yet, if the novelty of the policies accepted in the Declaration of Intent should not be exaggerated, they none the less indicated a preparedness on the part of the Labour Party to accede to the economic philosophy of those who preached the virtues of fiscal rectitude and monetary control.

So, with the AES in effect emasculated and Keynesianism on the retreat, the Labour Government was left, in the period until its demise (May 1979), with little in terms of an economic philosophy by reference to which it could determine policy. It is true that some within that government were, undoubtedly, "frustrated Keynesians"[25] but they were Keynesians whose frustration did not, for the most part, vent itself in the search for alternative ways forward when the traditional Keynesian road was manifestly, if temporarily, blocked. In that respect they were of course markedly different from Keynes himself. As regards the conduct of policy there was, in fact, a tendency to continue to edge down the monetarist road with the occasional tentative reversion to Keynesianism. Thus along with the setting of targets for Domestic Credit Expansion, there went the retention of the "corset" until November 1977 and then its reactivation in June 1978. There was also the adoption in 1977 of targets for money supply (M3) growth, the decision in the autumn of 1977 to retain IMF surveillance of the economy, and continuing affirmations of the government's determination to adhere to a counter-inflationary monetary policy, most notably in a "Letter of Intent" to the IMF in December 1977.

On the public expenditure front the Labour Government not only accepted the need to cut planned public expenditure but also to reduce it over time as a percentage of GDP and this did indeed fall from 45.6 per cent in 1975–6 to 39.8 per cent in 1977–8 (though it rose again to 41.1 per cent in 1978–9). Moreover, the Labour Government was successful in reducing the PSBR as a percentage of GDP from 9.6 per cent in 1975 to 4.9 per cent in 1978; while much greater control was exercised over the expenditure of individual government departments by the imposition of "cash limits" in this period.

At the same time, however, with unemployment remaining above 5 per cent throughout most of the 1975–9 period, tentative efforts were made to stimulate the economy, principally by way of reductions in personal taxation. In fact, the budgets of April 1977 and April 1978 were moderately expansionary, though, interestingly, tax cuts were justified in the supply-side language of incentives rather than that of demand management. This fiscal policy was also pursued in conjunction with the old expedient of a pay and prices policy. Indeed the cuts in personal taxation were seen as an important carrot that could be offered to the trade union movement in return for its co-operation in a voluntary, "social contract" policy of wage restraint. For a time this policy did prove successful in holding down the level of wage claims. However, in July 1978, the government published a White Paper, *Winning the battle against inflation*, which proposed a 5 per cent ceiling for pay settlements, excluding what could be awarded for productivity gains, and in attempting to implement this phase of the incomes policy it came comprehensively unstuck. The TUC rejected the 5 per cent proposal at its annual conference in September 1978; and at its annual conference the following month, the Labour Party itself passed overwhelmingly a motion rejecting any form of wage restraint. The scene was then set for a winter of widespread industrial unrest – the "winter of discontent" – and the effective destruction of a central element in what was left of the government's economic strategy.

One commentator has categorized the policies pursued as "not Keynesian" but "very different from the policies followed later under the Conservatives in that the exchange rate was allowed to depreciate to help exports and incomes policy remained a central component of the economic strategy".[26] Denis

Healey has himself written of his "eclectic pragmatism" and a trial and error approach that, as he put it, owed more to Karl Popper than either Maynard Keynes or Milton Friedman. Others have described the period as one of "frustrated Keynesianism"[27] and it is the case, despite Callaghan's 1976 speech quoted above, that policy might well have been conducted under the slogan "Keynesianism if we may, monetarism if we must", the "must" being determined by the onset of sterling crises and the need to win back international confidence or at least the confidence of those whose opinion mattered. In that respect, as regards the impact of ideas on policy, the ones that really mattered in this period were those subscribed to by the IMF, the US Treasury and the US Federal Reserve.

One is left, though, with the overwhelming impression that in this period economic ideas and economic philosophies proved influential to the extent that they contributed to political survival. When they did so they were embraced or modified, when they did not they were jettisoned. Economic policy did not so much bear the imprint of ideas as the scars of expediency.

As regards the AES it was however not dead, only dormant, and in the late 1970s and the early 1980s, it and its proponents emerged rejuvenated. There were a number of reasons for this. First, the sterling crisis of 1976, the intervention of the IMF, its government by proxy and the public expenditure cuts that ensued, seemed to many within the Party to signal the end, once and for all, of Croslandite revisionism and the Keynesian social democracy in which it was rooted. In the past, this economic philosophy could be indicted by the Left for failing to produce an economic performance and thence a rise in living standards comparable to other major industrial powers. By the mid-1970s, however, it seemed that it could no longer even furnish the material basis for policies that would permit the maintenance of what, in social and economic terms, had been won by the working class since 1945, let alone any extension of those gains. Thus the two years after the crisis (1976–8) had seen, "for the first time since the war, public expenditure cut back not only below planned levels of increase, but absolutely in real terms".[28] Further, as Michael Meacher put it, "recent history suggests that the present economic system can no longer consistently guarantee a sufficient annual rise in the standard of living to satisfy the expectations of its wage-earning majority and indeed the survival of the system itself seems dependent precisely on the downgrading of this objective."[29] Thus, under the pressure of adverse economic circumstances Keynesian social democracy had, in the words of Tony Benn, degenerated into "a permanent statutory incomes policy; legislation to restrict and centralise the power of trade unions" and moves "to restructure capitalism within a federal Europe".[30]

British capitalism, run on Keynesian social democratic lines, was no longer capable of the dynamism necessary to provide the wherewithal to finance a programme of social reform. The likelihood that it would ever again attain such dynamism, in the aftermath of 1976, looked increasingly remote. As Benn wrote, "if socialist policies could be mounted piggy-back on the shoulders of a revived capitalism" it was clear that "they would soon overburden it."[31] Literally and metaphorically the economic philosophy of the Party's Right had been shown to be bankrupt. As Geoff Hodgson put it in *Labour at the crossroads* (1981), while "the social democratic Right still retained control of the Parliamentary Labour Party and its leadership", it no longer possessed "the coherent and forceful ideology with which it had set the terms of debate in the 1950s and 1960s."[32] What the Left offered had ceased to be an "alternative" economic strategy; it had become the only coherent economic strategy available. For, if 1974–9 had revealed the bankruptcy of the economic philosophy underpinning liberal socialism, the AES remained essentially untainted by that failure. While its key elements had, for a time, loomed large in policy documents, the political manoeuvring of Wilson and other members of the Shadow Cabinet had ensured that it had had a limited impact upon actual economic policy. Tony Benn's move to the Department of Energy in June 1975 had brought the Industry Bill under the control of Harold Wilson and, from that point on, there was never any likelihood that a radical industrial strategy would be pursued, whatever documents or resolutions Conference might approve.

Further, if the Left had been outmanoeuvred politically in the 1970s, by the early 1980s they were in a much more powerful political position than before. The left-of-centre Michael Foot had replaced the avuncular, right-of-centre, James Callaghan as leader in 1980, while Tony Benn, making the AES a key plank in his platform, had run Denis Healey desperately close for the post of Deputy. In addition, the liberal socialist Right had been weakened by the death of Crosland in 1977, shortly after the crisis of 1976 had seemed finally to destroy the basis of that Croslandite vision of socialism that *The future of socialism* had encapsulated. In losing Crosland, liberal socialism lost its most effective ideologue and its influence within the Party was to be further diminished by the exit of Bill Rodgers, David Owen and Shirley Williams to form, in 1981, the Social Democratic Party.

The arrival of a Conservative government proposing a radical, right wing, free market/monetarist alternative to what had gone before also, for a time, strengthened the position of the Left. In some respects they enjoyed a symbiotic relationship at the expense of the much thinned and ideologically damaged ranks of the Keynesian liberal socialists. After all, there was much on which they agreed. Demand management, given the structural weaknesses of the British economy, did more harm than good. A radical economic strategy was required to repair those structural weaknesses. That strategy must look to increase the efficiency and productivity of the economy's supply side. All this was common ground. Where they differed violently, of course, was over the respective role of the state and the market in effecting a supply-side revolution and over who should be its beneficiaries. That said, both sides derived profit and pleasure from attacking Keynesian social democracy.

Also, the desperate economic crisis into which Britain was plunged soon after the Conservatives took office further reinforced the claims of the Left that a radical alternative was required. In the early 1980s unemployment rose to over 3 million, industrial production fell by almost 20 per cent, manufacturing capacity declined by one third and double-digit inflation again made an appearance. "As things crumble on all sides", wrote Hodgson, "possibilities loom large". Thus the scale of the economic crisis was such that it seemed to present a "greater probability of socialist change than at any time in its [Britain's] history".[33]

One further point here as regards the strengthening position of those who supported the AES. Up to the early 1980s the trade unions remained a potent force. In fact in the period 1969–79, the proportion of the workforce unionized rose from 46 per cent to about 55 per cent. It had also been trade union action during the winter of discontent that had brought about the electoral demise of the Callaghan government. The trade union movement looked, therefore, to be an increasingly potent force and one that any viable economic strategy would have to accommodate. As we have seen, key elements of the AES, e.g. planning agreements, the accountability of enterprises and increasing industrial democracy, did just that.

So, for these reasons, the proponents of the AES were in a strong position in the period until 1983 and their strength is reflected in the literature produced by the Party, Party members and those who sought to influence Party opinion. Sam Aaronovitch's *The road from Thatcherism, the alternative economic strategy* (1981), the Conference of Socialist Economists' *The alternative economic strategy* (1980), Michael Meacher's *Socialism with a human face* (1980), Geoff Hodgson's *Labour at the crossroads* (1981) and *The democratic economy* (1984), Eric Heffer's *Labour's future* (1986) and Tony Benn's *Arguments for socialism* (1980) and *Arguments for democracy* (1981) all advocated acceptance of the essential elements of the AES, the objectives of which were, perhaps, most neatly summarized by Aaronovitch as being,

> to expand the economy especially through large-scale public investment and current spending, including direct and indirect support for massive investment in industry. To increase democratic control and planning over the main levers of the economy through the extension and democratization of publicly owned industry and through planning agreements with all large enterprises, public and private. To launch a new social strategy based on reshaping the welfare system and social services through radical reform of the tax system.

> To ensure *controlled growth* of imports so as to help domestic economic growth,[34]

the last involving the adoption of protectionism and the abandonment of the EEC. This was, in essence, to be the economic policy stance assumed by the Labour Party in the early 1980s and adhered to until its election defeat in 1983. *Labour's programme, 1982* and its election manifesto *The new hope for Britain* (1983) make that abundantly clear: their ideological roots were firmly anchored in the AES.

However, while the Alternative Economic Strategy was at the heart of the political economy of all these socialist writers and while it set the agenda for policy debate within the Party in the early 1980s, there were those such as Michael Meacher and Geoff Hodgson who at the same time as embodying it in their work also sought, in some measure, to transcend it. Indeed the political economy of these writers, particularly in Meacher's *Socialism with a human face* and Hodgson's *The democratic economy*, was part of an efflorescence of creative economic thinking on the Left of the Party in the early 1980s – the kind of flaring up of a candle that often precedes its extinction.

Meacher's work undoubtedly accepted the general thrust and major components of the AES. It would, he believed, lay the basis for a higher rate of growth and that would dampen inflationary pressures, effect a sustained rise in real earnings and "enable public expenditure to increase again at an annual rate of about the average for the post-war period".[35] In short, it would once again make possible Labour's pursuit of some of its traditional economic objectives. Yet, parallel with this ran arguments highly critical of the contemporary preoccupation of "nearly all politicians" with "quantitative growth";[36] arguments which, in fact, sit uneasily beside the trumpeting of the virtues of economic expansion that is at the heart of the AES. Further, this scepticism as regards the unrelenting pursuit of economic growth, pointed, for Meacher, to the need for a much more revolutionary transformation of the British economy and society than that implied by the AES itself.

Here, Meacher believed that he saw in the powerful and insistent demand for the extension of industrial democracy an indication of working-class revulsion against "that reckless and relentless pressure to maximise economic growth at all costs" which had produced "a grossly materialistic distortion of the human personality and in the longer run, almost certainly, an ecologically unsustainable goal".[37] The demand also represented, in Meacher's eyes, a prioritization of self-determination and job satisfaction over "output maximisation"; a recognition that "at a certain level of affluence, security of income . . . a sense of purpose in one's occupation, shared control over decision-making . . . and satisfaction from the intrinsic interest of work become more important than raising output for its own sake."[38] This, he believed, was the lesson to be drawn from the actions of the Lucas aerospace shop stewards "who in 1976 challenged the strategy of their company with an alternative, detailed, full-length, corporate plan involving new products and techniques".[39] The goals of that strategy were not the maximization of output *per se*, still less the maximization of profit, but the production of products, such as medical equipment, which would satisfy pressing social needs. As Meacher saw it, British socialism must accommodate such aspirations.

All this would entail not just an extension of industrial democracy to give effect to such specific grassroots initiatives, but also a fundamental re-ordering of national policy priorities. Thus, for Meacher, what was required was a general re-orientation of production to the traditional socialist objective of satisfying definite social needs, rather than, as was the case at present, production geared to the maximization of profit, the enhancement of international competitiveness or the highest attainable rate of output. For example, as regards the objective of job security: "while capitalism aims to provide as many jobs as are compatible with organising production and pricing to maximise profits, socialism seeks to achieve the most efficient production of goods and services *as is compatible with ensuring that all adults seeking employment are indeed offered a job.*"[40] In short, because of its social and human, as well as economic implications, the objective of full employment must prevail over narrowly conceived growth objectives such as profit maximization and the rapid accumulation of capital in private hands.

There was a need, too, for socialists to come to terms with the resource and pollution implications of the current commitment to rapid output growth. Thus the dramatic rise in oil prices of 1973–4 and 1978–9 was seen by Meacher as a foretaste of the future, unless environmental considerations became an integral part of policy formulation. Here he put forward the possibility of "a steady-state economy"; "one in which the total population and the total stock of physical wealth are maintained roughly constant at some desired levels".[41] Elsewhere Meacher writes of "non-material growth", which would involve increased opportunity for "creative leisure, sports, arts, education", qualitative growth of a kind that would not put pressure on the environment by way of depleting scarce natural resources or increasing pollution.

However, the successful pursuit by a socialist Britain of such non-capitalist, non-materialistic objectives would require a number of complementary policies. To begin with, it would be necessary to insulate the British economy, in some measure, from the international pressures of competitive capitalism and that meant protection from an unregulated inflow of foreign imports and closer control over inward and outward investment flows. As regards the former, Meacher looked to the setting of "actual volume targets for specific products, with a division between domestic production and imports that suited [Britain's] particular national capabilities, resources and employment requirements".[42] As regards foreign investment, he suggested much closer scrutiny of inward and outward movements of capital with an eye to their impact upon exports, employment, the dissemination of technology, industrial efficiency and the viability of domestic undertakings. Meacher denied advocating a siege economy. But there can be no doubt that he looked to one that would enjoy a greater and growing measure of self-sufficiency. Thus "if satisfying people's needs is seen as the purpose of production, the British economy is large enough for *most* requirements to be produced economically"; "in the last analysis socialism in Britain means using resources in a planned way to serve the needs of the people. For this to be possible Britain must *become more self-reliant* . . . cutting down the import of goods that could perfectly well be produced at home."[43] Here he defended the Cambridge Economic Policy Group input to the AES and like them he stressed that "other countries would not lose, in fact would gain, because they would increase their exports to Britain compared with what they can hope to achieve while the government's highly deflationary policies remain in force."[44] Thus a high growth economy with import controls would *ultimately* suck in more imports than a low growth economy pursuing free trade policies. Yet such statements sit uneasily beside the autarkic and steady-state sentiments already quoted.

Meacher also argued that if a steady-state economy were to be created, it would require the detailed planning of economic activity by reference to a price/value system that did not function solely on the basis of market forces. "It is here", Meacher argued, "that ecological and socialist perspectives begin to dovetail. Industrial production would have to be systematised, and employment and investment would need to be channelled towards the nation's most essential requirements"[45] – presumably those of the qualitative, environmentally friendly kind mentioned above. To promote this development, it would also be necessary to establish the "true relative value of different projects"; something that would require the application of a system of taxes and subsidies to ensure that "the full, finite resource and environmental costs of all goods and services would be reflected in their prices".[46] All this, Meacher admitted, would necessitate "meticulous planning, firm controls and probably a reduction in all the traditional ways of accumulating capital, making profits and spending wealth".[47] But that was an acceptable price to pay for an ecologically sustainable socialism.

However, Meacher was at pains to deny the need for a "central bureaucratic apparatus" to give effect to such calculations and planning. Thus to the extent that "the spread of incomes is more equal", as it would be under socialism, the market could be used by planners to provide some *initial* indication of the "social needs of the community".[48] The dangers of the growth of a centralized bureaucracy would be countered too, both by the extension of industrial democracy and the devolution of decision-making powers. Here, Meacher recognized the hazards that attended the Yugoslav model, where enterprise autonomy had made for growing inequality; but, as he saw it, that still left open the possibility of a "diversified distribution of power", with what he termed the "community" as "the basis for a larger framework of regional and national co-ordinating institutions". In general he believed that a socialist government should "leave as many functions as possible to localities, elevating what is absolutely essential to the higher unit".[49]

Thus *Socialism with a human face*, while it proceeded from a clear articulation and defence of the AES, also developed a much longer-term and, in many respects, more radical strategy involving substantial insulation of the British economy from international pressures and the pursuit of non-capitalist and, in effect, green objectives, within the general framework of a decentralized socialism.

Given that this decentralized, community-based, ascetic socialism represented such a radical departure from almost every aspect of existing economic and social arrangements, it is understandable that Meacher believed it would require what he termed a "counter-ideology" to secure the support necessary for its implementation and survival. "At least as important as constructing an alternative strategy is the launching of a counter-ideology to facilitate the transfer."[50] For Meacher the central, indeed the organizing concept of that ideology must be the ideal of social service. For, in effect, what socialists sought was to replace a society organized around the motive of "self-advancement" by a society in which "service to a cause and to the wider community" was what directed activity. "Sharing, altruism and co-operation" must replace "elitism, materialism and excess competitiveness". Capitalism had failed not just, or even fundamentally, in a material sense; it had failed because it had left people "starved of moral or spiritual values by the sheer unbalanced weight of materialistic propaganda grossly distorting the value system of society in the economic interests of the capitalist establishment".[51] What underpinned the whole, therefore, was a moral critique and an ethical vision not dissimilar from those of R. H. Tawney and the ethical socialists of an earlier era. There was too more than a dash of William Morris in the brew.

Like Meacher, Hodgson also saw in the pressure for industrial democracy an indication of a working-class desire for a qualitative rather than a quantitative enrichment of their lives. However, while Meacher proceeded from this to the idea of a steady-state, environmentally balanced and increasingly self-sufficient economy, Hodgson, in *Labour at the crossroads* and, in particular, in *The democratic economy*, focused more on the implications for socialist political economy of the idea of democracy *per se*. Thus while taking as his starting point the notion of industrial democracy that formed such a central component of the AES, what he ultimately advanced was a view of the business of building socialism more radical than that to be found in that Strategy.

For the Hodgson of *Labour at the crossroads*, the AES was an "economic strategy [that] not only addresses the central problems of the British politico-economic crisis; it provides a means of moving towards socialism in the coming decades". It was, in effect, "*an excellent starting point*".[52] However, for all its strengths, *The democratic economy* makes clear that, for Hodgson, it was just that: a starting point for a radical, socialist transformation of society. In that work, Hodgson's argument was this. The extension of economic democracy and socialist advance must be seen as synonymous. The fact was that the "character" of an economic "system as a whole is determined by the general pattern of relations of power". In terms of altering those relations, the extension of "collectivist forms of property" was, in itself, of subsidiary importance: the central and most contentious feature of the AES became "a secondary issue". What, therefore, became "the *primary* objective of a radical socialist programme", for Hodgson, was the "rebuild[ing]" of "these relations *in a democratic mode*".[53] Democracy and the extension of democracy became the central agents of social transformation because that transformation must be about empowerment, about a genuine decentralization of decision-making power into the hands of the working class. Of course the extension of public ownership had a role to play here; but *only* in so far as it brought a changed relationship between workers and management. Thus, where it obstructed the progress of industrial democracy collectivism could be as inimical to the growth of socialism as capitalism itself. The socialization of the economic base did not necessarily entail a socialist transformation of society.

For Hodgson, therefore, the extension of democratic practice, both in the economic and political spheres, was *the* transformative agency. It was so because it would *make* socialists – the only way, in fact, in which socialism could become a reality. Thus the extension of democratic practice advocated by Hodgson would, he believed, dissolve the social barriers of hierarchy and deference that obstructed the growth of a classless, egalitarian society. It would ensure too that production was directed to the satisfaction of social needs because democratic participation would guarantee that those needs were fed into decision-making processes. As Hodgson put it, "one of the objectives of economic democracy is to make not only production itself but the *purpose* of production accountable to society at large".[54] Democratic participation in decision-making was also the antidote, the sole antidote, to the alienation experienced by the workforce within all large-scale enterprises, whether in public or private ownership. Like Meacher, and echoing E. F. Schumacher, Hodgson wrote that "economics" should not simply be "concerned with the production of more material goods". Rather it should focus on the means by which *all* human needs can be satisfied and that included the psychic need of the producer for creative labour. Schumacher, perhaps, but one can again detect in all this the renaissance of ideas that underpinned the political economy of John

Ruskin and William Morris. Thus there was, at the core of Hodgson's work, the desire that socialism should embody a humanistic political economy.

The extension of industrial democracy would also force the trade union movement to broaden the scope of its activities. It could no longer concern itself primarily with pay and conditions but would need to cultivate an involvement with the whole nature and purpose of productive activity. To the extent that trade union representatives were involved in investment and production decisions, they would be determining corporate strategy. Given that, they would be in a position both to do what the shop stewards at Lucas Aerospace had done and, moreover, to actually implement plans that redirected productive activity so that it focused on social need rather than profit maximization.

Yet while emphasizing the social transformation that the extension of democratic practice could effect, Hodgson made clear that he also saw it as the means of transforming Britain's economic fortunes. The AES had correctly directed attention to supply-side deficiencies as the root cause of the British disease. For Hodgson, therefore, what was needed to circumvent the crisis in which the British economy found itself in the early 1980s, what was needed to lay the basis for future growth, was a substantial and sustained increase in labour productivity and "any attempt to improve productivity and bring economic revival must engage in a process to transform relations of production within the British economy".[55] Increased investment, the extension of public ownership into profitable sectors, increased public expenditure might all be necessary prerequisites, but economic democracy was the indispensable condition of economic rejuvenation. Thus, for Hodgson, participation in decision-making was crucial to the enhancement of "collective and interactive effort": there existed "very strong evidence to support the conclusion that substantial increases in productivity are possible through extended worker participation."[56] It was, quite simply, *the* means of unleashing the creative and productive energies of the workforce and, thence, *the* means of transforming the economy's supply side.

Economic democracy was also a necessary corrective to the ignorance of decision-makers in general and economic planners in particular, and was, therefore, a fundamental means of improving the flow of information. Thus, as regards planning, history evidenced that a technocratic approach, where discussion and decision-making were confined to a professional or political elite, "exacerbate[d] the problem of uncertainty and incomplete information" (which all planners confronted) by a failure "to create open and informed debate".[57] In such circumstances, where information transmission and feedback were circumscribed, mistakes were more likely to be made and more difficult to rectify. Further, "without democracy" and with "the planning elite peering into a pit of ignorance", "the way is open for the assertion of priorities by and for the elite instead of by and for the people".[58] In the absence of democracy, planning objectives reflected what the planners or a political elite desired, not what society wanted.

It is with respect to this prioritization of the extension of democracy that Hodgson's discussion of public ownership, planning and the price mechanism must be understood. Socialism involved the dispersal and democratic exercise of power. The extension of public enterprise must accommodate that. While, then, Hodgson was clear that public enterprise must ultimately predominate, he was equally emphatic that it must assume a variety of forms (some experimental) and involve "parallel and competing public firms"; moreover, "such a solution implies competition and it implies a market."[59] Thus, as regards the public sector, he envisaged a competitive pluralism not dissimilar, in some respects, from that of an earlier generation of liberal socialists.

The existence of a market did not, however, preclude the need for extensive planning. On the contrary Hodgson saw planning, rather than the uncoordinated, market-mediated decisions of individuals, as the dominant form of decision-making. Further, for the future, "as the economic system becomes more and more complex and dependent on the efficient transmission of information, *the market system becomes of less and less use for the purpose.* We enter a world where much information has to be readily available from central institutions, where a large proportion of the population are occupied in its processing and distribution and where market trading of much of the economic output does not occur in a normal manner."[60] Nevertheless, "despite the limitations of the market mechanism . . . there is some force in the argument for market relations in certain spheres, where planning itself is insensitive to needs."[61] Further, Hodgson accepted that "the decentralisation of control over industry", a key characteristic of his vision of socialism, "inevitably means the establishment of a market mechanism: no realistic alternative has been found". Thus the market would have a fundamental role to play, if a subordinate one. In that respect Hodgson posited a solution to a problem that other decentralists such as the guild socialists had preferred to ignore: the problem, in Hodgson's words, of "maximising autonomy while retaining social coherence . . . decentralising decision-making while retaining a measure of overall democratic control". Such a society had to be one "in which both the state and the market exist" with both "subordinate to democracy".[62]

Taking the AES as their starting point, therefore, Meacher and Hodgson sought to make a radical break from both Keynesian social democracy and a fundamentalist state collectivism. They also sought to transcend what they viewed as the rather narrow materialism of the Strategy itself. Their political economies give a flavour of the fertility and the intellectual self-confidence of the Left, even after Labour's election defeat(s). Indeed the economic disaster that followed close on the heels of Mrs Thatcher's 1979 election triumph seemed to lend force to their view that an immediate radical departure from past thinking and policy was now imperative. It was also believed, as relative economic decline accelerated into the catastrophe of the early 1980s, that such a radical socialist alternative would secure the popular support of a despairing electorate and thus transform the Labour Party's political fortunes.

Yet however strident the blast, it is rare that theoretical systems fall, like the walls of Jericho, after the first notes of the assailants' trumpets. If Keynesian liberal socialism was on the ropes in the mid-1970s it was very far from surrendering the ring and the period after 1983 was to see it mount an effective counterattack. At the same time, by the mid-1980s left revisionism was in retreat in the wake of the rapidly diminishing strength of the Left within the Labour Party. It is with the reasons for and the consequences of these developments that the final two chapters are concerned.

Chapter 17
Liberal socialism rejuvenated, the 1980s

> The community . . . is yielding up rather than discharging the responsibility for the provision of necessary public services . . . The government is withdrawing from its role as overall director of economic strategy and from its responsibility to maintain full employment.
>
> Bryan Gould, *Socialism and freedom*, 1986

> The norms of the post-war Labour government, public spending, state intervention, regional policy, welfare, Keynesian economics, ha[ve] given Britain a rising standard of living in the age of affluence. They are as relevant to the problems of the New Depression as they were to the old . . . The problem is to make these policies work better.
>
> Austin Mitchell, *The case for Labour*, 1983

> With the re-emergence of the old problems, there is even greater need for the old Labour Party.
>
> Austin Mitchell, *The case for Labour*, 1983

After 1983, the political tide within the Labour Party began to ebb strongly against the Left and the economic policies embodied in the AES. Overwhelming defeat in the 1983 General Election was one crucial factor here. Not only did it precipitate the replacement of Michael Foot by Neil Kinnock, it also forced the Party to begin to consider why, despite all the failings of its economic policies, Thatcherism had evoked a positive response in at least a part of the working-class electorate that had previously voted Labour. Socialist writers might complain that what Thatcherism had done was to tap into the rich veins of popular prejudice exposed in periods of economic crisis, that it had engendered, articulated and exploited an aggressive cupidity in the British populace, but the fact remained that it had managed to do so in an economic and political language that elicited the cross-class support necessary to return it to power with one of the largest majorities of the post-war period. That at least was something that had to be taken seriously by those who sought to formulate the Party's future political economy. Specifically here, they had to come to terms with the rhetoric of economic liberty that Thatcherism had so effectively deployed to penetrate that social constituency which Labour had previously regarded as its own. That the Party was under pressure to do so, in itself militated against the kind of political economy being offered by the Left and gave the whip hand to those who preached a liberal market socialism that more easily accommodated the language of economic freedom.

In addition, the defeat of the miners' strike of 1984–5, the consequent acceleration in an erosion of trade union power already set in train by Tory legislation and the rapid rise in the level of unemployment consequent upon a savagely deflationary monetary policy and an overvalued currency, all had a bearing on the outcome of the struggle in the 1980s between the alternative-economic-strategy Left and the Keynesian, liberal socialist Right. Much of what the Left had offered – planning agreements, encroaching workers' control, participation in the business of national economic planning – had been predicated upon the existence and growth of trade union power. However, in the 1980s, that was no longer warranted. Trade union power was palpably declining and, in the economic circumstances that prevailed, the major concern of the trade union member increasingly became that of retaining employment, rather than the eroding of managerial prerogatives. History may not repeat itself but there would certainly seem to be strong parallels here with the comparable dissipation of forces pressing for industrial democracy in the period immediately following the Great War: they too, in part, fell victim to a government determined to deflate and strengthen the international position of sterling regardless of the cost in terms of employment.

It was also the case that the rise in unemployment, the massive underutilization of productive capacity, the fall in the mid-1980s in the rate of inflation and the insulation provided by North Sea oil against balance of payments crises, all suggested that conventional Keynesian remedies might once again be relevant and viable. As with the economy so with the political and economic debate: Thatcherism, in many respects, returned Britain to the 1930s and, in that context, it seemed that an opportunity had been created for the Keynesian revolution to be usefully re-enacted, with Keynesian liberal socialists able to savour all the moral fervour and psychic satisfaction that attaches to a revivalist crusade.

The gathering momentum of privatization in the mid-1980s also fundamentally altered the terrain upon which the debate over public ownership took place. In the 1970s and early 1980s debate revolved around how and where social ownership might be usefully extended. The assumption was that the extension would be considerable and that assumption was certainly integral to the "left" economic programme that the Labour Party embraced.

However, as privatization gathered momentum the debate was increasingly concerned with whether, how and to what extent there should be a return to the status quo. On this ground the liberal socialists were certainly more at home. Hence arguments that had seen service in the 1950s in constructing the socialist case for a more circumspect, imaginative and pluralistic expansion of the public sector could be dusted off and deployed to some effect in a situation where the extension of public ownership was more problematic and the climate of opinion more hostile to it. The same could not be said of the arguments for social ownership that had figured prominently in the AES.

In effect, the deliberate, systematic and relatively successful destruction in the 1980s of what had been built up on the basis of Keynesian social democracy, provided a golden opportunity to fight, fight and win again the battles of a previous epoch. The Keynesian demand management that Jim Callaghan had dismissed as history suddenly acquired a future and Mrs Thatcher made possible a born-again liberal socialism that rested heavily on the same political economy that had supported its post-war predecessor. Thus Giles Radice wrote that "a Labour government, elected in the 1990s" would be "entitled to have confidence in sensible, moderately applied and well-balanced Keynesian policies". Austin Mitchell too looked to "Keynesian management revived" as the way forward. "The argument that the spending way out of depression is no longer open was wrong in 1976 and even more so now when things are so much worse." As he perceptively put it, "mass unemployment, widening gaps in society, increasingly inadequate welfare provision, a threatened industrial base, a welfare system that is creaking and undermined . . . all make it necessary for Labour *to resume its task*."[1] Bryan Gould and his co-authors in *Monetarism or prosperity?* (1981) also highlighted the return to full employment as the "essence" of the Labour Party's economic strategy with increased public expenditure being "an important element in getting the economy moving".[2] Further, all these writers were at one in arguing that demand management, rather than the kind of industrial planning on offer from the Left, was to be the crucial factor promoting productivity gains and thence a return to sustained economic growth. The tools of economic management embraced by an earlier generation of Keynesian socialists were once more enthusiastically proffered.

But how could past failings be avoided and Keynesianism rendered the basis of an effective macroeconomic strategy? Here, writers such as Bryan Gould, Roy Hattersley, Austin Mitchell and Giles Radice had to confront again the problems of inflationary pressure and balance of payments crises that had proved fatal in the past. For Mitchell, they obviated any simple revamping of Keynesianism. That "offer[ed] only increased inflation and rising imports unless the framework in which the strategies operate can be changed"[3] and to this end he, and others, proposed that an expansionary strategy should be pursued only in conjunction with a substantial devaluation of sterling and, thereafter, in the context of a flexible exchange rate regime. Indeed, throughout the 1980s, Mitchell's emphasis remained the same. The exchange rate was "more important than any other single instrument"; "everything depends on the correct positioning of the exchange rate". If it was not a sufficient condition for full employment, economic growth and the reconstruction of Britain's manufacturing base, then it was, most certainly, a vital one.[4]

Both Mitchell and Gould believed a substantial devaluation was necessary to reverse what they correctly identified as an extraordinarily damaging appreciation of the international value of sterling, that had begun with the tight monetary policies pursued by the Labour government after the 1976 sterling crisis and continued apace in the deflationary aftermath of the electoral success of Mrs Thatcher in 1979. Thus by the first quarter of 1981 the international value of sterling was 46 per cent up on that for the fourth quarter of 1976. That in itself had inflicted severe damage on Britain's export industries, exacerbated her balance of payments problems and rendered more difficult the pursuit of expansionary policies; for, in such circumstances, they could be guaranteed to suck in imports at an even more alarming rate than previously. A devaluation of around 30–35 per cent in the real exchange rate would go some way to reverse this substantial loss of competitiveness and restore the fortunes of Britain's export industries. Thus "a correctly aligned exchange rate [was] the key to international competitiveness" and thence to the creation of jobs in the export sector.[5]

As important, however, was the fact that it would provide the British economy with that measure of insulation necessary, if a government-initiated expansion of aggregate demand was to prove successful in terms of employment creation and growth. So while, for the Cambridge Economic Policy Group, insulation was to be furnished by import controls (tariffs and/or quotas), for Mitchell, Gould and others the exchange rate could be used to achieve this objective. In effect, they favoured insulation by the price mechanism. Without it they were adamant that a substantial proportion of any increase in demand would leak abroad and that would diminish both its impact on the level of employment and output in the domestic economy and precipitate, as in the past, a damaging sterling crisis. A competitive and flexible exchange rate would go a long way to prevent such problems by ensuring the competitiveness of British goods in domestic markets and thereby diminishing the propensity to import. As Mitchell summarized it: "the economy must be insulated in order to expand and in this respect the exchange rate is the key to both competitiveness and insulation."[6] In this context it is also interesting to note Mitchell's vehement opposition to EEC membership and any possibility of Britain joining the Exchange Rate Mechanism (ERM). For Mitchell the EEC was to be opposed on many grounds but in particular because its institutions and mechanisms such as the ERM limited Britain's freedom of manoeuvre with respect to its management of sterling's international value, its control over commercial policy and, therefore, its conduct of macroeconomic policy in general. For these reasons he considered that entry into the ERM "would be disastrous for the nation".[7]

For Gould and Mitchell, the expansion of international and domestic demand for British goods would lay the basis not only for a solution to the problem of unemployment but also for the transformation of Britain's economic performance. As regards international demand, Gould saw it in this way:

> Higher growth springs from the cumulative increases in market share as export sectors become progressively more competitive and past successes become the platform for the next round of market penetration. Nothing succeeds like success and nothing raises labour productivity, reduces costs and enhances price competitiveness like the full utilisation of productive capacity resulting from buoyant foreign demand.

Of itself, therefore, such demand would solve many of the supply-side problems that afflicted British industry. The expansion of output, and thence the full utilization of existing productive capacity, would make for a well-rewarded, co-operative labour force in the internationally traded goods sector. In raising profitability it would also provide the wherewithal to improve sales promotion, the servicing of products, the speed of delivery and other non-price aspects of competitiveness.[8] As Austin Mitchell put it, British industrialists would be in a position to seize the opportunity created by a competitive exchange rate and increased profit flow "to improve investment, production and productivity, design, research and development and delivery".[9] The socialist advance towards a rejuvenated economy was to be export led.

These writers also confronted the argument that devaluation had not worked in the past, in particular in 1967, and could not therefore be expected to effect a transformation of the British economy in the future. In response, they argued that the devaluation of 1967 had been a reflex reaction to crisis rather than part of a coherent strategy aimed at export and demand-led growth. Further, Mitchell, in both *The case for Labour* (1983) and *Competitive socialism* (1989), was at pains to defend the Barber/Heath dash for growth of 1972–4, which, on the basis of rapidly expanding domestic demand and a floating (or more accurately sinking) exchange rate, had produced a marked increase in industrial output. As he saw it, only its unfortunate coincidence with a marked increase in oil and raw material prices had blown the strategy off course. Also, Mitchell referred to Britain's economic experience, post-1932, when recourse to devaluation, cheap money, economic insulation and expanded domestic demand had produced a marked increase in the level of economic activity, at least until 1937. He and others had, therefore, no doubts about the "cumulative improvement" which would result from a competitive exchange rate and a policy of demand management pursued with full employment and growth, rather than balance of payments equilibrium, as its central objective.

They were also adamant that what they proposed was a policy for industry. A rejuvenated manufacturing base was, for them, the key to economic growth. Deindustrialization of the kind that was occurring under the Conservatives in the 1980s was not inevitable and certainly not something to be lightly accepted. Service industries might have expanded and might continue to grow but in terms of employment, output and exports, they were no substitute for a thriving manufacturing sector. The problem was that in the past "the interests of the real economy – of manufacturing industry – have been subordinated to the monetary economy and to the international role of sterling", with the result that "an overvalued pound and the deflationary policies needed to support it [had] been entirely destructive of our international competitiveness".[10] Manufacturing had been "sacrificed to City interests". For Gould and Mitchell, therefore, their reconstructed Keynesianism would involve a fundamental switch in the interests that economic policy sought to serve. As Gould and his co-authors put it in 1981, "the whole balance of the economy would be tilted in favour of those sectors [manufacturing] which offer the greatest chance of expansion and improved productivity."[11]

The essence of these writers' strategy was a return to the use of Keynesian demand management tools to attain the objectives of full employment and sustained economic growth. Such tools had been largely abandoned by the Callaghan Government, dismissed as inadequate for socialist purposes by the Labour Left and denigrated as damaging by Thatcherite Conservatives intent on the microeconomic reinvigoration of the supply side. However, as regards the born-again Keynesians the plight of manufacturing industry was a "macro not a micro" problem.[12] Industry could only flourish in a climate of demand-generated growth.

Those who advocated an expansionist strategy in the 1980s did not see inflation or the threat of inflation as a constraint. In part this was due to the fact that the decade saw a fall in the rate of price inflation but also, given the high level of unemployment and the underutilization of productive capacity, any increase in aggregate demand was seen as pulling productive factors back into employment rather than bidding up their price. Their position was that of Keynes in *Can Lloyd George do it?* (1929) – "to bring up the bogey of inflation in the present circumstances is like warning a man dying of emaciation of the dangers of excessive corpulence"; or, as Austin Mitchell put it, "inflation will probably be low when Labour comes to power – it usually is in graveyards."[13]

Further an increase in output resulting from an expansion of demand was seen as imparting a downward pressure on the price level. This was so because, it was believed, a fuller utilization of capacity would reduce overhead costs per unit of output – something that would also help to restore profitability.

Even so, the Keynesian socialists of the 1980s, like their post-war predecessors, saw a place for a prices and incomes policy, though all were agreed, given the experience of the previous Labour government, that it should not be of a statutory kind. In many ways the major obstacle here was the folk memory of 1974–9 and, in particular, the 1978–9 "winter of discontent". For Roy Hattersley, many workers had benefited from the "social contract". In particular, the lower paid had benefited from the period in the late 1970s when a £6 flat-rate limit on wage increases prevailed. "But the experiences of that period so prejudiced the Labour Party against 'incomes policy' that socialists who believed in that system had to search desperately for another name with which to describe the object of their enthusiasm."[14] Hattersley's preferred term was "income planning" and what he proposed was an incomes policy of the loosest kind. Thus, as part of an overall process of indicative planning (which will be discussed below) there would emerge "a national view on the overall level and general distribution of wages".[15] The trade union movement would play a part in the formulation of this view and that should militate in favour of its acceptance by individual unions. There was, however, to be no element of coercion; coercion would destroy the possibility of "income planning" becoming "a permanent feature of a socialist society". By the same token, it should be made clear that an adherence to free collective bargaining was in no sense essential to socialist democracy.[16]

Giles Radice too saw great virtues in the ill-fated "social contract", which he described as "an ambitious attempt to link together incomes, output, employment, tax and welfare policy".[17] Like Hattersley, what he hoped for, in the context of a Labour government, was the emergence of "a consensus on income and wage increases". Such a consensus should, however, be "backed by non-accommodating fiscal, monetary and exchange rate policies and the use of the tax system to deter strategic employers from conceding inflationary wage increases".[18] This latter was an idea that had already been mooted by James Meade and, indeed, a number of writers in the 1980s including Meade and Richard Layard advocated using the tax system to give bite to a non-statutory incomes policy, though their advice was directed more to the SDP than to the Labour Party.

If Hattersley wrote of "income planning", Mitchell preferred to speak of a "social compact"; something embracing the elements of the social contract but without any provocative tinge of statutory compulsion. Voluntary wage restraint would form part of a package that included full employment, increased social welfare expenditure and redistributive measures. The policy would be policed by the trade union movement itself. It would be "an honour system which they themselves operate and which encourages them to build up the kind of collective decision-making and collective discipline by which trade union movements can claim the right to participate nationally".[19] Thus adherence to such an honour system would give the trade union movement the right to be involved in the more general business of shaping the social compact. As Mitchell put it in *Competitive socialism*, there would be a commitment to accept responsibility for adherence to "agreed norms in return for influence on spending and tax changes".[20] Given such a "social compact" government could deliver its commitment to economic expansion free from the fear of crippling inflationary pressures.

The position of writers here is recognizably that of a previous generation of liberal socialists who saw incomes policy as an essential, anti-inflationary component of a demand-driven full employment strategy. In particular these ideas are redolent of the kind of neo-corporatism that was such a characteristic feature of Labour governments in the 1960s and 1970s, with its attendant faith in the emergence of an employer/trade union/state consensus with respect to both the objective of full employment and the distribution of the rewards that full employment would bring. This faith was particularly manifest in the unanimous rejection of a statutory incomes policy and (with the exception of Mitchell) in the rejection of any element of coercion. Indeed, even with Mitchell, the fiscal stick is absent from his later work, *Competitive socialism*. The language too is of a consensual and corporatist character. Hattersley's reference to "a *national* view" on "general distribution" is indicative of that. So too is Mitchell's view that: "Unions and industry [could] be enmeshed in both the preparation and fulfilment of the *national programme for recovery* . . . gearing industries' expectations, government plans and union hopes in one *collective effort*."[21] The fact that the whole growth strategy was to rest on distinctively Keynesian foundations further suggests that, as regards this genre of socialist political economy, it was a case of back to the future with a vengeance.

These writers' views on planning were also couched in the consensual language of influence and co-operation rather than the alternative-strategy rhetoric of compulsion. Thus Mitchell wrote of "enmeshing national priorities with major corporate strategies" by means of "a mutual information flow between the two" and rejected the idea of compulsory planning agreements.[22] Planning would be essentially indicative in form and would take place through a Department of Economic Expansion, which Mitchell envisaged in terms of an expanded National Economic Development Council with its trade union, employer and government representatives. This would provide the institutional forum within which information as to government, entrepreneurial and union intentions and expectations could be exchanged. A National Planning

Council, again involving both sides of industry and the government, would be responsible for a National Economic Assessment, which would set "an annual norm for wage increases, investment, profits and taxes as well as the social dividend of benefit and transfer payments".[23] This would constitute the institutional framework for the operation of the Social Compact. It was the right to participate in the deliberations of this body that trade unions would win by adherence to the "honour system" discussed above. This is how they would participate in the business of economic planning.

Ideas on how such indicative planning might be applied to the British economy were developed by a number of writers in this period. One of note was Saul Estrin who in a contribution to a work entitled *Labour into the eighties* (1980) provided an exposition of this conception of planning, which in many ways is representative of the rejuvenated liberal socialism of the period.[24] For Estrin "pure indicative planning" was a method by means of which the state added to the information flow of individual enterprises by indicating the economic shape of things to come on the basis of its knowledge of the investment and production intentions of the public and private sector. It was, in effect, an attempt to create a consistent set of expectations about the economic future and was "intended to reduce the resource misallocation that would otherwise arise because of inconsistencies between current choices about future production".[25] The problem was, as Estrin and others recognized, that producers might refuse to accept the expectations on the basis of which the indicative plan was constructed and consequently act in a manner that prevented its fulfilment. What he proposed, therefore, was that the Labour Party should adopt "investment planning" that would provide an "incentive structure" (taxes, subsidies, state-sponsored production) to bring about those decisions and actions that would ensure that the indicated objectives of the plan were attained and expectations fulfilled. Again, the structures within which this would occur would be of an essentially corporatist kind. Here Estrin suggested a systematization of the work of the NEDC (a body shortly to be abolished by Mrs Thatcher) and the economic development councils (the so-called "little Neddies") that already involved the co-operation of the state, trade unions and employers. Within such an institutional structure those responsible for planning (a sub-committee of the Cabinet) would set "annual targets for each sector over a fixed period (say six years) and [provide] a related incentive structure". "Industrial committees", comprising members from all enterprises and trade unions in a sector would then disaggregate these targets to the enterprise level and be responsible for distributing "the available rewards to firms according to their individual rate of implementation. If the assumptions underlying the Plan prove to have been false, the [industrial] committees inform the planners who must alter the relevant targets and incentives accordingly".[26]

What Estrin and others had in mind, therefore, was not the state control of investment decisions – something that lay at the heart of the AES – but first, the dissemination of information as to planners' expectations and secondly, the provision of incentives to encourage firms to act on the basis of that information. In the final analysis therefore, decisions, right or wrong, still lay in the hands of private agents. Such a view of planning, with its emphasis on influence rather than control, its stress on a consensus evolved within a corporatist framework and its conception of the state's economic responsibilities in macro not micro terms, epitomizes the position of most 1980s liberal socialists. Thus Giles Radice writing of the need for an "industrial policy" pointed to the possibility of governments intervening not to replace markets but to "encourage" and "cajole" market players "to take a longer term view than that dictated by narrowly defined market requirements". As Radice put it, "the role of government is not to try and run industry or 'second guess' business but to act as an enabler, as a midwife of change."[27] Here again the conception is clearly indicative and voluntarist.

Given this, it is not surprising that all these writers acknowledged, if sometimes in qualified fashion, the virtues of market forces. Hattersley went so far as to suggest that "socialists are not opposed to the market allocation of *most* goods and services".[28] Market forces were a "protection against bureaucratic inefficiencies" and, to the extent that incomes and wealth were more equally distributed, they provided "a more accurate indication of social need".[29] Gould argued that while there should be checks and controls on the exploitative use of market power and while the market was a poor determinant of strategic economic decisions with long-term consequences, "yet the market remains a substantially more efficient means of allocating resources at the level of the microeconomy than any bureaucratically controlled system of planning."[30] Other writers echoed the sentiments of Hattersley and Gould or, as in the case of the Mitchell of *Competitive socialism*, trumpeted the merits of the market even louder. "The *main weight* of any policy needs to be the free market, for prices and market motivate and we compete in a market world." Of course the state had a role in "managing" market forces. But its role was very much that of an "agent of co-ordination, an instigating force, the *manager* of markets".[31] Indeed at times Mitchell's discussion verges on eulogy and is clearly illustrative of the extent to which, by the late 1980s, some within the Labour Party were not so much on the ideological defensive as on the intellectual run. Thus he wrote of: "an expansionary strategy which is market driven stimulat[ing] development by *liberating the dynamic forces of the economy rather than using the fiat of state power.*" In this context, "the state . . . comes to play the role of facilitator . . . within a framework of co-operation, support and sustenance." Elsewhere he was to summarize his position on the state's economic role in the aphorism – "as much market as possible, as much state as necessary".[32]

Radice too saw the state's role in terms of liberating and canalizing market forces, in particular, by promoting competition through a "tough competition, mergers and monopolies policy". It was a view articulated by a number of socialist writers in the 1980s. Gone then were the Wilsonian days of the Industrial Reorganisation Corporation, when big was beautiful and the concentration of industrial ownership was something to be welcomed. That said, Radice was none the less adamant that while competition had its virtues markets should "operate within a framework of civic responsibilities and values."[33]

Along with this emphasis on the socialist role of a freer and genuinely competitive market went an attempt to reappropriate the language of liberty for the socialist cause. This did not involve the abandonment of the goals of equality and fraternity but rather a tendency to see them as a means to the prioritized end of freedom. Socialism's mission was then defined not in egalitarian or communitarian terms but rather in those of the empowerment of previously powerless individuals and the provision of "real" choice and "real" freedom. The trinity of liberty, equality and fraternity is collapsed into the one goal of freedom. The very title of Hattersley's work *Choose freedom* speaks volumes, even if its reversal of Milton Friedman's *Freedom to choose* was intentionally ironic. As Hattersley saw it, socialism was now about "a commitment to organise society in a way that ensures the greatest sum of *freedom*, the highest total amount of real *choice* and, *in consequence, the most happiness*"; "the duty of socialists is to organise the State . . . in a way which demonstrably *increases the sum of liberty*"; "socialists attempt to organise society in a way which allows increasing numbers of men and women to make . . . *choices for themselves*", and so on.[34] The same insistence can be found in the work of Radice, who wrote of the need for Labour's firm "commitment to the expansion of *freedom*, opportunity and *choice* and defended the market on grounds of 'efficiency' and 'liberty' ".[35]

Bryan Gould's book *Socialism and freedom* (1986) covered similar ground and with similar intent. As with Radice and Hattersley, he sought to reformulate socialist objectives in terms of individual liberty and, more specifically, to derive from the liberal philosopher John Rawls's *Theory of justice* (1972), a philosophical basis for a distinctively socialist reconciliation of the goals of liberty and equality. What he did, in fact, was to cover much of the ground already traversed by the late-nineteenth-/early-twentieth-century new liberals. The negative conception of freedom embraced by the right libertarians was dismissed and replaced by a positive conception that saw freedom not in terms of what individuals were left free to do but rather in terms of what they could be put in a position to do, freedom "having no meaning or worth unless it can be exercised".[36] Here the state had a positive, interventionist role to play in removing the causes of the social and economic deprivation that eroded the possibility of "real" freedom. To achieve that end it would be necessary, above all else, to mount an "attack on the concentration of power" and effect a "diffusion and equalisation of power amongst all members of society". That, for Gould, was "the essence of socialism". This view of what socialism was about was reiterated throughout the book – "Socialism is a constant struggle against the forces in society which naturally tend towards concentration of power."[37]

In this focus upon the distribution of economic power there is a certain resonance with the concerns of the alternative-economic-strategy Left. But it is a superficial one. Their objective, for the most part, was the social appropriation of concentrations of power and their democratically determined use. For Gould the aim was their dispersal, which he saw as a crucial prerequisite for the extension of freedom. As he wrote "there is a close connection between the maximisation of freedom and the achievement of *a socialism whose main objective is the diffusion of power.*" Further, by concentrations of power, Gould had in mind not only "the current dominance of capital and property" but also those "promoted and encouraged by government bodies *and trade unions*".[38] Little fellow-feeling here with those who saw trade unions as a major agent of socialist transformation.

For Gould, freedom meant the freedom of the individual from collective coercion from whatever source. As he phrased it the true concern of the socialist *is the individual* in society. Socialists had all too often failed to grasp this and thereby paid too "little attention to *the enlargement of choice* and *the liberation of the individual*".[39] The concerns and the rhetoric are markedly similar to those of Hattersley and Radice and again we see the extent to which the political triumph of the Right had transformed the language of socialist political economy, precipitating a collapse of the trinity of socialist ideals – liberty, equality, fraternity – into the one godhead of freedom.

Of course, underneath the libertarian rhetoric, the old economic and social goals of liberal socialism remained, if somewhat diluted to suit the taste of an electorate whose instincts were perceived as more individualistic, more acquisitive and less communitarian than had previously been the case. Freedom to choose did involve the creation of a greater equality of wealth and power and here the state had a positive, and recognizably socialist, role to play. Nevertheless, the constant refrain of "freedom" and "choice", which runs as a leitmotif through the work of all these writers, indicates the degree to which "Mrs Thatcher has succeeded to a considerable extent in changing the terms and meaning of the debate so that the emphasis is more on freedom than equality than it was in the 1960s and 1970s."[40] The devil had not only stolen a good tune but had got the righteous to dance to its rhythms.

It was in such a context that these writers advanced their ideas on the extension of public ownership. These did not differ radically from the liberal socialism of the early 1950s and early 1970s but Mitchell's choice of *Competitive socialism* as a title is surely revealing; for it was in terms of the competitive stimulus it provided, and the competitive environment it created, that the case for public enterprise was now most often advanced. Thus Radice saw a role for public corporations as "price leaders and pace-setters providing a yardstick of efficiency". For Mitchell, their objective should be "to compete with, to stimulate, to supplement and to complement the private sector". Specifically, public ownership could be used "to break monopolies and stimulate competition".[41]

To this end, public ownership should assume a variety of forms. The autonomous public corporation might be fine for "the essentially monopolistic public utilities" but for other kinds of economic activity public ownership, where it was deemed necessary, could often usefully take a different form. Gould stressed the role, in particular the competitive role, that could be played by co-operatives and municipal enterprises. Hattersley too suggested the encouragement of co-operatives through the creation of a British Investment Bank, Local Authority Enterprise Boards and "a whole swathe of fiscal measures". In addition, Radice argued that state shareholding should be considered as a form of public ownership that allowed control without the costs and administrative difficulties of outright nationalization.[42] Thus he believed such involvement would frequently be sufficient to allow the state to achieve its objectives and, indeed, it was in terms of expanding public shareownership, and the use of the influence and control it would bring, that these writers saw the future role of a State Holding Company/National Enterprise Board. For Mitchell, for instance, such a board or company was to play the role of shareholder, adviser and financier, not only saving failing firms but "participating in joint ventures". What was wanted, as regards ownership, was a "healthy pluralism" of forms with the state eschewing a dominant role, its general objective being "to manage and work with capital to the benefit of all, not to expropriate it".[43]

There was little here that was new, though Radice did moot the idea of a new type of enterprise that he termed a "public interest company whose targets on consumer service, investment [and] pricing policy" would be monitored "by powerful regulatory authorities",[44] the object being to achieve what was wanted through regulation rather than ownership. Further, as regards the public sector itself, Radice suggested "an enforceable system of citizen and consumer rights in public services and industries". This was one means of guaranteeing that existing public enterprises ran efficiently, thereby ensuring public support; it also prefigures, though with different motives, the idea of a "citizens' charter", which was to be embraced by the Conservatives under John Major in the 1990s. That said, the vision of the mixed, pluralistic, competitive market economy, with an emphasis on social control not ownership, which pervaded the work of all these writers, did not differ in any significant sense from that of Crosland, Gaitskell and others writing in the 1950s.

Understandably, such writers had little time for the AES and its proponents, dismissed variously as "the army of political riff-raff who infiltrated the Labour

Party in the late sixties and early seventies" and "Trotskyists of all IQs".[45] In their less *ad hominem* and more reflective moments, criticism focused on the economic role and powers that Holland and others had ascribed to multinationals. For Mitchell, Britain's decline had been "cushioned" rather than precipitated by multinationals. They had brought investment, jobs, better management and innovative ideas to the British economy. They provided a fundamental part of Britain's industrial base and played a vital role in linking Britain with the global economy. To the extent that they did exercise a dominating role in the economy, that was a consequence not of any coercive intent on their part but of "the failure of smaller firms to grow in the vigorous way they [had] in Germany and the USA",[46] a failure that was primarily caused by the over-valuation of the exchange rate and the general anti-manufacturing bias that distinguished the conduct of British economic policy. Some regulation of their activity was required. But when transfer pricing and "currency fiddles" were practised it was almost invariably as part of a defensive response to a declining economy. In contrast, "in an expansionary economy they are anxious to come, keener to stay, desperate to share in its benefits" and, therefore, likely to act in a manner beneficial to Britain's economic prospects, without substantial financial inducements. It should, therefore, be the objective of government economic policy to create such a macroeconomic climate rather than to take these companies into public ownership or severely circumscribe their activities by compulsory planning agreements. In that respect the attitude of the 1980s liberal socialists to multinationals was consistent with their attitude to capitalist enterprise as a whole.

As regards the traditional goal of redistribution these writers also had little that was new to offer. They were, it is true, possessed of an acute sense of how much had yet to be done and how profoundly difficult it would be to do it. Like Jenkins, Crosland and others in the 1970s, they were aware of the considerable evidence which showed that the real beneficiaries of the welfare state had been not the poor, but the middle class. They were conscious too of how the existing benefit and tax system combined to penalize those on low incomes, with effective marginal rates of tax of 100 per cent or more. In addition, they also knew that the policies of the Thatcher governments had compounded the problem of income inequality, though, for Mitchell, it was the crisis of 1976, with its substantial cuts in public expenditure, that saw the demise of the progressive welfarism that had characterized the post-war period. Further, the rapid rise in unemployment in the 1980s and the consequent weakening in trade union bargaining power also served to block any advance towards a more egalitarian society.

Hattersley expressed scepticism about the power of the tax system to "adequately" redistribute income and wealth "to the point that meets the needs and aims of socialism", arguing that "to increase equality we need to create more equal primary incomes". That should not preclude "a massive programme of redistribution" but it also necessitated a truly socialist incomes policy, one component of which might be a statutory minimum wage.[47] Only by the implementation of such measures could such concepts as "freedom" and "choice" be invested with any substance. Gould proposed that socialists should aim for what he termed an "equality of social benefit" as a means of eroding or eliminating those marked material inequalities that threatened the increase of individual freedom. Thus he suggested in 1986 that "each person, as his condition for entering society, could insist upon a sort of social dividend, which because each person entered society on the same basis, would have to mean *an equal share of total benefits produced by social co-operation.*"[48] Gould's aim was undoubtedly redistributive and egalitarian, indeed radically so, even if, like all else in the 1986 work, his argument was formulated in the language of freedom and choice. There are hints here of the early Fabian notion of a surplus that emerged as a consequence of social arrangements rather than individual effort and that could, therefore, be legitimately and efficaciously appropriated and used for social/egalitarian purposes. But the concept of "total benefits" is never clearly formulated and certainly not developed in such a way as to permit specific policy prescriptions.

For Mitchell also, the way forward was through the payment of a social dividend of a kind similar to that already discussed in relation to the work of James Meade in the early 1970s. "This comprehensive dividend", argued Mitchell, "should eventually replace all National Insurance and Social Security benefits, being set at a level appropriate for family need and type." If a "means tested system" was desired, then the dividend "should be taxable when aggregated with other income". Such a dividend would get round the problem of take-up associated with means-tested benefits and would also circumvent the problem of the poverty trap. In the interim, though, measures should be implemented that "open[ed] up the gap between the level at which tax is paid and benefit received".[49] That said, whatever egalitarian policies were adopted they could only be effectively pursued in a context of growth. Unlike Crosland, Mitchell did not believe that growth itself would solve the problem of income inequality but he was also certain that "altruism is generated by affluence". Greater material abundance "*set*[*s*] *people free to care* for their fellow men": the generosity of spirit that permitted a redistribution of wealth was more likely when people had the wherewithal to be generous.[50] Egalitarianism became feasible when it no longer entailed sacrifice or economic loss. One wonders what the early-century ethical socialist would have made of such circumspect idealism.

As regards the idea of a minimum wage, Mitchell argued that it could not be "introduced until we are nearer full employment", otherwise it would "deprive the poor of jobs by pricing them out of the labour market".[51] This was a view that was shared by others. Radice, for example, warned that "it would be wrong to ignore the consequences for employment" of statutory minimum wage legislation and suggested, instead, reinforcing and extending the power and remit of wage councils.[52] Such views illustrate the division of opinion within the Labour Party on this issue and the resulting policy ambivalence that persisted into the 1990s.

Modified Keynesianism, corporatism, a cross-class consensus, redistributive welfarism, competitive public enterprise and the positive role of market forces in a mixed economy purged of the exploitative and coercive exercise of oligopoly power: these were the key components of the dominant strain of socialist political economy in Britain in the period after 1983. *Plus ça change plus c'est la même chose.* If a decade of Thatcherism had done nothing else it seemed, for a time, to have induced in Labour's political economists a mood of 1950s nostalgia.

Chapter 18

Supply side socialism: the political economy of New Labour, 1987–95

> These strategies for economic prosperity do not only generate the wealth on which social justice depends; in themselves they constitute elements in any plan for social justice.
>
> *Social justice: strategies for national renewal, the Report of the Commission on Social Justice*, 1994

> It is a good and desirable thing, truly, to make many pins in a day. But if we could only see with what crystal sand their points are polished – sand of human soul – we should think there might be some loss in it also. We blanch cotton and strengthen steel and refine sugar and shape pottery; but to brighten, to strengthen, to refine or to form a single living spirit never enters into our estimate of advantages.
>
> John Ruskin, *The stones of Venice*, 1851

If the 1983 election witnessed the swan song of the AES and, in its aftermath, the appearance within the Labour Party of a rejuvenated Keynesianism, defeat in the 1987 election was the prelude to further ideological developments anathema to many on the Left. These were encapsulated in the emergence of a *supply-side socialism* deploying the economic language of competition, productivity, profitability and cost effectiveness, a language that, from the late 1980s onwards, came to dominate the literature of the Labour Party. Such a patois was, for some, alarmingly redolent of the political economy of the "New Right" as indeed was the very use of the term "supply side".

The central objective of supply side socialism's proponents was to enhance the quality and improve the use of factor inputs, thereby increasing labour productivity, reducing unit costs and, crucially, improving Britain's international competitiveness. It also embodied the concomitant belief that more than mere manipulation of aggregate demand was necessary to ensure sustained economic growth, full employment and rising living standards. This emphasis on the supply side of the British economy was lent a particular force in the 1980s by a number of developments. To begin with, there was the dramatic erosion of Britain's manufacturing base that occurred in the early part of the decade. Not only did this precipitate a substantial increase in unemployment, it also turned Britain into a net importer of manufactured goods for the first time since the late eighteenth century. This increase in the post-war British propensity to suck in (manufactured) imports convinced many that, for the future, any recourse to Keynesian remedies for mass unemployment would prove utterly ineffectual. In addition, from the point of view of employment and future economic survival, there was now clearly an urgent need to pursue policies that directly tackled the deficiencies of the supply side of the British economy, thereby facilitating the reconstruction of Britain's industrial base and enhancing her competitive position.

It was also the case that, like the proponents of the AES, supply-side socialists believed that the globalization of business (transnational corporations) and finance meant that a unilateral pursuit of Keynesian demand management policies would almost inevitably precipitate the kind of response from the international financial community that was guaranteed to subvert them. Thus, for many, the failure of the expansionary economic strategy pursued by the French socialists under François Mitterrand (1981–6) made clear the likely consequences of trying to go it alone. Moreover, greater openness in the world economy made it virtually impossible to resort to those protectionist and exchange control measures by which Keynesians had previously suggested Britain's balance of payments blushes might be spared. The creation of the Single European Market in 1992 was one manifestation of this, while Britain's membership of the Exchange Rate Mechanism in the early 1990s emphasized still further, if for a short time, the severe limitations on any British government's freedom to manage aggregate demand, with employment objectives to the fore.

For supply-siders, such developments did not eliminate the need for macroeconomic management but they did suggest that, for the future, if such management was to prove effective in securing low inflation, low unemployment and ironing out the economic cycle, then it could do so only on the basis of two preconditions. First, a substantial improvement in Britain's international competitiveness and a rejuvenation of her industrial base to curb the increasing inflow of high-value manufactured goods, and secondly, the co-ordination of macroeconomic management policies at either a European or a G7 level. Specifically, as it was expressed in the Labour Party's *Rebuilding the economy* (1994), "The only way in which recovery can be sustained without inflation accelerating is if an internationally co-ordinated expansion of demand is combined with supply-side policies to boost investment in industry, skills and infrastructure". There was a need, in effect, for "an interaction between supply-side policies and [co-ordinated] demand management".[1]

Thus the literature envisaged the existence of a symbiotic relationship between short-run (demand-managed lower unemployment) and longer-term (supply-side rejuvenation) objectives. This notion was expressed with particular clarity in *Social justice, strategies for national renewal* (1994), the final report of the Commission on Social Justice, set up by the Labour Party in 1992, a document that may be seen as both reflecting and influencing thinking within the Party on economic and social questions. The Report stated that "the need to run the economy at a higher level of demand", in order to move towards the goal of full employment, would only be met "if we build competitive strength in the tradeable sector". At the same time, it insisted that "we must find ways to transmit the wealth earned in competitive markets to job creation in the rest of the economy." To this end the Report suggested government-financed expansion of labour-intensive, non-tradeable-goods sectors, wage subsidies, the development of intermediate labour markets (combining jobs and training) and the creation "of tax and benefits systems which provide incentives to employment". However, the strong implication was that expenditure upon, and thence the scale of, employment-creating initiatives would be determined by what the success (or otherwise) of supply-side policies made available. In effect the long run would govern the short run; the problem here being that the long run might be very long indeed and the wherewithal for short-run employment-creating measures initially scarce.[2] There are echoes here of 1929, when the Party had a long-run vision but lacked a short-run or intermediate strategy that would improve the material lot of its constituency while laying the basis for future social progress.

As regards the Party's thinking on demand management, it should be noted too that Labour now gave particular emphasis to the need to use macroeconomic policy not just, or even primarily, to attain full employment but also to win the battle against inflation. Here a number of expedients were suggested. For a time the Exchange Rate Mechanism was seen as providing the basis for a successful anti-inflationary strategy and the Labour Party was vociferous in its support. In *Made in Britain, a new economic policy for the 1990s* (1991), it was stressed that Labour's "commitment to macroeconomic stability and the Exchange Rate Mechanism [would] help to secure low inflation, competitive interest rates and a stable exchange rate". Similarly, the 1992 Manifesto promised that "to curb inflation, Labour [would] maintain the value of the pound within the Exchange Rate Mechanism", membership of the ERM having its salutary anti-inflationary impact through the constraints it imposed upon the government as regards the conduct of monetary and fiscal policy. Indeed, in the early 1990s Labour emphasized the importance of exchange rate stability as an antidote to inflation with an almost Snowdenian relish.[3]

However, it was recognized that if the relative exchange rate stability attendant upon ERM membership was not to undermine the competitive position of Britain's export industries then the level of real wage increases could not move far out of line with those in the economies of our major industrial competitors. If they did, and given exchange rate stability, the relative rise in unit wage costs would be likely to have an adverse impact on exports and thence the balance of payments. Of course, it was believed that exchange rate stability in itself would militate against the kind of trade union reaction to the imported inflation resulting from a depreciating exchange rate, which had previously sparked off wage inflation. Also, the damage to trade unions done by the Conservatives' anti-trade union legislation and the high level of unemployment that had prevailed in the 1980s would also militate in favour of wage restraint. Nevertheless it was believed that more was needed and to this end the idea of a National Economic Summit or National Economic Assessment was proposed. Indeed, as early as 1986 Neil Kinnock had suggested the idea of "gaining and maintaining a national consensus for the distribution of our national product [which] will have clear implications for wages and profits and . . . will establish a direct link between the achievement of targets in investment, output and job creation and wages and prices".[4] Suggestions for this kind of implementation of an informal wages policy were subsequently to loom large in the economic literature of the Labour Party in the late 1980s and early 1990s: a co-ordinated, wage bargaining arrangement of a non-statutory kind.

However, with respect to the battle against inflation and the other macroeconomic objectives of economic growth, balance of payments equilibrium and full employment, it was upon the rejuvenation of the supply side and the enhancement of Britain's international competitiveness that the overriding emphasis was placed in the Party literature of this period. As one pamphlet put it, while demand management might have its part to play, "the best way to cut unemployment and create jobs that last is to modernise our economy and build competitive industries that can succeed all round the world." "Export-led growth [was] the only guarantee of sustainable growth." It was necessary to face the fact that, as the 1992 Manifesto phrased it, "Britain [was] in a race for economic survival and success. Faced with intense competition, companies and countries can succeed only by constantly improving their performance" and that meant more "cost-effective production, continuous product and process innovation, the flexibility of a highly skilled workforce and the ability to translate the achievements of modern science into commercially viable projects." Only in this way could the objective of "a prosperous manufacturing sector producing *high profits for investment*" be secured and "more industrial companies [restored] to the front rank of innovation, *productivity and profit*" – things that were regarded by Labour as fundamental prerequisites for permanent, well-remunerated employment and thence for a sustained rise in living standards.[5]

To this end, a number of things became important. To begin with, and fundamentally, the level of investment in the British economy had to be raised and its nature altered. In the early 1990s Britain was investing less of its GDP in manufacturing than all but two of the 24 OECD nations. Further, it was investing a low percentage of GDP in research and development when compared with its major industrial rivals, while a high proportion of what was invested was channelled into defence and defence-related activity. There was also the problem of short-termism with respect to the investment that did take place, with emphasis placed by investors on quick gains, rather than the long-term expansion and underlying strength of companies.

To remedy this state of affairs Labour, in the late 1980s and early 1990s, proposed a number of measures, some fiscal and some institutional. As regards raising the level of investment, the Party advocated a substantial improvement in tax allowances for investment in new technology, innovation, product design and product development. On the institutional side it identified the need for regional investment banks: financial intermediaries with local knowledge of investment opportunities that would, among other things, serve as an antidote to the concentration of financial expertise and decision-making in London. In addition, to facilitate investment in smaller businesses, it proposed the creation of a Business Development Bank.

Another major element of Labour's proposals with respect to investment was concerned with the evil of short-termism. Here the Party's avowed objective was "to create the structures that produce a larger number of committed owners supporting a longer-term view of the company's future".[6] To this end a number of proposals were made. First, given that the major corporate investors in stocks and shares were the pension funds it was suggested that pension fund trustees might be trained to exercise closer control over their fund managers with a view to ensuring that they took a long-term view of their investments in British industry. In addition as "shareholders . . . often have little commitment to the long-term survival of the enterprise they own", it was suggested that fiscal measures to discourage speculative share buying might go some way to effect a change in attitudes.[7] The fundamental problem however was seen as altering a situation where "financial institutions appear to regard themselves as dealers in company shares rather than long-term owners" and here the Party made a number of proposals.[8]

First, "to break through short-termism", the possibility of "long-term investment agreements between companies and financial institutions" was mooted.[9] Secondly, the provision of a wider range of company information on research and development, capital investment, growth, etc. would, much Party literature argued, provide an antidote to a short-term and overly narrow focus on dividends, on the part of investment managers. Thirdly, the Party sought measures to counter the encouragement that the prevailing takeover culture had given to short-termism on the part of company managers. Thus it was argued that long-term investment, vital to the underlying strength of a firm, could be discouraged because managers were aware that, in the short run, it might have an adverse impact on dividend and share price and so render their company vulnerable to hostile takeover. To tackle this, the Labour Party put forward the idea of legislation to ensure that the "bidding company" proved that the proposed takeover "would increase efficiency and serve the public interest".[10] Thus, rather than the onus being on a Monopolies Commission to substantiate that the takeover was not in the national interest, the burden of proof would rest with the predatory company. This, it was argued, would insulate company managers, in some measure, from the short-term pressures mentioned and it would also encourage companies to seek to grow by way of investment and efficiency gains rather than simply by acquisition, as had all too often been the case in the past.

The rise in the level and change in the nature of investment effected by such policies would lay the basis for that upgrading of industrial and human capital which Party literature in the late 1980s and early 1990s increasingly stressed was the key to international competitiveness and thence prosperity. Here, emphasis was placed on an acceleration in the pace of technological innovation – a stress strongly reminiscent, in many respects, of the Wilsonian vision of the 1960s. However, as regards improving the quality of factor inputs it was upon investment in people that the greatest emphasis was laid. Indeed it has been argued repeatedly in recent party literature that it is the quality of the workforce that is now the essential determinant of international competitiveness. Thus according to *Labour's economic approach* (1993), as "capital is more than ever a global commodity, *highly skilled labour is now finally acknowledged to be the critical resource.*" Given this, to "enhance the value of labour [is] a policy objective which is the key . . . to a successful economy." The point was also made forcefully in a recent Fabian pamphlet by the shadow chancellor Gordon Brown. As he saw it, "in the modern global economy, where capital, raw materials and technology are internationally mobile and tradeable worldwide, it is people – their education and skills – that are necessarily *the most important determinant of economic growth.*"[11] The consequent policy corollary, pushed strongly by Labour, was that there should be a substantial increase in investment in education and training and to that end it proposed, among other things, that "all employers, except for small businesses, [should] be obliged to invest a minimum amount on training their workforce" or be required to "make a contribution to the local or national training effort"; such a penalty being essential to prevent "free riders" who poach the human products of the training investment of others.[12]

All this is undoubtedly laudable. Given that, as regards its labour force, "two thirds of workers have no vocational or professional qualification at all" and that Britain is almost at the bottom of the OECD skills league table, the implementation of such a policy can be seen as long overdue.[13] For all that it must be said in passing that the central proposition upon which these proposals rest is problematic: the view that skilled labour is the decisive determinant of competitiveness because of its immobility must be seen as a questionable assumption. For, if capital is mobile, so too are the well trained and highly skilled. This has two implications. First, highly skilled labour once trained, can flow out. Alternatively, if, as Labour's most recent policy document argues, "technology, raw materials and capital can be bought from anywhere", so too, presumably, can high-grade human capital.[14] As a case in point, the Commission on Social Justice itself noticed the fact that "highly skilled computer software designers" in Bangalore were "linked by satellite to western clients". [15] Further, to write of the mobility of international capital does not distinguish between capital as investment funds and capital as new technology. The former is undoubtedly mobile if the requisite price is paid; the mobility of the latter depends on a number of factors, in particular government policy, and cannot be taken for granted. Thus, in this second sense, Gordon Brown's view that "capital" is "internationally mobile" is certainly open to question. This is not to decry the need for a substantial increase in investment in training to circumvent bottlenecks in the supply of skilled labour but to place such emphasis upon it as *the* key to enhanced competitive performance is an unnecessary overstatement of the case reminiscent, in a peculiar way, of the labour theory of value. In particular, it ignores, or at least downplays, all that has to be in place before a supply of high-grade human capital can be effectively utilized. It should be said though that such an overemphasis is avoided by the Commission on Social Justice, which specifically stated that "it would be foolish to believe that skills are enough to build competitive strength. However good the skills they will be wasted if tools are poor."[16]

This critical point aside, what strikes one powerfully when reading the most recent economic literature of the Labour Party is the magnitude of the shift in policy emphasis that has occurred in recent years and the extent of the hegemony of the supply-side philosophy. A new economic discourse dominates. The socialist project is now articulated in the language of competition, efficiency, productivity, economic dynamism, profitability and, above all, that of individual choice and self-fulfilment in the context of a market economy. Of course, as regards Labour Party literature, it could be argued that such a discourse is not new. Elements of it can be found in the technocratic enthusiasms of the Wilson years and, to a lesser extent, in Webbian Fabianism. Further, a preparedness to use the competitive market for socialist ends has, as we have seen, loomed large in policy documents from the late 1930s onwards. What is different, though, is the extent to which this language now infuses all discussion of economic questions – often to the exclusion of those ideological markers which traditionally indicated that what was being read was the literature of a putatively socialist Party.

Along with competition and efficiency, choice and freedom are now the words most often engraved by New Labour on its signposts to the New Jerusalem. A few examples from the literature must suffice. The Party's *Agenda for change* (1992) looked to "a society in which it is possible for everyone to make *choices* that lead to *personal fulfilment and self-expression*" and emphasized the importance of giving people the "freedom to choose". "At the core of our convictions", stated the 1992 Manifesto, "is *a belief in individual liberty*" and consistent with this, there runs through Party literature a reiterated adherence to the kind of rational individualism akin to that to be found in classical political economy. Thus "because people have diverse needs and because *they are almost always the best judges of their own needs*, they must have a greater say in determining how needs are met."[17] Of course freedom has always been the fundamental socialist goal. But the pursuit of that goal has usually been seen as inseparably linked with ideas of equality and community, while in recent Labour Party literature that link has certainly become less apparent and more tenuous.

The link has also been made still weaker by the Party's continual emphasis on competition and by an increasing tendency to downplay the importance of public provision. The stress on increasing international competitiveness has already been noted. More generally discussion of the virtues of "competition" has sometimes verged on the kind of eulogy associated more often with the political economy of the Manchester School than with socialism. Thus the most recent economic policy document produced by the Party states: "Effective and fair competition in product markets reduces the prices that millions pay for the goods they buy and prevents the growth of entrenched and privileged institutions . . . Competition is also required between firms as a spur to innovation, investment and improved productivity – the real organs of a dynamic economy." In addition, "competition" is seen as having a fundamental role to play "in helping increase choice and raise standards". Giles Radice's desire for "as much competition as possible, government intervention where necessary" may be a somewhat crude rendition of New Labour's position but it does not fundamentally distort it.[18]

One wonders here what many of the socialist thinkers whose work has been discussed in this volume would have made of such panegyrics. Certainly these celebrations of a competitive ethos turn a blind or at least a myopic eye to some of the dangers that socialist thinkers have traditionally stressed – that by concentrating ownership, competition persistently threatens its own destruction and the growth of coercive monopoly power; that its casualties may be many while its winners are few; that it can foster instincts inimical to those that should prevail in a socialist community; that it can engender social antagonism and de-moralize society.

In this context too, it should be noted that the roles of public ownership and public provision have been played down. This has sometimes been portrayed as a pragmatic response to the intense and competing demands upon resources that will confront a Labour government: as one commentator has put it, given the scale of privatization and "given the constraints on resources it would simply be impossible for a Labour government to take large manufacturing and service companies into public ownership. There would be far more urgent priorities for resources available to a Labour government."[19] Yet, given the general thrust of New Labour's political economy one suspects that such views make a pragmatic virtue out of an ideological predilection. Now, in Labour Party literature, the emphasis is on the regulation of private utilities such as electricity, gas and water, rather than their return to the public sector – an emphasis which, if it predates, has certainly been reinforced by the recent (1995) abandonment of Clause IV. Thus stress is now placed on the need for a tighter regulatory framework with greater opportunity for enforcing consumer rights and with institutional devices such as public hearings prior to price rises, to prevent the abuse of monopoly power.[20] More generally, the Labour Party has proposed regulation as an essential antidote to market failure. As it was put in *Labour's objects, socialist values in the modern world* (1994):

> it does not follow that common ownership is our reflex answer to all market failures. The central question should always be how we protect and advance the public interest in the efficient and equitable production of goods and services . . . ownership is not the only way to advance our goals, *regulation* affects how markets operate . . . The mixed economy depends on the *rules that govern markets* as well as on the size of the public sector[21]

or, as the Commission on Social Justice phrased it: "markets need to be *shaped and regulated in the common interest*, not abolished."[22] Fair competition, regulated markets, regulations governing the actions of producers, consumers' charters: these are the means by which New Labour seeks to guide the market to socialist ends and it is to a sanitized market that it now looks, primarily, to achieve its economic objectives.

Further, the idea has been mooted, within the Party, that social welfare provision might come from a plurality of sources – public, private and voluntary; that "some public services will be owned and run by government" while others will be "contracted to private or voluntary sectors".[23] Thus the Commission on Social Justice has envisaged a 'mixed economy' of "public service provision, combining the efforts of public, non-profit and private sectors" and the virtues of competition and choice are stressed in the defence of such recommendations.[24] Also, it has been argued that those services which remain in government and local authority hands should be subjected to pseudo-market pressures by way of institutions such as a Quality Commission, which "will ensure councils provide high quality, value-for-money services, with clear avenues of complaint and redress".[25] Where market forces do not exist, therefore, comparable consumer-generated pressures will be institutionally created and brought to bear on public providers.

As regards major infrastructural projects the Labour Party is also now insistent that these can best be undertaken through the partnership of public and private capital. Specifically, "public and private capital" should be brought "together to regenerate our public services". There should be "imaginative, new, public–private partnerships" to fund infrastructural projects such as high-speed railways, telecommunications and housing.[26] Thus there would be private sector involvement even in those areas of economic activity traditionally regarded by Labour as best left to the state and local authorities.

In general, it should be noted too that this language of partnership is part and parcel of a new corporatist rhetoric that often does service for the traditional ideals of fellowship and fraternity in the literature of New Labour. The old corporatism of the Keynesian consensus might be dead and buried but there are shades of a modern one in many of the Party's recent policy statements. That said, the new one is built around an altered set of objectives and, in consequence, the dynamics of the relationship between the participants which it presupposes are fundamentally different from those that characterized the corporatism and consensus of the 1950s and 1960s. If the old consensus was founded on an acceptance of full employment, enhanced social welfare provision and rising living standards as the essential objectives to be pursued, the consensual objective around which the new corporatism is to be constructed is that of international competitiveness or, to cite the title of a recent policy document, the objective of "*Winning for Britain*". In consequence, while in the 1950s and 1960s the crucial relationship in the corporatist triangle was that between government and the trade union movement, particularly when Labour was in power, now, with international competitiveness the overriding goal, the crucial relationship is seen as that between the government, the City and the CBI."Our first move in government", stated *Made in Britain* on the eve of the 1992 election, "will . . . be to bring together industry and finance into manufacturing partnership . . . Its goal will be to define the policies which industry needs; *to help the Department of Trade and Industry become an active, effective, department*; to ensure the consistency of government policy which British industry so badly needs."[27] In *A new economic future for Britain* (1995), the theme is very much the same. "We are sure", the document states, "that only through partnership, with government playing its *proper* role alongside shareholders, managers and workers, can success be realised."[28] In this instance, workers are at least mentioned as an element in the partnership necessary for industrial success, though it is interesting that the term "workers" is preferred to that of trade unions. Even so, under the new corporatism, it is quite clear the crucial relationship is to be that between the providers of finance, the providers of industrial leadership and the government. Certainly it is the views and the good opinion of these two groupings that the Party's leadership has been most assiduously acquiring and cultivating in recent years; at the same time it has sought to escape from its traditional relationship with, and dependency on, the trade union movement.

In this context, government's contribution to the partnership is largely conceived of in terms of framework provision; providing a framework within which business and finance can function freely, fairly and in an effectively competitive fashion. As it was put in the 1992 Manifesto, "Modern government has a strategic role, not to replace the market but to ensure that markets work *properly*." This might entail intervention "to set standards to protect consumers" to "improve training or safeguard the environment" but not intervention of a kind to short-circuit or supplant market forces.[29] Thus, with respect to the Party's overriding objective of economic modernization, "to achieve this in the new global market place, the job of government is neither to suppress markets nor to surrender to them but to equip people, companies and countries to succeed within them." In short, the objective is for government to play a facilitating role, ensuring that market participants are winners not victims.[30]

To what extent therefore can the charge be levelled against the Labour Party that it now seeks simply to manage a more competitive and a more efficient British capitalism better than the Tories? Do the policy developments that have been detailed represent the demise of anything that might be termed a socialist political economy within the Labour Party? Does the saga of socialist political economy and the Labour Party end here?

Against those who would answer in the affirmative New Labour's supply-siders have mounted a vigorous counterattack, the central argument of which is that efficiency and competitiveness and the classic socialist objectives of social justice, co-operation and even environmental concern are, essentially, two sides of the same ideological coin. By way of illustration, a few statements from Labour Party literature, before consideration is given to the implications for policy of this position. "Democratic socialism", stated *Labour's objects,* "sees *economic efficiency and social justice as complementary to one another, not opposites*; and links together action to attack poverty, increase employment, counter discrimination, curb unaccountable power and protect the environment." Or again, "in the modern economy, *social justice and economic efficiency are inseparable* . . . In today's world *fairness and efficiency go hand in hand.*"

Likewise co-operation and social cohesion are seen as productive of an enhanced competitive performance. For example: "co-operation between companies is as important as competition . . . The players in a modern economy . . . are interlinked and mutually dependent. Their success depends on the strength of the networks between producers, suppliers and investors. *Competitiveness is as much the product of co-operation as competition.*"[31] Similarly, it is argued by Gordon Brown that "businesses increasingly understand that in a modern, global economy, the policies necessary *to tackle growing inequality and social dislocation are the very same which are necessary to produce a dynamic and competitive economy.*" "At the heart of Labour's economic approach", therefore, there is now "a belief that a strong and flourishing economy demands a *strong* and socially just *society.*"[32] Or, in the words of the Commission on Social Justice: "social capital", which it defines as social "networks, norms and trust that facilitate co-ordination and co-operation for mutual benefit", "improves the efficiency with which market economies operate."[33] Further, to the extent that social cohesion prevails, the costs of social dislocation and discontent are minimized; "social cohesion has economic value, social division has economic cost."[34] As a riposte to the Thatcherite dictum that there is no such thing as society, New Labour has embraced the belief that without a cohesive society there can be no such thing as economic success.

Finally here, as regards environmental concern, there is an analogous equation of virtue and economic expediency. Thus in *Labour's economic approach*, it is clearly stated that: "social justice, *economic efficiency and environmental improvement go hand in hand.*"[35]

In this way the economic literature of New Labour conflates co-operation and competition, social cohesion and efficiency, social justice and economic success, social concern and economic advantage. What many socialists have seen, at least in some measure, as antagonistic the Labour Party in the 1990s portrays as mutually supportive. Where others have seen a tension or the possibility of conflict, supply-side socialists envisage a necessary consonance. But how, in policy terms, is the circle to be squared? How are traditional socialist goals and values to be reconciled with efficiency, competitiveness and winning for Britain?

As regards efficiency and social justice, emphasis has been placed, in large measure, on the expansion of economic opportunity and the higher remuneration that will result from increased investment in people. Thus a substantial part of the inequality that characterizes British society is seen as stemming from the fact that many have failed to receive the education and training that is a prerequisite for skilled, high-wage employment. In consequence, in an age when the accelerating pace of technological advance has created a surfeit of unskilled and semi-skilled, the disparities in "in-work" income have increased considerably. Further, it is argued, a significant part of the high levels of unemployment that have been experienced in the 1980s and 1990s derive from a diminution in unskilled or semi-skilled occupations. Investment in training and education would therefore result in a more fully-employed and better-remunerated labour force, in contrast to the low-wage, bargain-basement economy that Conservative policy has created. Investment in people will therefore, of itself, promote greater equality of incomes and social cohesion.

At the same time the creation of a highly skilled labour force will enhance the efficiency and thence the competitiveness of the British economy. As has already been pointed out, recent Labour literature has repeatedly stressed that suitably skilled labour is, and will be for the future, the crucial input in securing commercial advantage. Thus the same policies that expand opportunity and promote greater equity, as regards the remuneration of labour, will also serve to sharpen Britain's competitive edge. In the title of a Fabian pamphlet by Gordon Brown, "fair *is* efficient". Escape from a bargain basement economy is to be achieved by hopping on the elevator of social justice. "By investing in skills", through "lifelong learning", "we raise people's capacity to add value to the economy"; "the best indicator of the capacity of our economy tomorrow is the quality of our children today."[36]

Of course such a reconciliation of justice and efficiency also has its pedigree within the socialist tradition. Not all have seen these ideals as essentially antagonistic. Thus the "old" Fabians also saw inequality of remuneration as stemming, in large measure, from a "rent of ability": that is as a rental payment that derived from the monopoly of scarce talents or skills by a few. Under socialism, with a widening of educational opportunity and the general skilling of the population, they believed this rental element of wages would be eliminated, or at least greatly reduced. The Fabians also considered, as do New Labour theoreticians, that the material gains deriving from greater efficiency would provide the wherewithal for the provision of those social services that were considered a vital element of the socialist project. Only efficiency could breathe life back into a gradualist social democratic pursuit of social justice.

However, the crucial difference between the Fabians and New Labour is that the former predicated what they proposed on the transference of economic power to the state and municipalities; something that would give socialists command over the necessary resources to effect a widening of educational opportunity and the expansion of social welfare provision. Thus when it came to allocating scarce resources amongst competing ends, it was to be a socialist government or socialist municipalities that would determine what those ends would be. Any tendency on the part of the private sector to short-termism or free-riding would simply not exist as private enterprise itself would be of limited significance. Also, with a substantial extension of public ownership, the early Fabians could be assured that whatever economic surplus derived from the efforts of an effectively trained labour force would accrue not to those who employed it but to society as a whole. Thus, if the early Fabians reconciled or sought to reconcile justice and efficiency/competitiveness, it was with a macroeconomy in mind very different from that envisaged by New Labour, specifically one through which they could feel certain that a Labour government would have the power to ensure the requisite investment in increasing efficiency and to guarantee that what was created by social production would be used for social ends.

As regards promoting social justice through the enhanced social provision that a more efficient, competitive economy would resource, the New Labour position must give the socialist reader of recent literature some cause for concern. Thus Giles Radice, in one of a series of Fabian Society pamphlets that focus upon the need to win back Essex Man to the Labour fold, advocated that: "future spending commitments, if they have to be made, should be made very cautiously indeed *and always with the maximum attention to electoral advantage.*"[37] Now it is true that there may not be an inevitable conflict between policies that promote greater social equity and those that advance the electoral prospects of the Labour Party but there is, at the very least, a tension. Further, one might expect a recognition of that fact to lead on to an unambiguous declaration in favour of prioritizing the former over the latter. In fact, Radice implied the opposite when he expressed scepticism as to the electoral advantage secured in southern England in the 1992 election from Labour's proposals to increase pensions and child benefits. Such proposals had not been cost-effective in electoral terms and that is something the Labour Party should bear in mind for the future when formulating its position on public expenditure. Thus the impression is conveyed that the economic gains that accrue to a Labour government from a reinvigoration of the supply side would not necessarily be utilized by reference to criteria that prioritized social equality.

Of course Radice may not be entirely representative of mainstream New Labour opinion, but where attempts are made to reconcile potentially antagonistic principles such as competitiveness and fairness, efficiency and equity, the absence from Labour Party literature of a unambiguous socialist language of priorities can lead to the kind of pitfall into which Radice has jumped with such enthusiasm. There is, at the very least, a tension between justice and efficiency and failure to acknowledge that leaves the reader of recent Party literature unclear as to which way a Labour government will bend when priorities have to be established and choices made. When the chips are down, as they so often are in relation to the British economy, just what will be regarded as essential in its economic and social programme and what is it prepared to jettison as superfluous to the success of the supply-side revolution it seeks?

If we take, for example, its avowed determination to expand the sphere of freedom and self-fulfilment, New Labour has been adamant that that is what socialism should be about. "We want", states *Agenda for change*, "a society which liberates people."[38] But what if the education or skilling necessary for personal liberation is not that required to produce a more efficient and competitive workforce? How will such a tension be resolved where it emerges? In many cases, it is true, there may indeed be no conflict. Thus where personal liberation is seen as residing in the greater access to high-wage employment that education provides, there may be no antagonism between freedom and efficiency. But one does not have to be an unrepentant Morrisite to suggest that education may, and in some respects must, be liberating in ways that have nothing to do with and may even conflict with the drive for efficiency. Indeed a cursory reading of R. H. Tawney, a name all too often on the lips and in the pamphlets of the present Labour leadership, would be sufficient to convince one on that score.

As regards co-operation and competitiveness, mention has already been made of the language of partnership and it has been argued that the location of power in the kind of partnership that Labour proposes casts doubt on its use of this term. As to policies, Labour has suggested the creation of many institutions that will promote the kind of co-operation or partnership that it has in mind: a Business Development Bank, regional investment banks, regional development agencies and, central to new Labour thinking, a National Economic Assessment that "will . . . allow employers, trade unions and other social partners to consider Britain's competitiveness and the competing claims on national output. These considerations will be an important influence on collective bargaining."[39] There is here, in microcosm, an illuminating juxtaposition of partnership/co-operation and competitiveness. Thus the "social partners" will co-operate in the discussion of resource allocation but, crucially, in the light of Britain's competitive position. That some benefit might accrue from it need not be queried, but the possibility of co-operation or social partnership where "competitiveness" is the sole, or at least the primary, point of reference must certainly be open to question. Again, there is an unacknowledged tension in this juxtaposition of potentially conflicting principles – co-operation and competition. In this context some resolution of the potential antagonism might have been sought by suggesting that discussions about competing demands upon resources could be pursued with reference *both* to Britain's competitive position *and* the pursuit of social equality. In fact the agenda of the national economic assessment is weighted in such a way as to militate against true partnership and real co-operation; it is also weighted in such a manner as to bias the outcome in favour of one set of interests. In general, New Labour in its conflation of antagonistic principles eschews the language of prioritization. But here, where such language is used, it is competitiveness that it is given precedence.

One final point should be made here with respect to co-operation and partnership. When such terms are used in Labour literature what is envisaged is not the ideal to which many nineteenth- and twentieth-century socialists would have subscribed, but much more the kind of functional interdependence that Adam Smith recognized as deriving from the enlightened pursuit of material self-interest. Thus in *Winning for Britain*, "the *players* in a modern economy" are seen as "*interlinked and mutually dependent.* Their success depends on the strength of the networks between producers, suppliers and investment. *Competitiveness is as much the product of co-operation as competition.*"[40] This is, in essence, co-operation in pursuit of private gain and while it may be unwise to decry the competitiveness it produces, co-operation of this kind has more in common with the collaboration of a pack intent on the kill than with the kind of co-operation or fellowship that someone like Tawney or Morris had in mind. This may not be a deliberate misappropriation of socialist vocabulary, but it still involves its debasement or, at the very least, its misuse.

Nor, in relation to partnership, is there any significant emphasis in Labour Party literature upon making efforts to redress the balance of power in the labour market that has, since 1979, swung so heavily in favour of employers. No suggestion, therefore, as to what might be done, as regards a restoration of trade union power, to lay the basis for a genuine partnership of equals. There are, of course, allusions to the repeal of some of the more offensive pieces of Tory, anti-trade-union legislation. There is also in the literature mention of increasing worker share-ownership. In addition, Labour seems to have committed itself to a national minimum wage of £3.40 per hour though debate still rumbles on within the Party with, on the one hand, concern being expressed as to the impact of this on employment and on the other trade union disgruntlement that a higher figure of £4.15 has not been accepted. But, as regards effecting a substantial shift of decision-making power within enterprises, it can be said that the kind of industrial democracy put forward by the Party in the 1970s and early 1980s is history. Now the emphasis is much more upon expanding the power and the freedom of the working class as consumers rather than producers. Further, in marked contrast to the guild socialists, for whom the interests of producers and consumers clash, many within the Party now believe that it is those of the consumer that must prevail. As one commentator has succinctly phrased it, "The freedom of consumers creates . . . imperatives that workers *cannot* escape." Here, at least, the consequences of adherence to the competitive ideal are made clear. It is the interests and "life-styles of the affluent and aspirant working-class" that must be accommodated. The problem has been that "Labour's proper concern with deprivation, injustice and poverty has meant that it seems out of touch with the culture of consumerism."[41] But what happens when the culture of compassion and sacrifice and the culture of consumerism come into conflict? Will the Labour Party ask Essex Man to accept a tithe on his affluence to mitigate the impoverishment of those less fleet of foot in the competitive race? If decisions on these matters are made solely with reference to what Radice has termed Labour's "southern [electoral] discomfort"[42] the answer to the latter question will surely be in the negative and then, in truth, those who subsequently write on the history of socialist political economy and the Labour

Party will take their story no further than where this text ends.

Lastly, as regards clean, green socialism, the literature suggests that that too can be reconciled, in policy terms, with efficiency and competitiveness because new environmental standards give scope for the development of environmental technologies – technologies that are seen as having a prosperous and growing future in the twenty-first century. "Environmental improvement offers an opportunity for British industry to move into the new environmental market."[43] This is an opportunity that the British government could promote by ensuring that it is in the vanguard as regards the setting and enforcement of environmental standards. This would give those companies specializing in environmental technologies the home market necessary to support the kind of productive capacity that would give them a competitive edge in global markets. It has also been argued, by the Commission on Social Justice, that "companies and countries which lead the way in raising environmental standards, gain a competitive advantage in increasingly environmentally aware markets".[44] But, if adherence to high environmental standards were to impinge upon the goal of international competitiveness, it is not immediately apparent how the Labour Party would suggest such a conflict should be resolved. Again, one searches in the literature for an unambiguous language of priorities.

All then is for the best in the best of all possible economic worlds. Virtue can be squared with material advancement and principle with expediency. Of course, where "fair *is* efficient", this must be so and socialism no longer entails prioritization in a context of conflicting objectives. In such circumstances the interest of the strong and that of the weak become essentially the same and a basis is laid for a social consensus and a social cohesion that will militate in favour of economic success. All will participate in "winning for Britain" when all see winning as promoting the general good. In such circumstances there would be no basis for social conflict and the way would lie open for a socialism without sacrifice and without tears.

What place, then, will the welfare state occupy in this scheme of things and the general pursuit of social justice? Here, it is clear that one of the salient characteristics of New Labour literature is its emphasis on equality of opportunity rather than equality of outcome. Of course the argument is that to the extent that the former is really achieved the latter will follow or at least be approached. Thus, Labour's social welfare proposals are integrally related to their emphasis on investment in human capital. To the extent that education and training furnish an adaptable, well-motivated, highly skilled and well-remunerated labour force – to that extent the problems of poverty and social injustice will be considerably reduced. As the Commission on Social Justice has put it, "social justice cannot be achieved through the social security system alone; employment [and] education . . . are at least as important as tax and benefit policy in promoting financial independence." "At the heart of the strategy is the belief that the extension of economic opportunity is not only the source of economic prosperity but also the basis of social justice."[45]

It is in this context, it is argued, that the role of the welfare state should be seen; social welfare policies should be used to put people in a position where they can take advantage of the opportunities that a rejuvenated supply side will create. What is wanted is a system of social welfare provision that will furnish the requisite support and incentives to move people back into gainful employment: a welfare to work strategy. To that end the Commission on Social Justice has sought in its proposals on social insurance and child benefit "to reduce dependence on means-tested benefits to a minimum" and so eliminate the situation where those who secure gainful employment may find, "with the withdrawal of means-tested benefits" that they are paying marginal rates of tax of 70 per cent plus. Rather than thus encouraging dependence, social welfare provision should be seen as a "fitness centre to make possible the extension of life chances"; a means of enabling individuals to seize the opportunities available whether in the form of education and training or in intermediate labour markets, or in part-time or full-time employment. Welfare to work and the greater equality and range of opportunity which that would provide – this is the unifying theme that runs through New Labour's vision of the future welfare state. "The welfare state needs actively to facilitate change and reduce rigidity by promoting opportunities and life chances across the life-cycle for all citizens."[46] There is also a clear indication in Party literature that those who fail to accept the opportunities provided will be penalized by the reduction of benefits. If its function is still seen as that of providing support, the emphasis is now more on its role as enabler. What would happen if the costs of fulfilling the latter function impinged on its capacity to fulfil the former is not immediately apparent. Again there seems to be an unwillingness to confront the tensions and potential conflicts inherent in what is proposed.[47]

Such is the economic world of New Labour, where potential conflicts between objectives are resolved by the simple expedient of insisting that if only we look hard enough we will see that all goals are, in fact, complementary. But as regards the future conduct of economic policy New Labour's supply-side socialists would do well to bear three things in minds. First, the economic world can be a wicked place, wicked in its unpredictability and particularly wicked to the economically weak. In such a world it may be salutary to remember that the Labour Party was created to protect that constituency and, in a situation where resources are always scarce in relation to competing ends, New Labour should acknowledge that sacrifices, when required, must be made by the economically powerful. Secondly, supply-side socialists should recognize too that "winning for Britain" is a means, not an end, and a language of priorities must ultimately be used in determining what ends are to be seen as primary. Finally, the New Labour supply-siders, in their unrelenting pursuit of an economically dynamic Britain, would do well, on occasion, to meditate upon the words of John Ruskin. "It is a good and desirable thing truly to make many pins in a day. But if we could only see with what crystal sand their points are polished – sand of human soul – we should think there might be some loss in it also. We blanch cotton and strengthen steel and refine sugar and shape pottery; but to brighten, to strengthen, to refine or to form a single living spirit never enters into our estimate of advantage."[48] Of course, to the extent that they do so, the quest for the Holy Grail of international competitiveness may come to seem an unutterably empty one.

Notes

Chapter 1

1. M. Morris (ed.), *William Morris, writer, artist, socialist,* [2 vols] (New York: Russell & Russell, 1966) vol.2, p. 113. Hyndman read a French translation of *Capital* in 1880.
2. H. M. Hyndman, *The economics of socialism* (London: Twentieth Century Press, 1896), p. 69.
3. *ibid.*, p. 157.
4. *ibid.*, p. 151.
5. *ibid.*, p. 179.
6. *ibid.*, p. 253.
7. E. J. Hobsbawm, "Hyndman and the S. D. F.", in *Labouring men, studies in the history of labour* (London: Weidenfeld & Nicolson, 1964), p. 234.
8. H. M. Hyndman & W. Morris, *A summary of the principles of socialism* (London: Modern Press, 1884), p. 23.
9. G. D. H. Cole, *Marxism and anarchism, 1850–1890* (London: Macmillan, 1974), p. 410.
10. S. D. Macintyre, *A proletarian science, Marxism in Britain, 1917–33* (Cambridge: Cambridge University Press, 1980), p. 221.
11. William Morris, "How I became a socialist", 1894, in *Lectures on socialism,* vol.23 of *Collected works* [24 vols], (London: Longman, 1915), p. 277; written by William Morris in his diary, 15 February 1887, in *William Morris*, M. Morris (ed.), vol.2, p. 173.
12. William Morris, "Art and the people", 1883, in *William Morris*, M. Morris (ed.), vol.2, p. 383; *Liberty*, May 1895, in *ibid.*, vol.2, p. 525.
13. See, for example, William Morris, "Useful work and useless toil", 1884, in *Signs of change*, vol.23 of *Collected works*, pp. 98–120.
14. William Morris, "How we live and how we might live" in *ibid.*, p. 118.
15. William Morris, "Dawn of an epoch" in *ibid.*, p. 136.
16. William Morris, "At a picture show", 1884, in *William Morris*, M. Morris (ed.), vol.2, p. 129.
17. Morris, "How we live", p. 5.
18. *ibid.*, p. 7.
19. William Morris, review of Edward Bellamy's *Looking backward*, *Commonweal*, 22 June 1889 in A. L. Morton, *The political writings of William Morris* (London: Lawrence & Wishart,1984), p. 253.
20. William Morris, "What socialists want", 1888, in E. Lemire, *The unpublished lectures of William Morris* (Detroit: Wayne State University Press, 1989), p. 236.

21. William Morris, "True or false society", in *Lectures on Socialism*, pp. 233–4.
22. Morris, "What socialists want", p. 231.
23. William Morris, "Makeshift" in *William Morris*, M. Morris (ed.), p. 480, my emphasis.
24. A. N. Lyons, *Robert Blatchford* (London: Clarion, 1910), p. 108.
25. *Clarion*, 10 June 1899, my emphasis; *ibid.*, 28 February 1913.
26. R. Blatchford, *Merrie England* (London: Clarion, 1894), pp. 43–4, my emphasis.
27. R. Blatchford, *The living wage and the law of supply and demand* (London: Clarion, 1895), p. 4, my emphasis.
28. Blatchford, *Merrie England*, pp. 20, 38, 134, my emphasis.
29. Blatchford, *The living wage*, p. 3.
30. A reprint of the *Manifesto of the Socialist League* can be found in E. P. Thompson, *William Morris, romantic and revolutionary* (London: Lawrence & Wishart, 1955).
31. Blatchford, *Merrie England*, p. 33.
32. Blatchford, *Britain for the British* (London: Clarion, 1906), p. 143, my emphasis.
33. Blatchford, *Merrie England*, p. 100.

Chapter 2

1. G. B. Shaw, "The common sense of municipal trading", 1902, in *Essays in Fabian socialism*, G. B. Shaw (ed.) (London: Constable, 1949), p. 199.
2. See, for example, J. A. Hobson, *The problem of the unemployed* (London: Methuen, 1896); *The economics of distribution* (London: Macmillan, 1900); and *Imperialism, a study* (London: Allen & Unwin, 1902).
3. S. Olivier, "Capital and land", *Fabian Tract*, 7, 6th edn, 1904, p. 12.
4. S. Webb, "English progress towards social democracy", *Fabian Tract*, 15, London, 1892, p. 5.
5. J. Burns, "The unemployed", *Fabian Tract*, 47, London, 1893, p. 6; G. B. Shaw, "Report on Fabian policy", *Fabian Tract*, 70, London, 1896, p. 11; A. Besant, "Industry under socialism", 1889, in *Fabian essays*, G. B. Shaw (ed.) (London, Allen & Unwin, 1962), p. 192.
6. S. & B. Webb, *A constitution for the socialist commonwealth of Great Britain* (London: Longmans, 1920), p. 342.
7. A. Maude, "Municipal trading", *Fabian Tract*, 138, London 1908, p. 18.
8. S. & B. Webb, *Industrial democracy*, 2nd edn (London: Longman, 1920), p. 674.
9. G. B. Shaw, "The economic basis of socialism" in *Fabian essays*, p. 43.
10. Besant, "Industry under socialism", p. 190; S. Webb, "The difficulties of individualism", *Fabian Tract*, 69, London, 1896, p. 5.
11. Shaw, "The economic basis of socialism", p. 52.
12. G. B. Shaw, "The transition to social democracy", in *Essays in Fabian socialism*, p. 40.
13. Besant, "Industry under socialism", p. 191.
14. G. B. Shaw, "Fabian Election Manifesto", *Fabian Tract*, 40, London, 1892, p. 4.
15. Webb, "The difficulties of individualism", p. 5.
16. Fabianism has sometimes been categorized as, literally, "milk and water socialism" in that these (and gas) were the kind of municipal enterprises that they supported and encouraged.
17. Webb, "English progress towards social democracy", p. 14; Besant, "Industry under

socialism", p. 185, my emphasis.
18. *The Minority Report of the Poor Law Commission, Part 2: The unemployed* (London: HMSO, 1909), pp. 1195, 1198, my emphasis.
19. *ibid.*, p. 1177, my emphasis.

Chapter 3

1. A. J. Penty, *The restoration of the gild system* (London: Swan & Sonnenschien, 1906), p. 7, my emphasis.
2. *ibid.*, p. 57.
3. *ibid.*, p. 77.
4. *ibid.*, p. 95.
5. *ibid.*, pp. 73, 100.
6. S. G. Hobson, *National guilds, an inquiry into the wage system and the way out* (London: Bell, 1914), p. 54.
7. *ibid.*, p. 153.
8. *ibid.*, p. 219.
9. *ibid.*, pp. 100, 222.
10. *ibid.*, p. 278.
11. *ibid.*, pp. 5, 171.
12. *ibid.*, p. 135.
13. *ibid.*, pp. 132, 225.
14. *ibid.*, p. 273.
15. G. D. H. Cole, *Self-government in industry* (London: Bell, 1917), p. 207.
16. *ibid.*, p. 280.
17. *ibid.*, p. 302.
18. *ibid.*, p. 53.
19. *ibid.*, pp. 8, 20.
20. *ibid.*, pp. 192–3.
21. *ibid.*, p. 272.
22. B. Holton, *British syndicalism, 1900–14, myths and realities* (London: Pluto, 1976).

Chapter 4

1. J. A. Hobson, *The economics of unemployment* (London: Allen & Unwin, 1922), pp. 8–9.
2. J. A. Hobson, *The evolution of modern capitalism, a study of machine production*, 4th edn (London: Allen & Unwin, 1926), pp. 407, 413.
3. *ibid.*
4. J. A. Hobson, *The crisis of liberalism* (London: King, 1909), p. 132.
5. J. A. Hobson, H. N. Brailsford, E. F. Wise, A. Creech Jones, *The living wage* (London: Independent Labour Party, 1926), p. 3.
6. *ibid.*, p. 10.
7. *ibid.*, p. 33.
8. *ibid.*
9. *ibid.*, pp. 33–4.

10. *ibid.*, p. 45.
11. Labour Party, *Report of the Labour Party Annual Conference* (London, 1928), p. 221.
12. J. A. Hobson, *Incentives in the new industrial order* (London: Parsons, 1922), pp. 36, 114.
13. *ibid.*, p. 159.
14. *ibid.*, p. 91.
15. Hobson et al., *The living wage*, p. 46.
16. *ibid.*
17. J. Strachey, *Revolution by reason* (London: Parsons, 1925), pp. 223–4, Strachey's emphasis.
18. *ibid.*, pp. 229–30.
19. *ibid.*, p. 35.
20. *ibid.*, pp. 135–6.
21. *ibid.*, p. 145.
22. *ibid.*, pp. 150, 179, my emphasis.
23. *ibid.*
24. *Report of the Labour Party Annual Conference* (1928), p. 264.

Chapter 5

1. R. H. Tawney, "Labour and capital after the war", 1910, in *The radical tradition, twelve essays on politics, education and literature* (London: Allen & Unwin, 1964), p. 101.
2. J. M. Winter & D. M. Joslin (eds), *R. H. Tawney's commonplace book* (Cambridge: Cambridge University Press, 1972), pp. 10, 68.
3. R. H. Tawney, *Equality* (London: Allen & Unwin, 1938), p. 212.
4. R. H. Tawney, *The acquisitive society* (London: Bell, 1921), p. 74.
5. *ibid.*, p. 81.
6. *ibid.*, p. 29.
7. Tawney, "Labour and capital after the war", p. 114.
8. Winter & Joslin, *R. H. Tawney's commonplace book*, p. 40.
9. *ibid.*, p. 18.
10. *ibid.*, pp. 56, 37, my emphasis.
11. Tawney, *Equality*, p. 208.
12. Tawney, *The acquisitive society*, p. 81, my emphasis.
13. Tawney, *Equality*, p. 141.
14. *ibid.*, p. 236.
15. Tawney, *Equality*, pp. 192, 237.
16. Tawney, "Labour and capital after the war", pp. 112, 107.
17. *ibid.*, p. 105, my emphasis.
18. *ibid.*, p. 113.
19. *ibid.*, p. 42.
20. Tawney, *Equality*, p. 273.
21. Tawney, *The acquisitive society*, p. 131.
22. Winter & Joslin, *R. H. Tawney's commonplace book*, p. 9.
23. *ibid.*, p. 62.

Chapter 6

1. J. R. MacDonald, *Socialism and society* (London: Independent Labour Party, 1905), p. 87.
2. *ibid.*
3. *ibid.*, p. 76; J. R. MacDonald, *Socialism, critical and constructive* (London: Waverley, 1921), p. 34.
4. MacDonald, *Socialism and society*, p. 103.
5. *ibid.*, p. 127, my emphasis.
6. *ibid.*, p. 156, my emphasis.
7. J. R. MacDonald, *Socialism*, 1907, in *Ramsay MacDonald's political writings*, B. Barker (ed.) (London: Allen Lane, 1972), p. 158, my emphasis; *Socialism and society*, p. 130.
8. *ibid.*, p. 57, my emphasis.
9. *ibid.*, p. 127, my emphasis.
10. *ibid.*, p. 172.
11. MacDonald, *Socialism*, p. 149; *Socialism, critical and constructive*, p. 152.
12. MacDonald, *Socialism and society*, p. 42.
13. *ibid.*, p. 154.
14. *ibid.*, my emphasis.
15. J. R. MacDonald, *Socialism after the war* (London: National Labour Press, 1918), p. 8.
16. *ibid.*, p. 11.
17. MacDonald, *Socialism, critical and constructive*, p. 143.
18. *ibid.*
19. MacDonald, *Socialism after the war*, p. 20, my emphasis.
20. MacDonald, *Socialism, critical and constructive*, pp. 148–9, my emphasis.
21. D. Marquand, *Ramsay MacDonald* (London: Jonathan Cape, 1976).
22. MacDonald, *Socialism, critical and constructive*, p. 115.
23. *ibid.*, p. 17, my emphasis.
24. MacDonald, *Socialism and society*, pp. 4, 5, my emphasis.
25. MacDonald, *Socialism*, p. 163; *Socialism and society*, pp. 87, 36.
26. *ibid.*, pp. 6–7, 183.
27. MacDonald, *Socialism, critical and constructive*, p. 153.
28. P. Snowden, *Socialism and syndicalism* (London: Collins, 1913), pp. 80, 42.
29. P. Snowden, *Labour and the new world* (London: Waverley, 1921), p. 2.
30. Snowden, *Socialism and syndicalism*, p. 133.
31. *ibid.*, p. 57.
32. *ibid.*, pp. 106–71.
33. Snowden, *Labour and the new world*, p. 111.
34. *ibid.*
35. Snowden, *Socialism and syndicalism*, p. 117.
36. P. Snowden, "The socialist budget, 1907", in James Kier Hardie, *From socialism to serfdom* (Hassocks: Harvester, 1974), p. 7.
37. Snowden, *Labour and the new world*, p. 9.
38. *ibid.*, pp. 180–81.
39. Snowden, *Socialism and syndicalism*, p. 89.
40. *ibid.*, p. 80.
41. Snowden, *Labour and the new world*, p. 183, my emphasis.

42. *ibid.*, p. 185.
43. *ibid.*, p. 187, my emphasis.
44. Snowden, *Socialism and syndicalism*, p. 78.
45. *ibid.*, pp. 15, 80.
46. *ibid.*, pp. 133–4.
47. *ibid.*, p. 84.
48. *ibid.*, pp. 174–5; *Labour and the new world*, p. 162.

Chapter 7

1. Labour Party, *Labour and the new social order* (London, 1918), pp. 20–21, my emphasis.
2. *ibid.*
3. *ibid.*, p. 43.
4. *ibid.*, p. 4.
5. *ibid.*, p. 12.
6. *ibid.*, p. 5.
7. *ibid.*, p. 9.
8. *ibid.*
9. Reprinted in the Labour Party's *Unemployment, a Labour policy* (London, 1921), pp. 10–11.
10. *Labour and the new social order*, p. 10.
11. Labour Party, *Unemployment, the Peace and the indemnity* (London, 1921), p. 3.
12. *ibid.*, p. 6.
13. *Unemployment, a Labour policy*, p. 8.
14. *ibid.*
15. *ibid.*
16. *ibid.*, p. 9.
17. *ibid.*, p. 9, my emphasis.
18. Labour Party, *On the dole or off?* (London, 1926), p. 12.
19. *ibid.*
20. *ibid.*, my emphasis.
21. *On the dole or off?* pp. 12–13.
22. *ibid.*
23. Labour Party, *Work for the workless* (London, 1924), p. 10, my emphasis.
24. Labour Party, *Labour and the nation* (London, 1928), pp. 8, 16, 31, 8, my emphasis.
25. *ibid.*, p. 25.
26. *ibid.*, p. 23.
27. *ibid.*, p. 42.
28. Labour Party, *How to conquer unemployment* (London, 1929), p. 10.
29. *ibid.*, p. 5.
30. *ibid.*, p. 7.
31. Labour Party, *Report of the Labour Party Annual Conference* (London, 1928), p. 231, my emphasis.
32. *Labour and the nation*, p. 43.
33. *ibid.*, p. 7, my emphasis.
34. *ibid.*, pp. 16, 8, 35.

Chapter 8

1. Winston Churchill, Budget Speech, April 1925.
2. See, for example, R. McKibbin, "The economic policy of the second Labour government, 1929–31", *Past and Present* **68**, 1975, pp. 85–123.
3. J. Strachey, "The future of the parties", *Week-End Review* (22 March 1930), p. 51; J. Strachey, "The coming session – and after", *Week-End Review* (25 October 1930), p. 571.
4. See R. Skidelsky, *Oswald Mosley* (London: Macmillan, 1975), p. 199. By the time of the publication of the Manifesto this Executive Committee was to be comprised of five "economic overlords".
5. On the political and administrative dimensions of Mosley's proposals see J. Strachey & C. E. M. Joad, "Parliamentary reform; the New Party's proposals", *Political Quarterly* **2**, 1931, pp. 319–36.
6. Quoted from W. F. Mandle, "Sir Oswald Mosley leaves the Labour Party, March 1931", *Labour History* **12**, 1967, p. 37.
7. Labour Party, *Report of the Labour Party Annual Conference* (London, 1930), p. 172.
8. A. Bevan, A. Young, W. J. Brown, J. Strachey, *A national policy, an account of the emergency programme advanced by Sir Oswald Mosley* (London: Macmillan, 1931), p. 12.
9. *ibid.*, p. 17.
10. O. Mosley, *Daily Telegraph* (8 December 1930).

Chapter 9

1. E. Durbin, *New Jerusalems, the Labour Party and the economics of democratic socialism* (London: Routledge & Kegan Paul, 1985), p. 83. This is the definitive study of socialist political economy and the Labour Party in the inter-war period and this and the next chapter are heavily indebted to it.
2. M. Cole, "The society for socialist inquiry and propaganda", in *Essays in Labour history, 1918–39*, A. Briggs & J. Saville (eds) (London: Croom Helm, 1977), p. 201.
3. E. F. M. Durbin, *Purchasing power and trade depression: a critique of underconsumption theories* (London: Cape, 1933), p. 155.
4. *ibid.*, pp. 155–7, my emphasis.
5. *ibid.*, p. 159.
6. *ibid.*, p. 163.
7. *ibid.*
8. *ibid.*
9. *ibid.*, p. 109.
10. *ibid.*, p. 161, my emphasis.
11. *ibid.*, p. 177.
12. E. F. M. Durbin, *The problem of credit policy* (London: Chapman & Hall, 1935), pp. 239–40.
13. *ibid.*, pp. 136–7.
14. *ibid.*, p. 219.
15. *ibid.*, p. 226.
16. *ibid.*, p. 230.

17. *ibid.*, p. 237.
18. E. F. M. Durbin, *The politics of democratic socialism, an essay on social policy* (London: Routledge, 1940), p. 305.
19. *ibid.*
20. Durbin, *The problem of credit policy*, p. 217.
21. J. Meade, *An introduction to economic analysis and policy*, 2nd edn (Oxford: Oxford University Press, 1937), p. 2.
22. *ibid.*, pp. 38–9.
23. *ibid.*, p. 50.
24. *ibid.*, p. 57.
25. *ibid.*, pp. 77–8.
26. D. Jay, *The socialist case* (London: Faber, 1937).
27. *ibid.*, p. 192.
28. *ibid.*, pp. 219–20.
29. *ibid.*, p. 217.
30. J. Strachey, *A programme for progress* (London: Gollancz, 1940), pp. 54–5.
31. *ibid.*, p. 154.
32. G. D. H. Cole, *The next ten years in British economic and social policy* (London: Macmillan, 1929), p. 7.
33. G. D. H. Cole & E. Bevin, "The crisis", 1931, in G. D. H. Cole, *Economic Tracts for the Times* (London: Macmillan, 1932), p. 13, my emphasis.
34. *ibid.*
35. *ibid.*, p. 48–9.
36. G. D. H. Cole, "Public opinion and monetary policy", 1932, in Cole, *Economic Tracts*, p. 97.
37. *ibid.*, p. 99.
38. Cole & Bevin, "The crisis", p. 48.
39. Cole, "Public opinion and monetary policy", p. 101, my emphasis.
40. G. D. H. Cole, "The monetary factor and other factors", 1933, in *What everybody wants to know about money* (London: Gollancz, 1933), p. 523.
41. *ibid.*, p. 526, my emphasis.
42. G. D. H. Cole, *The intelligent man's guide through world chaos* (London: Gollancz, 1932), p. 338.
43. G. D. H. Cole, "The problem of consumers' credit", in *Studies in world economics* (London: Macmillan, 1934), pp. 110–11.
44. *ibid.*, Cole's emphasis.
45. G. D. H. Cole, "A study in world economics", in *Studies in world economics*, p. 4.
46. G. D. H. Cole, "Money and the world crisis", in *What everybody wants to know about money*, p. 113, my emphasis.

Chapter 10

1. Cole, *The intelligent man's guide*, p. 571.
2. B. Wootton, *Plan or no plan* (London: Gollancz, 1934), pp. 37, 102.
3. *ibid.*, p. 106.
4. *ibid.*, pp. 107–8.

5. *ibid.*, p. 31.
6. *ibid.*, p. 105.
7. *ibid.*, p. 149.
8. *ibid.*, p. 131.
9. *ibid.*, p. 143.
10. *ibid.*, p. 133.
11. *ibid.*, p. 246.
12. *ibid.*, pp. 243, 244, my emphasis.
13. *ibid.*, p. 271, my emphasis.
14. She was also very much in favour of the Morrisonian mode of extending it; see *Plan or no plan*, pp. 273–4.
15. *ibid.*, p. 303.
16. *ibid.*, p. 311.
17. *ibid.*, pp. 60–61.
18. *ibid.*, p. 283.
19. E. F. M. Durbin, *The politics of democratic socialism*, pp. 96, 91, 103, 93.
20. *ibid.*, p. 87.
21. Quoted from E. Durbin, *New Jerusalems* p. 177.
22. Durbin, *The politics of democratic socialism*, p. 303, my emphasis.
23. *ibid.*
24. Quoted from Durbin, *New Jerusalems*, p. 179.
25. *ibid.*
26. Durbin, *The problem of credit policy*, p. 219.
27. Durbin, *The politics of democratic socialism*, p. 147.
28. See Durbin, *New Jerusalems*, p. 178.
29. *ibid.*, p. 135.
30. See Durbin, *New Jerusalems*, p. 176.
31. J. Meade, *An introduction to economic analysis*, p. 197.
32. *ibid.*, p. 251, my emphasis.
33. See Durbin, *New Jerusalems*, p. 213.
34. Jay, *The socialist case*, p. 142.
35. *ibid.*, p. 237.
36. *ibid.*, p. 298, my emphasis.
37. *ibid.*, p. 315.
38. *ibid.*, p. 313.
39. *ibid.*, p. 333.
40. *ibid.*, p. 335.
41. Cole, "The problem of consumers' credit", p. 121, my emphasis.
42. Cole, *The intelligent man's guide*, p. 571.
43. G. D. H. Cole, "The debacle of capitalism' in *Recovery through revolution*, S. D. Schinahausen (ed.) (New York: Covici, 1933), pp. 32–3.
44. G. D. H. Cole, *Practical economics, or studies in economic planning* (Harmondsworth: Penguin, 1937), p. 254.
45. G. D. H. Cole, *The principles of economic planning* (London: Macmillan, 1935), p. 405.
46. *ibid.*, pp. 304, 309.
47. *ibid.*, pp. 312–13.
48. Cole, "The problem of consumers' credit", pp. 120–1.
49. Cole, *The principles of economic planning*, p. 89.

50. Cole, *Practical economics*, p. 26.
51. Cole, *The principles of economic planning*, p. 220.
52. Cole, "Towards a new economic theory", in *Studies in world economics*, p. 261.
53. *ibid.*, p. 262, my emphasis.
54. *ibid.*, p. 256.
55. Cole, *The principles of economic planning*, p. 339.
56. *ibid.*, p. 228.
57. *ibid.*, pp. 312–13, my emphasis.
58. Cole, "Towards a new economic theory", p. 262.
59. Cole, "Free trade and tariffs", 1932 in Cole, *Economic Tracts*, p. 69.
60. Cole, *The principles of economic planning*, p. 281.
61. *ibid.*, p. 285.
62. See Bibliography, p. 316
63. O. Lange, "On the economic theory of socialism", 1936, in *On the economic theory of socialism,* O. Lange &. F. Taylor (eds) (Minneapolis: University of Minnesota, 1938), p. 71.
64. *ibid.*, p. 51.
65. H. Dickinson, "Price formation in a socialist community", *Economic Journal* **43**, 1933, pp. 237–50.
66. E. F. M. Durbin, "Economic calculus in a planned economy", in *Problems of economic planning* (London: Routledge & Kegan Paul, 1949), pp. 142–3.
67. A. Lerner, "Statics and dynamics in socialist economies", *Economic Journal* **47**, 1937, p. 253.
68. Quoted from E. Durbin, *New Jerusalems*, p. 179.
69. Labour Party, *For socialism and peace* (London, 1934), p. 6, my emphasis. As Elizabeth Durbin has pointed out Hugh Dalton was deeply involved in the writing of this pamphlet, *New Jerusalems*, p. 212. In Chapters 11 and 12 of that work Durbin furnishes a superb, detailed discussion of the economic literature of the Labour Party in the 1930s, the filtration of economic ideas into policy documents and the process of policy formation.
70. *For socialism and peace*, p. 21
71. Labour Party, *Socialism and the condition of the people* (London:1934), p. 5; *For socialism and peace*, pp. 12, 17.
72. *For socialism and peace*, p. 6.
73. Labour Party, *Labour's immediate programme* (London, 1937), p. 1.
74. The ideas of E. F. Wise, Nicholas Davenport and Vaughan Berry fed through into this document, while Dalton and Bevin played a crucial role in formulating the plans for national development that it contained. See Durbin, *New Jerusalems*, pp. 214–22.
75. *Socialism and the condition of the people*, p. 10, my emphasis.
76. Labour Party, *Labour's financial policy* (London, 1935), p. 3.
77. *Socialism and the condition of the people*, p. 10; *For socialism and peace*, p. 14.
78. *For socialism and peace*, p. 26, my emphasis.
79. See also J. M. Keynes & H. Henderson *Can Lloyd George do it?* (London: Nation and Athenaeum, 1929).
80. *Labour's financial policy*, p. 5.
81. *For socialism and peace*, p. 21; *Labour's immediate programme*, p. 3.
82. Durbin, *New Jerusalems*, p. 244.
83. *ibid.*, p. 247.

Chapter 11

1. Labour Party, "Let us face the future", 1945, in F. W. S. Craig, *British General Election Manifestos, 1918–66* (Chichester: Political Reference Publications, 1970), p. 99.
2. *ibid.*, p. 102, my emphasis.
3. *ibid.*, p. 100.
4. J. Tomlinson, "Mr. Attlee's supply-side socialism", *Economic History Review* **46**, 1993, pp. 1–26.
5. *Economic Survey of 1947*, Cmd. 7046, para 27.
6. See J. Tomlinson, "The Iron Quadrilateral, political obstacles to economic reform under the Attlee government", *Journal of British Studies* **24**, 1995, pp. 90–111.
7. *Economic Survey of 1947*, para 2
8. A device particularly favoured by James Meade.
9. A. Cairncross, *Years of recovery, British economic policy, 1945–51* (London: Methuen, 1985), pp. 328, 352.
10. On this point see Tomlinson, "Mr. Attlee's supply-side socialism", p. 13.
11. See Cairncross, *Years of recovery*, p. 414.
12. *ibid.*, p. 87.
13. *ibid.*, p. 509.

Chapter 12

1. M. Shanks, "Labour philosophy and the current position", *Political Quarterly* **31**, 1960, p. 244.
2. R. Crossman, "Socialist values in a changing civilisation", *Fabian Tract*, 286, London, 1950, p. 11.
3. Socialist Union, *Socialism, a new statement of principles* (Harmondsworth: Penguin, 1952), p. 41.
4. R. Jenkins, *In pursuit of progress, a critical analysis of the achievements and prospects of the Labour Party* (London: Heinemann, 1953), p. 169; "Equality" in *New Fabian essays*, M. Cole & R. Crossman (eds) (London: Turnstile, 1952), p. 72.
5. Crossman, "Socialist values in a changing civilisation" and J. Strachey, *Contemporary capitalism* (London: Gollancz, 1956).
6. This argument is most fully developed in the opening chapters of C. A. R. Crosland's *The future of socialism* (London: Cape, 1956).
7. R. Jenkins, "Equality", p. 72.
8. C. A. R. Crosland, *The future of socialism* (London: Cape, 1964), pp. 14–19.
9. *ibid.*, pp. 346–7.
10. *ibid.*, p. 346.
11. C. A. R. Crosland, *The Conservative enemy, a programme of radical social reform for the 1960s* (London: Cape, 1962), p. 121.
12. This was the clause that committed Labour to the common ownership of the means of production, distribution and exchange.
13. R. Acland, B. Castle, R. Crossman, I. Mikardo et al., *Keeping left* (London: New Statesman, 1950), p. 30.
14. A. Bevan, *In place of fear* (London: Heinemann, 1952), p. 30.

15. H. Gaitskell, "Socialism and nationalisation", *Fabian Tract*, 300, London, 1956, p. 25.
16. Socialist Union, *Socialism, a new statement of principles*, p. 55.
17. *ibid.*
18. Gaitskell, "Socialism and nationalisation", p. 27.
19. Socialist Union, *Twentieth century socialism* (Harmondsworth: Penguin, 1956), p. 91.
20. Jenkins, *In pursuit of progress*, p. 175.
21. Jenkins, "Equality", p. 84.
22. C. A. R. Crosland, "The function of public enterprise", *Socialist Commentary*, (February 1950), p. 28.
23. Crossman, "Socialist values in a changing civilisation", p. 11.
24. Gaitskell, "Socialism and nationalisation", p. 18.
25. *ibid.*, p. 10.
26. Jenkins, *In pursuit of progress*, p. 175.
27. *ibid.*, pp. 104–5, my emphasis.
28. Strachey, *Contemporary capitalism*, p. 180.
29. *Hansard*, vol. 539, col. 51, 28 March 1955.
30. J. Strachey, "Marxism revisited II", *New Statesman* (23 May 1953).
31. J. Strachey, "The object of further socialization", *Political Quarterly* **24**, 1953, pp. 74–5.
32. J. Strachey, "The new revisionist", *New Statesman* (6 October 1956); letter to *Socialist Commentary* (September 1957), p. 22, my emphasis.
33. A. Bevan, "Democratic values", *Fabian Tract*, 282, London, 1950, p. 9.
34. Acland et al., *Keeping left*, p. 4, my emphasis.
35. Gaitskell, "Socialism and nationalisation", p. 34.
36. Jenkins, "Equality", pp. 82–3.
37. J. Strachey, speech at Cumnock, 17 June 1951; *Contemporary capitalism*, p. 192.
38. Crosland, *The future of socialism*, pp. 351–2.
39. *ibid.*, p. 345.
40. *ibid.*, p. 346–7.
41. J. Meade, *Planning and the price mechanism, the liberal socialist tradition* (London: Allen & Unwin, 1948), p. 56.
42. *ibid.*, p. 5.
43. Jenkins, *In pursuit of progress*, p. 136.
44. J. Meade, "Maintenance of full employment", 1943, in S. Howson (ed.), *Employment and inflation*, vol.1 of *The collected papers of James Meade* (London: Unwin Hyman, 1988).
45. Jenkins, *In pursuit of progress*, p. 179, my emphasis.
46. Socialist Union, *Twentieth century socialism*, p. 77.
47. Meade, *Planning and the price mechanism*, p. ix.
48. Socialist Union, *Twentieth century socialism*, p. 70.
49. J. Strachey, "The British experiment: a social ejection mechanism", unpublished chapter of *Contemporary capitalism*, 1954.
50. Acland et al., *Keeping left*, p. 32.
51. R. Crossman, "Labour in the affluent society", *Fabian Tract*, 325, London, 1960, pp. 4–5.
52. G. D. H. Cole, *Socialist economics* (London: Gollancz, 1950), p. 47.
53. *ibid.*, pp. 49–50.
54. *ibid.*, p. 53, my emphasis.
55. B. Wootton, *Freedom and planning* (London: Allen & Unwin, 1945), p. 68.
56. *ibid.*, p. 63.

57. Cole, *Socialist economics*, p. 89.
58. Wootton, *Freedom and planning*, pp. 95, 98.
59. *ibid.*, p. 104.
60. Acland et al., *Keeping left*, p. 39, my emphasis.
61. Wootton, *Freedom and planning*, p. 106.
62. *ibid.*, p. 127.
63. *ibid.*
64. *ibid.*, p. 129.
65. *ibid.*, pp. 128, 130.
66. Crossman, "Labour in the affluent society", p. 24.
67. *ibid.*, p. 9, my emphasis.
68. *ibid.*, p. 11.
69. *ibid.*, p. 15.
70. *ibid.*, p. 23.
71. Bevan, *In place of fear*, 153, pp. 47–8.
72. *ibid.*, p. 14.
73. Cole, *Socialist economics*, p. 74.
74. *ibid.*, p. 76.
75. Crosland, "The function of public enterprise", p. 30.
76. Crosland, *The future of socialism*, p. 102.
77. *ibid.*, p. 124.
78. *ibid.*, pp. 208–16, my emphasis.
79. Crosland, *The Conservative enemy*, pp. 16–18.
80. Meade, *Planning and the price mechanism*, p. 40; Jenkins, "Equality", p. 76.
81. *ibid.*, p. 83.
82. Gaitskell, "Socialism and nationalisation", p. 34.
83. Strachey, "The object of further socialization", pp. 68, 71.
84. Strachey, *Contemporary capitalism*, p. 192.
85. D. Jay, *Socialism in the new society* (London: Longman, 1962), p. 190.
86. *ibid.* For some of the major works of these writers in this period see Bibliography Part III.
87. *ibid.*, pp. 20, 178, my emphasis.
88. *ibid.*, p. 25, my emphasis.
89. *ibid.*, pp. 21, 181, my emphasis.
90. Durbin, *The politics of democratic socialism*, p. 119; Crosland, *The Conservative enemy*, p. 115.
91. *ibid.*, p. 122.
92. Socialist Union, *Twentieth century socialism*, p. 108.
93. Crosland, *The Conservative enemy*, p. 123.
94. J. Strachey, "Marxism revisited IV", *New Statesman* (23 May 1953).
95. Jenkins, *In pursuit of progress*, p. 154.
96. Crossman, "Socialist values in a changing civilisation", p. 11.
97. R. Crossman, "Towards a philosophy of socialism", in *New Fabian Essays*, p. 10.
98. Socialist Union, *Twentieth century socialism*, p. 21.
99. Socialist Union, *Socialism, a new statement of principles*, p. 11; *Twentieth century socialism*, p. 17.
100. *ibid.*, p. 144.
101. Socialist Union, *Socialism, a new statement of principles*, p. 57.

102. Crosland, *The future of socialism*, pp. 128–9, my emphasis; *The Conservative enemy*, p. 8.
103. *ibid.*, p. 102.
104. Bevan, *In place of fear*, p. 153.

Chapter 13

1. Labour Party, *Industry and society, Labour's policy on future public ownership* (London, 1957), p. 47, my emphasis.
2. Craig, *British General Election Manifestos*, pp. 148, 180.
3. *Industry and Society*, p. 42, my emphasis.
4. Labour Party, *Plan for progress* (London, 1958), p. 40.
5. *ibid.*, p. 48.
6. Labour Party, *Britain belongs to you* (London, 1959), in Craig, *British General Election Manifestos*, p. 201.
7. *Industry and Society*, p. 56.
8. *Britain belongs to you*, p. 201.
9. *Plan for progress*, p. 9.
10. *ibid.*, pp. 16–17.
11. *ibid.*, p. 15.
12. In particular A. A. Berle, *The twentieth century capitalist revolution* (London: Macmillan, 1955) – see *Industry and Society*, p. 26.
13. *Plan for progress*, p. 16.
14. *Britain belongs to you*, p. 202, my emphasis.
15. *Plan for progress*, p. 40.
16. *ibid.*, p. 35–7.
17. Labour Party, *Forward with Labour*, 1955, and *Britain belongs to you*, 1959, in Craig, *British General Election Manifestos*, pp. 180, 178, 197.
18. *Britain belongs to you*, p. 201, my emphasis.
19. Labour Party, *Signposts for the sixties* (London, 1961), p. 10.
20. The influence of Thomas Balogh was important here. It should also be said that Balogh was an influence on policy-making within the Labour Party throughout the 1960s and 1970s.
21. *Signposts for the sixties*, p. 16.
22. H. Wilson, "A Four Year Plan for Britain", *New Statesman* (24 March 1961), pp. 464, 468.
23. *Signposts for the sixties*, p. 15.
24. *ibid.*, p. 14.
25. *Britain belongs to you*, p. 202; *Signposts for the sixties*, pp. 34–5.
26. *ibid.*, p. 10.
27. H. Wilson, *The New Britain, selected speeches* (Harmondsworth: Penguin, 1964), pp. 10, 13, 50, 14, 12.
28. *ibid.*, p. 12.
29. *ibid.*, p. 18.
30. The "little Neddies" had been established for particular industries by the previous Conservative government. They comprised employers, trade unionists and civil servants and met to consider ways in which the development of an industry might be

fostered. At a national level such tripartite discussion was promoted under the auspices of the National Economic Development Office set up in 1962. Thus some of the corporatist institutions that Labour envisaged using in the business of planning had already been established by the Conservatives.

31. *The national plan*, HMSO, 1965, Cmnd. 2764.
32. Quoted from A. Graham, "Industrial policy" in *The Labour Government's economic record, 1964–70*, W. Beckerman (ed.) (London: Duckworth, 1970), p. 189.
33. *The national plan*, pp. 1–2.
34. R. Opie, "Economic planning and growth", in *The Labour Government's economic record*, Beckerman (ed.), p. 172.
35. C. Ponting, *Breach of promise, Labour in power, 1964–70* (London: Hamish Hamilton, 1989), p. 272.
36. An excellent account of the travails of Mintech is provided in R. Jenkins, *Tony Benn, a political biography* (London: Writers & Readers, 1980), pp. 111–38.
37. *Hansard*, vol. 638, cols 1038, 1040; *ibid.*, vol. 656, col 51.
38. M. Stewart, "The distribution of income", in *The Labour Government's economic record*, Beckerman (ed.), p. 107.

Chapter 14

1. S. Holland, *Beyond capitalist planning* (London: Blackwell, 1978), p. 148.
2. *ibid.*, p. 140.
3. *ibid.*, p. 141.
4. S. Holland, *The socialist challenge* (London: Quartet, 1975), p. 368.
5. *ibid.*, p. 55.
6. *ibid.*, p. 9, my emphasis.
7. *ibid.*, p. 150.
8. *ibid.*, p. 177, my emphasis.
9. *ibid.*, p. 120.
10. *ibid.*, p. 159.
11. *ibid.*, pp. 195, 197.
12. S. Holland, "Introduction" in *The state as entrepreneur*, S. Holland (ed.) (London: Weidenfeld & Nicolson, 1972), p. 3.
13. *ibid.*, p. 230.
14. *ibid.*, p. 224.
15. *ibid.*, p. 271.
16. *ibid.*, p. 306.
17. M. B. Brown, *From Labourism to Socialism, a political economy for Labour in the 1970s* (Nottingham: Spokesman, 1972), p. 55.
18. *ibid.*, p. 65.
19. *ibid.*, p. 59.
20. *ibid.*, p. 67.
21. *ibid.*, p. 203.
22. *ibid.*, pp. 205–6.
23. *ibid.*, pp. 218, 227.
24. *ibid.*, pp. 185–6.

25. *ibid.*, p. 233.
26. *ibid.*, p. 240.
27. *ibid.*, p. 227, my emphasis.
28. K. Coates and T. Topham, *New unionism, the case for workers' control* (Harmondsworth: Penguin, 1974), p. 29.
29. *ibid.*, p. 140.
30. *ibid.*, p. 233.
31. *ibid.*, p. 184.
32. K. Coates, *The crisis of British socialism* (Nottingham: Spokesman, 1972), p. 202.
33. C. A. R. Crosland, *Socialism now and other essays* (London: Cape, 1974), p. 49.
34. Coates, *The crisis of British socialism*, p. 46.
35. Coates and Topham, *New unionism*, p. 68.
36. *ibid.*, p. 63.
37. *ibid.*, p. 7; see M. B. Brown, *UCS: the social audit* (Nottingham: Institute for Workers' Control, 1971).
38. J. Jones, *The right to participate*, 1970, quoted in Coates and. Topham, *New unionism*, p. 202.
39. The adoption of import controls was certainly the advice given by Nicholas Kaldor to the Labour government in the mid-1970s.

Chapter 15

1. Crosland, *Socialism now and other essays*, p. 15; J. Meade, *The intelligent radical's guide to economic policy, the mixed economy* (London: Allen & Unwin, 1975), Preface.
2. Crosland, *Socialism now*, p. 18.
3. *ibid.*, pp. 54, 56.
4. C. A. R. Crosland, "A Social Democratic Britain", 1971, in *Socialism now*, pp. 248–9.
5. R. Jenkins, *What matters now* (London: Fontana, 1972), p. 92.
6. *ibid.*, p. 93.
7. Meade, *The intelligent radical's guide*, p. 38.
8. *ibid.*, p. 46.
9. *ibid.*
10. *ibid.*, pp. 50–51.
11. *ibid.*, pp. 153–4.
12. *ibid.*, p. 65.
13. *ibid.*, p. 46.
14. As an example of anti-statist literature emanating from those in the Labour Party see E. Luard, *Socialism without the state* (London: Macmillan, 1979).
15. Crosland, *Socialism now*, p. 37.
16. R. Jenkins, *What matters now*, pp. 30–31.
17. *ibid.*, p. 30.
18. *ibid.*, p. 35.
19. Crosland, *Socialism now*, p. 29.
20. *ibid.*, p. 33.
21. *ibid.*, p. 26.
22. *ibid.*, p. 249.

23. *ibid.*, pp. 39, 38.
24. *ibid.*, p. 49.
25. *ibid.*, p. 53.
26. Jenkins, *What matters now*, p. 90, my emphasis.
27. *ibid.*, p. 84.
28. *ibid.*, p. 15.
29. *ibid.*, p. 39.
30. *ibid.*, p. 47, my emphasis.
31. *ibid.*, pp. 53, 57.
32. *ibid.*, pp. 115–17, my emphasis.
33. *ibid.*, p. 22.
34. Meade, *The intelligent radical's guide*, pp. 119–20.
35. *ibid.*, pp. 88–9.
36. *ibid.*, p. 89.
37. Hodgson, *Labour at the crossroads: the political and economic challenge to the Labour Party in the 1980s* (London: Robertson, 1981), p. 20.

Chapter 16

1. Quoted from M. Hatfield, *The house the left built: inside Labour policy making* (London: Gollancz, 1978), p. 128.
2. Labour Party, *Programme, 1973* (London, 1973), pp. 33–4.
3. *ibid.*, p. 18, my emphasis.
4. *ibid.*, p. 19.
5. *ibid.*
6. *ibid.*, p. 33.
7. *ibid.*, p. 18.
8. *ibid.*, pp. 7, 13, my emphasis.
9. *ibid.*, p. 15.
10. *ibid.*, p. 16.
11. For an excellent discussion of this exchange see Hatfield, *The house the left built*, pp. 202–6.
12. *Programme, 1973*, p. 24, my emphasis.
13. *ibid.*, p. 27.
14. Labour Party, *Let us work together* (London, 1974), p. 3.
15. *ibid.*, pp. 10–11.
16. *ibid.*, p. 9.
17. *ibid.*
18. Quoted from Hatfield, *The house the left built*, p. 238.
19. *ibid.*, p. 240.
20. The seminal work here is A. W. Phillips, "The relationship between unemployment and the rate of change of money wages in the United Kingdom, 1861–1957", *Economica* **25**, 1958, pp. 283–99.
21. D. Laidler, "United Kingdom inflation and its background: a monetarist perspective" in *Inflation in the United Kingdom*, M. Parkin and M. Sumner (eds) (Manchester: Manchester University Press, 1976), p. 52.

22. *ibid.*, p. 55.
23. H. Wilson, *Final term, the Labour government, 1974–76* (London: Weidenfeld & Nicolson & Michael Joseph, 1979), pp. 267–8; J. Callaghan, *Time and chance* (London: Collins, 1987), pp. 425–6.
24. The "corset" was an attempt to control the growth of bank lending, and thence the rate of growth of the money supply, by controlling banks' interest-bearing eligible liabilities. Excessive growth of this component of a bank's balance sheet would result in its having to lodge non-interest-bearing, supplementary special deposits with the Bank of England.
25. A label used by A. Britton, *Macroeconomic policy in Britain, 1974–87* (Cambridge: Cambridge University Press, 1991), p. 20.
26. Britton, *Macroeconomic policy in Britain*, p. 34.
27. *ibid.*, p. 20.
28. M. Meacher, *Socialism with a human face, the political economy of Britain in the 1980s* (London: Allen & Unwin, 1982), p. 228.
29. *ibid.*, p. 171.
30. T. Benn, *Arguments for socialism* (Harmondsworth: Penguin, 1980), p. 157.
31. *ibid.*, p. 218.
32. Hodgson, *Labour at the crossroads*, p. 125.
33. *ibid.*, pp. 7, 3.
34. S. Aaronovitch, *The road from Thatcherism: the alternative economic strategy* (London: Lawrence & Wishart, 1981), p. 3.
35. Meacher, *Socialism with a human face*, p. 170.
36. *ibid.*, p. 86.
37. *ibid.*, p. xiii.
38. *ibid.*, p. 14.
39. *ibid.*, p. 102.
40. *ibid.*, p. 157, my emphasis.
41. *ibid.*, p. 82.
42. *ibid.*, p. 104.
43. *ibid.*, pp. 190, 183, my emphasis.
44. *ibid.*, p. 170.
45. *ibid.*, p. 82.
46. *ibid.*, p. 86.
47. *ibid.*, p. 88.
48. *ibid.*, p. 100.
49. *ibid.*, p. 153.
50. *ibid.*, p. 196.
51. *ibid.*, p. 234.
52. Hodgson, *Labour at the crossroads*, pp. 198, 201, my emphasis.
53. G. Hodgson, *The democratic economy* (Harmondsworth: Penguin, 1984), p. 87.
54. Hodgson, *Labour at the crossroads*, p. 202.
55. *ibid.*, p. 171.
56. *ibid.*, pp. 199, 139.
57. Hodgson, *The democratic economy*, p. 161.
58. Hodgson, *Labour at the crossroads*, p. 224.
59. Hodgson, *The democratic economy*, pp. 109, 208, 207.
60. *ibid.*, p. 75, my emphasis.

61. *ibid.*, p. 16.
62. *ibid.*, p. 206.

Chapter 17

1. G. Radice, *Labour's path to power, the new revisionism* (London: Macmillan, 1989), p. 115; A. Mitchell, "Political aspects of unemployment : the alternative policy", in *Unemployment*, B. Crick (ed.) (London: Methuen, 1981), p. 48; A. Mitchell, *The case for Labour* (London: Longman, 1983), p. 50, my emphasis.
2. B. Gould, J. Mills, S. Stewart, *Monetarism or prosperity?* (London: Macmillan, 1981), pp. 192–3, 202.
3. Mitchell, *The case for Labour*, p. 83.
4. *ibid.*, pp. 88, 89. See also A. Mitchell, *Competitive socialism* (London: Unwin, 1989), p. 52.
5. Gould et al., *Monetarism or prosperity?*, p. 24
6. Mitchell, *Competitive socialism*, p. 52.
7. *ibid.*, p. 62.
8. Gould et al., *Monetarism or prosperity?*, p. 193.
9. Mitchell, *Competitive socialism*, p. 53.
10. Gould et al., *Monetarism or prosperity?*, p. 178.
11. *ibid.*, pp. 192–3.
12. Mitchell, *The case for Labour*, p. 60.
13. Mitchell, *Competitive socialism*, p. 90.
14. R. Hattersley, *Choose freedom, the future for democratic socialism* (Harmondsworth: Penguin, 1987), p. 237.
15. *ibid.*, p. 241.
16. *ibid.*, pp. 248, 240.
17. Radice, *Labour's path to power*, p. 130.
18. *ibid.*, p. 117.
19. Mitchell, *The case for Labour*, p. 102.
20. Mitchell, *Competitive socialism*, p. 91.
21. Mitchell, *The case for Labour*, p. 108, my emphasis.
22. *ibid.*, p. 109.
23. *ibid.*, p. 104.
24. But see also A. Nove, *The economics of feasible socialism* (London: Allen & Unwin, 1983).
25. S. Estrin, "Future planning in the United Kingdom", in *Labour into the eighties*, D. Bell (ed.) (London: Croom Helm, 1980), p. 51.
26. *ibid.*, pp. 58–9.
27. Radice, *Labour's path to power*, p. 121.
28. Hattersley, *Choose freedom*, p. 111, my emphasis.
29. *ibid.*, p. 167.
30. B. Gould, *Socialism and freedom* (London: Macmillan, 1985), p. 53.
31. Mitchell, *Competitive socialism*, p. 52, my emphasis.
32. *ibid.*, pp. 99, 84, my emphasis.
33. *ibid.*, p. 94.
34. Hattersley, *Choose freedom*, pp. 22, 86, 97, my emphasis.

35. Radice, *Labour's path to power*, p. 101, my emphasis.
36. Gould, *Socialism and freedom*, p. 90.
37. *ibid.*, pp. 56, 60.
38. *ibid.*, p. 70, my emphasis.
39. *ibid.*, p. 105, my emphasis.
40. *ibid.*, p. 65.
41. Radice, *Labour's path to power*, p. 103; Mitchell, *Competitive socialism*, pp. 114–15, 116.
42. Hattersley, *Choose freedom*, p. 196; Radice, *Labour's path to power*, p. 103.
43. Mitchell, *The case for Labour*, pp. 114–17.
44. Radice, *Labour's path to power*, p. 95.
45. Hattersley, *Choose freedom*, p. 4; Mitchell, *The case for Labour*, p. 57.
46. *ibid.*
47. Hattersley, *Choose freedom*, pp. 234–5.
48. Gould, *Socialism and freedom*, p. 97, my emphasis.
49. Mitchell, *The case for Labour*, pp. 153, 157.
50. *ibid.*
51. *ibid.*, p. 154.
52. Radice, *Labour's path to power*, p. 158.

Chapter 18

1. Labour Party, *Rebuilding the economy* (London, 1994), p. 7; *Labour's economic approach* (London, 1993), p. 10.
2. Commission on Social Justice, *Social justice: strategies for national renewal* (London: Vintage, 1994), pp. 166, 155. "Our vision of national renewal is long term; we are looking ahead to 2010 and beyond."
3. Labour Party, *Made in Britain* (London, 1992), p. 3; *It's time to get Britain working again* (London, 1992), p. 12.
4. N. Kinnock, *Making our way* (Oxford: Blackwell, 1986), pp. 55–7.
5. Labour Party, *Made in Britain*, pp. 17; *ibid.*, p. 16; *Britain working again*, p. 11; *Made in Britain*, p. 3; *Making Britain's future* (London, 1993), pp. 3, 10, my emphasis.
6. *Making Britain's future*, p. 11.
7. *ibid.*, p. 5.
8. Labour Party, *Winning for Britain, Labour's strategy for industrial success* (London, 1993), p. 1.
9. *Labour's economic approach*, p. 19.
10. Labour Party, *A new economic future for Britain* (London, 1995), p. 33.
11. *Labour's economic approach*, p. 9; G. Brown, "Fair is efficient: a socialist agenda for fairness", *Fabian Pamphlet*, 563, London, 1994, p. 1, my emphasis.
12. *Britain working again*, p. 13.
13. Commission on Social Justice, *Social justice*, p. 73.
14. *A new economic future*, p. 4.
15. Commission on Social Justice, *Social justice*, p. 70.
16. *ibid.*, p. 73.
17. Labour Party, *Agenda for change* (London, 1992), p. 2; *Britain working again*, p. 1; Commission on Social Justice, *Social justice*, p. 85, my emphasis throughout.

18. *A new economic future*, p. 38; *Agenda for change*, p. 13; G. Radice, "Southern discomfort", *Fabian Pamphlet*, 555, London, 1992, p. 19.
19. C. Leadbeater, "The politics of prosperity", *Fabian Tract*, 523, 1987, p. 11.
20. *A new economic future*, p. 39.
21. Labour Party, *Labour's objects, socialist values in the modern world* (London, 1994), pp. 8–9, my emphasis.
22. Commission on Social Justice, *Social justice*, p. 102, my emphasis.
23. See, for example, S. Crine, "Labour's first year: a sense of socialism", *Fabian Pamphlet*, 550, London, 1991, p. 12.
24. Commission on Social Justice, *Social justice*, p. 360.
25. *Britain working again*, p. 20.
26. *Rebuilding the economy*, p. 21; Commission on Social Justice, *Social justice*, p. 165.
27. *Made in Britain*, p. 13, my emphasis.
28. *A new economic future*, p. 4, my emphasis.
29. *Britain working again*, p. 11; *Made in Britain*, p. 6.
30. *A new economic future*, p. 14.
31. *Labour's objects, socialist values*, p. 2; *Rebuilding the economy*, p. 4; *Winning for Britain*, p. 4, my emphasis.
32. Brown, "Fair is efficient", p. 17, my emphasis.
33. Commission on Social Justice, *Social justice*, pp. 307, 309.
34. *ibid.*, p. 103.
35. *Labour's economic approach*, p. 17, my emphasis.
36. Commission on Social Justice, *Social justice*, pp. 120, 311.
37. Radice, "Southern discomfort", p. 21, my emphasis.
38. *Agenda for change*, p. 2.
39. *Britain working again*, p. 14.
40. *Winning for Britain*, p. 4, my emphasis.
41. Leadbeater, "The politics of prosperity", pp. 8, 7, my emphasis.
42. See Radice, "Southern discomfort".
43. *Labour's economic approach*, p. 17.
44. Commission on Social Justice, *Social justice*, p. 67.
45. *ibid.*, pp. 223, 95.
46. *ibid.*, pp. 250, 227, 110.
47. Though it is interesting to note that unlike most New Labour literature the Commission on Social Justice does stress the importance of influencing the popular perception of taxation so that people see it as "a desirable good, not a necessary evil. If they want the ends – higher standards in our schools, better health . . . we must be willing to pay the means. The public goods we pay for through taxation create social and private benefits", *ibid.*, p. 250.
48. J. Ruskin, *The stones of Venice*, [2 vols] (London: Dent, n.d.), vol. 2, p. 151.

Bibliography

Key primary texts

Part I 1884–1929

Chapter 1

Blatchford, R. *Merrie England* (London: Clarion, 1894).
Blatchford, R. *Britain for the British* (London: Clarion, 1906).
Hyndman, H. *The historical basis of socialism in England* (London: Kegan Paul, 1883).
Hyndman, H. *The economics of socialism* (London: Twentieth Century Press, 1896).
Morris, W. *Lectures on socialism*, vol. 23 of *Collected works* (London: Longman, 1915).
Morris, W. *Signs of change*, vol. 23 of *Collected works* (London: Longman, 1915).
Morris, W. *News from nowhere, or an epoch of rest* (London: Reeves & Turner, 1891).

Chapter 2

Fabian essays (London: Allen & Unwin, 1889).
Olivier, S. "Capital and land", *Fabian Tract*, 7, 6th edn, 1904.
Shaw, G. B. *Essays in Fabian socialism* (London: Constable, 1949).
Webb, S. "English progress towards social democracy", *Fabian Tract*, 15, London, 1892.
Webb, S. & B. *A constitution for the socialist Commonwealth of Great Britain* (London: Longman, 1920).
Webb, S. & B. *Industrial democracy*, 2nd edn (London: Longman, 1920).

Chapter 3

Cole, G. D. H. *Self-government in industry* (London: Bell, 1917).
Cole, G. D. H. *Guild socialism restated* (London: Parsons, 1920).
Hobson, S. G. *National Guilds, an inquiry into the wage system and the way out* (London: Bell, 1914).
Penty, A. J. *The restoration of the gild system* (London: Swan & Sonnenschien, 1906).

Chapter 4

Hobson, J. A. *The economics of unemployment* (London: Allen & Unwin, 1922).
Hobson, J. A. *Incentives in the new industrial order* (London: Parsons, 1922).
Hobson, J. A. *The evolution of modern capitalism, a study of machine production*, 4th edn (London: Allen & Unwin, 1926).
Strachey, J. *Revolution by reason* (London: Parsons, 1926).

Chapter 5

Tawney, R. *The acquisitive society* (London: Bell, 1921).

Tawney, R. *Equality* (London: Allen & Unwin, 1938).

Tawney, R. *The radical tradition, twelve essays on politics, education and literature* (London: Allen & Unwin, 1964).

Winter, J. M. and D. Joslin. *R. H. Tawney's Commonplace Book* (Cambridge: Cambridge University Press, 1972).

Chapter 6

MacDonald, J. R. *Socialism and society* (London: ILP, 1905).

MacDonald, J. R. *Socialism after the war* (London: National Labour Press, 1918).

MacDonald, J. R. *Socialism, critical and constructive* (London: Waverley, 1921).

MacDonald, J. R. *Socialism*, 1907, in *Ramsay MacDonald's political writings,* B. Barker (ed.) (London: Allen & Unwin, 1972).

Snowden, P. *Socialism and syndicalism* (London: Collins, 1913).

Snowden, P. *Labour and the new world* (London: Waverley, 1921).

Chapter 7

Labour Party. *Labour and the new social order* (London, 1918).

Labour Party. *Unemployment, a Labour policy* (London, 1921).

Labour Party. *Unemployment, the peace and the indemnity* (London, 1921).

Labour Party. *Work for the workless* (London, 1924).

Labour Party. *On the dole or off?* (London, 1926).

Labour Party. *Labour and the nation* (London, 1928).

Labour Party. *How to conquer unemployment* (London, 1929).

Part II 1929–45

Chapter 8

Bevan A., A. Young, W. J. Brown, J. Strachey. *A National policy, an account of the emergency programme advanced by Sir Oswald Mosley* (London: Macmillan, 1931).

Chapter 9

Cole, G. D. H. *The next ten years in British economic and social policy* (London: Macmillan, 1929).

Cole, G. D. H. *Economic tracts for the times* (London: Macmillan, 1932).

Cole, G. D. H. *The intelligent man's guide through world chaos* (London: Gollancz, 1932).

Cole, G. D. H. *What everybody wants to know about money* (London: Gollancz, 1933).

Cole, G. D. H. *Studies in world economics* (London: Macmillan, 1934).

Dalton, H. *Practical socialism* (London: Routledge, 1935).

Durbin, E. F. M. *Purchasing power and the trade depression: a critique of underconsumptionist theories* (London: Cape, 1933).

Durbin, E. F. M. *The problem of credit policy* (London: Chapman & Hall, 1935).

Durbin, E. F. M. *The politics of democratic socialism, an essay on social policy* (London: Routledge, 1940).

Jay, D. *The socialist case* (London: Faber, 1937).

Meade, J. *An introduction to economic analysis and policy*, 2nd edn (Oxford: Oxford University Press, 1937).
Strachey, J. *A programme for progress* (London: Gollancz, 1940).

Chapter 10

Cole, G. D. H. *The principles of economic planning* (London: Macmillan, 1935).
Cole, G. D. H. *Practical economics, or studies in economic planning* (Harmondsworth: Penguin, 1937).
Durbin, E. F. M. *Problems of economic planning* (London: Routledge & Kegan Paul, 1949).
Labour Party. *For socialism and peace* (London, 1934).
Labour Party. *Socialism and the condition of the people* (London, 1934).
Labour Party. *Labour's financial policy* (London, 1935).
Labour Party. *Why the banks should be nationalised* (London, 1936).
Labour Party. *Labour's immediate programme* (London, 1937).
Lange, O. & F. Taylor (eds). *On the economic theory of socialism* (Minneapolis: University of Minnesota, 1938).
Wootton, B. *Plan or no plan* (London: Gollancz, 1934).

Part III 1945–70

Chapter 11

Crossman, R. et al. *Keep left* (London: New Statesman, 1947).
Crossman, R. et al. *Keeping left* (London: New Statesman, 1950).
Labour Party. *Let us face the future* (London, 1945).
Labour Party. *Labour believes in Britain* (London, 1949).

Chapter 12

Bevan, A. *In place of fear* (London: Heinemann, 1952).
Cole, G. D. H. *Socialist economics* (London: Gollancz, 1950).
Crosland, C. A. R. "The function of public enterprise", *Socialist Commentary* (February 1950).
Crosland, C. A. R. *The future of socialism* (London: Cape, 1956).
Crosland, C. A. R. *The Conservative enemy, a programme of radical social reform for the 1960s* (London: Cape, 1962).
Crossman, R. "Socialist values in a changing civilisation", *Fabian Tract*, 286, 1950.
Crossman, R. "Labour in the affluent society", *Fabian Tract*, 325, London, 1960.
Crossman, R. & M. Cole (eds). *New Fabian essays* (London: Turnstile, 1952).
Gaitskell, H. "Socialism and nationalisation", *Fabian Tract*, 300, London, 1956.
Jenkins, R. *In pursuit of progress, a critical analysis of the achievements and prospects of the Labour Party* (London: Heinemann, 1953).
Meade, J. *Planning and the price mechanism, the liberal socialist tradition* (London: Allen & Unwin, 1948).
Socialist Union. *Socialism, a new statement of principles* (Harmondsworth: Penguin, 1952).
Socialist Union. *Twentieth century socialism* (Harmondsworth: Penguin, 1956).
Strachey, J. *Contemporary capitalism* (London: Gollancz, 1956).

Strachey, J. *The end of empire* (London: Gollancz, 1959).
Wootton, B. *Freedom and planning* (London: Allen & Unwin, 1945).

Chapter 13
Labour Party. *Let us win through together* (London, 1950).
Labour Party. *Forward with Labour* (London, 1955).
Labour Party. *Industry and society, Labour's policy on future public ownership* (London, 1957).
Labour Party. *Plan for progress* (London, 1958).
Labour Party. *Britain belongs to you* (London, 1959).
Labour Party. *Signposts for the sixties* (London, 1961).
The National Plan. Cmnd. 2764 (London: HMSO, 1965).
Wilson, H. "A four year plan for Britain", *New Statesman* (24 March 1961).
Wilson, H. *The new Britain, selected speeches* (Harmondsworth: Penguin, 1964).

Part IV 1970–95

Chapter 14
Brown, M. B. *UCS: the social audit* (Nottingham: Institute for Workers' Control, 1971).
Brown, M. B. *From Labourism to socialism, a political economy for Labour in the 1970s* (Nottingham: Spokesman, 1972).
Coates, K. *The crisis of British socialism* (Nottingham: Spokesman, 1972).
Coates, K. & T. Topham. *New unionism, the case for workers' control* (Harmondsworth: Penguin, 1974).
Holland, S. (ed.). *The state as entrepreneur* (London: Weidenfeld & Nicolson, 1972).
Holland, S. *The socialist challenge* (London: Quartet, 1975).
Holland, S. *Beyond capitalist planning* (Oxford: Blackwell, 1978).

Chapter 15
Crosland, C. A. R. *Socialism now and other essays* (London: Cape, 1974).
Jenkins, R. *What matters now* (London: Fontana, 1972).
Luard, E. *Socialism without the state* (London: Macmillan, 1979).
Meade, J. *The intelligent radical's guide to economic policy, the mixed economy* (London: Allen & Unwin, 1975).

Chapter 16
Aaronovitch, S. *The road from Thatcherism, the alternative economic strategy* (London: Lawrence & Wishart, 1981).
Benn, T. *Arguments for socialism* (Harmondsworth: Penguin, 1980).
Hodgson, G. *Labour at the crossroads, the political and economic challenge to the Labour Party in the 1980s* (London: Robertson, 1981).
Hodgson, G. *The democratic economy* (Harmondsworth: Penguin, 1984).
Labour Party. *Programme, 1973* (London, 1973).
Labour Party. *Let us work together* (London, 1974).
Labour Party. *Programme, 1982* (London, 1982).
Labour Party. *New hope for Britain* (London, 1983).

Meacher, M. *Socialism with a human face, the political economy of Britain in the 1980s* (London: Allen & Unwin, 1982).

Chapter 17

Gould, B. *Socialism and freedom* (London: Macmillan, 1985).
Gould, B. et al. *Monetarism or prosperity?* (London: Macmillan, 1981).
Hattersley, R. *Choose freedom, the future for democratic socialism* (Harmondsworth: Penguin, 1987).
Mitchell, A. *The case for Labour* (London: Longman, 1983).
Mitchell, A. *Competitive socialism* (London: Unwin Hyman, 1989).
Nove, A. *The economics of feasible socialism* (London: Allen & Unwin, 1983).
Radice, G. *Labour's path to power, the new revisionism* (London: Macmillan, 1989).

Chapter 18

Brown, G. "Fair is efficient, a socialist agenda for fairness", *Fabian Pamphlet*, 563, London, 1994.
Commission on Social Justice, *Social justice: strategies for national renewal* (London: Vintage, 1994).
Kinnock, N. *Making our way* (Oxford: Blackwell, 1986).
Labour Party. *Made in Britain, a new economic policy for the 1990s* (London, 1991).
Labour Party. *Agenda for change* (London, 1992).
Labour Party. *It's time to get Britain working again* (London, 1992).
Labour Party. *Labour's economic approach* (London, 1993).
Labour Party. *Making Britain's future* (London, 1993).
Labour Party. *Winning for Britain, Labour's strategy for industrial success* (London, 1993).
Labour Party. *Labour's objects, socialist values in the modern world* (London, 1994).
Labour Party. *Rebuilding the economy* (London, 1994).
Labour Party. *A new economic future for Britain* (London, 1995).

Secondary literature

This short bibliography aims to provide the reader with some indication of useful further reading, first with respect to many of the individual thinkers whose economic writing is discussed in this work; secondly in relation to the various socialist political economies that have been considered; and thirdly as regards the Labour Party's conduct of economic policy and the economic backdrop against which it sought to implement its ideas. I have also used the four-part structure of the book to organize my bibliographical suggestions, though there are, of course, many works relevant to more than one part.

As regards the biographies and intellectual biographies cited little need be added by way of commentary except to say that I have usually limited myself to one or two suggestions; the alternative would be a bibliography of unmanageable proportions. With respect to those books that discuss the different strains of socialist economic thinking and policy implementation I have given the reader some further guidance by way of an indication of what they offer.

Part I 1884–1929

Autobiography

Blatchford, R. *My eighty years* (London: Cassell, 1901).
Hyndman, H. *The record of an adventurous life* (London: Macmillan, 1911).
Hyndman, H. *Further reminiscences* (London: Macmillan, 1912).
Webb, B. *My apprenticeship* (London: Longman, 1948).
Webb, B. *Our partnership* (London: Longman, 1950).

Biography and intellectual biography

Allett, J. *New Liberalism, the political economy of J. A. Hobson* (Toronto: University of Toronto Press, 1981).
Anthony, P. D. *Ruskin's Labour, a study of Ruskin's social theory* (Cambridge: Cambridge University Press, 1983).
Carpenter, L. *G. D. H. Cole, an intellectual biography* (Cambridge: Cambridge University Press, 1973).
Cross, C. *Philip Snowden* (London: Rockcliff, 1966).
Hobsbawm, E. "Hyndman and the SDF", in *Labouring men* (London: Weidenfeld & Nicolson, 1964).
McCarthy, F. *William Morris, a life for our time* (London: Faber & Faber, 1994).
Marquand, D. *Ramsay MacDonald* (London: Cape, 1976).
Meier, P. *William Morris, the Marxist dreamer*, trans. F. Gubb (Hassocks: Harvester, 1978).
Radice, L. *Beatrice and Sidney Webb: Fabian socialists* (London: Macmillan, 1984).
Scherr, R. *Robert Blatchford and Clarion socialism, 1891–1914* (PhD thesis, University of Iowa, 1974).
Terrill, R. *Richard Tawney and his times, socialism as fellowship* (London: Deutsch, 1974).
Thompson, E. P. *William Morris, romantic to revolutionary* (London: Lawrence & Wishart, 1955).
Thompson, L. *Robert Blatchford, portrait of an Englishman* (London: Gollancz, 1951).
Thompson, N. *John Strachey, an intellectual biography* (London: Macmillan, 1993).
Tsuzuki, C. *H. M. Hyndman and British socialism* (Oxford: Oxford University Press, 1961).
Wright, A. *G. D. H. Cole and socialist democracy* (Oxford: Oxford University Press, 1968).
Wright, A. *R. H. Tawney* (Manchester: Manchester University Press, 1987).

Political economy and economic policy

One of the best discussions of Fabian political and economic thinking is to be found in A. McBriar, *Fabian socialism and English politics, 1884–1918* (Cambridge: Cambridge University Press, 1966). However, readers might also usefully refer to E. Durbin, "Fabian socialism and economic science" in *Fabian essays in socialist thought*, B. Pimlott (ed.) (London: Heinemann, 1984); N. Thompson, *The market and its critics, socialist political economy in nineteenth century Britain* (London: Routledge, 1988) and G. J. Stigler, "Bernard Shaw, Sidney Webb and the theory of Fabian socialism" in *Essays in the history of economics* (Chicago: University of Chicago Press, 1965). For more general discussions of the history of Fabianism see M. Cole, *The story of Fabian socialism* (London: Heinemann, 1961) and N. Mackenzie, *First Fabians* (London: Weidenfeld & Nicolson, 1977).

J. Allett, *New Liberalism, the political economy of J. A. Hobson* (Toronto: University of Toronto Press, 1981) provides an excellent study of Hobsonian liberal socialism. For more general studies of the interaction and interrelationship of socialism and "new liberalism" in this period see P. Clarke, *Liberals and Social Democrats* (Cambridge: Cambridge University Press, 1978) and M. Freeden, *Liberalism divided: a study in British political thought* (Oxford: Clarendon Press, 1986). In this context C. Cline, *Recruits to Labour: the British Labour Party, 1914–31* (Syracuse, NY: Syracuse University Press, 1963) furnishes an interesting study of those who moved from the Liberal to the Labour Party in that period.

For a detailed consideration of the ideas of the guild socialists see S. T. Glass, *The responsible society, the ideas of the English guild socialists* (London: Longman, 1966). On British Marxism see the excellent discussions provided by S. Macintyre, *A proletarian science, Marxism in Britain, 1917–33* (Cambridge: Cambridge University Press, 1980), S. Pierson, *Marxism and the origins of British socialism, the struggle for a new consciousness* (Cambridge: Cambridge University Press, 1973) and also the study of Hyndman by Tsuzuki cited above. More generally for a history of the evolution of Marxian economics covering this period see M. C. Howard and J. E. King, *A history of Marxian economics, 1883–1929* (London: Macmillan, 1989). On British syndicalism see B. Holton, *British syndicalism, 1900–14, myths and realities* (London: Pluto, 1976).

As regards the impact of ideas on policy documents, A. Booth, "The Labour Party and economics between the wars", *Bulletin of the Society for the Study of Labour History* **47**, 1983, pp. 36–42 provides a short but perceptive study; though for the 1920s specifically see also N. Thompson, "Hobson and the Fabians, two roads to socialism in the 1920s", *History of Political Economy* **26**, 1994, pp. 203–20; D. Mackay, D. Kelly, D. Forsyth, "The discussion of public works programmes, 1917–35; some remarks on the Labour Movement's contribution", *International Review of Social History* **11**, 1966, pp. 8–17 considers the discussion of public works in Labour Party literature, while as regards economic thinking within the ILP, see A. Oldfield, "The Independent Labour Party and planning, 1920–26", *International Review of Social History* **21**, 1976, pp. 1–29 and R. Dowse, *Left in the centre, the I. L. P. 1883–1940* (London: Longman, 1966). For thinking on the left of the Party in the 1930s see, in addition, B. Pimlott, *Labour and the Left in the 1930s* (Cambridge: Cambridge University Press, 1977).

Part II 1929–45

Autobiography

Brown, W. J. *So far* (London: Allen & Unwin, 1943).
Dalton, H. *The fateful years: memoirs 1931–45* (London: Muller, 1957).
Davenport, N. *Memoirs of a city radical* (London: Weidenfeld & Nicolson, 1974).
Mosley, O. *My life* (London: Nelson, 1968).
Wootton, B. *In a world I never made: autobiographical reflections* (London: Allen & Unwin, 1967).

Biography and intellectual biography

Donoughue, B. & G. Jones. *Herbert Morrison, portrait of a politician* (London: Weidenfeld & Nicolson, 1973).
Skidelsky, R. *Oswald Mosley* (London: Macmillan, 1978).
Thomas, H. *John Strachey* (London: Methuen, 1973).

Political economy and economic policy

R. Skidelsky, *Politicians and the slump 1929–31* (London: Macmillan, 1967), remains the best critical account of the conduct of economic policy by the second minority Labour government; though see also that in D. Winch, *Economics and policy* (London: Hodder & Stoughton, 1969). Winch's work also provides an excellent general account of economic thinking and the conduct of economic policy in the inter-war period. As an antidote to Skidelsky's critique see R. McKibbin, "The economic policy of the second Labour government, 1929–31", *Past and Present* **68**, 1975, pp. 85–123. S. Howson and D. Winch, *The Economic Advisory Council, 1930–39: a study of economic advice during depression and recovery* (Cambridge: Cambridge University Press, 1977) provides, among other things, a discussion of the variety of advice that the second Labour government received as the British economy plunged into depression.

E. Durbin's *New Jerusalems, the Labour Party and the economics of democratic socialism* (London: Routledge, 1985) provides a superlative account of economic thinking and the process of economic policy-making within the Labour Party in the 1930s. As regards the specific debate over bank nationalization see S. Pollard, "The nationalisation of the banks, the chequered history of a socialist proposal in *Ideology and the Labour movement, essays presented to John Saville*, D. Martin and D. Rubinstein (eds) (London: Croom Helm, 1978) and on the socialist economic calculation controversy, D. Lavoie, *Rivalry and central economic planning, the socialist calculation debate reconsidered* (Cambridge: Cambridge University Press, 1985). For the impact of Roosevelt's New Deal on economic thinking within the Labour movement see B. Malament, "British Labour and Roosevelt's New Deal: the response of the Left and the unions", *Journal of British Studies* **17**, 1978, pp. 85–123 and also H. Pelling, *America and the British Left, from Bright to Bevan* (London: A. & C. Black, 1956). M. Cole, "The Society for Socialist Inquiry and Propaganda" in *Essays in Labour History, 1918–39*, A. Briggs and J. Saville (eds) (London: Croom Helm, 1977), provides an interesting account of the origins and influence of one of the groups that helped to enliven the economic debate within the Labour Party after 1931.

On the general backdrop of economic thinking in the 1930s see, in addition to Winch's *Economics and policy* (London: Hodder & Stoughton, 1969), A. Booth and M. Pack, *Employment, capital and employment policy, 1918–39* (Oxford: Blackwell, 1985) and P. Clarke, *The Keynesian revolution in the making, 1924–36* (Oxford: Clarendon Press, 1988).

As regards Marxian economics in this period see M. C. Howard and J. E. King, *A history of Marxian economics, 1929–90* (London: Macmillan, 1992).

For an account of the intellectual and other currents feeding into the policy positions taken up by Labour in 1945 see P. Addison, *The road to 1945* (London: Cape, 1975) and, more specifically, S. Howson, "Socialist monetary policy: monetary thought in the Labour Party in the 1940s", *History of Political Economy* **20**, 1988, pp. 543–64.

Part III 1945–70

Autobiography

Benn, A. *Against the tide, diaries, 1973–77* (London: Deutsch, 1982).
Brown, G. *In my way: the political memoirs of Lord George Brown* (London: Gollancz, 1971).
Jay, D. *Change and fortune, a political record* (London: Hutchinson, 1980).
Jenkins, R. *A life at the centre* (London: Macmillan, 1991).
Wilson, H. *The Labour Government 1964–70* (London: Weidenfeld & Nicolson, 1972).

Biography and intellectual biography

Burridge, T. *Clement Attlee* (London: Cape, 1985).
Campbell, J. *Nye Bevan and the mirage of British socialism* (London: Weidenfeld & Nicolson, 1987).
Cooke, C. *The life of Richard Stafford Cripps* (London: Hodder & Stoughton, 1957).
Crosland, S. *Tony Crosland* (London: Cape, 1987).
Foot, M. *Aneurin Bevan* [2 vols] (London: Macgibbon & Kee, 1962, 1973).
Harris, K. *Attlee* (London: Weidenfeld & Nicolson, 1982).
Howard, A. *Crossman: the pursuit of power* (London: Cape, 1990).
Pimlott, B. *Hugh Dalton* (London: Cape, 1985).
Pimlott, B. *Harold Wilson* (London: Harper Collins, 1992).
Thirlwall, A. P. *Nicholas Kaldor* (Brighton: Wheatsheaf, 1987).
Williams, P. *Hugh Gaitskell* (London: Cape, 1979).
Ziegler, P. *Harold Wilson, the authorised life of Lord Wilson of Rievaulx* (London: Weidenfeld & Nicolson, 1993).

Political economy and economic policy

For a magisterial assessment of the post-war Labour government's economic record see A. Cairncross, *Years of recovery, British economic policy, 1945–51* (London: Methuen, 1985); also N. Tiratsoo (ed.), *The Attlee years* (London: Pinter, 1991) and K. O. Morgan, *Labour in power, 1945–51* (Oxford: Clarendon Press, 1984). For a more specific assessment of certain aspects of the conduct of policy and the theoretical basis upon which they rested see J. Tomlinson, "Mr. Attlee's supply-side socialism", *Economic History Review* **46**, 1993, pp. 1–26 and J. Tomlinson, "The Iron Quadrilateral: political obstacles to economic reform under the Attlee government", *Journal of British Studies* **34**, 1995, pp. 90–111.

For a fascinating general study of the influence of economists on policy-makers, which covers the period of the Attlee governments, see A. Cairncross and N. Watts, *The economic section, 1939–61: a study in economic advising* (London: Routledge, 1989).

As regards the evolution of socialist political economy in this period see in particular S. Haseler, *The Gaitskellites, revisionism in the British Labour Party* (London: Macmillan, 1969) and also G. Foote, *The Labour Party's political thought*, 2nd edn (London: Croom Helm, 1985) pp. 189–235. This work also, of course, provides a general account of the development of political thinking within the Labour Party for the whole of the period covered. For a discussion of the Labour Party strategy in the post-war period see A. Warde, *Consensus and beyond: the development of Labour Party strategy since World War II* (Manchester: Manchester University Press, 1982). More specifically for an excellent account of the ebb, flow and historical roots of the debate over nationalization see E. E. Barry, *Nationalisation in British politics, the historical background* (London: Cape, 1965).

For the work of those who challenged the Croslandite optimism of *The future of socialism*, see Richard Titmuss, *Essays on the Welfare State* (London: Allen & Unwin, 1958), *Income distribution and social change* (London: Allen & Unwin, 1962) and B. Abel-Smith & P. Townsend, *The poor and the poorest* (London: Bell, 1965).

For an excellent short account of the Keynesian consensus that emerged in the 1950s and 1960s see D. Marquand, *The unprincipled society, new demands and old politics* (London: Fontana, 1988), pp. 17–88.

On the economic record of Labour governments in the 1960s see W. Beckerman (ed.), *The Labour Government's Economic Record, 1964–70* (London: Duckworth, 1970); also R.

Coopey, S. Fielding & N. Tiratsoo (eds), *The Wilson governments, 1964–70* (London: Pinter, 1994) and B. Donoughue, *Prime minister: the conduct of policy under Harold Wilson and James Callaghan* (London: Cape, 1987).

For a more narrowly defined study discussing Labour's pursuit of an incomes policy see F. Blackaby, *Incomes policy in British economic policy, 1964–70* (Cambridge: Cambridge University Press, 1978). For two highly critical accounts of Labour's conduct in office, 1964–70, see C. Ponting, *Breach of promise: Labour in power, 1964–70* (London: Hamish Hamilton, 1987) and P. Foot, *The politics of Harold Wilson* (Harmondsworth: Penguin, 1968).

Part IV 1970–95

Autobiography

Callaghan, J. *Time and chance* (London: Collins, 1987).
Castle, B. *The Castle diaries, 1974–76* (London: Weidenfeld & Nicolson, 1980).
Healey, D. *The time of my life* (London: Joseph, 1989).
Wilson, H. *Final term: the Labour Government, 1974–76* (London: Weidenfeld & Nicolson and Michael Joseph, 1979).

Biography and intellectual biography

Jenkins, R. *Tony Benn, a political portrait* (London: Writers and Readers Publishing Co-operative, 1980).
Jones, E. *Neil Kinnock* (London: Hove, 1994).
Lipsey, D. (ed.). *The socialist agenda, Crosland's legacy* (London: Cape, 1981).
Sopel, J. *Tony Blair, the moderniser* (London: Michael Joseph, 1994).

Political economy and economic policy

On the general backdrop of economic thinking against which the Labour Party sought to formulate policy in this period see D. Smith, *The rise and fall of monetarism* (Harmondsworth: Penguin, 1987), M. Bleaney, *The rise and fall of Keynesian economics* (London: Macmillan, 1985) and, for the specialist economist, R. Backhouse, *A history of modern economic analysis* (Oxford: Blackwell, 1987).

For a discussion of the political economy of indicative planning see A. Nove, *The economics of feasible socialism* (London: Allen & Unwin, 1983) and S. Estrin, "Future planning in the United Kingdom" in *Labour into the eighties*, D. Bell (ed.) (London: Croom Helm, 1980), pp. 49–61.

On the rise of the Alternative Economic Strategy see M. Hatfield, *The house the Left built* (London: Gollancz, 1978) and on the rise and fall of the political forces supporting it, P. Seyd, *The rise and fall of the Labour Left* (London: Macmillan, 1987). More generally on the difficulties experienced by the Left in the 1980s see S. Hall, *The hard road to renewal: Thatcherism and the crisis of the Left* (London: Verso, 1988) and R. Hefferman, *Defeat from the jaws of victory: inside Kinnock's Labour Party* (London: Verso, 1992).

For an assessment of Labour's conduct of economic policy in the 1974–9 period see A. Britton, *Macroeconomic policy in Britain, 1974–87* (Cambridge: Cambridge University Press, 1991), which also furnishes an excellent discussion of the contemporary currents of economic thinking that impinged on policy formulation. See also M. Holmes, *The Labour*

Government, 1974–79 (London: Macmillan, 1985), M. Artis & D. Cobham (eds), *Labour's economic policies, 1974–79* (Manchester: Manchester University Press, 1991) and for a highly critical account, D. Coates, *Labour in power? A study of the Labour Government, 1974–79* (London: Longman, 1980). More specifically, on the manner in which the Labour Government handled economic affairs during the sterling crisis of 1976, see K. Burk & A. Cairncross, *Goodbye Great Britain, the 1976 I. M. F. Crisis* (New Haven: Yale University Press, 1991) and E. Dell, *A hard pounding, politics and economic crisis, 1974–76* (Oxford: Clarendon Press, 1991). For a discussion of the advice the government received and the process of advising see T. Blackstone and W. Plowden, *Inside the think tank: advising the Cabinet, 1971–83* (London: Heinemann, 1983), J. Barnett, *Inside the Treasury* (London: Deutsch, 1982) and D. MacDougall, *Don and Mandarin: memoirs of an economist* (London: Murray, 1987).

On the economic thinking of the New Right see G. Thompson, *The political economy of the new Right* (London: Pinter, 1990).

For a critique of the political economy of New Labour see N. Thompson, "Supply side socialism: the political economy of New Labour, *New Left Review* **216**, 1996, pp. 37–54.

Histories of the Labour Party

Jefferys, K. *The Labour Party since 1945* (London: Macmillan, 1994).
Pelling, H. *A short history of the Labour Party* (London: Macmillan, 1976).
Phillips, G. *The rise of the Labour Party* (London: Routledge, 1992).
Smith, M. & J. Spear (eds). *The changing Labour Party* (London: Routledge, 1992).
Thorpe, A. *A history of the British Labour Party* (London: Macmillan, 1995).

Useful general texts

G. Foote, *The political thought of the Labour Party* (London: Croom Helm, 1985) provides an excellent survey of political thinking within the Labour Party from its creation until the early 1980s.

K. O. Morgan, *The people's peace, British history, 1945–90* (Oxford: Oxford University Press, 1992) furnishes an excellent general history of post-war Britain.

W. H. Greenleaf, *The British political tradition* [4 vols] (London: Methuen), vol. 1 *The rise of collectivism* (1983); vol. 2, *The ideological heritage* (1983), provide a scholarly and beautifully written account of socialist political thinking in Britain from the late nineteenth century to the post-war period.

S. Walkland & A. Gamble, *The British party system and economic and policy, 1945–83: studies in adversarial politics* (Oxford: Oxford University Press, 1984) considers the manner in which the adversarial, two-party system has impinged on the formulation of economic policy in post-war Britain.

As regards economic histories of Britain that cover the period see S. Pollard, *The development of the British economy, 1914–90*, 4th edn. (London: Arnold, 1992) and R. Floud and D. McCloskey (eds), *The economic history of Britain since 1700* [3 vols] 2nd edn (Cambridge: Cambridge University Press, 1994), vol. 1, 1860–1939 and vol. 2, 1939–1992.

Index

5417